THE
SEC⚥ND
SEⵝ︎ISM

THE
SECOND
SEXISM

Discrimination
Against Men
and Boys

DAVID BENATAR

WILEY-BLACKWELL

A John Wiley & Sons, Ltd., Publication

This edition first published 2012
© 2012 John Wiley & Sons, Inc.

Wiley-Blackwell is an imprint of John Wiley & Sons, formed by the merger of Wiley's global
Scientific, Technical and Medical business with Blackwell Publishing.

Registered Office
John Wiley & Sons Ltd, The Atrium, Southern Gate, Chichester, West Sussex, PO19 8SQ, UK

Editorial Offices
350 Main Street, Malden, MA 02148-5020, USA
9600 Garsington Road, Oxford, OX4 2DQ, UK
The Atrium, Southern Gate, Chichester, West Sussex, PO19 8SQ, UK

For details of our global editorial offices, for customer services, and for information about how
to apply for permission to reuse the copyright material in this book please see our website at
www.wiley.com/wiley-blackwell.

The right of David Benatar to be identified as the author of this work has been asserted in
accordance with the UK Copyright, Designs and Patents Act 1988.

Library of Congress Cataloging-in-Publication Data

Benatar, David.
    The second sexism : discrimination against men and boys / David Benatar.
      p. cm.
    Includes bibliographical references and index.
    ISBN 978-0-470-67446-8 (hardcover : alk. paper) – ISBN 978-0-470-67451-2
(pbk. : alk. paper)
    1. Sex discrimination against men. 2. Men–Psychology. I. Title.
    HQ1090.B463 2012
    305.32–dc23
                                        2011038087

A catalogue record for this book is available from the British Library.

Set in 10/12pt Sabon by SPi Publisher Services, Pondicherry, India

1 2012

To my brothers

Contents

Preface

Sexism negatively affects not only women and girls, but also men and boys. While the former manifestation of sexism is widely acknowledged, few people recognize or take seriously the fact that males are the primary victims of many and quite serious forms of sex discrimination. The central purpose of this book is to draw attention to this "second sexism" and to respond to those who would deny that it exists.

It is worth pre-empting the joke that a book about discrimination against males must be a very short book. Although this *is* a relatively short book, this is not because the scope or seriousness of the problem it discusses is limited. Instead it is (partly) because a longer book is not required to show that there is an extensive and dangerous second sexism.

That said, the book develops, at much greater length, the arguments I advanced in an earlier paper on this topic. The editors of *Social Theory and Practice*, to which I had submitted that paper, invited four responses. These were published alongside my original article as well as my rejoinder in the April 2003 (vol. 29, no. 2) issue of the journal. I am grateful to the editors of the journal for permission to draw on those earlier papers of mine in writing this book. I also acknowledge the use of material used in Chapter 6 that is drawn but significantly adapted from two other previous works of mine: "Diversity limited," in Laurence Thomas (ed.), *Contemporary Debates in Social Philosophy*, Oxford: Blackwell, 2008, pp. 212–225; and "Justice, diversity and racial preference: a critique of affirmative action," *South African Law Journal*, 125(2), 2008, pp. 274–306.

The first draft of this book was written while I was a Laurence S. Rockefeller Visiting Fellow at Princeton's University Center for Human Values for the (northern hemisphere) 2009/2010 academic year. I want to thank the director, faculty and staff of the Center, both for awarding me this fellowship and for making my visit such an agreeable one. I could not have asked for a more stimulating environment in which to conduct my research and do my writing. The Princeton University libraries were also an invaluable resource and I appreciate the assistance provided by the library staff.

My thanks also go to the University of Cape Town for the period of sabbatical leave that enabled me to take up the fellowship and write the book.

Leo Boonzaier, Meghan Finn and Andrew Fisher provided very able research assistance. Jessica du Toit compiled the list of bibliographic references from my endnotes, and detected some typographical errors in the process. I am grateful to have had such excellent assistants.

I presented an overview of the book as the Morris Colloquium Speaker at the University of Colorado at Boulder. At a Laurence S. Rockefeller Fellows Seminar at the University Center for Human Values in Princeton, I presented parts of Chapter 5. In the Admiral Anderson Speaker Series at the United States Naval Academy, I presented the material on women and combat. I am grateful to those who attended these events for their comments.

Kingsley Browne kindly commented on my response (in Chapter 4) to his *Co-Ed Combat*. He and I still disagree on the question of women in combat, but his critical comments were most welcome. Nannerl Keohane provided helpful written comments on parts of Chapter 5.

I am especially grateful to Don Hubin and Iddo Landau, the two reviewers for Wiley-Blackwell, for their extensive and extremely helpful comments.

Finally, my thanks go to members of my family. The book is dedicated to my brothers.

DB
Cape Town
20 June 2011

1

Introduction

Many men are far more oppressed than many women, and any feminist who was determined to support women in all situations would certainly encounter some where her support of women against men would increase the level of injustice in the world. ... No feminist whose concern for women stems from concern for justice in general can ever legitimately allow her only interest to be the advantage of women.

Janet Radcliffe Richards, *The Sceptical Feminist*,
London: Penguin Books, 1994, p. 31.

What Is the Second Sexism?

In those societies in which sex discrimination has been recognized to be wrong, the response to this form of discrimination has targeted those attitudes and practices that (primarily) disadvantage women and girls. At the most, there has been only scant attention to those manifestations of sex discrimination whose primary victims are men and boys.[1] What little recognition there has been of discrimination against males[2] has very rarely resulted in amelioration. For these reasons, we might refer to discrimination against males as the "second sexism," to adapt Simone de Beauvoir's famous phrase.[3] The second sexism is the neglected sexism, the sexism that is not taken seriously even by most of those who oppose (or at least claim that they oppose) sex discrimination. This is regrettable not only because of its implications for ongoing discrimination against males but also, as I shall argue later, because discrimination against *females* cannot fully be addressed without attending to all forms of sexism.

The Second Sexism: Discrimination Against Men and Boys, First Edition. David Benatar.
© 2012 John Wiley & Sons, Inc. Published 2012 by John Wiley & Sons, Inc.

Disadvantage

So unrecognized is the second sexism that the mere mention of it will appear laughable to some. Such people cannot even think of any ways in which males are disadvantaged, and yet some of them are surprised, when provided with examples, that they never thought of these before. Male disadvantages include the absence of immunity, typically enjoyed by females, from conscription into military service. Men, unlike women, are not only conscripted but also sent into combat, where they risk injury, both physical and psychological, and death. Men are also disproportionately the victims of violence in most (but not all) non-combat contexts. For example, most victims of violent crime are male, and men are often (but again not always) specially targeted for mass killing. Males are more likely than females to be subject to corporal punishment. Indeed, sometimes such punishment of females is prohibited, while it is permitted, if not encouraged, for males. Although males are less often victims of sexual assault than are females, the sexual assault of males is typically taken less seriously and is thus even more significantly under-reported. Fathers are less likely than mothers to win custody of their children in the event of divorce. These and other examples will be presented in some, but by no means exhaustive detail, in Chapter 2.

However, demonstrating the existence of male disadvantage is, by itself, insufficient to show that males are the victims of sexism. Not all disadvantages somebody suffers on the basis of his or her sex amount to sexism. By way of illustration, consider the following. The disease called hereditary haemochromatosis is a genetic condition in which the body gradually absorbs too much iron, storing it in major organs. If the condition is not detected in time, serious organ damage and failure can result, often resulting in death. The treatment, if the condition is detected sufficiently early, is regular blood-letting.[4] Although both males and females can have this genetic condition, males are more likely to suffer from the resultant disease. This is because females, during their reproductive years, regularly lose blood, and thus iron, during menstruation.[5] It thus transpires that menstruation is an advantage for those females with haemochromatosis. But menstruation can also be a disadvantage. Because younger women do lose blood and iron, they are more prone than are men to iron deficiency anemia. Menstruation is thus an advantage for women with haemochromatosis, but a disadvantage for women who are susceptible to iron deficiency anemia. Similarly, the absence of menstruation is a health disadvantage for men with haemochromatosis, but an advantage for men who might otherwise be susceptible to iron deficiency.

The presence or absence of these disadvantages does not demonstrate that males with symptomatic haemochromatosis and females with iron deficiency anemia are the victims of *sexism*.

Discrimination

To understand the relationship between disadvantage (on the basis of sex) and sexism, there are a number of concepts we need to understand and distinguish. First, we need to distinguish disadvantage from discrimination. The man with haemochromatosis is disadvantaged by not menstruating, but he is not discriminated against. For there to be discrimination the disadvantage must be at least partly the product of agency, or, on some views, of social structures or practices. Thus an individual, an institution or a state might discriminate against people of one sex. Or it might be the case that particular social structures or practices have the effect of favoring one sex over the other. The disadvantage suffered by the man with haemochromatosis is not in itself the product of any of these. For example, nobody forbade or discouraged him from menstruating or removed the uterus he never had, or prevented him from acquiring one.[6]

We cannot conclude, however, that whenever some disadvantage is experienced as a result of discrimination on the basis of sex that the person suffering the disadvantage is the victim of sexism. This is because discrimination is sometimes entirely appropriate, if not desirable. The word "discrimination" is so often used in its pejorative sense that it is sometimes forgotten that it also has an entirely non-pejorative sense. To discriminate is to recognize a difference or to differentiate. Some discrimination in this sense is both necessary and desirable. Teachers, for example, must discriminate – discern the difference – between good- and bad-quality work submitted by their students. If teachers awarded first-class passes for all work, or failed all work, irrespective of its quality, they would not be acting in an appropriately discriminating way.

Wrongful discrimination

This brings us to a second distinction, namely between discrimination and unfair or wrongful discrimination. Whereas discrimination *per se* can be morally acceptable, wrongful discrimination is, by definition, morally problematic.

There are obviously many possible grounds on which one might wrongly discriminate. These include sex, race, religion, ethnic group, national origin and sexual orientation. Of interest in this book is wrongful discrimination on the basis of a person's sex.[7]

However, sex is not *always* an inappropriate basis on which to discriminate between people. Thus once one has established that a disadvantage is the product of discrimination on the basis of somebody's sex, one then needs to establish whether or not that discrimination is fair, just or justifiable. That is to say, one must determine whether or not a person's sex provides an appropriate basis for the differential treatment. For example, one might say that middle-aged males are discriminated against if their medical insurance does not cover them, but does cover females of similar age, for routine mammography. However, one might argue that the discrimination is not unfair on account of a relevant difference between men and women. Women, given the nature of their breasts, are more likely to get breast cancer, and thus the cost of routine scanning may be warranted for them but not for men. (We can imagine exceptions, of course. If some subset of males were known to have an elevated risk of breast cancer, we might think it unfair if they, unlike other men, were not covered.)

As we might expect, there is disagreement about the correct account of when discrimination is wrong. My preferred answer is that discrimination is wrong when people are treated differently without there being a relevant difference between the people that justifies the differential treatment. (When I speak of the differential treatment being *justified*, I do not mean that some or other reason is *offered* for the differential treatment, but rather that there is good objective reason for the differential treatment.) If, for example, a teacher were to fail work that deserves to pass and does so on account of its having been written by a student of a particular sex, race, religion, ethnic group or sexual orientation, then that teacher has also acted unfairly and wrongly. Such features of the author of a piece of written work are irrelevant to assessing the quality of that work.

Although this is my preferred account of what makes discrimination wrong, it is not necessary to accept this particular account in order to reach the conclusions for which I shall argue later in this book. It is possible for people with different accounts of what makes discrimination wrong to agree that specific instances of discrimination are wrongful. Thus my arguments in subsequent chapters will not presuppose a specific account of when discrimination is wrongful. In this way I hope to bypass at least some disagreement about what makes some discrimination wrong.

To give a specific example, we do not need to have an account of what makes discrimination wrong in order to know that excluding women from university (because they are women) amounts to wrongful discrimination. Similarly, we do not need to have such an account in order to know that laws permitting the corporal punishment of boys but not of girls amounts to wrongful discrimination. This is not to say that each of these discriminatory practices has not had its defenders. Instead it is to say that the best way to determine whether a given form of discrimination is wrong is to examine that specific treatment and all the considerations relevant to it. That is what I shall do in Chapter 4.

For this same reason it is not necessary, for those who do accept my preferred account, to give a more detailed account of *when* precisely a person's sex is irrelevant. This question too can be bypassed. Moreover, it is not clear, in any event, that any more precise account could be given. There are so many different ways of treating people and so many different conditions under which they may be treated. To expect that a precise account can be given to cover all these cases is to expect more than can be provided.[8] Consider, for example, the breast cancer screening example above. Determining whether that is a case of justifiable discrimination depends on the relative risks of breast cancer faced by men and women, on the costs of competing screening policies and on the rationing principles one uses to distribute scarce resources. This is just one of very many contexts in which we need to determine whether discrimination is fair.

Sexism

I shall refer to wrongful discrimination on the basis of sex as "sex discrimination," "sexist discrimination" or "sexism."[9] This seems like an entirely reasonable understanding of what sexism is. However, it is not uncontroversial and thus more needs to be said about this definition, its competitors and what is at stake between them.

The first thing to note is that there is no single, standard usage of the term "sexism." It is used in many different ways, even by those who are united in opposing it. For example, Janet Radcliffe Richards defines it, albeit in passing, as counting "sex as relevant in contexts in which it is not."[10] Mary Anne Warren says that sexism "is usually defined as wrongful discrimination on the basis of sex"[11] and that discrimination "based on sex may be wrong either because it is based on false and invidious beliefs about persons of one sex or the other, or because it unjustly harms those discriminated against."[12]

Others think that a definition of this kind is inadequate and that sexism involves at least one further element, which is variably described as the *subordination* of one sex to the other, the *domination* of one sex by another or the *oppression* of one sex.[13] Those who think that some such additional element is required for sexism to exist typically think that sexism must be a *systemic* phenomenon, because subordination, domination or oppression could not exist without systemic discrimination. They also think that such additional conditions for sexism preclude the possibility that males could be the victims of sexism. This is because they deny that males suffer from subordination or being dominated or oppressed. In addition they might deny that discrimination against males, even if it exists, is systemic in some other way.

There are innumerable versions and combinations of these views and I obviously cannot consider them all. However, I shall consider a few examples.

Richard Wasserstrom says that "racism and sexism should not be thought of as phenomena that consist simply in taking a person's race into account ... in an arbitrary way."[14] It must also be the case that this occur

> in the context of a specific set of institutional arrangements and a specific ideology which together create and maintain a specific *system* of institutions, role assignments, beliefs and attitudes. That system is one, and has been one, in which political, economic, and social power and advantage is concentrated in the hands of those who are white and male.[15]

According to this understanding of sexism, it must be systemic and the system must favor those who enjoy overall power.[16] Marilyn Frye is another who thinks that sexism must be systemic and to the overall advantage of some. She says that "the locus of sexism is primarily in the system or framework, not in the particular act"[17] and that the "term 'sexist' characterizes cultural and economic structures which create and enforce the elaborate and rigid patterns of sex-marking and sex-announcing which divide the species, along lines of sex, into dominators and subordinates."[18]

These definitions of sexism are, in one sense, broader than mine, but in another sense they are narrower. It will be recalled that I have defined "sexism" as wrongful discrimination on the basis of a person's sex. The definitions of Professors Frye and Wasserstrom are broader in the sense that they focus not on an individual act, but a system into which the act does (or does not) feed. However, their definitions are narrower than mine in another sense. If we follow their lead, fewer actions will count as sexist. This is because it is only a subset of actions that wrongly discriminate against people on the basis of their sex that creates or contributes to hegemonies.

What can be said in favor of the definitions that compete with mine? Professor Frye asks us to consider the following case:

> If a company is hiring a supervisor who will supervise a group of male workers who have always worked for male supervisors, it can scarcely be denied that the sex of a candidate for the job is relevant to the candidate's prospects of moving smoothly and successfully into an effective working relationship with the supervisees.[19]

This case is intended to show that unfair discrimination cannot consist merely in treating people differently on the basis of an arbitrary or irrelevant attribute such as their sex. This is because, it is said, sex is not irrelevant in this case to the ability to perform the job. What Professor Frye finds problematic about the case is that if a woman is not hired, this will feed into a broader system in which females are disempowered.

I agree that systems can be sexist and I agree that systematic exclusion of women from particular positions is sexist. However, I deny that unfair discrimination *must* reach the systemic level in order to constitute sexism. I shall say more about this later, but now I shall indicate why the "irrelevant characteristic" view is able to account for Professor Frye's case. First, we should note that the relevance of the applicant's sex in her case is dependent on the attitudes of those workers who will be supervised. If they had different attitudes to women or to female supervisors then a female supervisor would be able to function as effectively as a male one. Thus we need to ask whether the differential attitude that the workers have toward male and female supervisors was based on an irrelevant characteristic. The answer to that question is affirmative and thus we could conclude, following the view that Professor Frye rejects, that the workers have sexist attitudes.

There is now a secondary question whether the people hiring the supervisor should take those sexist attitudes as a given or whether they should override them. While I doubt that a categorical answer can be given to this question, I strongly suspect that much more often than not, they should not pander to the sexist views. For example, historical experience suggests that pandering to such views only reinforces them (which is problematic, independent of systemic concerns). By contrast, resisting prejudice by opening positions to people irrespective of their sex (or race), although it can have teething problems, helps to break down prejudicial attitudes. In all cases where those hiring should hire the woman despite the workers' attitudes, pandering to sexism could be said to be derivatively sexist.

Professor Wasserstrom provides a different case. He says that what was primarily wrong with human slavery was "not that the particular individuals who were assigned the place of slaves were assigned there arbitrarily because the assignment was made in virtue of an irrelevant characteristic, i.e., their race."[20] Instead, he says, the primary problem is with the practice itself – "the fact of some individuals being able to own other individuals and all that goes with that practice."[21]

Does the case of human slavery really show that the "irrelevant characteristic" account of racism or sexism fails? I do not think so. There are at least two possible alternative reasons. According to the first, it is precisely because what is primarily wrong about slavery is that people are treated as chattel that the wrong is not primarily one of discrimination. Given this, it should be unsurprising that racism fails to provide an exhaustive account of what is wrong with slavery. Of course, where race is the criterion for who may be enslaved, then racist discrimination is a further wrongful feature of slavery, but there is no reason to think that the underlying wrong of slavery must be explained in terms of racism and thus in terms of the "irrelevant characteristic" account of racism. What this nicely illustrates is that some actions may be wrong for more than one reason and that discrimination may sometimes be a compounding wrong rather than the primary wrong.

Alternatively, perhaps we *can* fully explain the wrong of slavery via the "irrelevant characteristic" account. There is no moral problem with humans owning machines and treating the machines as chattel. There *is* a problem with humans owning other humans and treating them as chattel. What explains this difference? It is the fact that there are relevant differences between machines and humans. It is these differences that make it wrong to own humans but not machines. When people have thought that some humans may be owned on account of their "race," they have mistakenly taken a person's "race" to be a relevant difference from those humans who may not be owned. They have mistakenly treated being black as being like a machine or some other object that may be owned. According to this explanation, it is wrongful discrimination that explains why the wrong of slavery is inflicted on particular people. A given person is enslaved only because of his race. Had he been a member of another race he would not have been enslaved.

Now, even if one rejects these responses to Professors Frye and Wasserstrom and maintains that sexism is not merely a matter of treating people differently on the basis of an irrelevant characteristic, one need not embrace their definitions of sexism. One could retain the view that sexism is unfair or wrongful discrimination on the basis of a person's sex, but deny that this consists of treating people differently on the basis of their sex when their sex is indeed irrelevant. One could prefer an alternative account of wrongful discrimination, while still identifying sexism as wrongful discrimination. Rejecting the "irrelevant characteristic" account of wrongful discrimination does not entail the view that sexism must satisfy a systemic criterion or must involve domination, subordination or oppression.

So far I have argued that we do not *need* to abandon the understanding of sexism as wrongful discrimination on the basis of a person's sex. Now I wish to say why we *should not* abandon it in favor of the alternatives I have outlined. Accepting the requirement that discrimination be systemic and involve subordination, domination or oppression would do violence to ordinary language.

In our ordinary usage, we speak of prejudicial and discriminatory "isms" in the absence of overall and systemic disempowerment. If a teacher were to assess a student's work more harshly merely because that student was white or male, we would ordinarily label that action racist or sexist (in addition to being wrong on other grounds). People *do* use the words "racism" and "sexism" in such contexts. Nor is this usage restricted to non-philosophers. Peter Singer, for example, understands speciesism and racism in terms of treating beings differently on the basis of arbitrary or irrelevant differences.[22]

Perhaps my opponents think that although we do use words like "sexism" and "racism" in these ways we should not do so. Perhaps they are recommending that we alter our usage and use the word "sexism" in a more restricted way. These definitional issues are difficult. We cannot categorically say that ordinary usage must prevail. Such usage is sometimes both confused and confusing. However, it is not clear that this is true in the case at hand. Moreover, there is a danger in stipulative definitions that depart too significantly from ordinary usage. They themselves can be confusing or misleading. If, to choose an extreme example, one defines Monday as the day *after* Tuesday, one will not be contributing positively to clearer thinking and communication.

It is possible to stipulate that males cannot be the victims of sexism or, less blatantly, that group members cannot be victims of sexism or racism unless those groups are disempowered or subordinated. However, it is hard to see why such stipulations should be made. Indeed, doing so seems to have implications that would be unpalatable even to many of those who make them. A racial epithet directed against a rich and powerful member of the Kenyan government would widely and rightly be recognized as racist, even though the epithet would not lead to an overall disempowerment or subordination of blacks in Kenya. Nor does the target group need to be a majority. Jews in the United States, for example, today enjoy a degree of equality and influence unprecedented in Jewish history. They are not (contrary to the view of some antisemites) controlling the country, but they are hardly disempowered or subordinated. Isolated anti-Jewish epithets in the United States do not plausibly effect an overall disempowering or subordination of Jews in that country, but they would nonetheless appropriately be recognized as instances of antisemitism.

In response to these examples, perhaps it will be suggested that they are instances of racism and antisemitism because there is a *history* of discrimination against blacks and Jews. According to this view, it does not matter whether, in a given place, that pattern of discrimination continues. It is sufficient that it did previously continue for a long time. Notice, however, that this pedigree criterion of racism and antisemitism is even more controversial than the other features of the alternative definitions I reject.

There is a further problem with stipulating that only disempowered, subordinate or oppressed groups can be the victims of sexism (or racism). It may well be the case that *females* are no longer systematically disempowered, subordinated or oppressed in developed countries. Many feminists will be outraged at this suggestion. I shall delay, until the concluding chapter, my defense of this suggestion. For now, it is sufficient to make two observations.

First, power is spectral rather than binary. One has more or less of it, rather than either having it or not having it. Accordingly, even if men still have overall power in the developed world, the erosion of male power has taken place gradually. On this trajectory, there comes a point at which men no longer hold most power and at which women, while still the victims of discrimination, are no longer subordinated or dominated. Those who assert that the term "sexism" only applies where one group is dominant or another subordinate must concede that discrimination against females would not constitute sexism once that point is reached. I find that implausible. If my critics recognized that that point had already been reached in some places, they would likely find it implausible too.

Second, some feminists have recognized that to say, for example, that women in the developed world are still oppressed, they must depart from the traditional understanding of "oppression" and employ a new understanding of this term.[23] In this way the definitional questions recur. We are asked to reinterpret "sexism" in such a way that oppression is a criterion for it, but then we are asked to reinterpret "oppression" in such a way that the word "sexism" can still be applied to contexts in which it still seems to have application. With all this reinterpretation that is required, one wonders why it would not be more economical – and truer to ordinary usage – just to stick with the common understanding of "sexism."

I have now presented and rejected some representative alternatives to my understanding of sexism. It is worth noting, however, that less rests on this disagreement than might first appear. Let us assume, merely for the sake of argument, that sexism should not be understood in the way I have suggested it should be understood. And let us assume further that for this reason men cannot be the victims of sexism. If that were the case then there could be no *second sexism*. However, nothing would follow from this about a *second sex discrimination*. Men and boys could still be the victims of wrongful sex discrimination.[24] Even if that were not appropriately called sexism it would still be worthy of moral concern and opposition. Wrongful discrimination is wrongful and could be quite seriously so. Thus the really important conclusion for which I need to argue is that males are the victims of wrongful discrimination (or even merely wrongful treatment) on the basis of their sex. I happen to think that such discrimination merits the name "sexism" but even if I were incorrect about that, my critics could not justify, on that basis, any complacency about the wrongful discrimination of which males are the victims.[25] It would still be a problem that should be recognized and confronted. It is much more important that wrongful discrimination against men and boys be identified and opposed than that we *call* it "sexism." The fact that labeling wrongful discrimination as "sexism" is not essential to its being wrong and worthy of opposition might explain why some feminists have either barely mentioned the word "sexism" or failed to give a full account of what it is.[26]

Having defended my understanding of sexism against alternative views (and having placed that disagreement in perspective), I now return to say more about my view. According to this view, sexism is by definition *wrongful* discrimination. This, I think, is in keeping with our ordinary understanding of the term "sexism." We do not, in normal parlance, think that sexism could be morally justifiable, at least in ordinary circumstances.[27]

Sexism is sometimes explicit, as it is when people of one sex are legally prohibited from performing certain jobs. However, as feminists have rightly noted, it can often be implicit, subtle and unintentional.[28] For example, there may be some policy or practice that appears neutral but in fact unjustifiably has a "disparate impact" on either women or men. Thus, a height requirement for a particular job may lead to many fewer women being employed. If there is not a good reason for that particular height requirement, then women are the victims of an indirect and often unintentional sexism. Or consider those powerful social forces that shape the expectations or preferences of men and women in ways that significantly disproportionate numbers of men and women aspire to particular positions.[29] If, for example, girls are led to think that a "woman's place is in the home," girls might not seek work or careers outside the home. Here subtle discrimination is operative. Given the nature of subtle discrimination, it is not always easy to tell *to what extent* it is operative – a matter that will be discussed in more detail later.

The second sexism is that sexism of which males are the primary victims. As a species of sexism, it is a form of *wrongful* discrimination. Thus, to show that there is a second sexism, I shall have to demonstrate not only that males are disadvantaged and that at least some of this disadvantage is the result of discrimination, but also that this discrimination is wrong. I shall do this in stages. In Chapter 2, I shall present examples of male disadvantage. Some, but not all, of these disadvantages are manifestly also instances of discrimination, and often *de jure* discrimination. However, I shall delay until Chapter 4 the arguments that at least some of the discrimination is *wrongful*. In Chapter 5 I shall, among other things, ward off objections that this discrimination does not amount to wrongful sex discrimination or sexism.

If would be tedious if, on every occasion that I refer to discrimination, I were to spell out whether I meant discrimination in the pejorative or non-pejorative sense and whether I was referring to sex discrimination or discrimination on some other basis. Very often the correct sense is implicit and does not require explicit statement. Thus, while I shall often speak of unfair or wrongful discrimination, I shall often shorten this simply to "discrimination" where an adjective is unnecessary, either because it is clear from the context that I am speaking about wrongful discrimination or because I am referring to both discrimination and wrongful discrimination. Similarly, I shall not usually qualify "discrimination" with the words "sex" or "sexist" because it will usually be obvious that I am speaking about such discrimination.

The First Sexism

This book is about the second sexism. Accordingly it is not about that sexism of which females are primary victims. This is *not* because I deny the existence of such sexism. It clearly exists and has existed for a very long time.

Girls and women, in some times and places, have been killed because they are female. Female infanticide is common in some of those countries with a strong preference for sons. And widows have sometimes been pressured, if not forced, to end their lives through such rituals as *sati* in India. Girls and women have also died through neglect. Where food is in short supply, cultures favoring sons have prioritized the feeding of boys, often allowing girls to die of malnutrition. In the developing world, women continue to die in significant numbers during childbirth. This is attributable to the absence of basic obstetric services. To some extent this is a product of their impoverished environment. However, sometimes limited services are available at some distance and insufficient priority is put on granting women access to those services. At least in such cases, the peri-partum deaths are the result of discrimination.

Millions of girls and women have had their genitals excised. Girls have regularly been deprived of education, even when boys have been provided with education. Even in many places where girls received primary and secondary education, young women were often barred from institutions of higher education. Millions of women and girls have been raped or sexually enslaved. Women have often been prohibited from owning or inheriting property and from voting and holding public office. Women are often required to cover up their bodies in ways that men are not. In the most extreme cases, a full burqa is required. Among the many restrictions imposed on women in such countries as Saudi Arabia is a prohibition on driving a car or riding a bicycle or motorcycle.

Some of these forms of discrimination are more serious than others, but none are trivial or justifiable. Their impact on the lives of women and girls should not be underestimated. However, all these forms of discrimination, as well as many others, have been widely discussed. Discrimination against females has been the subject of almost all discussion about sexism. I do not plan to add to it here. Instead I shall focus on the neglected side of sexism. My topic is the *second* sexism rather than the first sexism. This selectivity is not unfair. Because my aim is to show that there *is* a second sexism, rather than to show that there is not a first sexism, I need only cite cases of the second sexism to establish my conclusion. It is only if I were also arguing that females were not the victims of sexism that my failure to consider instances of unfair discrimination against them would be relevant.

Although I have distinguished between the first and second sexism, this distinction does not imply that they are unrelated. In the course of this book I shall point to various connections between them, while retaining my focus on the second sexism. It is worth mentioning now, however, that there are some instances of discrimination that arguably are simultaneously instances of both the first and second sexism.

Consider, for example, the United States Supreme Court case of *Frontiero v. Richardson*.[30] Sharon Frontiero, a lieutenant in the United States Air Force, had sought benefits for her husband that wives of military personnel automatically received under Federal law. By contrast, husbands of female members of the military were entitled to these benefits only if they were dependent on their wives for over half of their support. Lt. Frontiero's request was turned down because she failed to demonstrate her husband's dependency. A lower court ruled that the discrepant treatment did not amount to unconstitutional sex discrimination. Lt. Frontiero and her husband, Joseph Frontiero, appealed. The Supreme Court reversed the lower court's judgment.

Although the court ruled that female service members were discriminated against by the policy of differential treatment, it is far from clear that this is exclusively a case of the first sexism. One could as easily say that husbands of female service members are discriminated against because they are denied the benefits that wives of male service members automatically enjoy. Alternatively, one could say, as I think we should, that both female service members and their male spouses are discriminated against, in which case the discriminatory policy is an example of both the first and the second sexism. It is noteworthy, however, that the court noticed only the first sexism. This supports my claim that even though a second sexism exists and is often intertwined with the first sexism, the second sexism typically remains invisible.[31] The aim of this book is to make it visible.

Two Kinds of Denialist

Arguments showing that there is a second sexism raise objections from two main directions.[32] Most plentiful, at least within the academy, are objections from some (but not all) feminists. From the other side come objections from some conservatives. In each case, the objectors deny either there is such a thing as the second sexism or that it is as extensive as I shall argue it is.

Consider, first, those second sexism denialists from among the ranks of feminists. Feminists, of course, are not a monolithic group. There are numerous ways of categorizing varieties of feminist, but for my purposes only one distinction is crucial. It is the distinction between those feminists who are motivated by and interested in equality of the sexes and those feminists whose primary concern is the advancement of women and girls. Some feminists – those of the second kind – are likely to claim that this is a distinction without a difference. They will argue that equality of the sexes is promoted by advancing the interests of females, and vice versa. They are (only) partly right. Promoting equality of the sexes does often coincide with the promotion of women's interests. It does so when women are unfairly discriminated against. However, because men, as I shall argue, are sometimes the victims of unfair discrimination, the promotion of gender equality will sometimes require the advancement of men's rather than women's interests.

We might refer to those feminists who are fundamentally concerned with equality of the sexes as *egalitarian feminists*,[33] and those feminists who are basically concerned only with the promotion of women's and girls' interests as *partisan feminists*.[34] The latter are the feminist equivalent of those men's rights advocates who are interested only in advancing the interests and protecting the rights of males. Feminists are rightly critical of that view, but partisan feminists do not notice that the blinkered pursuit of one sex's interests that is characteristic of such (but not other) men's rights advocates is similarly true of their own position. This criticism does not extend to the egalitarian feminists.[35] Nothing that I say should be hostile to egalitarian feminism. Indeed, I endorse that form of feminism. Advocates of this view will recognize that opposing the second sexism is one part of the overall project of opposing sexism and promoting gender equality. What I shall say will be antagonistic only to partisan feminism.

In drawing the distinction between egalitarian and partisan feminists, I have not claimed that egalitarian feminists *must* recognize that there is a second sexism. Obviously, a commitment to equality of the sexes does not entail the belief that men are the victims of some unfair discrimination. The aim of this book is to argue that males are indeed the victims of sexism. The only point I am making now is that there is nothing in that claim that is inconsistent with egalitarian feminism.

In distinguishing egalitarian feminism from partisan feminism I have not proved that there are any partisan feminists. The distinction also does not prove that there are any egalitarian feminists, but it is the category of partisan feminists that some feminists might claim is empty. I intend to show at various points in the course of this book that there are indeed feminists of this kind. There are some, but not many, feminists who explicitly espouse what I have called partisan feminism.[36] Much more commonly, however, many of those who profess egalitarian feminism in fact slip into a partisan form of feminism. They interpret the evidence as proving that females are the victims of discrimination even when they are not – and even when it is instead males who are the victims of discrimination. They also engage in rationalizations to reach the conclusion in any given instance that it is female interests that ought to prevail.

I do not intend to identify particular feminists as egalitarian. One reason for this is that it is difficult at this stage to determine who the real egalitarian feminists are. Almost all feminists writing about sex discrimination have been concerned with discrimination against females. It is difficult to know whether any given feminist has ignored discrimination against males simply because she or he has not been aware of the problem. It remains to be seen what will happen once they are made aware of it. Once it is drawn to their attention, their (broad) options seem to be these:

(1) They could accept that there is some wrongful discrimination against males (and join me in opposing it).
(2) They could provide good arguments why, contrary to what I say, males are not the victims of any wrongful discrimination.
(3) They could reject the conclusion that males are the victims of wrongful discrimination but fail to provide good reasons for this conclusion and instead engage in the familiar rationalizations that I shall discuss later.
(4) They could declare that they are not interested in discrimination against men and boys even if it does exist.

The first two options are compatible with egalitarian feminism, while the second two either suggest (option 3) or explicitly declare (option 4) partisan feminism. Partly for this reason, those in the third category are likely to claim that they are actually in the second. I do not wish to prejudge how particular people will respond. Because many feminists who profess to be egalitarian slip into a partisan form of feminism when confronted with arguments that there is a second sexism, one often cannot easily tell (in advance) which of those who profess to be interested in equality of the sexes really are.

Nor do I *need* to identify particular egalitarian feminists (or discuss their work *qua egalitarian* feminists) in order to make my case. Egalitarian feminism is a possible view and one that many people profess. The question of who actually occupies this intellectual (and political) space is not relevant to determining whether there is a second sexism. Nor is it relevant to showing that recognition of and opposition to the second sexism is compatible with the view that I have called "egalitarian feminism."

As is the case with feminists, conservatives are not all of one stripe. Some of those who go by the name "conservative" may have no objection to the views I shall defend. This is because somebody might be conservative in one realm but not in another. Economic conservatism, for example, does not entail religious conservatism. The conservatives who will object to my arguments will most likely be those who endorse (the enforcement of) gender roles and the consequent differential treatment of the sexes, which I oppose. They will argue that many of the disadvantages that males suffer are not instances of sexism, because males ought to bear those burdens or at least that it is not unfair for males to bear them. These conservatives – whom we might call *gender-role conservatives* – think the same thing about various burdens borne by women, which should make them unreliable allies for partisan feminists who also deny that there is a second sexism. Indeed, gender-role conservatives may find *some* of what I shall argue – especially against partisan feminists – to be quite congenial. They might, for example, agree that there are the double standards that I shall demonstrate exist in the views of partisan feminists.

It should be clear, though, that *my* view is not conservative about gender roles. While there may well be average differences in some psychological traits between the sexes[37] I do not think that these justify all the differential treatment of the sexes that gender-role conservatives endorse. Because I think that the second sexism ought to be opposed along with the more widely recognized sexism, I am advocating change – doing things differently from the way they have been done historically. Moreover, the change I am recommending is quite radical. That is by no means conservative.

In defending the view that there is a second sexism, I shall respond to criticisms both from partisan feminists and from gender-role conservatives. However, my arguments will be directed more commonly against the former. This is not because I am more opposed to their position, but rather because it is the more common one in the academy.[38]

It cannot be emphasized enough, though, that I am not criticizing *all* feminists. I have found that this fact is often forgotten (or, on a less charitable reading, ignored) even when one states it clearly. Unfortunately, partisanship and other ideological excesses of feminism are rampant and I shall devote lots of attention to demonstrating the problems with such views. In doing so, however, I should not be construed as rejecting feminism in its purer egalitarian form.

Forestalling Some Fallacies

Given the prevailing orthodoxy in the academy and the sensitivity of the issues I shall be discussing, the views I defend in this book will be deemed threatening by many.[39] I am thus under no illusions. My position, no matter how clearly stated, is likely to be misunderstood. Where it is not merely dismissed (sometimes vituperatively, as inconsistent with received opinion), it is likely to be subject to numerous (sometimes overly confident) mistaken objections. Indeed, overly confident objections are very common among those defending orthodoxies.[40] One reason for this is that the responses to those objections by those defending heterodox views is so much harder for the orthodox to imagine, given either the rarity of unconventional views or the rarity of their being openly expressed. Orthodoxies are repeated endlessly and usually go unchallenged. The result is that they acquire a life of their own and become self-reinforcing. Thus those who hold orthodox positions have no felt need to justify their positions, which become entrenched by being shared by so many others around them.

It is obviously not possible to anticipate every objection that will be advanced. Indeed, some objections that have been leveled against earlier work on this topic are so outlandish that even in retrospect it is hard to imagine how they came to be raised. For example, one respondent to an earlier paper about the second sexism said that virtually every point in that paper had "been argued for in the men's rights movement in the late 1970s."[41] If he meant "virtually every point" literally, then he is mistaken. If, however, he meant virtually every example of male disadvantage then, indeed, I would be surprised if nobody had *ever* mentioned these before.[42] But what difference does it make if these examples have been mentioned before? The instances of female disadvantage are recited and repeated in thousands, if not hundreds of thousands of articles and books. Just as (many of) those works approach and probe them in different ways, shed different light on them and advance different arguments about them, so discussions of the second sexism can offer novel insights and arguments even if the phenomenon of discrimination against males has been mentioned before. It is certainly more novel to write about the second sexism than about the first sexism. Thus if the highest standards of novelty are required, critics should object first (or instead) to traditional feminist discussions of discrimination against women.

Unlike this objection another response to the claim that there is a second sexism is easy to predict. Perhaps the most common response to all disliked opinions is the *ad hominem* fallacy, in which one attacks the person who is offering the argument (instead of attacking the argument itself). Indeed, I have already been accused of being an "angry man" and an antifeminist.[43] This is a fallacy because even if I were an "angry man" and an "antifeminist," this would be irrelevant to determining whether my arguments are sound. Angry men and antifeminists can utter true statements and make valid inferences from them. And thus even if the charges stuck, they would tell us nothing about whether my conclusions ought to be accepted.

There is a second problem, however. Accusing males of being angry men and antifeminists is both regrettable and unfair for the very same reasons that leveling accusations of "man-hater" at all (female) feminists[44] is regrettable and unfair.[45] In other words the *ad hominem* argument is as unfair as the *ad feminam* argument. It does not facilitate an open-minded consideration of others' views, and it ignores the fact that while some feminists are man-haters and some men who are concerned about male disadvantage are "angry" antifeminists (if not outright misogynists), not all are.

The labeling is worrying for a third reason. Given the prevailing views, at least in the academy, the charges of "angry man" and "antifeminist," like the charge "conservative," can be anticipated to have the "chilling effect" that is antithetical to the kind of discussion that should go on in academia.[46]

Structure and Method of the Book

One way to have written this book would have been to devote a separate chapter to each of the disadvantages that males experience, arguing that it constitutes unfair discrimination and then responding to objections to those arguments. That is not the way I have written this book. Taking that route would have required unnecessary repetition of ideas and arguments. Thus I have opted for an alternative approach.

In Chapter 2, the chapter immediately following this introductory one, I present a range of disadvantages of being male. I do more than mention them. I also describe them in some detail in order to give a richer account, to convey the nature and seriousness of the disadvantages. I do this because some people have been inclined to dismiss the disadvantages as minor. They need to see why they are wrong. In some cases, the disadvantages are clearly the product of discrimination and sometimes *de jure* discrimination, but even in those cases further argument is required to show that the discrimination is wrongful. That further argument is delayed until Chapter 4.

Chapter 3 fulfills two purposes. First, I present what I take to be (some of) the beliefs and attitudes that play some role in explaining why males suffer the disadvantage they do, and I provide some argument why I take these beliefs and attitudes to play a role in bringing about those disadvantages. The third chapter also provides a framework for thinking about sex differences. Because disagreements about sex differences play such an important role in arguments about how men and women should be treated, it is crucial to avoid common mistakes in thinking about differences between the sexes.

In Chapter 4, I argue that most of the disadvantages of being male are also the result of wrongful discrimination. However, not every disadvantage, I shall argue, is attributable to wrongful discrimination. Some clearly are not. In other cases it is unclear whether they are, or the extent to which they are, the result of wrongful discrimination. However, even these cases are instructive because they have implications for some of those disadvantages of being female that are typically said to be instances of wrongful discrimination but may well not be.

Chapter 5 is devoted to considering various categories of objections to the claim that males are the victims of a second sexism. Thus my argument that there is a second sexism really develops over the course of a few chapters. It is only once the objections are considered and rejected in Chapter 5 that the bulk (but not all) of the argument for the existence of a second sexism is completed.

Chapter 6 examines sex-based affirmative action. Here I argue that those affirmative action policies and practices that involve giving preference to people of a particular sex are not an appropriate response to sexism. This is true irrespective of whether it is men or women who are the victims of the discrimination in question.

In Chapter 7, the concluding chapter, I consider such questions as the relative severity of the first and second sexism and whether feminism is bad for men. I also discuss the implications of taking the second sexism seriously.

This is not a work of armchair philosophy. My arguments, because they have to do with the real world, must be informed by the relevant facts about the world. However, the facts are often very difficult to establish and are sometimes in dispute. I have thus been as careful as I can be in my use of empirical data. Where I offer a citation in support of a claim I have endeavored, in most cases, to get to the most foundational authoritative source possible. For example, instead of citing a secondary source, I have attempted wherever possible to check a primary source directly and to cite that. (In a disturbing number of cases, I found, in checking the primary sources, they did not support the claim made in the secondary sources. In such cases I either sought alternative and appropriate evidence for the claim, or rejected the claim where the balance of evidence did not support it.)

Where it seems to me that the facts were unclear, I have indicated this and then either made conditional statements or found a way to bypass the dispute about the facts. Obviously I cannot claim, despite my efforts, to have avoided all error. I cover considerable ground and review empirical findings and data on many different issues. I cannot claim expertise in all these areas and it may turn out that I am ignorant of some relevant body of literature. Thus I would be grateful to be advised of any mistakes or lacunae that might be found.[47] It is also almost certainly the case that our knowledge about these matters will progress with the passage of time.

Moreover, the facts themselves may change. If men or women suffer some specific form of discrimination now, that might not be the case later. For that reason this book is unlikely to be a timeless work. Indeed, the hope is that it will not be. Instead the hope is that the problem the book raises will be addressed and either minimized or eliminated. However, given human nature and the way human societies function, it is also extremely unlikely that any of this will happen anytime soon. For that reason what I have to say will be more enduring than I would like it to be.

I have sought to be careful not only in the factual claims I make and the sources I cite in support of them, but also in the arguments I make. Many of those who argue that men are the victims of discrimination (along with many of those who claim that women are the victims of discrimination) resort to emotive polemics, in which bizarre claims and manifestly fallacious arguments are advanced. While my arguments are forthright and deal with issues to which many people will have emotional responses, I have attempted to maintain rigor in my argumentation. No doubt my critics will think I have failed to deliver satisfactory arguments, but then they must provide arguments of their own to say why they think that there is no second sexism.

Notes

1   This is not to say that men have not sometimes utilized anti-discrimination legis-lation and sought relief from the courts for discrimination against them. However, anti-discrimination legislation was not enacted to target this form of discrimina-tion. Moreover, there are those who seem to begrudge men this relief and make exaggerated claims about how much men have benefited. See, for example, Catharine A. MacKinnon, *Feminism Unmodified*, Cambridge, MA: Harvard University Press, 1987, p. 35.

2   Although men and boys are not the only males, when I use "males" in this book I am referring only to *human* males. Moreover, by "males" I mean those humans who are of the male *sex* rather than the male *gender* – that is to say, those who are anatomically rather than socially or psychologically male – in cases where sex and gender do not coincide. (For more on this, see note 7 below.)

3   As far as I know this term is my own. In a response to my earlier article by this name, Tom Digby disputes this. He writes: "By the way, the epigraph to [Christina Hoff] Sommers' article, 'The War against Boys' [*Atlantic Monthly*, May 2000, pp. 59–74], presumably not written by the author, proclaims 'it is boys who are the second sex'. So credit for that nasty inversion of Beauvoir's expression may actually go to an anonymous editor at *The Atlantic*" (Tom Digby, "Male trouble: are men victims of sexism?" *Social Theory and Practice*, 29(2), April 2003, p. 247, n. 3). Referring to boys as the second sex (which I encountered only after formu-lating my title) is an inversion or negation of the Beauvoirian phrase. My expres-sion is a derivation from it. It says that even if females are the second sex, males are the victims of the second sexism. Professor Digby seems not to have distin-guished between (a) a disagreement about whether boys or girls are the second sex, and (b) a claim that boys and men are the victims of a second sexism.

4   Blood-letting was once a standard medical treatment for dozens of conditions. Haemochromatosis is one of only a few conditions for which it is actually a suit-able treatment.

5   While older woman do not menstruate, the onset of iron accumulation in those with haemochromatosis tends to begin sufficiently late in their life that they either die of something else first or only suffer the symptoms very late.

6   Fans of Monty Python's *Life of Brian* will remember that a man's lack of a uterus is "nobody's fault, not even the Romans'."

7   As implied in note 2 above, I am interested in *sex* discrimination rather than *gender* discrimination. Although there are different ways of drawing the distinction, a common one is between the biological or anatomical condition of being male or female – a person's sex – and attributes that are socially designated as being masculine or feminine – a person's gender. Thus a person who is anatomically male might be feminine and a person who is masculine might be anatomically female. I am fundamentally interested in *sex* discrimination because I am interested in discrimination against people who are anatomically male (or who are perceived as such). This is the complement to concern about discrimination against people who are anatomically female. Of course, sex discrimination and gender discrimination are related. Sexists tend to assume that males should be masculine and females should be feminine, but the expectation is that people's gender matches their sex. Masculine women do not escape discrimination against females, and feminine men do not escape discrimination against males.

8   I am not the only one to think this. For example, Sophia Moreau ("What is discrimination?" *Philosophy and Public Affairs*, 38(2), 2010) says that her view of discrimination "does not offer a single reductive explanation of the wrong of discrimination – that is, an explanation that traces the wrong of discrimination to some further single kind of normative fact that is operative in all cases" (p. 157). That it cannot be so reduced, she says, "reflects the complex nature of the type of injustice that we are trying to explain" (p. 157). She says that we can only address such questions "on a case-by-case basis" (p. 159). And she says that this is no more problematic for her "account than for any other account of discrimination" (p. 160). Iris Marion Young makes a similar claim about oppression. She says that "it is not possible to give one essential definition of oppression" (Iris Marion Young, *Justice and the Politics of Difference*, Princeton: Princeton University Press, 1990, p. 42).

9   Some people use the term "sexual discrimination" but I prefer to avoid it as it is ambiguous between discrimination on the grounds of sexual orientation or activity and discrimination on the grounds of a person's sex.

10 Janet Radcliffe Richards, *The Sceptical Feminist*, London: Penguin Books, 1994, p. 37. Martha Nussbaum shares this view. Although she does not explicitly define sexism, she says that liberal feminism (which obviously stands in opposition to sexism) takes sex to be a morally irrelevant characteristic in determining how people should be treated. (*Sex and Social Justice*, New York: Oxford University Press, 1999, p. 10.)

11 Mary Anne Warren, *Gendercide*, Totowa, NJ: Rowman & Allanheld, 1985, p. 83.

12 Ibid., pp. 83–84.

13 See, for example, Marilyn Frye, *The Politics of Reality: Essays in Feminist Theory*, Freedom, CA: The Crossing Press, 1983, p. 38; Iris Marion Young, *Justice and the Politics of Difference*, especially pp. 39–65.

14 Richard Wasserstrom, "On racism and sexism," in Carol Gould (ed.), *Gender*, Atlantic Highlands, NJ: Humanities Press, 1997, pp. 337–358, at p. 347.

15 Ibid.

16 The "systemic" requirement is not sufficient. Discrimination against males may
    well be systemic. Those who deny the existence of a second sexism thus also
    require the condition that the system favors those who hold overall power. (This
    assumes that males hold overall power. I shall return to this assumption later.)
17 Marilyn Frye, *The Politics of Reality*, p. 19.
18 Ibid., p. 38. The precise wording of Professors Frye's and Wasserstrom's defini-
    tion allows the possibility that males could be victims of sexism if discrimina-
    tion against them were part of a system that concentrates power and advantage
    in the hands of (other?) males. However, it does not seem that either of them
    intended this loophole in their definitions.
19 Marilyn Frye, *The Politics of Reality*, p. 18.
20 Richard Wasserstrom, "On racism and sexism," p. 347.
21 Ibid.
22 Peter Singer, *Animal Liberation*, 2nd edn, New York: New York Review of
    Books, 1990, pp. 18–19.
23 Iris Marion Young, *Justice and the Politics of Difference*, pp. 40–41. I shall
    discuss these issues further in the final chapter.
24 And if anybody objects to that term, we might simply say that they are the
    victims of injustice, or simply that they are wrongly treated.
25 Some might suggest that if females are the greater victims of sex discrimination
    than males that we are, on that basis, justified in focusing on anti-female sex
    discrimination. I reject that argument in the "Distraction" section of Chapter 5.
26 For example, Betty Friedan, *The Feminine Mystique*, New York: Dell, 1974;
    Carole Pateman, *The Sexual Contract*, Cambridge: Polity Press, 1988; Deborah
    L. Rhode, *Speaking of Sex: The Denial of Gender Inequality*, Cambridge, MA:
    Harvard University Press, 1997.
27 Perhaps in extraordinary circumstances – to avoid some catastrophe, for exam-
    ple – a sexist act might be morally justified. Some might wish to say, under such
    circumstances, that the discrimination still wronged the person who was harmed
    by it, but that the wrong was justifiably inflicted. In this book I focus on ordi-
    nary rather than extraordinary circumstances.
28 Iris Marion Young, *Justice and the Politics of Difference*, pp. 41, 150; Nijole V.
    Benokraitis, *Subtle Sexism: Current Practices and Prospects for Change*,
    Thousand Oaks, CA: Sage Publications, 1997.
29 John Stuart Mill, "The subjection of women," in *On Liberty and Other Essays*,
    ed. J. Gray, Oxford: Oxford University Press, 1991, p. 486–487, 493–495;
    Martha C. Nussbaum, *Sex and Social Justice*, pp. 11, 13, 130–153.
30 *Frontiero v. Richardson*, 411 US 677 (1973).
31 I am grateful to Don Hubin for drawing my attention to this case and for sug-
    gesting the observations I have made in this paragraph.
32 There are some criticisms that do not presuppose either of the views I shall
    now outline. There are not many of these and I shall consider them too in
    due course.
33 Michael Levin would deny that egalitarian feminism really is feminism. This is
    because one of his conditions for a view to count as feminist is that it not be a
    "platitude which no reasonable person would dispute." He then says that views

like "opposition to sexism" fall foul of this condition. (*Feminism and Freedom*, New Brunswick, NJ: Transaction Books, 1987, p. 16.) The problem with his view, however, is that opposition to sexism has been, and still is, widely rejected. Even when people *say* that they are opposed to sexism their words often do not match their commitments. Thus it is not unreasonable to understand egalitarian feminism as a genuine commitment to equality of the sexes.

34 This distinction is not quite the same as Christina Hoff Sommers' distinction between equity feminism and gender feminism, even though there are similarities. (See *Who Stole Feminism?* New York: Simon & Schuster, 1994, p. 22.)

35 Janet Radcliffe Richards notes that there are partisan feminists (*The Sceptical Feminist*, p. 29), but judges such a view not to be true to feminism. She says, for example, that feminism "is not concerned with *a group of people it wants to benefit*, but with a *type of injustice it wants to eliminate*" (pp. 25–26). It is, she says, "far more reasonable to ask people to support a movement against injustice than a movement for women" (p. 26).

36 For example, the (no longer existent) "New York Radical Women" in a statement of principles said:

We take the woman's side in everything. We ask not if something is "reformist", "radical", "revolutionary", or "moral." We ask: is it good for women or bad for women?

(Robin Morgan (ed.), *Sisterhood is Powerful: An Anthology of Writings from the Women's Liberation Movement*, New York: Vintage Books, 1970, p. 520.)

37 I shall discuss this further in Chapter 3.

38 Indeed, when I first published an article on the second sexism, all four of the responses, invited by the journal editors, were feminist responses. Conservatives were not even invited to comment. This, I think, is very likely indicative of the current tendencies in social philosophy and of academia more generally.

39 Tom Digby ("Male trouble," p. 248) complains that I leave the nature of the threat unspecified. This is because its nature will depend on the particularities of any given reader's view.

40 I refer here to orthodoxies in general.

41 Kenneth Clatterbaugh, "Benatar's alleged second sexism," *Social Theory and Practice*, 29(2), April 2003, p. 211.

42 I have since discovered that many of them were mentioned well before the 1970s. See Ernest Belfort Bax, "The Legal Subjection of Men" (1908). Available at: http://en.wikisource.org/wiki/The_Legal_Subjection_of_Men (accessed July 1, 2010). Since this work claims that it is men *rather than* women who are (or, at the time of writing, were) subjugated, I do not endorse the conclusions of this broadside.

43 See, for example, Tom Digby, "Male trouble," p. 247. He says "antifeminism is a common theme in angry man discourse." He then says that this is my "approximate vantage point."

44 We should also reject, as an *ad hominem* fallacy, the possible accusation that *male* feminists hate men – or at least those men who do not agree with their particular feminist views.

45 It is ironic, indeed, that Professor Digby, who accuses others of being angry men, has previously objected to making the allegation that feminists hate men. See his "Do feminists hate men? Feminism, antifeminism and gender oppositionality," *Journal of Social Philosophy*, 29(2), Fall 1998, pp. 15–31.

46 Tom Digby tries a similar move when he taints, by association with racists and people who are insensitive to racism, those who disapprove of affirmative action (Tom Digby, "Male trouble," p. 258). I agree that those who oppose affirmative action (for blacks) include racists and those insensitive to racism, but there is another strand of opposition to affirmative action that is based on liberal, anti-racist premises.

47 My views have already evolved. In some cases, I previously thought that it was an open question whether a given disadvantage of being male was the product of discrimination, but subsequent reading suggested that it is.

2

Male Disadvantage

Now that females are no longer being felled by childbirth, it has become clear that they enjoy an advantage in both psychological and biological robustness.

Constance Holden, "Why do women live longer than men?"
Science, 238, October 9, 1987, p. 158.

Many people are unable to think of any ways in which males are disadvantaged. The aim of this chapter is to rectify that. I shall present a number of examples of such disadvantage and provide some details about them. Because some of those who deny that there is a second sexism are inclined to dismiss these as minor matters, I shall spend some time explaining just how substantial some of these disadvantages are, either in the number of males who are affected or by the severity of the impact. In other cases, I devote some attention to demonstrating that there is in fact a disadvantage, because the facts may be in dispute.

The disadvantages are presented under various headings. These categories are for convenience, but there is actually considerable overlap between a few of them. I do not pretend to be exhaustive. There has been so little attention to male disadvantage that it is very likely that we do not even know all the ways in which males are disadvantaged. My examples are thus either those where it is clear – to all except the most ideological deniers of the second sexism – that males are disadvantaged, or those where we have sufficient data to demonstrate male disadvantage. Not every example of male disadvantage I shall mention in this book will be covered in this chapter. Sometimes, I shall raise an example incidentally in subsequent chapters as part of my arguments that there is a second sexism.

The Second Sexism: Discrimination Against Men and Boys, First Edition. David Benatar.
© 2012 John Wiley & Sons, Inc. Published 2012 by John Wiley & Sons, Inc.

In presenting examples of male disadvantage, I draw on both historical and current examples. Both are relevant. Many of the historical examples continue until the present, at least in some parts of the world. Even where they do not, they demonstrate the historical depth of male disadvantage – that it is nothing new. Of primary interest, however, is the persistence of male disadvantage, or the development of new forms of disadvantage, and thus the current examples are crucial.

The incidence of male disadvantage varies not only from time to time, but also from place to place. There is considerable variation geographically. The disadvantages that males experience in some places are not experienced by males in all places. The same, of course, is true of female disadvantages, and thus those feminists who deny the existence of the second sexism should be careful about dismissing the significance of male disadvantage on the grounds that they are not experienced by all males in all times and places. The geographical and historical variation does not mean that the disadvantages are any less real or serious for those who experience them.

For the most part, my account of male disadvantage is general. That is to say, I describe laws, trends, quantitative data and common practices. Sometimes, however, I illustrate a point with an example about a specific person. I do this rarely and my argument does not rest on such specifics. The specific cases are illustrations of more widespread trends. I am thus not vulnerable to the charge of arguing by means of anecdote.

Although my aim in this chapter is to present only examples of male *disadvantage*, it should be clear, as I present these examples, that some of them are also the products of discrimination. However, the arguments for the claim that they are instances of *wrongful* discrimination will only be presented in subsequent chapters. Other examples I shall present, although clearly instances of disadvantage are not clearly examples of discrimination. I raise them nonetheless. One reason for this is that they parallel some forms of female disadvantage that feminists cite as instances of sexism. Thus I shall argue that either the relevant male disadvantages are instances of sexism or the comparable female disadvantages are not.

Conscription and Combat

Perhaps the most obvious example of male disadvantage is the long history of social and legal pressures on men, but not on women, to enter the military and to fight in war, thereby risking their lives and bodily and psychological health. Where the pressure to join the military has taken the form of conscription, the costs of avoidance have been self-imposed exile, imprisonment, physical assault or, in the most extreme circumstances, execution.[1]

Millions of men have been conscripted and forced into battle. Others have been press-ganged into naval service. While conscription has been abolished in an increasing number of countries – at least for now – it is still employed, in one form or another, in over 80 countries.[2] These include many developed liberal democracies, where the legal barriers to the advancement of women have (almost) all been broken down.

In those times and places where the pressures on men to join the military have been social rather than legal, the costs of not enlisting have been either shame or ostracism. It may be hard for people in contemporary western societies to understand how powerful those forces have been in other contexts. However, young men, and even boys, have felt, and been made to feel, that their manhood is impugned if they fail to enlist. In other words, they would be cowards if they failed to respond to the call to arms. Women, oblivious to their own privilege in being exempt from such pressures and expectations, have sometimes taken a lead in shaming men who they thought should already have volunteered.

One particularly graphic example of this is the campaign, during the First World War, of British women distributing white feathers – a symbol of cowardice – to young men who were not in uniform.[3] These were distributed even to adolescent boys who were technically too young to register.[4] One boy, Frederick Broome, who had succeeded in enlisting at age 15, fought in battle, was returned to England in a febrile state and then discharged at the insistence of his father, who produced his birth certificate to convince the authorities. Then, while walking over a bridge in town, then age 16, young Frederick was accosted by four girls who gave him three white feathers. He later recalled as follows:

> I felt very humiliated. I finished the walk over the bridge and there on the other side was the Thirty-seventh London Territorial Association of the Royal Field Artillery. I walked straight in and rejoined the army.[5]

Even in those few societies where women have been conscripted, they have almost invariably been treated more leniently. Thus, Israel, one of the few contemporary states (and perhaps the only liberal democratic state) currently to conscript women, is far less demanding of women than it is of men. Women are conscripted for under two years and men for a full three years.[6] While men serve in the reserves until age 54, women serve only until age 24.[7] Moreover, married women but not married men are exempt. Women are also much more likely to be exempt on other grounds (such as religious commitments).[8] Most important of all, women are not forced into combat and are thereby spared the worst of military life.[9] Indeed, they are largely placed in jobs that "free up" more men for combat.

Some have noted, quite correctly, that the definition of "combat" often changes, with the result that although women are often formally kept from combat conditions, they are *sometimes* effectively engaged in risky combat activity.[10] This is most pronounced in the case of the United States military where, *de facto* even though not *de jure*, women are increasingly in conditions where they come under enemy fire. Kingsley Browne acknowledges that these female soldiers are "in combat" in the sense that they face "combat risks" or are "in harm's way." However, he suggests that these women are not "in combat" in another, narrower sense which refers to "seeking out the enemy and closing with him for purposes of killing him."[11] In other words, the difference between being "in harm's way" and "in combat" (in the narrow sense) is the difference between hoping but failing to avoid contact with the enemy and seeking out such contact and engaging with the enemy. Moreover, it remains true that in those relatively few situations, both historically and geographically, in which women are permitted to take roles that expose them to greater risk, it is a result of their choice rather than coercion. Even then women are usually kept, insofar as possible, from the worst combat situations.

Others have noted that the exclusion of women from combat roles has not resulted in universal protection for women in times of war. Where wars are fought on home territory, women are regularly amongst the casualties of the combat. It remains true, however, that such scenarios are viewed by societies as being a deviation from the "ideal" conflict in which (male) combatants fight at a distance from the women and children whom they are supposed to be protecting. A society attempts to protect its own women but not its men from the life-threatening risks of war.

Nor should we forget just how terrible combat is. The conditions can be appalling. Consider, for example, the conditions faced by the English troops awaiting the battle of Agincourt on October 25, 1415:

> Waiting … must have been a cold, miserable and squalid business. It had been raining, the ground was recently ploughed, air temperature was probably in the forties or low fifties Fahrenheit and many in the army were suffering from diarrhoea. Since none would presumably have been allowed to leave the ranks while the army was deployed for action, sufferers would have had to relieve themselves where they stood. For any afflicted man-at-arms wearing mail leggings laced to his plate armour, even that may not have been possible.[12]

Nor is diarrhea a necessary condition for these excremental indignities:

> As contact with the enemy draws nearer, anticipation sharpens into fear. Its physical effects are striking. The heart beats rapidly, the face shines with sweat and the mouth grows dry – so dry that men often emerge from battle with

blackened mouths and chapped lips. The jaws gape or the teeth chatter, and in an effort to control himself a man may clench his jaw so tightly that it will ache for days afterwards. Many lose control of their bladder or bowels. Nearly a quarter of the soldiers of an American division interviewed in the South Pacific admitted that they had fouled themselves, and the spectacle of soldiers urgently urinating just before they go into action is as old as battle itself.[13]

Once battle begins so do the casualties.[14] Millions of men have been killed in combat. They have been clubbed with various instruments, decapitated with swords and cannonballs, hacked with axes, penetrated in every part of the body – the head, chest, abdomen, genitals and limbs – by arrows, bullets and shrapnel – and blown to smithereens.[15] They have been poisoned with gas, burned alive, crashed to their deaths in aircraft, drowned and hemorrhaged internally from the pressure of blasts.[16] Some die instantly. Others have bled to death, succumbed to infections or otherwise perished from their wounds over periods of varying duration. Some mortally wounded have died slowly on the battlefield because timely evacuation for medical treatment was impossible.

Not all casualties are fatal. Some are relatively mild, but nonetheless a disadvantage relative to women, who were spared such injuries by being exempt from combat. Serious injuries, however, are extremely common.[17] Men have lost limbs, jaws, noses, ears and eyes. They have been blinded, deafened, paralyzed and disfigured in innumerable ways. Nor are all the wounds physical. The trauma of combat, being injured, witnessing the gruesome deaths and wounds of comrades, and even inflicting such on enemies, can readily cause psychological trauma.[18] Soldiers can be haunted for decades by their combat experiences, impacting negatively on their lives in myriad ways.

The horrors of war are such that many soldiers – even those who volunteered, but more especially conscripts – would much rather leave battle than stay. The pressures against desertion are partially social. Men, if they are to save face, must act bravely and "honorably." But these pressures are insufficient to keep all men in rank, and thus steep penalties have been imposed for those who seek to hold back or run away. Deserters are regularly imprisoned but other penalties have included branding.[19] Deserters have often been executed, either summarily on the spot or following a court martial.[20] Among those who were executed for desertion are those who would today, at least in some societies, be recognized as having post-traumatic stress disorder.[21] However, there are still cases, even in enlightened societies, where the military is insufficiently attentive to the psychological stresses of combat. In 2003 an American soldier, on his second night in Iraq, saw an Iraqi who had been cut in half by machine-gun fire. The soldier vomited and "shook for hours. His head pounded and his chest hurt."[22] "When he informed his superior that he was having a panic attack and needed to see someone," he said he "was given two sleeping pills and told to go away."[23] Two days later he was shipped back to the United States and then charged with cowardice. "Coward is a pretty big stigma to carry around," he said.[24] Eventually all charges against him were dropped,[25] but not before causing him a great deal of distress.

Other soldiers, wishing to avoid both continued combat or the punishments for deserting, have feigned psychiatric illness, while others have resorted to self-mutilation, rendering themselves unfit for continued service.[26] Some are so desperate that they take their own lives.[27]

Some soldiers become prisoners of war. Although there are now conventions governing the treatment of prisoners, these are relatively new and even now are frequently breached. All prisoners of war are, by definition, prisoners and suffer the hardships that come with imprisonment. Some have been beaten, tortured, starved, put to hard labor. Some are executed.

Having fought, often unwillingly and under threat of severe punishment for refusing, surviving soldiers return home. While a hero's welcome sometimes awaits them, this does not last as long as the injuries many of them have suffered.[28] Their initial reception by civilian society is frequently less glorious. They can be feared because of how war has brutalized them.[29] They may even be met with hostility where the war in which they fought has become unpopular.[30] Indeed, they are sometimes rejected even before returning from such wars. For example, as the Vietnam War become more unpopular in the United States, "it became increasingly common for girlfriends, fiancées, and even wives to dump the soldiers who depended on them."[31]

Not all men who are conscripted see combat, but conscription even in the absence of combat is a significant disadvantage. Careers are interrupted. Conscripts are separated from their families. They are subjected to serious invasions of privacy, restrictions on freedom, demeaning treatment and harsh discipline.[32] Even today, in the Russian army for example, an "abusive system of discipline known as dedovshchina" is practiced.[33] Thousands of cases are reported every year and a number of soldiers die each year as a result of this discipline.[34] Hundreds take their own lives.[35]

Violence

Combat is by no means the only context in which men are the victims of violence. Indeed, with two exceptions, men are much more likely than women to be the targets of aggression and violence.[36]

The first exception is sexual assault. Although, as I shall show later, the incidence of sexual assault of males is significantly underestimated and taken insufficiently seriously, it is the case that women are more frequently the victims of sexual assault.

The second exception is one kind of domestic violence, but this is exceptional in an unusual way. In its spousal or "intimate partner" form,[37] the phrase "domestic violence" is routinely understood to refer to the violence husbands or boyfriends inflict on wives or girlfriends. The general perception is that spousal violence is almost exclusively the violent treatment of women by their husbands, boyfriends or other male partners. However, this perception is mistaken. Many studies have shown that wives use violence against their husbands at least as much as husbands use violence against their wives,[38] Given how unexpected such findings are to many people, at least one well-known author (who shared the prevailing prejudices prior to his quantitative research) examined the data in multiple ways in order to determine whether these could be reconciled with common views.[39] On almost every score, women were as violent as men. It was found that half the violence is mutual, and in the remaining half there were an equal number of female and male aggressors.[40] When a distinction was drawn between "normal violence" (pushing, shoving, slapping and throwing things) and "severe violence" (kicking, biting, punching, hitting with an object, "beating up" and attacking the spouse with a knife or gun), the rate of mutual violence dropped to a third, the rate of violence by only the husband remained the same but the rate of violence by only the wife *increased*.[41] Wives have been shown to initiate violence as often as husbands do.[42] At least some studies have suggested that there is a *higher* rate of wives assaulting husbands than husbands assaulting wives,[43] and most studies of dating violence show higher rates of female-inflicted violence.[44] It is thus not the case, as some have suggested, that female violence against intimate partners is usually in self-defense.

Research findings on the *effects* of spousal violence are mixed. Some have found that husbands inflict more damage on wives than wives do on husbands.[45] It has been suggested that this is because husbands are generally bigger and stronger than their wives.[46] However, other studies have found that wives inflict more damage on husbands.[47] If weapons are used, the smaller size of women would make no difference to their capacity to cause injury. Yet other studies have found no difference in the severity of injury caused by male and female partners.[48]

Thus spousal violence is an exception to the trend that men are at *greater* risk of being the victims of violence, not because men are at *lesser* risk but because they are at *comparable* risk. However, the mistaken perception that wives do not batter husbands itself causes further disadvantage to males. Abused men are taken less seriously than abused women when they complain of abuse or seek help. There are also fewer resources to aid abused men.

With the exception of sexual violence and intimate partner violence, males are more likely than females to be the victims of violence. Both men and women have been shown, in a majority of experimental studies, to behave more aggressively against men than toward women.[49] Outside the laboratory, men are also more often the victims of violence. This is true in a variety of contexts. Consider first violent crime. Data from the USA, for example, shows that nearly double the number of men as women are the victims of aggravated assault and more than three times more men than women are murdered.[50] Statistics from England and Wales show a similar phenomenon there. During the 2008–2009 year, men "were twice as likely as women to have been victims of violence."[51] Young men, aged 16 to 24 were particularly at risk. Thirteen percent of them had been the victims of violent crime, compared with 3% of all adults.

In cases of conflict, men, even when they are not combatants, suffer more violence. For example, the overwhelming majority of deaths during the Belgian "rubber terror" in the Congo were males. Although there is apparently no direct evidence of the numbers killed, the subsequent significant demographic imbalance between the number of adult males and females in the population at the end of this period reveals that it was primarily male lives that were taken.[52]

Men were also the majority of victims of the Stalinist purges. Examining data from the Soviet census of January 1959, Robert Conquest concluded that although the casualties of war explain some of the sex imbalance in the population, the more significant imbalances were in older age cohorts that were less affected by combat losses in the Second World War and more affected by the purges. Thus, in the 55–59 age group, only 33% of the population was male. In the adjacent age cohorts, the proportions are very similar. About 38% of 40- to 54-year-olds were male, and nearly 35% of 60- to 69-year-olds were male.[53]

In South Africa, the Truth and Reconciliation Commission found that the overwhelming majority of victims of gross violations of human rights – killing, torture, abduction and severe ill treatment – during the apartheid years (at the hands of both the government and its opponents) were males.[54] Testimony received by the Commission suggests that the number of men who died was six times that of women. Non-fatal gross violations of rights were inflicted on more than twice the number of men as women.[55] Nor can the Commission be accused of having ignored women and their testimony. The majority of the Commission's deponents (55.3%) were female,[56] and so sensitive was the Commission to the relatively small proportion of women amongst the victims of the most severe violations that it held a special hearing on women.[57]

In the Kosovo conflict of 1998–1989, according to one study, 90% of the war-related deaths were of men, and men constituted 96% of people reported missing.[58] According to the report of the Organization of Security and Co-operation in Europe (OSCE) Kosovo Verification Mission, "young men were the group that was by far the most targeted in the conflict in Kosovo."[59] While women and girls constituted the majority of rape victims, men and boys were tortured and killed in much greater numbers.

These are but a few recent examples, in the long history of human violence, in which males have been the primary victims of mass murder and other serious human rights violations.[60]

Corporal Punishment

One category of violence that merits separate attention is corporal punishment, the punitive infliction of pain on the body (by means of flogging, caning, beating or smacking, for example). This is because, unlike violent crime, which is by definition illegal, and much violence inflicted on non-combatants in times of conflict, which is often a breach of either law or local or international norms, corporal punishment is either imposed by the law or it is legally and socially permitted, if not encouraged.

Although corporal punishment has been inflicted on both males and females, it has been imposed, especially but not only in recent times, on males much more readily and severely than on females.[61] Distinct double standards exist.

One context in which corporal punishment has been inflicted – and still is inflicted in some countries – is the military. Because, as we have seen, the military has traditionally been an almost exclusively male preserve, females have been spared the brutal physical punishment, often for the most trivial of infractions, that has been inflicted on males in the military. Thousands of soldiers and sailors have been flogged. In the US Navy, for example, nearly 6000 floggings were inflicted in the period 1846–1847.[62] In any given flogging up to hundreds of lashes would be inflicted on a single man. The cat-o'-nine-tails, a whip made of "nine small, hard, twisted pieces of cotton or flax cord, with three knots in each, fixed to a short, thick rope handle,"[63] was used on the bare back, while the sailor on whom it was inflicted was tied with his arms elevated above his head. This punishment, which was administered in the presence of everybody on board, flayed the skin on the back and often also caused anterior damage as the whip curled round to the front of the sailor's body. Boy sailors were made to "kiss the gunner's daughter" – that is they were tied in a bending position, lengthways across the barrel of a cannon and then flogged on the (often naked) buttocks. Another penalty to which sailors were subjected was keelhauling,[64] in which a man was tied to a rope and dragged under a ship, from one side to the other. In this process the barnacle encrusted keel lacerated his skin. When hauled too slowly men drowned. In the nineteenth-century Russian army blows "from the officers, flogging with birch rods and with sticks, for the slightest fault, were normal affairs."[65] In contemporary Singapore, conscripts are caned (although the frequency is not known).[66] These are but a few examples drawn from many centuries and hundreds of countries in which men have been subject to harsh corporal punishment in the military.

Although corporal punishment is a judicially inflicted punishment in many fewer countries now than earlier, there are still over 30 countries in which the courts sentence people to corporal punishment.[67] In the overwhelming majority of these countries, this punishment is reserved for males and may not be inflicted on females. This double standard was also the norm in those countries that previously inflicted judicial punishment but no longer do.[68]

While the details of how the punishment is inflicted vary from jurisdiction to jurisdiction, judicial corporal punishment tends to be extremely severe. In Singapore, for example, the man is brought into the caning room, stripped naked and bound to a trestle. Protective material is placed over the kidney area to prevent organ damage in the event of a misplaced blow, but the buttocks are left exposed. The caning officers are powerful young men who are legally required to put their fullest force into each strike (a term I think preferable to the ambiguous, but commonly used "stroke"). The strikes are delivered with a rattan cane. The number of blows depends on the sentence, but the maximum is 24 (per offense) for adults and 10 for juveniles. The pain has been described as "beyond description," "stronger than excruciating" and "unbearable."[69] The blows draw blood and, if a sufficient number are delivered, the skin becomes lacerated, leaving open wounds in which the flesh is exposed. Permanent scarring is common. The number of caning sentences in Singapore has steadily increased over the years and now stands at over 6000 per year.[70] The Singapore Criminal Procedure Code specifically forbids the infliction of a caning on women,[71] which is also the case in most other countries where judicial corporal punishment is inflicted. Even where women are not exempt, the punishment is much less severe. Males are therefore at a disadvantage.

Many jurisdictions that no longer impose judicial corporal punishment still permit it in schools. Where it is (or has been) permitted in schools, it is often the case that only boys may be hit – that the corporal punishment of girls is prohibited.[72] This is true even in co-educational schools. In other words, if a boy and a girl in the same class commit the same offense, the boy may be subjected to corporal punishment, but the girl is treated more mildly. Indeed, a boy might be caned for a minor offense, while the girl is exempt even if she commits a serious wrongdoing. While the canings of boys is sometimes done in private, it is also often done in front of the class or even the whole school.[73] Thus a boy might be subjected to the humiliation of being caned in front of other children – including those (that is, girls) who are immune from that punishment. In one case a boy "was caned for sitting on the grass during break with his girl-friend's head on his lap."[74] This punishment was inflicted in the presence of the girlfriend, who was not caned even though it was her head that was in the boy's lap.[75]

As is the case with judicial corporal punishment, the way in which school corporal punishment is inflicted varies. The sadism in the following account of corporal punishment in a boys' boarding school, although not universal, has also not been uncommon:

> Cuts[76] were given after the evening meal and those due for punishment had to change into pajamas and dressing gowns and line up outside a small room in which all the boys' mackintoshes were hung.
>
> You would stand there in a state of terror wincing as the whistle and snap of Ploddy's[77] cane came through the door, each stroke a minute or two apart. Then the door would burst open and a white-faced boy would half run out of the place, trying like hell not to let tears take over and getting out of sight to where he would be able to rub his backside. Neither rubbing nor sob were tolerated by Ploddy. Either could earn an extra cut or two.
>
> Once inside that awful room ... [Ploddy] would make a deal out of choosing which cane he would use for you. Three of these thin curved yellow things stood in a metal rack, their ends in a well of linseed oil. Having chosen one, Ploddy would nod and the boy would have to bend down, grasp his ankles and stick his head into the hanging mackintoshes. Using the cane, Ploddy himself, lifted the dressing gown, folding it on to the boy's back.
>
> "And you do remember why you are here to be caned?" He would lightly tap the boy's backside, protected now by no more than thin pyjama material. Then would come a short explanation of your misdemeanour and, if Ploddy was in a good mood, the first of the cuts. He could stretch this out if he felt like it. Another short lecture on wrong and right would be proffered between each stroke while the threat of the cane was emphasised with little taps and strokings. Four cuts could take six minutes.[78]

While such treatment has sometimes been inflicted on girls, there have been very many places where it has been inconceivable to treat girls in this way, while it has been entirely normal and common to inflict such punishment on boys. I know of no places where the reverse has been true.

Where it is legally permissible to hit both boys and girls, there are nonetheless many disparities. Boys are hit much more often than girls.[79] Boys are often hit for more trivial offenses than girls. Among the very many trivial offenses (or "offenses") for which boys have been caned are: "not writing down homework; ... for being offside in a soccer match; for losing a rugby match; for not batting properly in a cricket match";[80] for not wearing the correct uniform; for running in the corridor;[81] "for stupidity";[82] for spelling and mathematical mistakes;[83] "for forgetting to change into house-shoes at six o'clock";[84] and for being a member of a class in which a wrongdoer had not been individually identified.[85]

There are also various other disparities – either matters of convention or of law. Thus, boys are often hit with a more severe implement – a cane instead of a slipper, for example. Sometimes the site on the body where the punishment is inflicted differs, boys suffering the more degrading posture of bending over and being hit on the buttocks – in some cases naked buttocks[86] – while girls are hit instead on the palms of their hands. Sometimes there are prohibitions on male teachers hitting female students but there are never, or almost never, parallel prohibitions on female teachers hitting male students.[87]

There are a small but increasing number of countries that prohibit all corporal punishment, including that inflicted by parents on their children. In most, countries, however, physical punishment of children by their parents is still permitted. Where parents do hit their children, both mothers and fathers are more likely to hit sons than daughters.[88]

To emphasize, it is not my claim that girls and women have never been subject to corporal punishment. Nor am I denying that some females have been subject to physical punishment that is as severe or degrading as that inflicted on any male. Instead my claim is that in general, corporal punishment has been inflicted much more often on males and has tended, in many contexts, to be inflicted more severely on males, while the reverse has not been true.

Sexual Assault

Although much sexual assault is violent, not all of it is. Fondling of genitals (without consent), for example, need not be violent or done under the threat of violence, even though it sometimes is. This is one reason to examine sexual assault separately from violence, which was discussed before.

The other reason is that male disadvantage in the realm of sexual assault is of a distinct kind. Although most victims of violence are males, females constitute the majority of victims of sexual assault, whether violent or otherwise. The greater likelihood of being sexually assaulted is a disadvantage of being female. However, males experience many unrecognized or under-recognized disadvantages pertaining to sexual assault. In general the problem can be characterized as a failure to take sexual assault of males as seriously as sexual assault of females.

In one illuminating study, the male and female experimental subjects were told that they were participating in a study on "Legal Decision Making."[89] They were told that the aim of the study was "concerned with the extent to which jury decision making in actual trials is based on the nature and strength of the evidence presented."[90] They were then given a detailed description of what the experimental subjects were told was a real case. The case concerned a hitchhiking 20-year-old college student who was picked up by two people who later pulled off the road in a deserted area, pulled a gun and forced the student to disrobe and then engage in mutual oral–genital sexual activity. The student was then left in a field. The assailants were later arrested and a gun found in their car. They were arrested and charged with rape. At trial they acknowledged that the sexual activity had occurred, but claimed it was consensual.

Unbeknownst to the experimental subjects, they were actually randomized to four different versions of the case. All details of the case, except the names of the assailants and victim, remained the same in each version. The effect of the variation in the names was to create four different permutations of the assailants' and victim's sex: male–female, male–male, female–female and female–male.

The experimental subjects were asked to complete a "Juror Questionnaire." These questions concerned the innocence or guilt of the defendants, the recommended sentence, the likelihood that the victim was forced, the likelihood that the victim encouraged or initiated the sexual activity, how pleasurable the incident was for the defendants and the victim and how personally responsible the victim was for the sexual episode.

While almost all subjects judged the defendants guilty, the "likelihood that the victim was forced to engage in the sex acts ... was perceived as higher when the victim was female" and the "highest likelihood of victim encouragement of the acts was attributed when the victim was male and the assailants female."[91] Victim stress was judged to be least when the victim was male and the assailants female, and greatest when there was a female victim (of either males or females).[92] Male victims were also judged to have derived more pleasure than female victims.[93] Significantly longer sentences were recommended when the defendants were male than when they were female.[94]

These effects were more pronounced in male than in female subjects – a matter to which I shall return in the next chapter – but the study still suggests that both males and females are less sympathetic to male victims of sexual assault than they are to female victims of such assault.[95] Male victims of sexual assault are disadvantaged by this phenomenon, which also manifests outside the laboratory.

Nor is it only the lay population that takes sexual assault less seriously when the victims are male. One study showed that clinical psychologists were more likely to hypothesize sexual assault in females than males.[96] In this study, clinical psychologists were given a "detailed summary of an adult client which incorporated a number of indicators that the client had been sexually abused."[97] In half the cases, the client was presented as male and in half as female. All other details of the case were the same, yet the clinical psychologists were twice as likely to hypothesize that female clients had been sexually abused.[98]

It is widely recognized that sexual assault in general is under-reported. This problem is particularly acute when the victims are males. Sexual assaults upon boys are less likely to be reported than are those upon girls.[99] It is unclear, however, what the ratio of abused girls and boys is. Some say it is as much as 9:1, while others say that girls are abused at only a slightly higher rate than boys.[100] Adult males are also less likely than women to report being sexually assaulted.[101] The under-reporting of sexual assault on males and the resultant misperception of the ratio of male to female victims may partially explain why people are less sympathetic to male victims. Because the phenomenon is less in the public consciousness it is less likely to be taken seriously. However, the reverse causal relationship is arguably greater: sexual assault on males is less likely to be reported in part because people are less likely to believe the report. There are other reasons too. Some of these have to do with the male gender role and these will be discussed in the next chapter.

There is some evidence that males are "more likely to be victims of multiple assailants, to sustain more physical trauma and to be held captive longer than female victims."[102] Their sexual identity is also threatened, irrespective of whether the assailant is male[103] or female,[104] although the experience tends to be worse when the assailant is male. Lest it be thought, in keeping with popular wisdom, that sexual assault of males by females is extremely rare, it should be said that it is actually not as uncommon as is generally thought.[105] It is unclear what exactly the rate of female abuse of males is. The scant existent data are very variable. A very small minority of studies have found that females are the perpetrators in no more than 2% of cases of sexual abuse of males.[106] An equally small number of studies put the rate as high as 60%.[107] Most studies, however, have found that the rate of abuse by females lies between the low and high rates just mentioned, with many studies finding the rate to be between a third and just under a half of all cases.[108] Given the under-reporting of sexual assault on males we cannot presume that the current rate of convictions is any indication of the actual rate. Indeed, there is some reason to think that the under-reporting of sexual assault on males may be particularly pronounced where the perpetrators are female. This is partly because of widespread incredulity that women, with a few highly aberrational exceptions, are capable of child sexual abuse.[109]

Both females and males can exhibit physiological sexual arousal without corresponding psychological arousal.[110] Thus both males and females can be physiologically aroused while being traumatized during and after a sexual assault or rape. Ignorance about this disjunction of physiological and psychological arousal (and ignorance about the disjunction between arousal of any kind and consent) can heighten trauma, leading victims who were physiologically aroused to be confused about whether they really were victims – or whether they really wanted the sexual experience. This effect is likely to be greater in males, perhaps in part because their physiological arousal is more apparent both to the assailant and to themselves.[111] Those heterosexual males who are victims of sexual assault by other males may be led, on account of their tumescent response, to bewilderment about their sexual orientation.

One context where sexual assault on males has received relatively more attention is that of incarceration. Although both females and males are subject to sexual assault in prisons, jails and other detention facilities, there are more male victims. This is partly a consequence of males constituting a disproportionate share of the prison population. However, there is also evidence that the rate of sexual abuse of male prisoners is higher. One study comparing sexual coercion of men and women in a Midwestern state prison system in the United States found that the sexual coercion incidence rate for males was 22%, while for females it was 7%.[112] It is also noteworthy that when the sexual assailant is a fellow prisoner, males are more likely than females to be infected by HIV as a result of being raped.

Very little has been done about this problem. In 2003 the United States passed the Prison Rape Elimination Act, one of the provisions of which was to establish the Prison Rape Elimination Commission, which monitors sexual assault statistics in United States detention facilities. It is unclear whether either the Act or the Commission has succeeded in reducing the numbers of sexual assaults in prison, but the mere existence of these initiatives is an advance over most other states, where the problem remains unaddressed. Indeed, in some parts of the world, rape is condoned if not actually approved as an act of torture.[113]

If we turn from the penal system to the criminal law, we find that there are other disadvantages to being male. Historically, rape has been defined in such a way that only females can be the victims of rape and males the only perpetrators of it. In some places, there is no comparable crime of which males could be the victims. This is true in China (excluding Hong Kong), where Article 236 of the Penal Code prohibits rape of women and sexual intercourse with underage girls, but has no provisions to prohibit comparable acts against men.[114] In other places, anal penetration of a man by a man is criminalized, but in many of those jurisdictions no distinction is drawn between consensual and non-consensual sodomy, which suggests that the law's concern is not with protecting males from rape but rather with prohibiting a certain kind of sexual activity, irrespective of whether the parties to it are consenting. In other jurisdictions a distinction is drawn between consensual and non-consensual sodomy, with only the latter being criminalized.

However, the penalty for sodomy of a man without his consent is sometimes less severe than the penalty for rape of a female. This is the case in Japan, for example, where the minimum penalty for forced "carnal knowledge of a woman or a girl" is more severe than the penalty for any sexual crime that can be committed against a male.[115]

In a few countries, primarily liberal democracies, the definition of rape has been broadened to include the possibility that males can be raped. The State of Michigan in the United States of America was an early jurisdiction to effect such a change[116] – in the mid-1970s. A number of other jurisdictions, both within the United States and elsewhere, have followed in making such a change. In some places, the reform has been effected only very recently. In South Africa the relevant Act was passed in 2007,[117] while in Scotland the change was made in 2009.[118]

Even where the law has been reformed to recognize that males can be raped, the reforms often fail to achieve full gender neutrality. Consider England, for example. Despite recent advances in sexual offenses law, English law still treats penetration by penis of vagina, anus or mouth as a necessary condition for rape.[119] Thus while the law now recognizes that males can be victims of rape by other men, it still does not recognize that females can be perpetrators of rape against males. Females can only be charged with other sexual offenses against men and boys. While some of these offenses could incur the same penalty as that for rape (namely, life imprisonment), other ways in which a woman could sexually assault a male incur lesser penalties. A man's penetrating a woman with his penis seems to be judged worse than what one would think is the equivalent offense committed by females on males – namely penile envelopment by vagina. Thus if a woman stimulates an unconscious or bound man and then has intercourse with him, she is liable only to a lesser penalty. In other words if the owner of a penis inserts it in a vagina without the consent of the woman whose vagina it is, he is committing rape and he is liable to life imprisonment, whereas if a woman inserts that penis into her vagina without the man's consent, she is guilty only of a lesser crime.[120]

Finally, statutory rape of boys by older females (or the equivalent of statutory rape where it is believed that females cannot rape males) is taken less seriously than when the sex of victim and assailant are reversed. There is a widespread belief that boys "are more likely than girls to be active collaborators rather than unwilling recipients of adult sexual attentions."[121] Now whether or not this belief is true, the whole point of making sex with minors a statutory offense is that minors are deemed not to have the capacity to consent. Willingness is thus not exculpatory. And insofar as a child's willingness mitigates the wrong, it should have equal mitigating force, irrespective of whether the willing party is a boy or a girl. In other words, even if there are more willing and fewer unwilling boys, they should be treated like willing and unwilling girls respectively.

Yet it seems that perceptions about the relative rates of willingness lead to male disadvantage. Because female abuse of boys is less likely to be reported, boys are less protected (which matters even if *they* do not want the protection). Sometimes, the blame is actually put on the boy rather than the adult woman. In one case, for example, a 10-year-old boy was repeatedly sexually assaulted by an older woman who looked after him when his parents were out of town or out for the evening. Eventually he plucked up the courage to tell his parents. In response, his father whipped him. He was then taken to a priest and then a psychiatrist, both of whom referred to his "shameful conduct."[122]

We do not know the full extent to which males are the victims of sexual assault. There has been far too little academic attention to this issue, with the possible exception of prison rape, and the data we have are conflicting. It is very likely, however, given attitudes to sexual assault on males, and males' greater reluctance to report their having been sexually assaulted, that the problem is bigger than we currently think.

Circumcision

In many African countries as well as in a few countries on other continents, female genital cutting is performed on women and girls. Although this practice is often referred to as female circumcision, this designation is misleading. As usually practiced, female genital cutting is a much more radical procedure than male circumcision. It is involves excision of part or all of the clitoris, and sometimes also the labia majori and minori. In the most extreme cases, which are by no means rare, the girl or woman is then infibulated – that is, what remains of her genitalia are sewed up, leaving only a tiny hole for voiding urine and menstrual blood. Girls who are subject to these procedures are disadvantaged. They endure considerable pain during and after the procedure. The risks of infection are high. There is obvious damage to the genitalia without any (known) medical benefit. Longer-term sequelae include limitation or obliteration of sexual pleasure and, in the more severe cases, even pain during intercourse. For these reasons, female genital cutting has rightly been condemned. In some places it has been banned, although in countries where the practice has been widespread such bans have often proven ineffective.

In the developed world, the practice is largely unknown. The exceptions are among immigrants who moved from societies where female genital cutting is practiced. Indeed, some western countries have introduced bans in order to deter the practice in such immigrant communities.

These same western societies permit circumcision of male infants. This is not problematic in itself. It is possible, without inconsistency, to disapprove of female genital cutting of the above kinds, while also approving, or at least tolerating, circumcision of males. This is because it is possible to think that the more severe procedure is unacceptable while the less severe procedure is acceptable.

Not all opponents of female genital cutting think that male circumcision is permissible. Some regard any form of genital alteration, at least of a minor, to be wrong unless it is done for a clear medical purpose. Such people tend to think that circumcision is medically indicated only rarely – indeed much more rarely than is usually thought. They argue that removal of the foreskin is mutilation and that it serves no medical purpose.

Contrary to this view, there is good reason to think that circumcision of boys is not morally wrong. I shall not provide a comprehensive argument for this claim here. One important reason for this is that it is not central to the thesis of this book – namely, establishing that there is a second sexism. If I am mistaken, and circumcision of boys is wrong, then this is a further way in which males are the victims of wrongful discrimination (in those places where female genital cutting is not practiced). That said, it is important to note when practices that may appear to be discriminatory are not in fact so. Thus I shall provide an overview of the argument that (male) circumcision *per se* is not wrong. Those who want further details of the argument can consult papers that focus specifically on this topic.[123]

Central to many arguments against circumcision is that it mutilates. However, the word "mutilation" can be used in different senses and these are not usually differentiated. In a descriptive sense it refers to the removal of part of the body. Alternatively, it can be used in an evaluative sense to refer to a wrongful removal of part of the body. If the word is used in the first sense then circumcision obviously constitutes mutilation, but it does not follow that it is wrong. This is because it is often necessary to remove part of the body, even healthy tissue, in order to advance the patient's interests. Consider, for example, the removal of an entire breast on account of a malignant lump within it. While this is disfiguring, it does not follow that it is wrong.[124]

If "mutilation" is used in the evaluative sense then one cannot designate circumcision as mutilation unless one establishes that it is not in the interest of the child who is circumcised. It is hard to show that circumcision does violate a boy's interests. This is because there is some evidence of modest medical benefits that could reasonably be thought to outweigh the even more modest costs and risks.

At least until recently, the benefits were not known to be sufficiently marked that one could claim with confidence that routine circumcision of male infants was medically indicated. However, they were sufficiently notable that one could not claim neonatal circumcision to be medically contra-indicated. In the last few years, the case *for* circumcision has become a *little* stronger, at least in some contexts. A number of studies have demonstrated that circumcision has a protective effect against HIV infection.[125] So clear was the evidence and so marked was the effect that the studies had to be ended early on ethical grounds: it was thought unacceptable to continue withholding the circumcision option to the control arm of each study. This finding does not entail, as some people think it does, that circumcision should be advocated as a public health measure. One reason for this is that the protective effects of circumcision might be offset by more risky behavior if people erroneously think that circumcision prevents rather than merely lowers the risk of contracting HIV. Nevertheless, the protective effect of circumcision does provide parents seeking to give their child the best chance in life some extra reason to circumcise their sons. Some might suggest that circumcision of children is still wrong because those children could decide, on reaching majority, whether or not they want to be circumcised. The primary problem with that argument is that the negative aspects of circumcision are minimized when performed in the neonatal period. Moreover, some of the benefits of circumcision occur in infancy and childhood.

This is not to deny that there is any disadvantage in circumcision. However, unlike the other disadvantages I have discussed so far, which I shall later show involve wrongful discrimination, the disadvantage of circumcision is not, in itself, impermissibly discriminatory. If circumcision has advantages for males and the only way of obtaining these advantages is to experience inevitable but lesser disadvantages, then males are not being wrongfully discriminated against in being circumcised.

That said, however, there are a few significant disadvantages to circumcision that are not inevitable and which do constitute the kind of disadvantage which can plausibly be described as inappropriate discrimination. Consider first circumcision in the western world. When circumcision is performed in this part of the world, it is usually done during the neonatal period. There is a widespread failure to use anaesthetic when a boy is circumcised at this age.

There was a time that this was justified by the belief that neonates were insufficiently neurologically developed to feel pain and thus the use of an anesthetic was thought unnecessary. This view is no longer tenable. Almost every expert in the area now maintains that the capacity for pain is developed quite late during gestation and thus, except in the cases of extremely premature babies, on whom circumcision would not be performed until later anyway, neonates are able to feel pain.[126] The removal of the prepuce without the use of anesthetic is a significant hardship. It is also avoidable.[127] A topical anesthetic cream is available, and there is no reason to avoid using at least that. This cream is not as effective as a penile dorsal nerve block, which is administered via injection. Obviously an injection involves a moderately greater risk than the use of a cream, but if done by a trained professional seems the right thing to do. When the procedure is performed on older boys or men in the developed world, appropriate anesthetics are used because any risk of anesthetic is more than outweighed by the benefit of not experiencing what would otherwise be quite considerable pain. We should employ the same reasoning in the case of neonates. Although they may not remember the pain later, they experience it intra-operatively, and that is unacceptable.

The equanimity with which infant boys are subjected to *painful* circumcision stands in contrast, in western societies, to the attitude taken to cutting female genitals. In western societies, where the practice of female genital cutting is not indigenous, there is intolerance not only of the common radical forms of female genital cutting, but also of the mildest forms. This is well illustrated in the United States. A group of immigrant Somalis in the Seattle area, mindful of the new cultural milieu in which they found themselves, but also wanting to preserve their own cultural traditions, sought a compromise. They sought to have their daughters symbolically cut at the Harborview Medical Center in Seattle.[128] The proposal was that the prepuce of the clitoris be nicked sufficiently to draw blood. No tissue would be removed and no scarring left. This practice, although far from the form of female genital cutting that takes place in Somalia, would evidently have satisfied at least some members of the Somali community in the Seattle area. The Somalis made it clear that they would have their daughters "circumcised" traditionally, either in Seattle or by sending them back to Somalia for the procedure, if the doctors did not oblige their request. The medical staff agreed to the proposal, which became known as the "Seattle Compromise."

When news of the compromise became public, the hospital received a barrage of criticism from feminist groups opposed to female genital cutting. One prominent critic was Patricia Schroeder, then a member of the United States House of Representatives, who had worked to enact federal legislation banning female genital cutting. In a letter to the hospital she claimed – evidently incorrectly[129] – that the Seattle Compromise would breach that legislation. Doctors also received communications that they described as "hate mail and death threats."[130] In the face of this pressure the hospital announced that it had decided not to perform the procedure. One upshot of this is that whereas the entire foreskin of a male infant may be removed without anesthetic, the much milder procedure of merely drawing blood from the clitoral prepuce has been rendered taboo. This discrepancy was not lost on the Somalis, who, quite reasonably, cannot understand this inconsistency.[131]

In April 2010 the American Academy of Pediatrics (AAP) published a policy statement on "Ritual Genital Cutting of Female Minors."[132] The statement noted that a ritual nick is not physically harmful and is much less extensive than routine newborn male genital cutting. There is reason to believe that offering such a compromise may build trust between hospitals and immigrant communities, save some girls from undergoing disfiguring and threatening procedures in their native countries, and play a role in eventual eradication of FGC. It might be more effective if federal and state laws enabled pediatricians to reach out to families by offering a ritual nick as a possible compromise to avoid greater harm.[133]

Barely a month later, the AAP, responding to an avalanche of criticism of the sort that thwarted the Seattle Compromise, issued a statement announcing that it had "retired its 2010 policy statement on female genital cutting."[134] The statement, explicitly backtracking, stated that:

> The AAP does not endorse the practice of offering a "clitoral nick." This minimal pinprick is forbidden under federal law and the AAP does not recommend it to its members.[135]

Commenting on this, a *New York Times* editorial described the clitoral nick as "a milder version of mutilation" and contended that "medicalizing violence against women would only legitimize it and undermine the force of the ban."[136] The claim that a mere nick of a girl's genitals constitutes a form of mutilation, even a milder form, is implausible in its own right, because it eviscerates the word "mutilation" of any meaning. The same may be said of the claim that this harmless procedure is "medicalized violence." (Do those who pierce their young daughters' ears also mutilate them? Are ear piercings medicalized violence if they are done under aseptic conditions by medical professionals?)

However, insofar as the much greater intervention that constitutes male circumcision is not deemed mutilation, there is also a consistency problem. It would be similarly inconsistent to describe a clitoral nick as medicalized violence if one fails to offer the same criticism of circumcising boys, especially without anesthesia. Now there are some people, of course, who think that both a clitoral nick and male circumcision are mutilation and medical violence. While they are consistent they are, for the reasons mentioned above, consistently wrong. Theirs is, in any event, a minority view in the United States at present, where the inconsistency prevails in public policy and practice.

Now it might be suggested that the explanation of this inconsistency is that male circumcision is commonplace in the United States and thus culturally familiar, whereas female genital cutting, even of the mildest kind, is culturally foreign to the dominant communities in the United States. This diagnosis is correct, I think. We see here a manifestation of intolerance towards the culturally unfamiliar. However, because the United States is a relatively tolerant country in many other ways, it matters that the intolerance is selective. It is relevant that the prevailing views grant no protection to infant boys against circumcision without anesthesia whereas they are hyper-concerned about the protection of baby girls from milder and less painful genital surgery. Whatever other errors are being made, male babies are disadvantaged relative to baby girls with regard to the infliction of pain upon the genitals.

Male disadvantage is still greater in those parts of the developing world where male circumcision is practiced but female genital cutting is not. Consider, for example, South Africa, where young Xhosa men are circumcised in an initiation ceremony that marks their passage from boyhood to manhood. Anesthetic is not used, in part because the young men are meant to demonstrate their manhood by enduring the pain. Moreover, the procedure is performed in non-sterile conditions. The same blade is often used on multiple men, increasing the risk of transmitting infection from one initiate to the other. It is not uncommon for men to suffer gangrenous damage to their penises, and there are a number of deaths each year.[137] Because the Xhosa (and other South Africans) do not perform genital cutting on females, young women are spared the pain and risk of death or genital mutilation to which Xhosa males are subject.

Circumcision has sometimes caused men to be disadvantaged in other ways. Consider, for example, those Jewish males attempting to pass as Christians during the Holocaust. Given that circumcision was practiced exclusively by Jews in the relevant countries at that time, any Jewish man could readily be exposed as a Jew in a way that a Jewess could not.[138]

Education

Through much of human history girls and women have been educationally disadvantaged. Boys have often been prioritized for education over girls. Sometimes girls have been barred even from primary or secondary education. More often they have been prohibited from attending universities. In some parts of the world girls and women are still significantly disadvantaged educationally. However, there are other parts of the world where, thanks to feminism and advances in the position of girls and women, this is no longer the case. Indeed, it seems that in such places males are now educationally disadvantaged according to some important metrics.

Before this evidence is presented, it should be noted that this is controversial terrain. A so-called "gender war" has been waged over the question of whether it is boys or girls who are now disadvantaged in the United States, for example. Sometimes it has seemed as though the facts were in dispute, and sometimes it has seemed as though the argument has been about the interpretation of the facts. I shall try to map out the issues in an attempt to show what we know and what is in dispute.

The first thing to note is that there are a number of possible competing claims one can make with regard to the question of who is educationally disadvantaged in those countries where the answer is disputed:

(1) Girls suffer all (or almost all) the disadvantages.
(2) Boys suffer all (or almost all) the disadvantages.
(3) Girls suffer some disadvantages and boys suffer others:
     (a) All things considered girls are more disadvantaged.
     (b) All things considered boys are more disadvantaged.
     (c) All things considered, boys and girls are equally disadvantaged, albeit in different ways.

For me to demonstrate that males suffer educational disadvantage, I need show only that (1) is false. In other words, even if (3a) were true – girls are more educationally disadvantaged than males – it would still be the case that boys suffer educational disadvantage. I do not think that (3a) is true in the places where the debate arises. However, if it were, male disadvantage would still be worthy of consideration in just the way that feminists would think that female disadvantage would be worthy of consideration if (3b) is true.

The evidence, as we shall see, makes the stronger interpretation of (1) – that is, (1) without the parenthetical "or almost all" – highly implausible and the weaker version only moderately less so. It really does not seem as though girls suffer *all* or even almost all the possible disadvantages in the educational realm. (2) is also false. There are at least some disadvantages of being female – arguably enough to make even the weaker interpretation of (2) false.

It is often difficult to know exactly which of the above claims is being made. Consider, for example, two reports commissioned by the American Association of University Women (AAUW) – *Shortchanging Girls, Shortchanging America* in 1991[139] and *How Schools Shortchange Girls* in 1992.[140] These both appear to be making the first claim. Although they mention the occasional male disadvantage, this is almost immediately either qualified or it is argued that it is not a real disadvantage. For example, while the 1992 report concedes that girls outperform boys on tests of verbal ability, it claims that the disparity has "decreased markedly."[141]

Christina Hoff Sommers, taking issue with these reports and other claims of female educational disadvantage in the United States, appears to defend (2).[142] Her challenge seems to have prompted the AAUW to moderate its position, at least somewhat, and to recognize that both girls and boys suffer disadvantage in schools. The report *Beyond the "Gender Wars": A Conversation about Girls, Boys, and Education* thus endorses (3), although it is arguably (3a) rather than (3b) or (3c) that is endorsed.[143] For example, this report claims that what looks like a disadvantage to males is "actually much more a race and ethnicity difference."[144]

Myra and David Sadker, in their book *Failing at Fairness*,[145] are more explicit in recognizing some male disadvantage, although they too endorse (3a), given that only one chapter in their book is devoted to male disadvantage and that the book's subtitle is *How America's Schools Cheat Girls*.

What are the facts? In the United States, boys drop out of high school at higher rates than girls. This has been true every year since 1977.[146] When one looks at individual "race" or ethnic groups, one finds the same trend, even though they are more marked among some groups than others.

Nor is the United States the only country in which boys drop out at higher rates. In Canada the drop-out rates for both males and females have declined, but the rate for females has declined more significantly, and from a lower base. In 1990–1991, 19.2% of boys and 14% of girls dropped out. By 2004–2005, the rates were, respectively, 12.2% and 7.2%. Thus boys are dropping out at nearly twice the rate of girls in the latter period.[147] Boys also graduate from high school at lower rates than girls in Chile, the Czech Republic, Denmark, Estonia, Finland, Greece, Hungary, Iceland, Ireland, Luxembourg, Mexico, New Zealand, Norway, Poland, Slovenia, Spain, Sweden and the United Kingdom, among other countries.[148]

In the Organisation for Economic Co-operation and Development (OECD) countries, boys obtain higher mathematics literacy scores than females.[149] In these countries boys also score slightly higher than girls on science literacy, although there are more exceptions to this trend – that is to say, quite a few countries where girls outperform boys on science literacy.[150] Girls outstrip boys on reading literacy (by a higher margin than boys exceed girls on the other scores).[151] Research conducted in North America, Europe and Asia, among other places, tends to indicate that overall females tend to perform academically better than males in childhood, adolescence and adulthood.[152]

In the United States, a greater proportion of females than males have enrolled in college every year since 1982.[153] More women are also graduating from colleges and universities in the United States.[154] For the year 2006–2007, women earned 62.2% of associate's degrees, 57.4% of bachelor's degrees and 60.6% of master's degrees. If one excludes non-resident aliens earning degrees, a smaller percentage of whom are women, the proportion would be still higher. These figures are also an increase over those in the 1996–1997 academic year, when females were already earning a majority of these degrees. Women now earn half of all first professional degrees and half of all doctorates. These proportions are increases since the 1996–1997 academic year, when women were still earning only about 40% of these degrees.

If the sexes in these statistics were reversed, feminists would take this to be evidence of overall female disadvantage. Indeed that is exactly what they did in the past, and still do with regard to other parts of the world. However, in those places where males are dropping out in greater numbers and earning fewer degrees than females many feminists have focused instead on other issues, thereby arguing that females are *still* disadvantaged.

For example, they say that "males receive more teacher attention than do females."[155] Receiving less teacher attention is, of course, a disadvantage, but the question is how this weighs relative to the male disadvantages mentioned above. If we assume that females are indeed receiving less teacher attention, it has not prevented them from enrolling in and graduating from colleges and universities in greater proportions than males. Indeed, if the tables were reversed – if most graduates were boys – and somebody were to object that girls were receiving more teacher attention, most feminists would argue that that is exactly what is required. Students who are doing worse, they would likely say, would require more attention. My aim here is not to deny that restricted teacher attention is a disadvantage. Instead, I mean only to show that it is not a sufficiently powerful consideration to support (1) or (3a) over (3b) or (3c).

It has also been noted that girls' self-esteem drops from elementary to high school at a greater rate than boys' self-esteem.[156] That too is a disadvantage, but there are a number of reasons for denying that this so vastly outweighs the educational disadvantages of boys as to show that females suffer greater educational disadvantage.

First, the self-esteem problem is only partly an *educational* disadvantage. Some of the problem does not arise in connection with education, but instead with issues about body image that arise during puberty. Schools can exacerbate or ameliorate these. It is also the case that these issues can impact on education. Nevertheless, they are not fundamentally measurements of educational disadvantage. "Black" girls were found not to have the same self-esteem problems as "white" girls, even though the former performed more poorly academically.

Second, given the fact that girls do better than boys in the ways mentioned above, it may well be that male self-esteem is partly misguided. If we are trying to determine where the educational disadvantage lies, we should put more weight on how well students are actually doing educationally and less weight on how good they feel about how they are doing. It is not that positive self-assessments are unimportant. Instead it is that we should not treat these as decisive in the face of (more) objective evidence about how well the sexes are doing.

In summary, then, a smaller proportion of males than females is succeeding educationally. That is a substantial educational disadvantage, irrespective of whatever educational disadvantages girls suffer.

Family and Other Relationships

Males suffer a number of disadvantages in the context of establishing and preserving close family and other relationships. Consider, for instance, the issue of child custody.

Custody

In a divorce, men are much less likely to gain custody of their children than are women. In the United States, fathers gain sole custody of children in about 10% of cases and women in nearly three-quarters of cases.[157] In New Zealand, fathers gain custody of children in about 11% of cases settled in Family Court, while mothers obtain custody in about 65% of cases.[158] In Canada, women gain sole custody in over 70% of cases.[159] Some people have suggested that men gain custody of their children so infrequently because so few men want custody. Whether or not it is true that fewer men than women seek custody of their children, it is the case that men fare less well than women even when they actively seek custody. In Canada, for instance, just over 93% of females petitioning for sole custody were granted this, whereas only two-fifths of male petitioners making such a request were granted it.[160]

Similarly, one United States study found that in 90% of cases where there was an uncontested request for maternal physical custody of the children, the mother was awarded this custody. However, in only 75% of cases in which there was an uncontested request for paternal physical custody was the father awarded such custody.[161] In cases of conflicting requests for physical custody, mothers' requests were granted twice as often as fathers' requests.[162] Similarly, when children were residing with the father at the time of the separation the father was more likely to gain custody than when the children were living with the mother at the time of separation, but his chances were not as high as a mother with whom children were living at the time of separation.[163] This study was undertaken in California, which is noted for its progressive legislation and attitudes and is thus possibly a state where men are less likely to be disadvantaged.

There is some evidence that divorced men also fare less well emotionally than do divorced women. For example they are more likely to be admitted to psychiatric hospitals than are divorced women.[164] While divorced women are no more likely to kill themselves than are married women, divorced men are twice as likely as married men to take their own lives.[165]

There are a number of possible explanations why men suffer greater emotional upheaval in the wake of divorce,[166] but they include the fact that fathers lose out on the close daily contact that they had with their children because they do not gain custody. Women also report greater satisfaction with the terms of divorce and a greater sense of control about the settlement process than do men.[167]

Fathers might not be the only males to suffer disadvantage from post-divorce and other custodial arrangements, although the evidence on this is mixed. Many studies have found that sons fare less well than daughters following the separation of their parents. In one study, for example, divorced mothers showed their sons less affection than their daughters, "treated their sons more harshly and gave them more threatening commands – though they did not systematically enforce them."[168] "Even after two years ... boys in ... divorced families were ... more aggressive, more impulsive and more disobedient with their mothers than either girls in divorced families or children in intact families."[169] In another study, "a significant proportion of boys who developed serious coping problems in adolescence, had lived in families in which their father was absent temporarily, either because of family discord or work."[170] The same was not true of girls who grew up with an absent father. In short, these and other studies suggest that boys tend to suffer more than girls as a result of divorce and of living with a single parent. Many scholars have suggested that this may be because children fare better when placed with the parent of their own sex, at least where that parent is amenable to having custody.[171]

However, not all studies have had these findings. Some have found that boys fare no worse than girls. This was also the conclusion of one meta-analysis.[172] Another study found that both boys and girls do better if in the father's custody, but the authors are appropriately cautious about making inferences from this finding.[173] They note, for example, that the fathers who do gain custody may be highly exceptional.

It seems then that the evidence is inconclusive and this is clearly an area that requires further research. It may turn out that boys are disadvantaged by divorce, but it might also turn out that this is not one of the disadvantages boys experience.

Paternity

Men have certainly been disadvantaged in a way that, short of draconian measures, was unavoidable until recent developments in science. Because women gestate and give birth, they have typically been as sure as one can be that the children they believe to be their biological offspring are indeed biologically theirs. Of course, there have been cases where babies have been switched at birth and a woman raises a child that she mistakenly thinks is hers. And today, with developments in assisted reproduction, there is more scope for uncertainty in some cases (although this is often because of conceptual rather than factual uncertainties[174]). Nevertheless, women generally enjoy high degrees of certainty that their children are biologically theirs.[175] Men have never had the same grounds for certainty. If a man has sex with a woman, he almost never knows as certainly as she does whether he is the only man with whom she is having sex. Chastity belts, genital infibulation and (eunuch-guarded) harems have been among the attempts to ensure a woman's fidelity, one of the consequences of which was greater confidence of paternity. However, these extreme measures are not employed by most men, who are left to rely on their wives' faithfulness. Most wives are faithful, but there are enough cases of cuckoldry, "non-paternity" or "paternity discrepancy" as it is variably designated, to create doubt.[176]

Until relatively recently a man's uncertainty about his (genetic) paternal status has been largely unavoidable. (Although a woman's fidelity was within her control, her husband's certainty of it was not.) However, we now have genetic paternity tests that can provide a man with extraordinarily high levels of confidence regarding whether or not he is the father of the identified children. At least two problems remain, however.

First, a man's knowledge about paternity does not come without cost. A test must be undertaken and many a man may be reluctant to undergo the test because it may be thought to cast aspersions on his wife and indicate a lack of trust in her. Because the suspicion is unwarranted in most cases, and most tests will prove positive, the affront to a wife will not usually be deemed worthwhile. Thus men face the dilemma of either knowing and affronting or not knowing and not affronting.

The second problem is that where scientific paternity testing could alleviate male disadvantage the law has not always caught up with the times. For example, in the law of the United States, any child born out of wedlock is automatically a citizen if the mother is a citizen of the United States. However, if the father but not the mother is a citizen, then the child becomes a citizen only if the father acknowledges paternity in writing or paternity is established in court of competent jurisdiction before the child's eighteenth birthday. One purported justification for this asymmetry is the relative uncertainty that a man is a father of a child, and the related concern about unverifiable claims of paternity as a means of obtaining citizenship. Even though paternity is something that could now readily be proved by a genetic test, the United States Supreme Court found that the relevant law did not violate the Equal Protection guarantee of the Fifth Amendment.[177] The case considered by the court was one of a young man who was born out of wedlock to a Vietnamese mother and a father who was a citizen of the United States. At age six the child moved to the United States, became a permanent resident and was raised by his father. The consequence of the court's decision is that fathers are disadvantaged relative to mothers with regard to their capacity to bestow citizenship on their children. In the case of mothers, citizenship of the offspring is presumptive. In the case of fathers, not only must it be proved, but it must be proved before the child reaches a certain age.

Thus far I have spoken about cases of paternity uncertainty where there is a child and the named or presumed father is not sure that the child is his genetic offspring. There is also a different kind of paternity uncertainty or even paternity ignorance. Whereas a (conscious and minimally competent) woman will always know that she has gestated and given birth to a child and thus whether she has become a genetic or a gestational mother, a man does not always know when he has become a genetic father. He may think he is childless, but in fact have offspring.

If, following a casual sexual encounter, the male and female parties to the act go their separate ways, the woman will know whether a child results. The man, by contrast, may not know. This is often portrayed as a disadvantage to women. They are often left, quite literally, carrying the baby. In other words, women but not men are said to pay the price of the sexual encounter. I do not mean to deny that this can be a disadvantage – that is, for those women who would rather not have the child. However, it is not the only possible disadvantage there is. Being unaware that one has become a parent can also be a disadvantage. Women, but not men, are capable, at least in ordinary circumstances, of preventing the other parent from knowing that their sexual union has produced a child.

Another paternity disadvantage is not epistemic. In many societies, males have less control than females over whether they will become parents. Both men and women can choose whether to have sex, but women have many more contraceptive options than men. Men have the condom and vasectomy, whereas women have "the pill," the diaphragm, the female condom, spermicide creams and gels, the intra-uterine device (IUD), the "morning-after pill" and tubal ligation.[178] Moreover, in the event of contraceptive failure, it is typically only women who can then decide whether to become parents. This is because women may still have the option of abortion. However, a man whose sexual partner has become pregnant may not override any decision of hers whether or not to abort.

Paternity leave

An increasing number of countries have included legal provision for paternity leave following the birth of a child. However, in almost all places, the leave benefits guaranteed to mothers exceed those guaranteed to fathers.[179] This legal discrimination disadvantages only those fathers who want greater paternity leave benefits than they are guaranteed by the law in their respective countries. It is not clear how many such men there are, but even if it is only a small proportion of fathers it remains true that those fathers are disadvantaged.

Homosexuals

Homosexual men suffer more victimization than do lesbians. For instance, male homosexual sex has been and continues to be criminalized or otherwise negatively targeted in more jurisdictions than is lesbian sex. In 2002, there were at least 30 countries in which homosexuality was illegal for men but female homosexuality was not explicitly criminalized.[180] Male homosexuals have a harder time adopting children than do lesbians,[181] even in those places where same-sex couples are permitted to adopt. Male homosexuals are much more frequently the victims of hate crimes than are lesbians.[182] For example, the United States Federal Bureau of Investigation (FBI) hate crime statistics show that in 2008, 58.6% of sexual-orientation crimes were motivated by bias against gay men, whereas 12% were motivated by anti-lesbian bias.[183]

Bodily Privacy

The bodily privacy of females is valued more than the bodily privacy of males. In many places and times this imposes a disadvantage on females who are *required* to cover their bodies more extensively than men are. For example, in some places women are required to cover themselves from head to toe in a burqa, while no comparable restriction is placed on males.

However, the greater value placed on the shielding of the female body from view has some significant disadvantages for males, who are more likely to be subjected by society to *unwanted* invasions of their bodily privacy. In other words, whereas females are sometimes forced to cover up their bodies, men are sometimes forced to uncover their bodies.

Consider, for example, the differential treatment of male and female prisoners, most especially in the context of cross-gender supervision. Many countries require that prison guards are the same sex as the prisoners they are guarding. There are exceptions to this trend, and the United States is one notable case. Male guards are found in female prisons and female guards are found in male prisons. In some cases, guards who are not of the same sex as the prisoners are restricted from some functions within the prison in order to protect the prisoners from undue invasion of their bodily privacy by guards of the opposite sex. Often these measures do not grant complete protection.

Four kinds of legal challenge have been raised against these arrangements:

(1) Male prisoners have objected to female guards searching their bodies or being able to view them in states of undress.
(2) Female prisoners have objected to male guards searching their bodies or being able to view them in states of undress.

(3) Male guards have objected, on equal opportunity grounds, to being excluded from certain positions or functions in female prisons.
(4) Female guards have objected, on equal opportunity grounds, to being excluded from certain positions and functions in male prisons.

In general the courts in the United States have given much more weight to the privacy interests of female inmates than they have to the privacy interests of male inmates.[184] Concomitantly, in balancing privacy interests of prisoners against employment interests of guards, the courts have put greater weight on the interests of female guards relative to male prisoners than they have on the interests of male guards relative to female prisoners. Privacy interests of female prisoners prevail over employment interests of male guards, but employment interests of female guards prevail over privacy interests of male inmates.

For example, when a male prisoner petitioned against the practice of female guards conducting pat-down searches of fully clothed male prisoners, including the groin area, the court ruled against the petitioner,[185] yet when female prisoners challenged a policy that permitted male guards to perform clothed pat-down searches, the court ruled in favor of the prisoners.[186] Similarly, when male guards appealed a District Court judgment against their complaint of sex discrimination because they were barred from select positions in a women's prison, the Court of Appeal ruled against them. The court said that excluding male guards was "reasonably necessary to accommodate the privacy interests of the female inmates."[187] However, when female guards had previously lodged the same kind of complaint, the court did not accord much weight to male privacy interests and ruled in favor of the guards.[188]

In cases where courts have ruled that male guards may continue to supervise female prisoners this is because arrangements have been made to protect the privacy of the prisoners to a considerable degree.[189]

There have been some exceptional court rulings, where the privacy interests of female prisoners have been treated in the same way as those of male prisoners,[190] but there do not seem to be any cases where the privacy interests of female prisoners have been treated less seriously than the same interests of male prisoners. Where the (lower) courts have been as sympathetic to male privacy interests as the courts typically are to female privacy interests, their rulings have been overturned by higher courts.[191]

It is strikingly clear that male inmates are much more likely to be subjected to cross-gender supervision invasions of their privacy than are female inmates. When they seek injunctive relief or damages from the courts, they are less likely to receive a favorable response from the courts. This is a considerable disadvantage.

Nor does this attitude seem to be localized to the United States, one of the few countries that allows cross-gender prison supervision.[192] The "Standard

Minimum Rules for the Treatment of Prisoners" adopted by the first United Nations Congress on the Prevention of Crime and the Treatment of Offenders and subsequently approved by the Economic and Social Council in 1957 and again in 1977, displays a clear gender bias. Rule 53 reads as follows:

> (1)   In an institution for both men and women, the part of the institution set aside for women shall be under the authority of a responsible woman officer who shall have the custody of the keys of all that part of the institution.
>
> (2)   No male member of the staff shall enter the part of the institution set aside for women unless accompanied by a woman officer.
>
> (3)   Women prisoners shall be attended and supervised only by women officers. This does not, however, preclude male members of the staff, particularly doctors and teachers, from carrying out their professional duties in institutions or parts of institutions set aside for women.[193]

In other words, the Rule explicitly prohibits male guards from supervising female inmates, but there is no rule prohibiting female guards from supervising male prisoners.

Nor is it the case that male privacy is valued less only if the males in question are prisoners. Some military personnel undergo SERE training, which is aimed to equip soldiers, who are at high risk of capture by the enemy to *survive* (if their aircraft is downed or they find themselves otherwise missing in enemy territory), to *evade* capture, to *resist* the enemy and to *escape* if captured. Part of this training can involve techniques for dealing with being searched. The training thus involves strip searches, inspection of the genitalia and body-cavity searches. In the Australian Army, female soldiers perform these searches on male soldiers in the training exercises, but male soldiers do not perform them on female trainees.[194]

In apartheid-era in South Africa, there were two in-takes of (male) conscripts per year. These inductions were regularly featured on the television news of the government-controlled South African Broadcasting Corporation. The visual footage would show the young conscripts arriving in their civilian clothes, bidding farewell to their families and then being paraded around in their underwear while they were weighed and measured and while they waited for their medical examinations. It is inconceivable that the nightly news would have entered into a changing room of 18-year-old females and filmed them, without their consent, in their bras and panties, and then aired the footage on national television.

Then, consider the configuration of single-sex toilets. Whereas males are provided with urinals, which are relatively exposed, females have stalls. Now, it is true that males also have stalls and thus males are not forced to use urinals. Nevertheless, the space taken up by urinals reduces the availability of stalls and there are social pressures on some males to use the more exposed facilities. Women often claim that because stalls take up more space, the queues for women's toilets are longer and they are thus disadvantaged. That may be true, but the point to note is that, contrary to what many feminists think, the disadvantages are not all in one direction. Could we imagine, in contemporary western societies, replacing some of the stalls in women's toilets with more closely spaced, but unpartitioned toilets, *à la* ancient Rome, in which women could urinate, only entering the stalls if they need to perform other functions?[195] While a woman who has to remove her trousers to urinate may be more exposed to other women than a man who has only to unzip his fly, a woman in a dress would be *less* exposed than the man. Our current practices are so entrenched that people rarely see how odd they are. Men are expected to urinate in the presence of other men, but women are not similarly expected to urinate in the presence of other women.

The different standards of privacy that obtain in male and female public toilets also have a differential impact on the parents of young children. Mothers are able to take both their daughters and young sons to female toilets without intruding excessively on the privacy of other females using public toilets and without exposing their children to the spectacle of women urinating. By contrast, fathers may be able to accompany their sons, but daughters present a greater problem. A father taking his young daughter (of, say, six, seven or eight years of age) to a male toilet will subject other men using the urinals to cross-gender invasions of privacy and expose his daughter to the spectacle of males urinating. Yet fathers caring for their young daughters may not want their daughters to enter (female) toilets unaccompanied by a trusted carer. This presents a problem when the mother, older sister or aunt, for example, is not present.

Life Expectancy

The life expectancy of females exceeds that of males almost everywhere. There are some exceptions. In Kenya, South Africa and Zimbabwe, male life expectancy, although short, is slightly higher than that of females.[196] In some other places, such as Nigeria and Pakistan, men and women have roughly the same life expectancy.[197] Almost everywhere else, however, females outlive males. In some countries, including some eastern European states, the differential is considerable. In Russia, for example, male life expectancy is 58.7 years, while that of females is 71.8.[198] Even in those places where both men and women have long life spans, women's are even longer. In Japan, for example, the life expectancy of males and females is, respectively, 79.1 and 86.4.[199]

While female life expectancy has not always been longer than that of males the phenomenon can be traced at least to the early decades of the twentieth century, and at least in some countries.[200] For example, in 1908 the life expectancy at birth in Spain was 40.41 for males and 42.27 for females. Australians born in 1921 had a life expectancy of 61.4 years if male and 63.24 years if female. Males born in 1922 in the United Kingdom had a life expectancy of 55.18 years, while females could expect to live for 58.86 years on average. In 1933, males born in the United States had a life expectancy of 59.17 years, in comparison with 62.83 years for females. Although the differential in life expectancy between Russian males and females has increased, it was nonetheless already significant in 1959. In that year females had a life expectancy of 71.14 years, roughly the same as today, whereas the life expectancy for males was 62.84, which is higher than today.[201]

Older reliable data are harder to obtain, particularly outside of developed countries. Where it exists at all, it is often "fragmentary" or unreliable.[202] Nevertheless there is some reason to think that it may not have been uncommon, or at least it may have been more common, for males to outlive females prior to the twentieth century.[203] On the other hand, this was not the case everywhere. In the late nineteenth century, the only data from the United States are for Massachusetts and New Hampshire.[204] In 1890 the life expectancies there for males and females were 42.5 and 44.46 respectively.[205] As far back as 1789, the respective life expectancies were 34.5 and 36.5.[206] However, whatever once was the case, it is clear that for at least about a century, and a lot longer in some places, women have been outliving men. Males are thus disadvantaged in this way, and have been for a while.

The difference in male and female life expectancy is explained by more than one factor. Although males may be biologically more susceptible to earlier death, this cannot explain all of the difference in male and female life expectancy. Given the geographic and historical variation, local factors are clearly influencing the extent of the difference between male and female life spans. These factors include the status of women. Where females are treated better – where, for example, there is no widespread female infanticide or the prioritizing of males for food under conditions of scarcity, and where women have access to obstetric care – their chances of survival are obviously higher than they otherwise would be.

However, it is not only female life span that is influenced by how well they are treated. The same is true of male life expectancy. The greater tolerance for, and incidence of lethal violence against males must constitute part of the explanation why males tend not to live as long as females. Not only are more men killed in wars and conflicts, but more males are also murdered, and male lives are more readily sacrificed. This surely contributes to shorter average male lifespan.

In almost all places males are also more likely than females to kill themselves. Throughout the west and in westernized Asian countries, the rate of suicide for males is at least twice that of females,[207] and sometimes even higher.[208] One notable exception is China, where females (particularly in the rural areas) have a higher suicide rate than males.[209]

Males also constitute the majority of workplace accident fatalities. In the United States, the fatality rate for men is about ten times that of women.[210] Although women account for 43% of hours worked for wages in the United States, they account for only 7% of work fatalities.[211] Matters are worse in Canada, where men account for about 95% of workplace fatalities. In that country, the incidence of workplace fatalities for men is about 10.4 per 100 000, whereas the incidence for women is 0.4 per 100 000.[212] In Taiwan, males account for about 93% of workplace fatalities.[213]

Wars, criminal violence, suicide and workplace fatalities are but a few of the factors that contribute to males' shorter life expectancy. A shorter life span is a disadvantage. While there are a few societies in which females suffer this disadvantage, in most places, and overall, it is women who live longer than men and thus men who are at a disadvantage.

Imprisonment and Capital Punishment

Men are also much more likely than women to be imprisoned or to be subjected to capital punishment. The overwhelming majority of the world's prison population is male. The same is true of those who are sentenced to death and those who are judicially executed.

In the United States, which has the largest prison population rate[214] (and possibly also the largest absolute prison population[215]) in the world, males constitute about 92% of all prison inmates, while females constitute only about 8%.[216] In England and Wales together, which have relatively low imprisonment rates, about 94% of prisoners are male.[217] In about 80% of prison systems worldwide, females constitute between 2% and 9% of the total prison population.[218] In only 12 systems is the percentage of female prisoners higher than that. Hong Kong is the highest at 22%, followed by Myanmar (18%).[219] The world median level is 4.3%.[220]

Being imprisoned is a serious harm (even when it is deserved). It involves massive restrictions on one's liberty and, as we have seen, on one's privacy. One runs a significantly elevated risk of sexual assault, including rape, along with the attendant risks of contracting sexually transmitted diseases. Of chief concern among these is HIV, which can transform a life sentence into a death sentence. This particular problem is especially acute for males, not only because they constitute the vast majority of prisoners but also because they, unlike female inmates, are much more likely to be infected as a consequence of sexual assault by fellow prisoners. Sexual assault by one female of another is less likely to transmit HIV. Of course, female inmates could contract HIV if raped by an HIV-positive male guard. However, in many places the guarding of female prisoners is performed only by other females. In any event, male prisoners can be infected both by male guards and by fellow prisoners.

An even greater proportion of those executed are male. In America, 568 women were executed in the 374 years from 1632 until the end of 2005.[221] This constitutes only 2.8% of all executions in America during this period. That is to say, 97.2% of those executed have been male. But this fact fails to capture trends over time. The rate at which women have been executed has actually declined. From 1973 (which marks the reintroduction of the death penalty in the United States after the Supreme Court had terminated it in its previous form in the 1972 decision of *Furman v. Georgia*) until the end of 2005, women were only 1.1% of all those executed.[222] Between 1973 and 1997 the rate was even lower (0.2%), but that seems to be atypical.[223] Thus men currently constitute about 98.9% of all those put to death in the United States.

Globally, women may constitute an even smaller proportion of all known executions.[224] According to one calculation, less than 1% of all those known to have been executed in recent years are females.[225]

Some countries explicitly exempt women from capital punishment. This was the case in the Soviet Union by 1991[226] and is today the case "in a few countries – mainly those associated with the former Soviet system – Belarus, Mongolia, Uzbekistan, and the Russian Federation."[227] A number of other countries prohibit the execution of pregnant women. While some of those simply treat this as a stay of execution, other countries, Kuwait being one example, "automatically commute the sentence to imprisonment for life."[228]

The death penalty has historically been inflicted for a range of crimes. In more oppressive societies, that trend continues. The United States is one of the few liberal democracies to retain capital punishment, which it inflicts only on murderers. While it is not difficult to have sympathy for those executed in oppressive societies for sexual misconduct, drug violations and political opposition, it is very hard to have sympathy for people who commit the sorts of crimes that carry the death penalty in the United States today. Moreover, executions account for an extremely small proportion of all deaths – a drop in the kicked bucket. Nevertheless, execution is a major disadvantage for those subjected to it (even when they do deserve it[229]). Not only does it cut short the condemned person's life (as death always does), but the prisoner endures the extreme anxiety and fear of knowing that he will face death at an appointed time. The clock ticks and he, powerless, awaits that awful date.

In Chapter 4 I shall consider the reasons why females constitute such a small proportion of prisoners and of the executed. More specifically, I shall consider whether this is attributable, even in part, to discrimination against males. For now, however, I am only interested in establishing the fact of disadvantage. The above statistics demonstrate as much. Being born male gives one a much higher chance of being incarcerated and of being executed.

Conclusion

In this chapter I have demonstrated that males suffer substantial disadvantage in many important ways. Obviously not *every* male suffers each of these disadvantages, but it is similarly the case that not every female suffers each of the well-known disadvantages generally suffered by females. For this reason we can conclude that some males are more disadvantaged by their sex than some females are disadvantaged by theirs, even if it is the case that women, in general, are more disadvantaged by their sex than men are by theirs. I am not suggesting that women *are* in general more disadvantaged. This too depends. There are times when and places where it certainly is the case that they are. However, there are other societies in which the disadvantages of being female are far fewer and less serious. The extent to which males are in general disadvantaged is also not constant. Thus whether males or females suffer more disadvantage in general may vary across space and time.

Even these modest claims, which I shall discuss further in the concluding chapter, are likely to be met with outrage by those who hold less complex views about the distribution of males' and females' disadvantage. Such people will be even more resistant to the further claim that at least many of the disadvantages males experience are the products of unfair discrimination, or sexism. My defense of that further claim will be provided in Chapter 4 and, by responding to objections, also in Chapter 5. First, however, there is some preliminary work to be done in understanding how male disadvantage arises and about how we should think about differences between the sexes.

Notes

1   Will Ellsworth-Jones, *We Will Not Fight: The Untold Story of the First World War's Conscientious Objectors*, London: Aurum, 2008.
2   At the time of writing these appear to include: Albania, Algeria, Angola, Armenia, Austria, Azerbaijan, Belarus, Benin (selective), Bhutan (selective), Bolivia, Bosnia and Herzegovina, Brazil, Burundi (selective), Cape Verde, Central African

Republic (selective), Chad (selective), Chile, China (selective), Colombia, Cuba, Cyprus, Democratic Republic of the Congo, Denmark, Ecuador, Egypt, Equatorial Guinea, Eritrea, Estonia, Finland, Georgia, Germany, Ghana, Greece, Guinea, Guinea-Bissau, Indonesia (selective), Iran, Iraq, Israel, Ivory Coast, Kazakhstan, Kuwait, Kyrgyzstan, Laos, Lebanon, Libya, Lithuania, Madagascar, Mali (selective), Mexico, Moldova, Mongolia, Montenegro, Morocco, Mozambique, Myanmar, Niger (selective), North Korea, Norway, Paraguay, Peru, Philippines, Poland, Russia, Senegal (selective), Serbia, Singapore, South Korea, Sudan, Switzerland, Syria, Taiwan, Tajikistan, Tanzania, Thailand, Togo (selective), Tunisia, Turkey, Turkmenistan, Ukraine, Uzbekistan, Venezuela, Vietnam and Yemen. It is very difficult to get reliable, comprehensive, up-to-date information on which countries still conscript. The above list is drawn from a few different sources and involves a measure of verification (or falsification) between them and independently. The full list of sources is too long to include here, but the initial, general sources were: http://www.nationmaster.com/graph/mil_con-military-conscription; http://www.wri-irg.org/programmes/world_survey; and http://en.wikipedia.org/wiki/Conscription.

3   Will Ellsworth-Jones, *We Will Not Fight*, especially chapter 4.
4   For more on adolescent soldiers in the First World War, see Richard van Emden, *Boy Soldiers of the Great War*, London: Headline, 2005.
5   Quoted in Will Ellsworth-Jones, *We Will Not Fight*, p. 47. Ironically, the feminist icon Virginia Woolf claimed – falsely, the evidence shows – that relatively few white feathers had been handed out and that "it was more a product of male hysteria than actual practice" (ibid., p. 46).
6   Originally women were conscripted for 24 months and men for 30 months. However, the period of women's service was reduced to less than 21 months and men's was increased to 36 months. Dafna N. Izraeli, "Gendering military service in the Israel Defense Force," *Israel Social Science Research*, 12(1), 1997, p. 139.
7   Ibid., p. 138.
8   Ibid., and Nira Yuval-Davis, "Front and rear: the sexual division of labor in the Israeli Army," *Feminist Studies*, 11(3), Fall 1985, pp. 666–668.
9   Women did serve (voluntarily) in combat in Israel's War of Independence, and women are now admitted to combat units, but only voluntarily.
10 Judith Wagner DeCew, "Women, equality, and the military," in Dana E. Bushnell (ed.), *Nagging Questions: Feminist Ethics in Everyday Life*, Lanham, MD: Rowman & Littlefield, 1995, p. 131.
11 Kingsley Browne, *Co-Ed Combat: The New Evidence That Women Shouldn't Fight the Nation's Wars*, New York: Sentinel, 2007, p. 72. Mary Wechsler Segal makes a similar point. She distinguishes military jobs by the degree to which they "involve offensive or defensive combat potential." "The arguments for female combatants," in Nancy Loring Goldman (ed.), *Female Soldiers: Combatants or Noncombatants? Historical and Contemporary Perspectives*, Westport: Greenwood Press, 1982, p. 267.
12 John Keegan, *The Face of Battle*, New York: Penguin Books, 1978, p. 89.
13 John Keegan and Richard Holmes, *Soldiers: A History of Men in Battle*, London: Hamish Hamilton, 1985, p. 261.

14 At least they begin on a larger scale. Casualties also occur in training, well before combat begins.

15 Joanna Bourke, *Dismembering the Male: Men's Bodies, Britain and the Great War*, Chicago: University of Chicago Press, 1996, p. 228.

16 Not all drown at sea. At the Battle of Agincourt, for example, when "the heavily armored French men-at-arms fell wounded, many could not get up and simply drowned in the mud as other men stumbled over them." James Glanz, "Historians Reassess Battle of Agincourt," *New York Times*, 25 October 2009, http://www.nytimes.com/2009/10/25/world/europe/25agincourt.html?pagewanted=all (accessed October 25, 2009).

17 For harrowing images of injuries suffered by twenty-first-century soldiers see Shawn Christian Nessen, Dave Edmond Lounsbury and Stephen P. Hetz (eds), *War Surgery in Afghanistan and Iraq*, Falls Church, VA: Office of the Surgeon General, United States Army, and Washington, DC: Borden Institute, Walter Reed Army Medical Center, 2008.

18 Joanna Bourke, *An Intimate History of Killing: Face-to-Face Killing in Twentieth-Century Warfare*, New York: Basic Books, 1999, pp. 235–236.

19 Scott Claver, *Under the Lash: A History of Corporal Punishment in the British Armed Forces*, London: Torchstream Books, 1954, p. 67; James E. Valle, *Rocks and Shoals: Order and Discipline in the Old Navy, 1800–1861*, Annapolis: Naval Institute Press, 1980, p. 38.

20 Joanna Bourke, *Dismembering the Male*, pp. 94ff.

21 David Sharp, "Shocked, shot, and pardoned," *The Lancet*, 368, September 26, 2006, pp. 975–976. Although earlier terms such as "shell shock," "neurasthenia" and "Vietnam War syndrome" referred to some similar symptoms, it is only more recently that the condition has been understood more fully and (relatively more) sympathetically.

22 Jeffrey Gettleman, "Soldier Accused as Coward Says He Is Guilty Only of Panic Attack," *New York Times*, November 6, 2003.

23 Ibid.

24 Ibid.

25 "Army drops all legal action against SSG Georg-Andreas Pogany." Statement by Anderson & Travis, PC, July 16, 2004.

26 Joanna Bourke, *Dismembering the Male*, pp. 38, 83ff.

27 Ibid., p. 77.

28 Ibid., p. 31, 70.

29 Joanna Bourke, *An Intimate History of Killing*, pp. 339ff.

30 Ibid., p. 350.

31 Dave Grossman, *On Killing: The Psychological Cost of Learning to Kill in War and Society*, Boston: Back Bay Books, 1995, p. 277.

32 Joanna Bourke, *An Intimate History of Killing*, pp. 67–68. See also James E. Valle, *Rocks and Shoals*, p. 76.

33 Steven Lee Myers, "Hazing Trial Bares Dark Side of Russia's Military," *New York Times*, August 13, 2006.

34 Ibid.

35 Ibid.

36   Saying that men are more *likely* to be the victims of aggression and violence is not
      to say that they are *always* over-represented among such victims. Nazi genocide
      of Jews and others, for example, eventually targeted men and women equally.
37   As distinct from parent–child or sibling violence.
38   For a comprehensive list of studies see Martin S. Fiebert, "References examining
      assaults by women on their spouses or male partners: an annotated bibli-
      ography," available at http://www.csulb.edu/~mfiebert/assault.htm (accessed
      March 5, 2010). Here are a few examples: Murray Straus, "Victims and
      aggressors in marital violence," *American Behavioral Scientist*, 23(5), May/
      June 1980, pp. 681–704; Murray A. Straus and Richard J. Gelles, "Societal
      change and change in family violence from 1975 to 1985 as revealed by two
      national surveys," *Journal of Marriage and the Family*, 48, August 1986,
      pp. 465–479. For similar findings in Canada see Merlin B. Brinkeroff and Eugen
      Lupri, "Interspousal violence," *Canadian Journal of Sociology*, 13(4), 1988,
      pp. 407–430.
39   This, of course, heightens one's confidence in the findings. They are clearly not
      the product of preconceived notions or ideological bias.
40   Murray Straus, "Victims and aggressors in marital violence," p. 683.
41   Ibid., p. 684.
42   Jan E. Stets and Murray A. Straus, "The marriage license as a hitting license:
      a comparison of assaults in dating, cohabiting, and married couples," *Journal
      of Family Violence*, 4(2), 1989, p. 163. Jean Malone, Andrea Tyree and
      K. Daniel O'Leary ("Generalization and containment: different effects of past
      aggression for wives and husbands," *Journal of Marriage and the Family*, 51,
      1989, p. 690) found that women are more likely to throw an object, slap,
      kick, bite, hit with a fist and hit with an object. For a survey of other findings
      to this effect, see Donald Dutton and Tonia Nicholls, "The gender paradigm
      in domestic violence research and theory. Part 1: the conflict of theory and
      data," *Aggression and Violent Behavior*, 10, 2005, pp. 680–714 (especially
      pp. 687–689).
43   K. Daniel O'Leary, Julian Barling, Ileana Arias *et al.*, "Prevalence and stability
      of physical aggression between spouses: a longitudinal analysis," *Journal of
      Consulting and Clinical Psychology*, 57(2), 1989, pp. 264–266.
44   David B. Sugarman and Gerald T. Hotaling, "Dating violence: a review of con-
      textual and risk factors," in Barrie Levy (ed.), *Dating Violence: Young Women
      in Danger*, Seattle: Seal Press, 1991, p. 104.
45   See, for example, Jan E. Stets and Murray A. Straus, "Gender differences in
      reporting marital violence and its medical and psychological consequences," in
      Murray A. Straus and Richard J. Gelles (eds), *Physical Violence in American
      Families*, New Brunswick, NJ: Transaction Publishers, 1990, pp. 151–165;
      Michele Cascardi, Jennifer Langhinrischen and Dina Vivian, "Marital aggres-
      sion: impact, injury, and health correlates for husbands and wives," *Archives of
      Internal Medicine*, 152, 1992, pp. 1178–1184; Daniel J. Whitaker, Tadesse
      Halleyesus, Monica Swahn and Linda S. Saltzman, "Differences in frequency of
      violence and reported injury between relationships with reciprocal and nonre-
      ciprocal intimate partner violence," *American Journal of Public Health*, 97(5),
      2007, pp. 941–947.

46   Murray Straus, "Victims and aggressors in marital violence," p. 681; Murray A. Straus and Richard J. Gelles, "Societal change and change in family violence," p. 468; K. Daniel O'Leary Julian Barling, Ileana Arias *et al.*, "Prevalence and stability of physical aggression," p. 267.

47   See, for example, Maureen McLeod, "Women against men: an examination of domestic violence based on an analysis of official data and national victimization data," *Justice Quarterly*, 1, 1984, pp. 171–193; Donald Vasquez and Robert E. Falcone, "Cross-gender violence," *Annals of Emergency Medicine*, 29(3), 1997, pp. 427–428.

48   See, for example, K. Daniel O'Leary, Amy M. Smith Slep, Sarah Avery-Leaf and Michele Cascardi, "Gender differences in dating aggression among multiethnic high school students," *Journal of Adolescent Health*, 42, 2008, pp. 473–479; David M. Fergusson, L. John Horwood and Elizabeth M. Ridder, "Partner violence and mental health outcomes in a New Zealand birth cohort," *Journal of Marriage and the Family*, 67, 2005, pp. 1103–1119.

49   Ann Frodi, Jacqueline Macaulay and Pauline Ropert Thome, "Are women always less aggressive than men? A review of the experimental literature," *Psychological Bulletin*, 1977, 84(4), p. 642; Alice H. Eagly and Valerie J. Steffen, "Gender and aggressive behavior: a meta-analytic review of social psychological literature," *Psychological Bulletin*, 100(3), 1986, pp. 321–322.

50   Diane Craven, "Sex Differences in Violent Victimization, 1994." Bureau of Justice Statistics Special Report, September 1997.

51   Home Office, *Crime in England and Wales 2008/9: A Summary of the Main Findings*, London: HMSO, 2009, p. 8.

52   Adam Hochschild, *King Leopold's Ghost*, Boston: Mariner Books, 1999, p. 232.

53   Robert Conquest, *The Great Terror: Stalin's Purge of the Thirties*, Toronto: Macmillan, 1968, pp. 533–535. He explains why the differential is not (significantly) attributable to combat deaths in the *First* World War.

54   Truth and Reconciliation Commission of South Africa, *Truth and Reconciliation Commission of South Africa Report*, Cape Town: Truth and Reconciliation Commission, 1998, vol. 1, p. 171; vol. 4, pp. 259–266.

55   Ibid., vol. 1, p. 171.

56   Ibid., p. 169.

57   Ibid., vol. 4, Chapter 10.

58   Paul. B. Spiegel and Peter Salama, "War and mortality in Kosovo, 1988–9: an epidemiological testimony," *The Lancet*, 355, June 24, 2000, pp. 2205–2206.

59   Organization for Security and Co-operation in Europe, *Kosovo: As Seen, As Told: An Analysis of the Human Rights Findings of the OSCE Kosovo Verification Missions, October 1998 to June 1999*, Warsaw: OSCE, Office for Democratic Institutions and Human Rights, 1999, p. 196.

60   Adam Jones has written at length about ways in which males have been targeted in genocide and mass-killing. See, for example, the following collection of his essays: Adam Jones, *Gender Inclusive: Essays on Violence, Men, and Feminist International Relations*, New York: Routledge, 2009.

61   For argument against sex discrimination in the infliction of corporal punishment see David Benatar, "The child, the rod and the law," *Acta Juridica*, 1996,

pp. 197–214; David Benatar, "Corporal punishment," *Social Theory and Practice*, 24(2), Summer 1998, pp. 237–260.

62 James E. Valle, *Rocks and Shoals*, p. 79.

63 Ibid., p. 81.

64 Ibid., p. 38.

65 Prince Peter Alekseevich Kropotkin, "Discipline in the Russian Army," *New York Times*, October 16, 1898. Online at nytimes.com/mem/archive-free/pdf (accessed October 7, 2009).

66 http://en.wikipedia.org/wiki/Caning_in_Singapore#Military_Caning (accessed October 12, 2009).

67 http://en.wikipedia.org/wiki/Judicial_corporal_punishment (accessed October 12, 2009).

68 Here are two examples: South Africa: J. Sloth-Nielsen, "Legal violence: corporal and capital punishment," in Brian McKendrick and Wilma Hoffmann (eds), *People and Violence in South Africa*, Cape Town: Oxford University Press, 1990, p. 77; United Kingdom: Section 56(1) of the (UK) Petty Sessions and Summary Jurisdiction Act 1927 (as amended by s. 8 of the Summary Jurisdiction Act 1960), quoted in *Tyrer v. United Kingdom, European Human Rights Reports*, 1978, p. 4.

69 http://www.corpun.com/singfeat.htm (accessed October 12, 2009).

70 Ibid.

71 Singapore Criminal Procedure Code 2010, Part XVI, Division 2, 325(1)(a). This replaced the (now repealed) Singapore Criminal Procedure Code, Chapter 25, 231(a), which also explicitly forbade caning of women.

72 See, for example, Singapore's Regulation No. 88 under the Schools Regulation Act 1957. Quoted at http://corpun.com/sgscr1.htm (accessed February 18, 2002.)

73 http://www.corpun.com/rules2.htm#singsch (accessed October 13, 2009).

74 T.L. Holdstock, "Violence in schools: discipline," in Brian McKendrick and Wilma Hoffman (eds), *People and Violence in South Africa*, p. 349.

75 Revealingly, the person who recounted this case wrote that the girlfriend "was compelled to witness the caning in the principal's office" (ibid.) In presenting the fact this way rather than by noting that not only was the boy caned but that he was subjected to the further indignity of being caned in the presence of his girlfriend, the focus is placed on the unpleasantness for the girl instead of on the greater unpleasantness for the boy.

76 "Cuts" is a term for strikes with a cane.

77 "Ploddy," the author of this account explains elsewhere, was the nickname the pupils gave the headmaster.

78 Robert Kirby, "Spoil the Rod, Spare the Child," *Mail & Guardian* (Johannesburg), December 22, 2000–January 4, 2001, p. 41. For other accounts see, for example: "Eton beating," in Michael Rosen (ed.), *The Penguin Book of Childhood*, London: Penguin Books, 1995, pp. 102–103; Roald Dahl, *Boy: Tales of Childhood*, London: Puffin Books, 1984, pp. 46–51, 119–121, 141, 145–146; Edward Said, *Out of Place*, New York: Alfred A. Knopf, 2000, pp. 41–42, 183, 187.

79 Steven R. Shaw and Jeffrey P. Braden, "Race and gender bias in the administration of corporal punishment," *School Psychology Review*, 19(3), 1990,

pp. 378–383; Irwin A. Hyman, *Reading, Writing, and the Hickory Stick*, Lexington, MA: Lexington Books, 1990, p. 65; John R. Slate, Emilio Perez, Phillip B. Waldrop and Joseph E. Justen III, "Corporal punishment: used in discriminatory manner?" *Clearing House*, 64, July/August 1991, pp. 362–364.

80   T.L. Holdstock, "Violence in schools: discipline," p. 349.

81   Ibid.

82   F. Spender, *An Inspector's Testament*, London: English Universities Press, 1938, cited in Jacob Middleton, "The experience of corporal punishment in schools, 1890–1940," *History of Education*, 37(2), March 2008, p. 264.

83   Joseph Mercurio, *Caning: Educational Rite and Tradition*, Syracuse, NY: Syracuse University Press, 1972, p. 50.

84   Roald Dahl, *Boy*, p. 141.

85   Colin McGinn, *The Making of a Philosopher*, New York: Perennial, 2003, p. 4.

86   For example, at Eton College, boys had to remove their pants and underwear for beatings until as late as 1970. See http://en.wikipedia.org/wiki/Eton_College#Corporal_punishment (accessed December 24, 2010).

87   See, for example, Rick Lyman, "In Many Public Schools, the Paddle Is No Relic," *New York Times*, September 30, 2006. Online at http://www.nytimes.com/2006/09/30/education/30punish.html (accessed October 3, 2006).

88   Håkan Stattin, Harald Janson, Ingrid Klackenberg-Larsson and David Magnusson, "Corporal punishment in everyday life: an intergenerational perspective," in Joan McCord (ed.), *Coercion and Punishment in Long-Term Perspectives*, Cambridge: Cambridge University Press, 1995, pp. 321–323; Murray A. Straus, *Beating the Devil Out of Them: Corporal Punishment in American Families*, New York: Lexington Books, 1994, pp. 29–30.

89   Ronald E. Smith, Charles J. Pine and Mark E. Hawley, "Social cognitions about adult male victims of female sexual assault," *Journal of Sex Research*, 24, 1988, pp. 101–112.

90   Ibid., p. 104.

91   Ibid., p. 107.

92   Ibid., p. 109.

93   Ibid.

94   Ibid., p. 107.

95   A later study of college students (Cindy Struckman-Johnson and David Struckman-Johnson, "Acceptance of male rape myths among college men and women," *Sex Roles*, 27(3/4), 1992, pp. 85–100), revealed somewhat less disturbing results. In this study subjects rejected most (but not all) myths about the rape of males, albeit to varying degrees. However, because the subjects were asked explicitly to endorse or reject statements, the responses might not be as revealing as the study of Ronald Smith and colleagues, which was more likely to determine latent rather than explicit attitudes. Cindy Struckman-Johnson and David Struckman-Johnson had another methodological concern about their study in retrospect (p. 96). Even their study, however, found that "male rape myths do operate more strongly when the perpetrator is described as a woman" (p. 97). For example 40% of male subjects thought that a man raped by a woman "was to blame for being careless or for not escaping" (p. 97). Moreover, 35% of men and 22% of women agreed that a man would not be

upset about being raped by a woman (p. 97). See also, H. Douglas Smith, Mary Ellen Fromouth and C. Craig Morris, "Effects of gender on perceptions of child sexual abuse," *Journal of Child Sexual Abuse*, 6(4), 1997, pp. 51–62.

96 Guy Holmes and Liz Offen, "Clinicians' hypothesis regarding clients' problems: are they less likely to hypothesize sexual abuse in male compared to female clients?" *Child Abuse & Neglect*, 20(6), 1996, pp. 493–501.

97 Ibid., p. 493.

98 Ibid., p. 498.

99 Almost every scholar working in the area makes this claim. They cannot all be listed, but here are some examples: William C. Holmes and Gail B. Slap, "Sexual abuse of boys: definition, prevalence, correlates, sequelae, and management," *Journal of the American Medical Association*, 280(21), December 2, 1998, pp. 1855–1862; Bill Watkins and Arnon Bentovim, "Male children and adolescents as victims: a review of current knowledge," in Gillian C. Mezey and Michael B. King (eds), *Male Victims of Sexual Assault*, 2nd edn, Oxford: Oxford University Press, 2000, pp. 40–42; Matthew Parynik Mendel, *The Male Survivor: The Impact of Sexual Abuse*, Thousand Oaks, CA: Sage Publications, 1995, pp. 40–51.

100 An outline of some of the discrepant data is provided by Bill Watkins and Arnon Bentovim, "Male children and adolescents as victims," p. 38. See also Matthew Parynik Mendel, *The Male Survivor*, pp. 48–51.

101 Nathan W. Pino and Robert F. Meier, "Gender differences in rape reporting," *Sex Roles*, 40(11/12), 1999, pp. 979–990; see also Gillian C. Mezey and Michael B. King (eds), *Male Victims of Sexual Assault*.

102 Arthur Kaufman, Peter Divasto, Rebecca Jackson *et al.*, "Male rape victims: noninstitutionalized assault," *American Journal of Psychiatry*, 137(2), February 1980, pp. 221–223.

103 Nicholas Groth and Wolbert Burgess, "Male rape: offenders and victims," *American Journal of Psychiatry*, 137(7), July 1980, p. 808; Cindy Struckman-Johnson and David Struckman-Johnson, "Men pressured and forced into sexual experience," *Archives of Sexual Behavior*, 23(1), 1994, p. 112.

104 Cindy Struckman-Johnson and David Struckman-Johnson, "Men pressured and forced into sexual experience," and Philip M. Sarrel and William H. Masters, "Sexual molestation of men by women," *Archives of Sexual Behavior*, 11(2), 1982, p. 121.

105 For a summary of findings about female abuse of boys see Bill Watkins and Arnon Bentovim, "Male children and adolescents as victims," pp. 43–45. See also Michael King, Adrian Coxell and Gill Mezey, "The prevalence and characteristics of male sexual assault," in Gillian C. Mezey and Michael B. King (eds), *Male Victims of Sexual Assault*, p. 12.

106 See, for example, Mary Spencer and Patricia Dunklee, "Sexual abuse of boys," *Pediatrics*, 78(1), July 1986, pp. 133–137.

107 Gregory S. Fritz, Kim Stoll and Nathaniel N. Wagner, "A comparison of males and females who were sexually molested as children," *Journal of Sex and Marital Therapy*, 7(1), Spring 1981, pp. 54–59.

108 For an overview of data from a range of studies see Matthew Parynik Mendel, *The Male Survivor*, pp. 62–63.

109   For a discussion of various possible explanations of why women are not recognized as perpetrators of sexual abuse see Craig M. Allen, "Women as perpetrators of child sexual abuse: recognition barriers," in Anne L. Horton, Barry L. Johnson, Lynn M. Roundy and Doran Williams (eds), *The Incest Perpetrator: A Family Member No One Wants to Treat*, Newbury Park, CA: Sage Publications, 1990, pp. 108–125.

110   The explanation for this may differ in the two sexes. For details on the phenomenon in the female see Meredith Chivers and J. Michael Bailey, "A sex difference in features that elicit genital response," *Biological Psychology*, 70(2), October 2005, pp. 115–120. For details of the non-sexual stimuli to physiological arousal in pre-adolescent and early adolescent males see Glenn V. Ramsey, "The sexual development of boys," *American Journal of Psychology*, 56(2), April 1943, pp. 217–233. For case studies of physiological arousal in men sexually molested by women, see Philip M. Sarrel and William H. Masters, "Sexual molestation of men by women."

111   Meredith Chivers and J. Michael Bailey, "A sex difference in features that elicit genital response."

112   Cindy Struckman-Johnson, David Struckman-Johnson, Lila Rucker *et al.*, "Sexual coercion reported by men and women in prison," *Journal of Sex Research*, 33(1), 1996, pp. 67–76. The male rate was consistent with that found in another study that looked only at sexual coercion rates in male prisons. (Cindy Struckman-Johnson and David Struckman-Johnson, "Sexual coercion rates in seven prison facilities for men," *Prison Journal*, 80(4), December 2000, pp. 379–389.) This study found that 21% of inmates "had experienced at least one episode of pressured or forced sexual contact since incarcerated in their state."

113   M. Peel, A. Mahtani, G. Hinshelwood and D. Forrest, "The sexual abuse of men in detention in Sri Lanka," *The Lancet*, 355, June 10, 2000, pp. 2069–2070; Michael Slackman, "Reformer in Iran Publishes Account of a Prison Rape," *New York Times*, August 25, 2009.

114   Criminal Law of the People's Republic of China, enacted by the National People's Congress on July 1, 1979, as amended. Online at http://www.cecc.gov/pages/newLaws/criminalLawENG.php (accessed December 1, 2009).

115   Compare Articles 177 and 176 of the Penal Code of Japan (Act No.45 of 1907, as amended). Online at http://www.cas.go.jp/jp/seisaku/hourei/data/PC_2.pdf (accessed December 1, 2009).

116   1974 amendment of Section 750.520 of the Michigan Penal Code Act 328 of 1931.Online at http://www.legislature.mi.gov/(S(24i0ub45icnmus55zkfdd32r))/documents/mcl/pdf/mcl-750-520a.pdf (accessed December 2, 2009). See also Maria Bevacqua, *Rape on the Public Agenda: Feminism and the Politics of Sexual Assault*, Boston: Northeastern University Press, 2000, pp. 99–100.

117   Criminal Law (Sexual Offences and Related Matters) Amendment Act 32 of 2007. Online at http://www.justice.gov.za/legislation/acts/2007-032.pdf (accessed December 1, 2009).

118   Sexual Offences (Scotland) Act 2009 (asp 9). Online at http://www.opsi.gov.uk/legislation/scotland/acts2009/pdf/asp_20090009_en.pdf (accessed December 1, 2009).

119 According to Section 1 of the Sexual Offences Act of 2003:

> (1) A person (A) commits an offence if –
> (a) he intentionally penetrates the vagina, anus or mouth of another person (B) with his penis,
> (b) B does not consent to the penetration, and
> (c) A does not reasonably believe that B consents.

Online at http://www.opsi.gov.uk/Acts/acts2003/ukpga_20030042_en_2#pt1-pb1-l1g1 (accessed October 19, 2009).

120 Ibid. She could be charged under Section 4, "Causing a person to engage in sexual activity without consent" and under Section 3, "Sexual assault," which criminalizes non-consensual "sexual touching." Both of these offenses lead "to imprisonment for a term not exceeding 10 years," whereas a conviction for rape would lead "to imprisonment for life."

121 Howard League Working Party, *Unlawful Sex*, London: Waterlow Publishers, 1985, p. 27.

122 Philip M. Sarrel and William H. Masters, "Sexual molestation of men by women," p. 122.

123 Michael Benatar and David Benatar, "Between prophylaxis and child abuse: the ethics of neonatal circumcision," *American Journal of Bioethics*, 3(2), Spring 2003, pp. 35–48. See also David Benatar and Michael Benatar, "How not to argue about circumcision," *American Journal of Bioethics*, 3(2), Spring 2003, online edition: http://www.bioethics.net/journal/pdf/3_2_LT_w01_Benetar.pdf (accessed August 29, 2011).

124 Whether it is permissible depends, in part, on the relative therapeutic success of lumpectomy versus full mastectomy.

125 See, for example: Bertran Auvert, Dirk Taljaard, Emmanuel Lagarde *et al.*, "Randomized, controlled intervention trial of male circumcision for reduction of HIV infection risk: the ANRS 1265 trial," *PLoS Medicine*, 2(11), 2005, pp. 1112–1122; Robert C. Bailey, Stephen Moses, Corrette B. Parker *et al.*, "Male circumcision for HIV prevention in young men in Kisumu, Kenya: a randomised controlled trial," *The Lancet*, 369, February 24, 2007, pp. 643–656; Ronald H. Gray, Godfrey Kigozi, David Serwadda *et al.*, "Male circumcision for HIV prevention in men in Rakai, Uganda: a randomised trial," *The Lancet*, 369, February 24, 2007, pp. 657–666.

126 For a survey of the evidence see David Benatar and Michael Benatar, "A pain in the fetus: toward ending confusion about fetal pain," *Bioethics*, 15(1), 2001, pp. 57–76.

127 For more on the data about circumcision anesthetic see Michael Benatar and David Benatar, "Between prophylaxis and child abuse," pp. 37–38.

128 Doriane Lambelet Coleman, "The Seattle compromise: multicultural sensitivity and Americanization," *Duke Law Journal*, 47, 1998, pp. 717–783.

129 Ibid., pp. 749ff. However, even if her claim is correct, that would only show that the double standard to which I shall refer is one that is enshrined in law.

130 Ibid., p. 748.

131 Ibid., p. 749.

132 American Academy of Pediatrics, Committee on Bioethics, "Policy Statement – Ritual Genital Cutting of Female Minors," *Pediatrics*, published online April 26, 2010. DOI: 10.1542/peds.2010-0187.

133 Ibid., p. 1092.

134 American Academy of Pediatrics, "American Academy of Pediatrics Withdraws Policy Statement on Female Genital Cutting," May 27, 2010. Online at www.aap.org/advocacy/releases/fgc-may27-2010.htm (accessed July 4, 2010)

135 Ibid.

136 "Not Anyone's Daughter," *New York Times* Online, June 30, 2010. Online at http://www.nytimes.com/2010/07/01/opinion/01thu4.html?scp=1&sq=not%20anyone's%20daughter&st=cse (accessed July 1, 2010).

137 "Circumcisions Have Claimed 102 Lives since 1996," Cape Times, Thursday, October 5, 2006, p. 6.

138 For one survivor's harrowing account of evading detection, see Emanuel Tanay, *Passport to Life*, Ann Arbor, MI: Forensic Press, 2004. See also Solomon Perel, *Europa Europa*, New York: John Wiley & Sons, 1997.

139 American Association of University Women, *Shortchanging Girls, Shortchanging America*, Washington, DC: American Association of University Women, 1991.

140 American Association of University Women, The *AAUW Report: How Schools Shortchange Girls*, Washington, DC: American Association of University Women, 1992.

141 Ibid., p. 22.

142 Christina Hoff Sommers, *The War against Boys: How Misguided Feminism is Harming Our Young Men*, New York: Simon & Schuster, 2000; and "The War against Boys," *Atlantic Monthly*, May 2000, pp. 59–74.

143 American Association of University Women, *Beyond the "Gender Wars": A Conversation about Girls, Boys, and Education*, Washington, DC: American Association of University Women, 2001.

144 Ibid., p. 4.

145 Myra and David Sadker, *Failing at Fairness: How America's Schools Cheat Girls*, New York: Charles Scribner's Sons, 1994.

146 Digest of Educational Statistics, 2008, "Table 109: Percentage of high school dropouts among persons 16 through 24 years old (status dropout rate), by sex and race/ethnicity: Selected years, 1960 through 2007." Online at http://nces.ed.gov/programs/digest/d08/tables/dt08_109.asp (accessed October 25, 2009).

147 G. Bowlby, "Provincial drop-out rates: trends and consequences," http://www.statcan.gc.ca/pub/81-004-x/2005004/8984-eng.htm (accessed December 2, 2009).

148 OECD, *Education at a Glance 2008: OECD Indicators*, Paris: OECD. Online at http://www.oecd.org/document/9/0,3343,en_2649_39263238_41266761_1_1_1_1,00.html (accessed June 16, 2011). See also Indicator A2, in OECD, *Education at a Glance 2009: OECD Indicators*, Paris: OECD, p. 56.

149 In 2006, Iceland was the one exception.

150 Digest of Educational Statistics, 2008, "Table 403: Average mathematics literacy, reading literacy, and science literacy scores of 15-year-olds, by sex and

country: 2006." Online at http://nces.ed.gov/programms/digest/d08/tables/
dt08_403.asp (accessed October 25, 2009).

151   Ibid. In 2006, there were no exceptions to this trend, although data for the US
are not listed.

152   There are some data that suggest that males do better and some data that suggest no significant difference between the sexes, but the bulk of the data support the conclusion that females do better. See Lee Ellis, Scott Herschberger,
Evelyn Field *et al., Sex Differences: Summarizing More Than a Century of
Scientific Research*, New York: Psychology Press, 2008, pp. 278–279.

153   Digest of Educational Statistics, 2007, "Table 191: College enrolment
and enrolment rates of recent high school completers, by sex: 1950 through
2006." Online at http://nces.ed.gov/programms/digest/d07/tables/dt07_191.
asp (accessed October 25, 2009).

154   The following statistics are drawn from US Institute of Education Sciences,
National Center for Education Statistics, "Fast facts: what is the percentage of
degrees conferred by sex and race?" Online at http://nces.ed.gov/fastfacts/dis-
play.asp?id=72 (accessed October 25, 2009).

155   American Association of University Women, *The AAUW Report*, p. 68.

156   American Association of University Women, *Shortchanging Girls, Shortchanging
America*, pp. 7ff.

157   These are statistics from a 1995 report, Centers for Disease Control and
Prevention, *Monthly Vital Statistics Report*, 43(9), Supplement, March 22,
1995, pp. 24–25. As far as I can tell the CDC no longer collects or publishes
data on the proportions of maternal and paternal custody of children following divorce and thus I cannot cite more recent data from this source. The US
Census has more recent data, but because the percentages listed in the Census
reports total 100%, there is reason to think that unlike the earlier CDC reports,
they are also factoring in joint custody. Thus the report for 2007 says that
82.6% of custodial parents were mothers, and 17.4% were fathers. (Timothy
S. Grall, "Custodial Mothers and Fathers and Their Child Support: 2007,"
Washington, DC: US Census Bureau, November 2009, p. 2). Even if fathers
now account for a slightly greater proportion of (sole residential) custody parents than in the early 1990s, they are still a small minority of such parents.

158   This comes from a ministerial answer to a parliamentary question in New
Zealand. Question available at http://www.parliament.nz/en-NZ/PB/Business/
QWA/0/f/d/QWA_09643_2006-9643-2006-Judy-Turner-to-the-Minister-for-
Courts.htm (accessed April 5, 2011). The answer links from that page. I am
grateful to Stuart Birks for directing me to this source.

159   There has been some fluctuation: 73% in 1970, rising to 79% in 1976 and
then dropping to 72% in 1986. See Department of Justice, *Evaluation of the
Divorce Act. Phase II: Monitoring and Evaluation*, Ottawa: Department of
Justice Canada, Bureau of Review, May 1990, p. 99.

160   Ibid., p. 103.

161   Eleanor E. Maccoby and Robert H. Mnookin, *Dividing the Child: Social and
Legal Dilemmas of Custody*, Cambridge, MA: Harvard University Press, 1992,
p. 103.

162   Ibid.

163 Ibid., p. 105.

164 See, for example, Bernard L. Bloom, Shirley J. Asher and Stephen W. White, "Marital disruption as a stressor: a review and analysis," *Psychological Bulletin*, 85(4), 1978, pp. 867–894.

165 Augustine J. Kposowa, "Marital status and suicide in the National Longitudinal Mortality Study," *Journal of Epidemiological Community Health*, 54, 2000, pp. 254–261.

166 For a number of suggestions see Sanford L. Braver, *Divorced Dads: Shattering the Myths*, New York: Jeremy P. Tarcher/Putnam, 1998, pp. 112–121.

167 Ibid., pp. 87–107.

168 Cited by Ross D. Parke, *Fathers*, Cambridge, MA: Harvard University Press, 1981, pp. 81–82.

169 Ibid.

170 Emmy E. Werner and Ruth S. Smith, *Vulnerable but Invincible: A Longitudinal Study of Resilient Children and Youth*, New York: Adams Bannister Cox, 1982, p. 80.

171 Ibid., pp. 94–95.

172 Paul R. Amato and Bruce Keith, "Parental divorce and adult well-being: a meta-analysis," *Journal of Marriage and the Family*, 53, February 1991, pp. 43–58.

173 K. Alison Clarke-Steward and Craig Hayward, "Advantages of father custody and contact for the psychological well-being of school-age children," *Journal of Applied Developmental Psychology*, 17, 1996, pp. 239–270.

174 For example, who is the mother of a child that is formed from the ovum of one woman but gestated in the womb of another?

175 When women adopt, then, they obviously know that their children are not their genetic offspring, but the same is true of men.

176 The precise rate of non-paternity is very difficult to calculate. Studies have shown considerable variation. See, for example, Kermyt G. Anderson, "How well does paternity confidence match actual paternity?" *Current Anthropology*, 47(3), June 2006, pp. 513–520.

177 *Tuan Anh Nguyen v. I.N.S*, 121 S.Ct 2053 (2001). I am grateful to Alex Guerrero for drawing my attention to this case.

178 Men technically also have castration, but then we can add hysterectomy and oophorectomy for women.

179 For a detailed (and relatively up-to-date) tabulation of parental leave benefits by country, see http://en.wikipedia.org/wiki/Parental_leave (accessed January 3, 2011).

180 Dan Smith, *The State of the World Atlas*, Brighton: Earthscan, 2003, pp. 62–63.

181 Kath O'Donnell, "Lesbian and gay families," in Gill Jagger and Caroline Wright (eds), *Changing Family Values*, London: Routledge, 1999, p. 90.

182 D.J. West, "Homophobia: covert and overt," in Gillian C. Mezey and Michael B. King, *Male Victims of Sexual Assault*, p. 29.

183 FBI, "Hate Crime Statistics, 2008." Online at http://www.fbi.gov/ucr/hc2008/documents/incidentsandoffenses.pdf (accessed December 21, 2009). (The sum of these is not 100% because some crimes were motivated by bias against

homosexuals in general, some were motivated by bias against bisexuals and a small proportion were motivated by bias against heterosexuals.)

184   For surveys, see Rebecca Jurado, "The essence of her womanhood: defining the privacy rights of women prisoners and the employment rights of women guards," *Journal of Gender, Social Policy and the Law,* 7(1), 1998/1999, pp. 1–53; and Brenda V. Smith, "Watching you, watching me," *Yale Journal of Law and Feminism,* 15, 2003, pp. 225–288.

185   *Smith v. Fairman,* 678 F.2d 52 (7th Cir. 1982).

186   *Jordan v. Gardner,* 986 F.2d 1521 (9th Cir. 1993).

187   *Robino v. Iranon,* 145 F.3d 1109 (9th Cir. 1998), at p. 1110.

188   *Bagley v. Watson,* 579 F. Supp 1099 (D.C.Or., 1983).

189   See, for example, *Forts v. Ward,* 621 F.2d 1210 (2nd Cir. 1980); and *Torres v. Wisconsin Department of Health & Social Services,* 838 F. 2d 944 (7th Cir. 1988).

190   *Carlin v. Manu,* 72 F.Supp.2d 1177 (D.Or., 1999).

191   See, for example, *Timm v. Gunter,* 917 F.2d 1093 (8th Cir. 1990).

192   Canada is another, but male prisoners have been similarly disadvantaged there. See *Weatherall v. Canada (Attorney General),* [1993] 2 S.C.R. 872.

193   "Standard Minimum Rules for the Treatment of Prisoners," adopted by the First United Nations Congress on the Prevention of Crime and the Treatment of Offenders, held in Geneva in 1955, and approved by the Economic and Social Council by its resolutions 663 C (XXIV) of July 31, 1957 and 2076 (LXII) of May 13, 1977. Online at http://www2.ohchr.org/english/law/pdf/treatmentprisoners.pdf (accessed January 6, 2010).

194   Martin van Creveld, *Men, Women and War,* London: Cassell & Co., 2001, p. 216 (citing a personal communication from Lt.-Col. Ian Wing, Australian Army).

195   In ancient Rome, *all* functions were performed in full view of others using the toilets.

196   *The Economist, Pocket World in Figures, 2007 Edition,* London: Profile Books, 2006, pp. 170, 212, 240.

197   Ibid., pp. 186, 190.

198   Ibid., p. 202.

199   Ibid., p. 168.

200   George Stolnitz, "A century of international mortality trends: I," *Population Studies,* 9(1), 1955, pp. 24–55; George Stolnitz, "A century of international mortality trends: II," *Population Studies,* 10(1), 1956, pp. 17–42.

201   All the foregoing statistics in this paragraph are from the Human Mortality Database, University of California, Berkeley (USA) and Max Planck Institute for Demographic Research (Germany). Available at www.mortality.org (accessed January 28, 2010).

202   George Stolnitz, "A century of international mortality trends: II," pp. 23ff.

203   Ibid. It was also true that male survival rates were higher than those of females at specific ages (even when female longevity was overall greater than that of males). However, over time female survival rates at those ages outstripped that of males. Ibid. See also, George Stolnitz, "A century of international mortality trends: I," pp. 44–45.

204 US Bureau of the Census, *Historical Statistics of the United States, 1789–1945*, Washington, DC, 1949, p. 45.

205 Ibid.

206 Ibid.

207 Colin Pritchard, *Suicide – The Ultimate Rejection? A Psycho-Social Study*, Buckingham: Open University Press, 1995, p. 59.

208 Ibid. See tables on pp. 61, 64–67.

209 Ibid., pp. 114–115.

210 US Department of Labor, "Fatal occupational injuries, total hours, and rates of fatal occupational injuries by selected worker characteristics, occupations, and industries, civilian workers, 2008," p. 1. Online at: http://www.bls.gov/iif/oshwc/cfoi/cfoi_rates_2008hb.pdf (accessed January 17, 2010).

211 US Department of Labor, Bureau of Labor Statistics, "Current Population Survey, and Census of Fatal Occupational Injuries, 2009," p. 8. Online at www.bls.gov/iif/oshwc/cfoi/cfch0007.pdf (accessed January 17, 2010).

212 Andrew Sharpe and Jill Hardt, "Five Deaths a Day: Workplace Fatalities in Canada, 1993–2005," Ottawa: Centre for the Study of Living Standards, 2006. See Table 4a.

213 Yen-Hui Lin, Chih-Yong Chen and Jin-Lan Luo, "Gender and age distribution of occupational fatalities in Taiwan," *Accident Analysis and Prevention*, 40, 2008, p. 1606.

214 Roy Walmsley, "World Prison Population List," 4th edn, London: Home Office, 2003, p. 1.

215 Ibid. I say "possibly" because the data show that the USA has about 1.96 million prisoners *including* pre-trial prisoners and that China has about 1.43 million *excluding* pre-trial prisoners. It is possible that if the pre-trial detainees were added to the China figures, they would exceed those of the USA.

216 There is obviously some fluctuation. Roy Walmsley, "World Female Imprisonment List," London: International Centre for Prison Studies, 2006, p. 3 (lists the female proportion as 8.6%, based on information available at the end of April 2006). US Department of Justice, "Prison Inmates at Midyear 2007," Washington, DC, June 2008, p. 1 (lists the female proportion as 7.2% based on information available at the end of June 2007).

217 UK Office of National Statistics, "Prison Population, 2003," March 22, 2005. Online at http://www.statistics.gov.uk/cci/nugget.asp?id=1101 (accessed February 3, 2010).

218 Roy Walmsley, "World Female Imprisonment List," p. 1.

219 Ibid.

220 Ibid.

221 Victor L. Streib, "Rare and inconsistent: the death penalty for women," *Fordham Urban Law Journal*, 33, 2006, pp. 609–636, at p. 621. Some of Professor Streib's data are drawn from his "Death penalty for female offenders," *University of Cincinnati Law Review*, 58, 1990, pp. 845–880.

222 Victor L. Streib, "Rare and inconsistent," p. 622.

223 Ibid.

224 I say "known" because China, which carries out many executions, is notoriously secretive about the precise numbers.

225   See http://www.capitalpunishmentuk.org/women.html (accessed February 24, 2010). The author of this site, Richard Clark, advises me that his claim of less than 1% is made in the light of his "detailed analysis of executions worldwide published every month." His figures exclude China because "there are no definitive numbers for that country for either sex." He also indicates that his "site lists the names of all verifiable and reported executions in the 21st century" (personal communication, February 23, 2010).

226   Roger Hood and Carolyn Hoyle, *The Death Penalty: A Worldwide Perspective*, 4th edn, Oxford: Oxford University Press, 2008, p. 54.

227   Ibid., p. 196.

228   Ibid., p. 195.

229   Not all do deserve it, as it has not been unknown for wrongfully convicted people to be sentenced to death.

3

Explaining Male Disadvantage and Thinking about Sex Differences

What are little boys made of?
Snips and snails, and puppy dogs' tails,
That's what little boys are made of!

What are little girls made of?
Sugar and spice and all things nice,
That's what little girls are made of!

English nursery rhyme

Although some of the male disadvantages outlined in the previous chapter may be the result of unfortunate facts about the world that do not amount to discrimination, most are at least partly the products of people's beliefs about and attitudes towards males and are thus a result of discrimination. Whether this discrimination is wrongful is a separate question.

This chapter has two purposes. I shall first outline the main beliefs about and attitudes towards males that partly explain why they are discriminated against. (For the sake of simplicity I shall refer henceforth either to beliefs or to attitudes rather than to both.) I shall then provide a framework for thinking about those beliefs and their relevance to the differential treatment of males and females. With this background, I shall revisit, in Chapter 4, the disadvantage males suffer and argue that much but not all of it is the product of wrongful discrimination.

Beliefs about Males

The beliefs I shall discuss are *about* males and they disadvantage males. They are also held *by* males as well as by females. That members of a group could hold beliefs that cause themselves disadvantage should not be news.

The Second Sexism: Discrimination Against Men and Boys, First Edition. David Benatar.
© 2012 John Wiley & Sons, Inc. Published 2012 by John Wiley & Sons, Inc.

Feminists have long argued, quite correctly, that females can hold beliefs about themselves that cause them disadvantage.[1] There is no reason why the same should not be true of males.

Of course, there are also beliefs about males that work to their advantage (just as there are beliefs about females that advantage women and girls). While I shall not talk specifically about the beliefs that redound to male advantage, I shall show in Chapter 5 that discrimination against both males and females is linked to beliefs about the differences between them and that it is therefore unlikely that discrimination against one sex can be eliminated entirely without also addressing discrimination against the other group.

The beliefs about males that contribute to explaining many of their disadvantages are either normative or descriptive or some combination of the two. The normative beliefs are ones that make evaluative judgments about males. They make judgments either about the extent to which male interests should count or about what males should do or what attributes they should have. By contrast, the descriptive beliefs are beliefs about what attributes males actually have or what they actually do. In other words, whereas the normative beliefs are about what should be the case, the descriptive beliefs are about what is the case.

Sometimes, as we shall see, the descriptive beliefs are cited in support of the normative beliefs. On other occasions, the distinction between the two kinds of beliefs is ignored and people slip between descriptive and normative versions of a belief. That is to say, they slip between saying that males are a certain way and saying that males should be that way.

What are the beliefs that contribute to explaining many of the disadvantages that men and boys experience? First, male life is often believed to be less valuable than female life. I do not mean by this that *every* society unequivocally values male lives less than female lives. This cannot be true, because there are some societies in which female infants are killed precisely because they are female. However, even in many such societies, the lives of adult males seem to be valued less than those of adult females. The situation is less ambiguous in other societies, including but not limited to contemporary liberal democracies. It is not my claim that every single person in these societies values male life less, but that these societies generally do. Although, of course, there are countless examples in such societies of fatal violence against women, this tends to be viewed as worse than the killing of men. For instance, arguing in favor of a combat exemption-exclusion for women, one representative in the US House of Representatives said: "We do not want our women killed."[2] This attitude partly explains why societies have been prepared to send males to war but have been extremely reluctant to send females.

It is true that this attitude has *partially* eroded in some places. A number of countries (including Canada and Denmark) now allow female soldiers into combat positions, although until these countries engage large numbers of troops in actual combat, the presence of women in combat *positions* does not demonstrate just how far the greater valuing of female lives has been eroded. Although the United States preserves a formal prohibition against females participating in combat, it is the United States military where, in practice, female soldiers have experienced actual combat conditions in the greatest numbers. Female US soldiers have increasingly been placed in more dangerous situations, and there has been gradually increasing acceptance of female military fatalities. However, the old attitudes are far from eliminated. The formal prohibition against females participating in combat is still in force in the United States, and disproportionately few of the fatalities are female. As of February 28, 2009, less than 2.5% of fatalities of the wars still current at the time of writing were female,[3] even though females constitute 14% of the US Armed Forces.[4] Most importantly, no country forces women into combat, but many countries have forced or do force men.

It has been suggested that the reason why men and not women are sent to war is not that male lives are valued less but rather that too many fatalities of women of reproductive years would inhibit a society's ability to produce a new generation and thus threaten its own survival.[5] The facts of reproduction are such that an individual man can father thousands of children if there were fertile women to gestate them, whereas an individual woman can produce only one child per year or so (depending in part on how and how long she breastfeeds the previous child), and then only as long as she still has ova and has not reached menopause. Because of this asymmetry, more women than men are required to produce new generations.

The problem with this suggestion is that instead of showing that male life is not valued less than female life, it (at least partially) explains *why* male life is less valued. In other words, there is a good evolutionary explanation why male lives are regarded as more expendable. Large numbers of male fatalities need not impede a society's ability to reproduce, whereas large numbers of female fatalities would. This was more true in our evolutionary past, when there were so many fewer human beings and societies were consequently so much smaller. Today, given how many more humans there are, societies could survive with higher female fatality rates, but it is in our species' distant past that the attitudes to male and female life evolved.

The greater valuing of female life is evidenced in other ways too. Where some lives must be endangered or lost, as a result of a disaster, men are the first to be sacrificed or put at risk. There is a long, but still thriving tradition (at least in western societies) of "women and children first," whereby the preservation of adult female lives is given priority over the preservation of adult male lives. Two famous examples are those of the ships *Birkenhead* and *Titanic*. When they were wrecked, in 1852 and 1912 respectively, women and children were given priority in access to the lifeboats, while adult men were expected to stay on board knowing full well that they would die.[6]

As we saw in the previous chapter, people are also more inclined to kill males than females. This is why, for example, men are so often singled out for murder and mass murder. Even in those so-called "root-and-branch" genocides, which aimed at destroying an entire people rather than just the males, extermination of males has often been a prelude to the more expansive program of killing.[7] Thus, Daniel Jonah Goldhagen, speaking about the early phases of the Holocaust, writes:

> The *Einsatzgruppen* officers ... could habituate their men into their new vocation as genocidal executioners through a stepwise escalation of the killing. First, by shooting primarily teenage and adult Jewish males, they would be able to acclimate themselves to mass executions without the shock of killing women, young children and the infirm.[8]

Indeed, the noted Holocaust historian Christopher Browning quotes an order from Colonel Montua of the Police Regiment Center directing that "all male Jews between the ages of 17 and 45 convicted as plunderers are to be shot."[9] Professor Browning goes on to say that there "was, of course, no investigation, trial, and conviction of so-called plunderers."[10] Instead male Jews "who appeared to be between the ages of seventeen and forty-five were simply rounded up" and then shot.[11] Professor Browning also notes, in another of his books, that "it is generally accepted that in the first weeks of Operation Barbarossa the Jewish victims were primarily adult male Jews, and that ... the killing was gradually expanded to encompass all Jews except indispensable workers."[12]

It is thus unsurprising that Leo Kuper notes, in his book on genocide, that while "unarmed men seem fair game, the killing of women and children arouses general revulsion."[13] When it comes to the perpetrators, this underlying attitude is usually implicit, but sometimes it is explicit. Consider, for example, the words of a Russian soldier describing his actions and attitudes during the 2000 offensive in Chechnya:

> I killed a lot. I wouldn't touch women or children, as long as they didn't fire at me. But I would kill all the men I met during mopping-up operations. I didn't feel sorry for them one bit. They deserved it.[14]

Nor is it only the perpetrators who take the loss (or even endangerment) of female lives to be worse. If violence or tragedy threatens or takes the lives of "women and children" that is thought to be worthy of special mention.[15] We are told that X number of people died (or are endangered), including Y number of women and children. That betrays a special concern, the depravity of which would be more widely denounced if newsreaders, politicians, poets and others commonly saw fit to note the number of "men and children" who had lost their lives in a tragedy. Even when violence is being enjoined, it is thought necessary to stipulate that the victims should also include "women and children" presumably because the assumption would otherwise be that it should be directed only against men.[16]

When men are the main victims of some tragedy or attack, this is rarely thought worthy of mention and even more rarely thought worthy of detailed examination. Thus, Adam Jones notes that in covering the atrocities against the Kosovars, neither the *New York Times* nor the *Washington Post* "published a single story or editorial focused on the phenomenon of gender-selective mass executions."[17] Nor is the problem restricted to that particular episode. To see how the maltreatment of males more generally is covered, he previously conducted a careful analysis of the Toronto *Globe and Mail*'s content (between March 10 and June 15, 1990)[18] and showed that it engaged in "denigrating, de-emphasizing, or ignoring male suffering and victimization."[19] This is but one newspaper. However, one suspects that if similar analyses were to be conducted of other newspapers and other periods, similar results would be found. Indeed, one of the problems is that whereas there are hundreds of thousands of studies investigating bias against females, inquiries into discrimination against males is in its infancy. It remains to be seen whether it survives into adulthood.

Now, it might be suggested that it is not a greater valuing of female life that explains the exemption of women from combat, the greater willingness to put male lives at risk and the greater concern when female lives are lost. Instead, it might be suggested, these phenomena are explained by beliefs that men are "tough, active agents," while women are "passive victims who need protecting." I think that this alternative suggestion is inadequate and must at least be supplemented by the explanation I have provided. There are at least two reasons for this. The first is that the combined evidence does not support the alternative suggestion. Consider, for example, the greater concern about women who are (unintentionally) killed in disasters, such as the explosion of the space shuttle Challenger. There may well be some people who believe that women should be protected from the dangers of space travel by being excluded from such positions. However, even many of those who do not think that women should be protected by such exclusions nonetheless think that the subsequent deaths of female astronauts are more noteworthy.

The second reason why the alternative suggestion fails is that it does not adequately explain why men are less in need of protection. It is difficult to sustain the view that the deaths of defenseless male victims of mass killings are less remarkable because men are "tough, active agents." These male victims are clearly passive rather than active, their purported toughness is no protection against an armed murderer, and it is absolutely clear that men who are victims of mass killing were in need of the protection they never received. Perhaps some will suggest that although the belief that males are (always) tough, active agents is false, it is nonetheless what explains the phenomena to which I have referred. But this suggestion also fails. To ascribe such obviously false beliefs to people is not the most charitable alternative. There is good evolutionary reason, as we saw earlier, to expect that female life would be valued more.[20] We have also seen that female lives are in practice valued more. It is thus more reasonable to conclude that this is because they *are* actually valued more.

A second contributor to male disadvantage is the greater social acceptance of non-fatal violence against males. This is not to deny the obvious truth that women are frequently the victims of violence. Nor is it to deny that there are *some* ways in which violence against women is accepted. I suggest only that violence against men is much more socially accepted, at least in many parts of the world.

One author has taken issue with the claim that violence against men is regarded as more acceptable. He has said that those who think it is so regarded "never offer a criterion for determining when a social practice is acceptable."[21] He says that "sometimes they slide from the fact that violence with men as victims is very widespread to the conclusion that it is acceptable."[22] He notes, quite correctly, that a practice can be widespread without its being deemed acceptable. He also thinks that the "penalties for violent acts, social instructions against violent acts, and moral codes prohibiting violent acts"[23] constitute evidence that violence against men is not acceptable.

It is doubtful that a single criterion of the greater acceptability of violence can be provided. However, there can be various kinds of evidence for such a claim. For instance, although violent acts against men do usually carry penalties (as do violent acts against women), the law does reveal bias. When the law prohibits physical punishment of women, but permits such punishment of men, it indicates a level of greater societal acceptance of violence against men. Similarly, when the law does not punish male homosexual rape with the same severity as it punishes heterosexual rape of women, it sends a similar message. But the law is not the only evidence of societal bias. There are penalties for wife-batterers and for rape, yet this (appropriately) has not stopped feminists from showing how both legal and extra-legal factors can indicate societal tolerance of such activities.[24] If, for instance, police do not take charges of wife-battery or rape seriously or if there are social impediments to the reporting of such crimes, this can sometimes constitute evidence of societal complacency and therefore some implicit acceptance of such violence. If that can be true when women are the victims, why can it not be true when men are?

Moreover, there is some social scientific research that lends support to the claim that a man who strikes a woman is subject to much more disapproval than a man who strikes another man. For example, a number of surveys have shown that people have a more negative view of husbands' violence against wives than vice versa.[25] Commenting on these surveys one author has noted that the fact that "some respondents may be giving a socially desirable response only adds further support to the notion that respondents consider violence against wives deviant behavior."[26]

In experimental research, which demonstrates what people will do rather than what they say, both male and female subjects have been found to inflict shocks on males more readily than on females. Nor was this only true when the female opponents were not aggressive. One study found that "subjects of both sexes facing aggressive females exhibited far less aggression than when facing equally aggressive males."[27] The authors of this study report that when they asked one male subject why he had not attempted to hurt his female opponent, he answered that it was "because she was a girl."[28]

A third belief about males has both descriptive and normative forms. It is the belief that males are, or at least should be, tough. They are thought to be able to endure pain and other hardships better than women. Whether or not they do take pain and other hardships "like a man," it is certainly thought that they *should*. When it is said that they should take pain and hardships "like a man," the word "man" clearly means more than "adult male human," but rather one who stoically, unflinchingly bears whatever pain or suffering he experiences, including that which is inflicted on him precisely because he is a "man." This is true even when he is not a man, but rather a boy. Boys are taught early that they must act like men. Crying, they are told, is what girls do. They are discouraged from expressing hurt, sadness, fear, disappointment, insecurity, embarrassment and other such emotions. It is because males are thought to be and are expected to be tough that they may be treated more harshly. Thus, corporal punishment and various other forms of harshness may be inflicted on them but often not on females, who are purportedly more sensitive.

Males are also believed to be more aggressive and violent, and less caring and nurturing than females. This is partly why men are thought, for example, to be better suited than women to combat and to be less suited than their ex-wives to taking custody of their children at the time of a divorce.

Sexually, men are thought to be more assertive and voracious, and thus less discerning that women. This, combined with a belief about the relative strength of men and women, explains why so many people have greater difficulty in thinking that a male could be a victim of female sexual assault than vice versa. First, as we saw in Chapter 2, people are more inclined to think that sexual assault was welcomed or enjoyed by the victim if the victim was male. Second, because women are believed to be so much less sexually aggressive than males, people have greater difficulty in believing that females would make unwanted sexual advances, much less force themselves on unwilling males. The beliefs about men and women also extend, respectively, to boys and girls. Thus, when a man has sex with a girl, the girl is likely to be seen as a victim. By contrast, when a woman has sex with a boy, the boy is likely to be seen as "lucky."

Because men are believed to be stronger and tougher than women and because the safety of women is thought more important than that of men, it is also believed that men must serve as protectors of women (and children). This too contributes to the belief that it is men rather than women who should be sent into battle. It is also a contributory factor to the disproportionate number of males who are the victims of violence. Because men believe that they must be protectors, and are expected by others to be so, they are more likely to place themselves in harm's way.

Questions about the Beliefs

While some people, as I have suggested, deny that these are indeed beliefs held about males, the evidence against this position is compelling. For example, people *do* express greater concern about female deaths in combat and other contexts. They *do* demand greater toughness from boys than from girls. Because their actions match their words, there is no reason to doubt that this is what they believe.

Once we recognize that these beliefs exist, there is a series of questions we can ask about them:

(1) To what extent, if at all, are the beliefs true?
(2) If they are true, what makes them true?
(3) Are there any moral, legal or other implications of the answers to the previous questions? If so, what are they?

All three of these questions are regularly asked, although one common mistake is to fail to distinguish each from the others. There are clearly problems with conflating these questions. If they are not differentiated, it is unlikely that the answers will be.

In what follows I shall say something about each of the questions. The aim is twofold. I wish to clarify the questions and their (purported) relevance, and I wish to go some way to answering them. I do not pretend to provide comprehensive answers to all of the questions. Among the many reasons for this is that we do not actually have all the knowledge required to answer the first two questions in full. Even outlining everything that is known would be a mammoth undertaking – and one that is not necessary for my purposes. Thus, in clarifying the first two questions and what the substance of the debate about them is, I hope to show how the way to answering the third question is thereby cleared. I shall make some general remarks about the third question in what then remains of this chapter. In the next chapter I shall show how the specific disadvantages that males suffer are the result of wrongful sex discrimination.

To what extent, if at all, are the beliefs true?

To answer this question we need to note again that some of the beliefs are normative whereas others are descriptive. These are very different kinds of beliefs and the methodology for answering them is different. Determining whether male lives are less valuable or whether boys should be tough is a different kind of project from determining whether males are more violent or more resistant to pain. For this reason, it is best to consider the two kinds of belief separately.

Consider first the normative beliefs about males. I suggest that these should be rejected. Male lives are not less valuable than female lives.[29] Nor is violence against males *per se* more morally acceptable than violence against females. There may be cases when violence against a male is more justified than violence against a female, but there will also be cases where the reverse is true. I think we should also reject the view that boys and men *should* be tougher, more aggressive and violent, more assertive, less caring and nurturing and sexually more assertive and voracious than women.[30] What argument can be advanced for these conclusions?

It will be remembered that my claim that there is a second sexism is opposed by two groups of people – partisan feminists on the one hand and some conservatives on the other. Although those feminists who deny that there is a second sexism are more interested in advancing the interests of females than in gender equality, most of them at least profess commitment to gender equality. For this reason, they are unlikely to object to my rejection of the normative beliefs about males. Indeed, it would be impossible for them to accept the claim that, for example, males should be more assertive than females, without also accepting the claim that females should be less assertive than males. The latter kind of claim is certainly one that they would want to reject. Even where feminists think that females should be less *violent* than males, this is only because they think males are too violent.

It is thus against gender-role conservatives that I need to defend my rejection of the normative beliefs. Those who accept the normative beliefs typically do so on the basis of the descriptive beliefs. For example, they might take their cue from nature, arguing that there are certain normative implications of these natural facts. For this reason, as well as others, much of my argument against the conservative endorsement of the normative beliefs will be implicit in my discussion (later in this chapter and in the next) of the descriptive beliefs and of the problem of defending discriminatory behavior against males on the basis of them.

However, there are a number of general observations that can be made now. These can all be subsumed under a more general point about the problem of deriving normative conclusions from descriptive premises. This is not to suggest that descriptive claims are not relevant to and should not inform normative conclusions, but rather that straightforward derivations of the latter from the former are notoriously problematic.

For example, explanations, such as the one mentioned earlier, of why male lives are valued less than female lives do not entail that male lives are less valuable. Perhaps it is the case that people value male lives less because fewer males than females are required to preserve the species or some smaller human grouping. However, we cannot conclude from this explanation that male lives are less valuable.

At the very least, that conclusion assumes that the preservation of the species through reproduction is desirable – something which at least some of us dispute.[31] I recognize that rejecting this assumption is a minority view and so we might grant, for the sake of argument, that the continuation of humanity would be desirable. It still does not follow that male lives are less valuable. There are many circumstances in which the population is sufficiently large that many female lives could be lost without the future of humanity or a particular society being compromised. Indeed, in circumstances of overpopulation, a reduction in population growth might actually enhance humanity's chances of survival because, for example, of the strains that increased population growth puts on the environment. It does not help to suggest at this point that the favoring of female lives evolved in circumstances in which the human population was much smaller and more precarious. This is because there is a difference between an explanation and a justification. The fact that fewer male lives are required to preserve the species when the human population is small might *explain* why people favor female lives, but it does not *justify* their doing so. *A fortiori* in circumstances in which we do not need a large proportion of existing females to preserve the species. In such circumstances it is even clearer that one cannot justify the greater value of female lives by the fact that in some other circumstances more females would be necessary.

In any event, the inference from a greater need for female lives to the greater value of these lives ignores the distinction between instrumental and intrinsic value. Perhaps it is the case in some circumstances that female lives are instrumentally more valuable, at least if one values the preservation of the species. It certainly does not follow that female lives are intrinsically more valuable. If, in a given society, there is an overabundance of a certain profession, then members of that profession will be instrumentally less valuable than members of some profession that is in short supply. But it does not follow that the lives of those in the more abundant profession have less intrinsic worth and may thus be sacrificed more readily.

When it comes to intrinsic value, there do not seem to be any relevant differences between the sexes to warrant the view that male lives are less valuable or that violence against males is more acceptable. Men and women have the same levels of sentience and sapience. They are as invested in their own lives. Whatever differences there might be between the sexes in perception or cognition, for example, they are certainly not sufficiently marked to say that male lives are worth less or that violence towards them is more acceptable. The idea of moral equality, it bears reminding, does not rest on the dubious claim that all people are identical in every way. Instead it is the idea that people's interests count equally despite variation in their aptitudes and despite differences in sex, sexual orientation, race, religion, ethnicity, disability and so forth.

Those normative beliefs that concern what attributes males should have and how they should act fare no better. If some attributes are found disproportionately among males it does not follow that those males lacking these attributes (to the same extent) *ought* to have them. Sometimes people think otherwise because they confuse two senses of the word "normative." In the sense I am using the term, it refers to the setting of a (moral) standard – something that ought to be met. But there is another sense, namely what is statistically normal. Thus it is normally the case that males are taller than females. Or, to take an attribute that is chosen, boys' hair tends (at least in many societies) to be shorter than girls' hair. We can say of a boy with long hair that he is not normal in the sense of deviating from the normal hair length for boys. But it certainly doesn't follow that he is abnormal in some moral sense – that he is doing something wrong. Put another way, the fact that most boys have shorter hair does not make some boys' deviation from that norm wrong or undesirable. The same can be said about deviations from whatever psychological or behavioral attributes most males may have.

Consider next the descriptive beliefs about males. Why should we be interested in whether they are true? The answer is that although we should be cautious, as I have suggested, in drawing conclusions from the purported truth of descriptive beliefs about males (and about females), the extent to which they are true or false is at least relevant. A false belief cannot be used for justificatory purposes. By contrast, true beliefs can have justificatory power. Nevertheless, there are constraints here too. A true belief might simply be irrelevant in a given justification. If it is relevant, there may be few inferences to draw, or any inferences might also require the truth of a number of other beliefs.

To determine the truth of a belief, one must first get clarity on what exactly the belief is. The beliefs about males and about the purported difference between males and females need to be clarified in a variety of ways.

First, we are not talking about obvious physical differences between males and females – that they have different genitalia, that women have breasts and men more bodily hair, or even that men tend to be taller than women. These differences are (generally) not in dispute. Instead, we are talking about psychological and behavior differences. Henceforth, when I speak about differences between the sexes or about sex differences I refer to the psychological and behavioral rather than the anatomical or sexual.

Second, when people claim that there are differences between males and females they are not claiming that all males can neatly be distinguished from all females with regard to the property in question. Thus, if people say that men are more aggressive than women, they do not mean that *all* men are more aggressive than *all* women. The claim that there is such a sharp distinction would be no less odd than the claim that all men are taller than all women. This is not what is meant when people say that men are taller than women. Claims about sex differences are statistical claims. They are generalizations. I shall say more about this later.

Third, we should realize that terms like "aggressive," "assertive" and "tough" are not without ambiguity. Sometimes people use these words synonymously. Other times they mean different things by them. Even when they are distinguished, how exactly we pick out the attributes they describe could influence whether or not somebody is described as having the attributes in question, or the extent to which they have them. Consider, for example, the claim that males are "tough." According to the *Oxford English Dictionary*, somebody or something is tough if he, she, or it is "capable of great physical endurance; strongly resisting force, injury; fatigue, etc.; not easily overcome, tired, or impaired; hardy, stout, sturdy." There are some ways in which men are clearly less tough than females. As we saw earlier, male life expectancy is typically lower than that of females. While some of this is attributable to greater violence against males, at least some of males' shorter life span is attributable to male biology. Males die in greater numbers at all ages, including during the fetal period,[32] (usually) before they are the victims of greater violence. But the kind of physical toughness that is commonly attributed to males is different. It is that they are better able to endure pain and hardship.

Fourth, we need to be clear about the *extent* of the purported differences. For example, when it is said that males are more aggressive and violent than females, how much more aggressive and violent are they thought to be? Depending on the answer to this question, the claim is either true or false. Although males *do* account for more aggression and violence than do females, the difference is not as great as it is usually thought to be. This is borne out by some laboratory studies.[33] In real life, we find that there are at least some circumstances, most notably within the family, in which women behave as aggressively and violently and sometimes even more so than men.

Thus, we saw earlier that, contrary to received wisdom, wives are at least as violent towards husbands as husbands are towards wives. We also saw that mothers inflict more corporal punishment on children than do fathers. Although mothers generally spend more time with children and thus have more opportunity, parallel claims can be made about some other situations in which men cause more violence (such as war). When women have had the opportunity they have proved capable of the brutalities usually perpetrated by men. Female participation in the Rwandan genocide is one example,[34] but there are many others.[35] It seems, then, that people generally underestimate the amount of female aggression and violence relative to male aggression and violence. Although the differential is very likely exaggerated, it is true that males exhibit more aggression and violence than females.

In summary, I have provided a preliminary argument that the normative beliefs about males ought to be rejected. However, I have suggested that, although sometimes exaggerated, at least some of the descriptive beliefs are true. I have not provided a long argument for this latter conclusion, primarily because it is not in dispute. Most of the debate concerning beliefs about males and females, and about the differences between them, has not focused on whether the beliefs are true. Indeed, most people have assumed that there are some (average) differences between males and females. Instead the focus has been on what accounts for these differences.

What makes the beliefs true?

It is in explaining the origins of sex differences that the hoary nature–nurture question arises. Insofar as this question is understood as a dichotomous choice, it seems unhelpful – indeed a false dichotomy, for it should be clear that some traits could be a product of both nature and nurture. But instead of requiring us to reject the nature–nurture question, recognition of this might instead prompt us to interpret the question in a different way. That is to say, we might interpret it as a question about *the extent* to which a given trait is the product of nature and the extent to which it is a product of nurture. This form of the question recognizes that a given trait might be influenced by both biology and socialization. Even this formulation of the question might be challenged. The worry might be that it ignores the *interaction* between the two. However, that just gives rise to a more sophisticated form of the question – one about how nature and nurture interact to produce a particular trait. It is unclear whether this version of the question can be answered with any precision, at least at this time. Fortunately, and contrary to what some people think, we do not need to answer it in order to demonstrate that there is a second sexism (just as we do not need to answer it in order to demonstrate that there is sexism against females). Knowing the precise extent of the second sexism (like the precise extent of the more familiar sexism) may require knowledge that we do not yet have. However, it is possible to show that there is a substantial second sexism in the absence of the knowledge not yet available to us.

The nature–nurture debate about differences between males and females is usually characterized as a debate between those who think that the differences are attributable exclusively to nature, those who think that they are exclusively attributable to nurture, and those who think that they are a product of the interaction of nature and the nurture. Although these are all logically possible positions, the actual debate, is restricted to a portion of this spectrum, as I shall now explain.

The view that sex differences are the product of nature alone is not one seriously entertained by anybody. It is not hard to see why this view – biological determinism – has no serious advocates. Although there are some traits, such as eye color, that are genetically[36] determined and to which the environment appears to make no contribution (or at least no contribution that is not mediated via genes), other physical traits involve some interaction with environment. One's height, for example, is partly genetic. There is some upper limit to how tall one can grow, given one's genes. However, environmental factors, such as one's nutrition level especially during the developmental years, also play a part. If that is true for relatively straightforward physical traits, it seems extremely unlikely that more complex traits such as aggression and assertiveness are uninfluenced by the environment. Moreover, it is clear that all the differences we see between the sexes are not *fully* explicable by innate biology. It is manifestly obvious that socialization into gender roles is occurring. Even if there is a greater biological tendency towards, for example, toughness in males, this is clearly being amplified by gender role expectations that males will be tough. It would not be necessary to tell boys not to cry like girls if their natures fully determined how tough they would be. There would be no point to gender role socialization if it would occur without prompting.[37]

In contrast to biological determinism, there do seem to be those who hold the opposite view – or, at the very least, something extremely close to it. Such people maintain that the differences between the sexes are entirely the product of "social construction." On this view, the traits of males and females have no biological basis. They have nothing to do with nature and are instead entirely the result of nurture. On this view masculinity and femininity are moulded by society, and nature plays no role.

The actual opponents of the social construction view are sociobiologists and evolutionary psychologists. While critics of these latter views often describe them as biological determinism, that is a mischaracterization. Instead, sociobiologists and evolutionary psychologists espouse the view that there are innate sex differences – tendencies – that interact with the environment to yield particular traits and behaviors. They provide an evolutionary account of sex selection, arguing that males and females have different reproductive strategies. A consequence of this is that some psychological and behavioral differentiation will occur. Some traits that are more adaptive for males are less so for females, and vice versa.

It is sometimes difficult to say for sure whether a particular view constitutes social constructionism. This is because it is unclear how extreme somebody's position must be before it qualifies to be designated as a social construction view. Some of those who oppose sociobiology and evolutionary psychology allow the *possibility* that there might just be some very *minor* differences between the sexes. Consider, for example, Anne Fausto-Sterling's *Myths of Gender*, which is devoted to rejecting the view that there are innate cognitive, affective and other psychological differences between males and females. However, she does not close off the possibility that there could be some differences. She says that if "sex differences in cognition exist at all they are quite small and the question of their possible origins remains unanswered"[38] and that she remains "open to the idea that some small fraction of an already tiny sex-related difference could result from hormonal differences between male and female."[39]

Another difficulty is determining what sociobiologists and evolutionary psychologists take the magnitude of the biological contribution to sex differences to be. Presumably there is some disagreement between individual proponents of these views, but at least some of them may be overestimating the biological contribution. The problem arises, in part, because of a failure to distinguish two questions. The first is whether there is a particular biological basis for some attribute. On the assumption that there is, the second question concerns its extent. The focus is usually on the first question. This is quite understandable. It is the prior question, and is also a difficult enough question to answer. However, an answer to this question does not entail an answer to the second one.

Consider, for example, the purported link between aggression and androgens, particularly testosterone. Although testosterone is also found in females, it is typically present at much higher levels in males, which is why it is known as a "male hormone." Androgens are often said to influence aggression (and other kinds of behavior) in two ways.[40] During gestation it is thought to have an organizing effect on the developing brain.[41] Then, later in life, during puberty and also afterwards, testosterone circulating in a person's blood system is said to influence behavior.

In the case of circulating androgens the evidence of an effect on behavior is weaker. The administering of antiandrogens (and the resultant reduction of circulating testosterone levels) has been successful in curbing compulsive paraphilic sexual thoughts and impulsive and violent sexual behaviors.

However, the drugs were not very effective in reducing non-sexual violence.[42] Increasing testosterone levels in women or hypogonadal men to normal or supranormal levels has not been shown to increase aggression consistently. Lowering testosterone levels in men, by castration or antiandrogens, does not consistently decrease aggression.[43]

Some of those reviewing the literature have concluded that the evidence does not support a link between circulating testosterone and human aggression.[44] The inability to establish this link, claim some authors,[45] stands in striking contrast to the ease with which relations have been shown between testosterone and other phenomena, including sexual activity. In those few studies which do suggest connections between circulating testosterone and human aggression, the links are correlational and there is some reason to think that it is the aggressive and dominant behaviors that cause testosterone levels to rise, rather than vice versa.[46]

The evidence for an effect of prenatal androgen exposure on aggression in later life is stronger, even though not at all conclusive. There are clearly moral constraints on experimentally altering the androgen levels to which fetuses and infants are exposed. As a result, one of the few ways of testing the hypothesis that prenatal androgen exposure increases aggression later is by examining girls with congenital adrenal hyperplasia (CAH), a condition causing them to be exposed to unusually high levels of androgens *in utero* and until diagnosis soon after birth. Some studies have indeed found CAH girls to be more aggressive than control females,[47] but some found "the difference was not significant."[48] Other studies found no difference in aggression levels between CAH females and control females, even though affected females were, in other ways, found to be behaviorally similar to boys and unlike control females.[49] The latter studies suggest that even if prenatal androgen exposure has other behavioral effects, the influence on aggression is not unequivocal.

This is not to deny a biological basis for human aggression. It is possible, for example, that human aggression is rooted in some biological phenomenon other than androgens. There is some evidence that human aggression has many features in common with what is called "defensive aggression" (as distinct from "hormone-dependent aggression") in non-primate mammals and that this kind of aggression is rooted in the limbic system of the brain.[50] One of the distinctive features of defensive aggression in non-primate mammals, however, is that it is quantitatively similar in males and females.[51]

It is also possible that there *is* a connection between androgens and aggression even though none has yet been demonstrated conclusively. One possible explanation for this is that the posited connection is a complex one. One obvious feature of this complexity is the interaction with environmental factors.

However, even if it is demonstrated that there is a specified biological basis for aggression, we would have answered only the first question to which I referred earlier. We would not have established anything about the *extent* to which aggression is attributable to the specified biological phenomenon. Discerning the approximate contribution it makes is no easy task. However, unless we recognize that this is not resolved by an answer to the first question, the temptation is to think that because one has established a biological basis, one has also demonstrated that it plays a large role in aggression.

While sociobiologists and evolutionary psychologists sometimes overestimate how far differences between men and women are attributable to biology or how conclusive the evidence for a particular link is, the extreme social construction view faces the following challenge: if one rejects a dualist separation of mind and brain and accepts that the mind is the product of the brain, it is wildly implausible to think that while every other part of the body is influenced by biology, our psychological features are not. Of course, it does not follow from this that one's sex does make a difference. However, it would be surprising if *every* psychological attribute were distributed equally between males and females. It would be especially surprising, given that there are behavioral differences between the sexes in other species. To think that there are none in humans would be to posit a massive evolutionary discontinuity between our species and others.[52] But acknowledging this leaves open the question which attributes are unequally distributed and how unequally.

What, if any, implications are there?

One reason why there is so much disagreement about the origin of differences between the sexes is that the scientific questions are often examined with an eye to the hypothesized moral and social implications of finding or refuting innate psychological differences between males and females.

The assumption is often made that to the extent that differences between the sexes are socially constructed they are alterable whereas to the extent the differences are innate they cannot be changed. Put another way, many people assume that whereas social constructionism facilitates liberal or revolutionary views, evolutionary psychology has conservative or reactionary implications. According to this reasoning, if the traits of males and females are attributable to socialization, we can decide to socialize children differently in future. By contrast, if the differences are biological then there is no point trying to change what cannot be changed.

The assumption that these conclusions follow from the respective views about the origin of sex differences is mistaken and there are certainly people who accept evolutionary explanations of human traits but who draw conclusions associated with the political left rather than right.[53] There are many reasons why such a position is coherent.

First, biology may sometimes be more malleable than society. For example, in some societies a woman equipped with oral contraceptives that act biologically to suppress her fertility will be more successful using these pills to limit her fecundity than she would be if she were to attempt to alter social expectations that women produce as many children as possible.

Second, as we have already seen, just as biology can influence society so society can exert an influence on biology. For example, social factors can affect levels of nutrition and exercise, which can impact on physical characteristics such as height, neurological and muscular development, age of the onset of puberty and so forth. Insofar as nutrition and opportunities for exercise are distributed on the basis of a person's sex, biological differences between the sexes will be increased or decreased even if not eliminated.

Third, even if it were the case that biological differences were unalterable, we would need to be careful about the *extent* to which the differences between the sexes were biological. After all, there is good reason to think that innate differences would be amplified by society. The amplification mechanism could be this: people perceive modest differences between the sexes. As a result they come to have certain expectations of males and others of females. Males and females are pressured to conform to those expectations. This magnifies the differences between the sexes, thereby entrenching the expectations that further amplify the differences.

It is very unlikely that the differences we see between the sexes are fully attributable to biology. As evidence for this, consider the great variation in the magnitude of sex differences across different societies. Consider, for example, the fact that we are biologically very similar to our human ancestors tens of thousands of years ago. However, the traits of the average man and average woman then and now – including those traits that would once have been thought natural – differ considerably. Or consider differences between contemporary women and men of Afghanistan in comparison with the differences between the female and male American soldiers interacting with them. If one knew only the female role of Afghan women and how they differed from Afghan men, one might well think the female soldiers from America a biological impossibility. Or consider what Adam Jones has said about female participation in the Rwandan genocide:

> If women anywhere can participate in genocide on such a scale, and with such evidence enthusiasm and savagery, then it seems a valid prima facie assumption that they are capable of such participation everywhere. The search then

becomes one not for some essential "difference" in women's approach to war and peace, but for the range of cultural and policy mechanisms that either allow or, more frequently, inhibit the expression of women's aggressive and genocidal potential.[54]

Fourth, whatever natural psychological and behavioral differences there are between men and women, these are only statistical. They are tendencies. We cannot say, for example, that all men are more aggressive than all women. Thus, one important question concerns how some attribute is distributed across males and females. Put another way, how much overlap is there between the distribution curves? Moreover, it might be argued that we should, as far as possible, treat people as individuals rather than as members of a group to which they belong. Thus if a particular job has a height requirement,[55] one should, as far as possible, seek individuals of the right height rather than use a person's sex as a proxy for determining his or her height.

Finally, whether or not biological and social factors are malleable does not tell us anything about whether they are desirable and thus about whether they should be altered if this becomes possible in the future. Some desirable form of government might be socially constructed but not something we should seek to change. Other things, like horrible congenital diseases, might be biologically unalterable but nonetheless something we would seek to be able to alter or to avoid. As I noted earlier, we cannot infer from the fact that things are a certain way that that is the way they should be. This is true irrespective of whether the claims are about biology or about society. Both biological and social matters might be either desirable or undesirable, good or bad, worthy of changing or preserving (if we are able to do so).

It should now be apparent that the nature–nurture distinction is a proxy for and less important than the distinction between traits that are less alterable and those that are more alterable. In other words, what matters is not whether a trait is the product of nature or of nurture but rather whether it can be changed. Insofar as a trait cannot be altered we ignore that fact at our peril.

This is not to say that we are unable to do anything in the face of some unalterable trait. As the famous dictum notes, power tends to corrupt (and absolute power corrupts absolutely). Let us imagine that this tendency is unalterable. It does not follow that we cannot do anything about it. One thing we can do is design institutions that acknowledge this fact and seek to minimize the damage it can do. This is one reason why democracy is preferable to dictatorship. Dictatorship indulges a dangerous tendency whereas democracy puts limits on the expression of the tendency (rather than eliminating the tendency itself). The same is true of sex differences. Failure to recognize any unalterable differences between the sexes is dangerous, but this does not mean that we can do nothing to limit undesirable traits and promote desirable ones.

Conclusion

I began this chapter by identifying a number of beliefs about males that explain why males suffer the disadvantages they do. I do not claim that this list is exhaustive, but it is both substantial and representative. The rest of the chapter was devoted to a discussion of how we should think about these beliefs. I noted that there are differences between the sexes, although the extent of these may be exaggerated. The real controversy, I suggested, lies in the origins of these differences. Some people attribute them entirely to socialization, while others think that nature plays a role. The latter is the more plausible view, but there is disagreement about just how much of a role nature plays. Competing answers to this question must be very general, however, because at this time we lack sufficient knowledge to determine with any precision what the relative roles and interactions are. That said, I have offered a general caution against hasty moral and political inferences from the fact that a trait has a biological component.

In the next chapter, I turn from these sorts of general comments to more specific ones. I do this by returning to each of the disadvantages outlined in Chapter 2. My aim is to show why many of them are the product of wrongful discrimination. Making this case depends in part on showing that sex differences do not justify the discrimination.

Notes

1   See, for example, Martha Nussbaum, *Sex and Social Justice*, New York: Oxford University Press, 1999, p. 29.
2   Quoted by Judith Wagner DeCew, "The combat exclusion and the role of women in the military," *Hypatia*, 10(1), Winter 1995, p. 62.
3   Hannah Fischer, "United States Military Casualty Statistics: Operation Iraqi Freedom and Operation Enduring Freedom," Washington, DC: Congressional Research Service, March 25, 2009, p. 2.
4   US Department of Commerce, US Census Bureau News, "Women's History Month, 2010," Washington, DC, January 5, 2010. Online at http://www.census.gov/Press-Release/www/releases/pdf/cb10ff-03_womenshistory.pdf (accessed March 21, 2010).
5   This suggestion was first made to me on one of the occasions on which I spoke about this topic. It also appears in Tom Digby, "Male trouble: are men victims of sexism?" *Social Theory and Practice*, 29(2), 2003, p. 256.

6   See David Bevan, *Drums of the Birkenhead*, Cape Town: Purnell & Sons, 1972; Mark Giroud, *The Return to Camelot: Chivalry and the English Gentleman*, London: Yale University Press, 1981. Sex and age are not the only relevant variables. Class is another. For statistics on the percentages of surviving men, women and children in each of the three classes on the *Titanic*, see Ian Jack, "Leonardo's grave," *Granta*, 67, Autumn, 1999, p. 32.

7   Adam Jones has made this point repeatedly. See, for example, "Gender and genocide in Rwanda," in Adam Jones (ed.), *Gendercide and Genocide*, Nashville: Vanderbilt University Press, 2004, pp. 126–127; Adam Jones, *Gender Inclusive*, London: Routledge, 2009, pp. 255 and 257. In the next three paragraphs, I provide some of his examples by following his citations to their source.

8   Daniel Jonah Goldhagen, *Hitler's Willing Executioners: Ordinary Germans and the Holocaust*, New York: Vintage Books, 1997, p. 149.

9   Christopher Browning, *Ordinary Men: Reserve Police Battalion 101 and the Final Solution in Poland*, New York: HarperCollins, 1992, p. 13.

10   Ibid., p. 14.

11   Ibid.

12   Christopher Browning, *Nazi Policy, Jewish Workers, German Killers*, New York: Cambridge University Press, 2000, p. 30.

13   Leo Kuper, *Genocide: Its Political Use in the Twentieth Century*, New Haven: Yale University Press, 1981, p. 204.

14   Maura Reynolds, "War Has No Rules for Russian Forces Fighting in Chechnya," *Los Angeles Times*, September 17, 2000.

15   The following are a few of hundreds, if not thousands, of possible examples. (1) In a report about South Koreans kidnapped by Afghan militants, it was said that "authorities believed that 22, including 18 women, were still being held" (Choe Sang-Hun, "Spirits Sag in South Korea at Death of Hostage," *New York Times*, July 27, 2007). (2) The caption to a photograph in another *New York Times* article read: "Children related to five people, including three women, who died Feb. 12 in a night raid near Gardez in Paktia Province, Afghanistan, stood at their graves last week" (R. Oppel and R. Nordland, "U.S. Is Reining In Special Forces in Afghanistan," *New York Times*, March 16, 2010). (3) A newspaper infographic about the Khmer Rouge, referring to the Tuoi Sleng Prison, read: "At least 14 000 people passed through, fewer than 10 are thought to have survived … Women, children and babies were among those killed" (Reuters, "Khmer Rouge Prison Chief Sentenced," *Cape Times*, July 27, 2010, p. 2). (4) The headline of a front-page article about *all* the victims of the space shuttle Challenger explosion read "Two Women among Victims" (*Cape Times*, January 23, 1986, p. 1). (5) The Iraqi human rights minister is quoted as saying that authorities had found "a mass grave with the bodies of more than 800 people, including women and children" ("Mass Grave Contains 800 Saddam Victims," *Cape Times*, April 15, 2011, p. 2).

16   Judy Dempsey, "East German Shoot-to-Kill Order Is Found," *New York Times*, August 13, 2007. Online at http://www.nytimes.com/2007/08/13/world/europe/13germany.html (accessed August 13, 2007).

17   Adam Jones, *Gender Inclusive*, pp. 100–101.

18   Adam Jones, "*The Globe* and males," in *Gender Inclusive*, pp. 3–24.

19 Ibid., p. 5.
20 Good evolutionary reason is not the same as good moral reason. I shall say more about this later.
21 Kenneth Clatterbaugh, "Are men oppressed?" in Larry May, Robert Strikwerda and Patrick D. Hopkins (eds), *Rethinking Masculinity: Philosophical Explorations in the Light of Feminism*, 2nd edn, Lanham, MD: Rowman & Littlefield, 1996, p. 301.
22 Ibid.
23 Ibid.
24 Susan Estrich, *Real Rape*, Cambridge, MA: Harvard University Press, 1987.
25 See, for example, Ileana Arias and Patti Johnson, "Evaluations of physical aggression among intimate dyads," *Journal of Interpersonal Violence*, 4(3), September 1989, pp. 298–307; Cathy Stein Greenblat, "A hit is a hit is a hit … or is it? Approval and tolerance of the use of physical force by spouses," in David Finkelhor, Richard J. Gelles, Gerald T. Hotaling and Murray A. Straus (eds), *The Dark Side of Families: Current Family Violence Research*, Beverly Hills: Sage Publications, 1983, pp. 235–260.
26 Richard B. Felson, "The normative protection of women from violence," *Sociological Forum*, 15(1), 2000, p. 95.
27 Stuart P. Taylor and Seymour Epstein, "Aggression as a function of the interaction of the sex of the aggressor and the sex of the victim," *Journal of Personality*, 35, 1967, p. 481.
28 Ibid.
29 To clarify, the claim that male lives are not less *valuable* is different from the descriptive claim that male lives are not less *valued*. I have shown that people do value male lives less. I am now arguing that they are wrong to do so.
30 In rejecting the view that they should have these attributes, I am not arguing that they should not have them.
31 David Benatar, *Better Never to Have Been*, Oxford: Oxford University Press, 2006.
32 Males are conceived at substantially higher rates. Some studies put the primary sex ratio at 160 males to every 100 females. Since the secondary sex ratio – the ratio of male to females at birth is around 105 : 100, it is evident that many more males succumb during gestation. (See Lee Ellis, Scott Herschberger, Evelyn Field *et al.*, *Sex Differences: Summarizing More Than a Century of Scientific Research*, New York: Psychology Press, 2008, pp. 1–2.
33 D.J. Albert, M.L. Walsh and R.H. Jonik, "Aggression in humans: what is its biological foundation?" *Neuroscience and Biobehavioral Reviews*, 17, 1993, p. 417; Ann Frodi *et al.* say that "[c]ommonly held hypotheses that men are almost always more physically aggressive than women and that women display more indirect or displaced aggression were not supported." Ann Frodi, Jacqueline Macaulay and Pauline Ropert Thome, "Are women always less aggressive than men? A review of the experimental literature," *Psychological Bulletin*, 1977, 84(4), p. 634.
34 African Rights, *Rwanda: Not So Innocent – When Women Become Killers*, London: African Rights, 1995.
35 Patricia Pearson, *When She Was Bad: Violent Women and the Myth of Innocence*, New York: Viking, 1997.

36 "Biological determinism" is not synonymous with "genetic determinism." However, genetic determinism is an example or component of biological determinism.

37 It is a separate question whether such gender role reinforcement is desirable. Michael Levin is one who thinks that it is desirable because it encourages boys and girls to do what they will find most fulfilling. (See *Feminism and Freedom*, New Brunswick, NJ: Transaction Books, 1987, pp. 59–60.) My response is as follows: traits can be possessed to varying extents. (One can be more or less generous, courageous, patient, etc.) The degree of a trait that is found fulfilling will vary. That is to say, some people will find having trait Z to degree X fulfilling, while others might find having trait Z to degree Y fulfilling. Even if such variation will occur between the sexes it will also occur within the sexes. Thus imposing certain traits on those people who are atypical for their sex will threaten rather than foster their fulfillment.

38 Anne Fausto-Sterling, *Myths of Gender: Biological Theories about Men and Women*, rev. edn, New York: Basic Books, 1985, p. 14.

39 Ibid., p. 36.

40 See, for example, Kingsley Browne, *Co-Ed Combat: The New Evidence That Women Shouldn't Fight the Nation's Wars*, New York: Sentinel, 2007, pp. 43–46.

41 The elevated prenatal androgen levels in boys do not drop immediately at birth, but taper off in the months after birth. Thus the androgens generated *in utero* may continue to influence development postnatally for a few months.

42 Robert T. Rubin, "The neuroendocrinology and neurochemistry of antisocial behavior," in Sarnoff A. Mednick, Terrie A. Moffit and Susan A. Stack (eds), *The Causes of Crime: New Biological Approaches*, Cambridge: Cambridge University Press, 1987, p. 248.

43 D.J. Albert, M.L. Walsh and R.H. Jonik, "Aggression in humans," pp. 407–410.

44 Robert T. Rubin, "The neuroendocrinology and neurochemistry of antisocial behavior," says "there remains a definite controversy concerning the role of androgenic hormones in human aggressive and violent behaviors" (p. 248) and "the data on the neuroendocrine correlates of aggression and violence, with particular reference to the most thoroughly studied relation, that of testosterone in men, are sparse and conflicting" (p. 250). D.J. Albert, M.L. Walsh and R.H. Jonik, "Aggression in humans," say that "[a]ttempts to demonstrate a correlation between testosterone and aggression in humans have been in progress for almost 30 years. Yet, a clear relation remains to be established" (p. 406). Leslie Brody, *Gender, Emotion, and the Family*, Cambridge, MA: Harvard University Press, 1999, says "there is very little basis to the widely accepted idea that there is a causal relationship between testosterone levels and human aggression" (p. 107).

45 D.J. Albert, M.L. Walsh and R.H. Jonik, "Aggression in humans," p. 417.

46 Leslie Brody, *Gender, Emotion, and the Family*, p. 111. Ruth Bleier, *Science and Gender: A Critique of Biology and Its Theories on Women*, New York: Pergamon Press, 1984, p. 97.

47 Sheri A. Berenbaum and Susan M. Resnick, "Early androgen effects on aggression in children and adults with congenital adrenal hyperplasia,"

Psychoneuroendochrinology, 22(7), 1997, pp. 505–515; Vickie Pasterski, Peter Hindmarch, Mitchell Geffner *et al.*, "Increased aggression and activity level in 3- to 11-year-old girls with congenital adrenal hyperplasia (CAH)," *Hormones and Behavior*, 52, 2007, pp. 368–374.

48 Anke A. Ehrhardt and Susan W. Baker, "Fetal androgens, human central nervous system differentiation, and behavior sex differences," in Richard C. Friedman, Ralph M. Richart and Raymond L. Vande Wiele (eds), *Sex Differences in Behavior*, Huntington, NY: Robert E. Krieger Publishing Co., 1978, p. 41.

49 John Money and Anke A. Ehrhardt, *Man and Woman, Boy and Girl*, Baltimore: Johns Hopkins University Press, 1972, p. 99. John Money and Mark Schwartz, "Fetal androgens in early treated adrenogenital syndrome of 46XX hermaphroditism: influence on assertive and aggressive types of behavior," *Aggressive Behavior*, 2, 1976, pp. 19–30 (esp. pp. 22–23). Melissa Hines and Francine R. Kaufman, "Androgen and the development of human sex-typical behavior: rough-and-tumble play and sex of preferred playmates in children with congenital adrenal hyperplasia (CAH)," *Child Development*, 65, 1994, pp. 1042–1053.

50 D.J. Albert, M.L. Walsh and R.H. Jonik, "Aggression in humans."

51 Ibid., p. 414.

52 There are many behaviors that are characteristic of one sex across many and unrelated species. For example, both territoriality and courtship display are usually male, while mate choice is usually female. There are exceptions, however, and thus the point about evolutionary discontinuity is not that if some specific behavior is characteristically male in most species we should expect the same behavior to be characteristic of human males. Instead the point is that if at least some behaviors are distributed unequally between the sexes in other species, it would be strange if *no* behaviors were distributed unequally between human males and females.

53 See, for example, Peter Singer, *A Darwinian Left: Politics, Evolution and Cooperation*, New Haven: Yale University Press, 1999.

54 Adam Jones, "Gender and Genocide in Rwanda," p. 127.

55 By this, I do not mean an arbitrary height requirement, but rather a height requirement that is materially connected to the nature of the job.

4

From Disadvantage to Wrongful Discrimination

And Pharaoh commanded his people, saying: "Every son that is born, you shall throw into the Nile, and every daughter you shall let live."

Exodus 1:22

Men and boys, as I demonstrated in Chapter 2, are disadvantaged in a number of significant ways. Some of these disadvantages were clearly the result of discrimination. However, neither disadvantage nor discrimination is the same as wrongful discrimination. Many of those who accept that males are disadvantaged deny that males are the victims of wrongful discrimination. One of the most common ways to do this is to appeal to differences between males and females. According to this kind of argument, some of the disadvantages that males experience do not constitute discrimination, because they are the products of biology rather than of people, institutions or states discriminating against them. In the case of other disadvantages, it is acknowledged that discrimination contributes to the disadvantage, but it is argued that the discrimination is not unfair on account of purported differences between the sexes.

In appealing to sex differences to deny that males are the victims of unfair discrimination, people are prone to many confusions and errors. For this reason I devoted Chapter 3 to discussing the relevance (and the limits on the relevance) of sex differences to how we should treat males and females. More specifically, I argued that from the differences between men and women no immediate inferences can be drawn about how they should be treated. That discussion was quite general. In the current chapter, the aim is to return to the specific disadvantages discussed in Chapter 2 and argue that many of them are the product of unfair or wrongful sex discrimination. In

The Second Sexism: Discrimination Against Men and Boys, First Edition. David Benatar.
© 2012 John Wiley & Sons, Inc. Published 2012 by John Wiley & Sons, Inc.

making that case, I shall consider various contrary arguments, including some that appeal to differences between the sexes. Some of these arguments are familiar and expected. Others are so outrageous that it is hard to anticipate them until one hears them.

I shall not contend that every disadvantage outlined in Chapter 2 is the consequence of unfair discrimination, but rather that many of them are. Other disadvantages are nonetheless worthy of consideration. In some cases this is because it is unclear whether they result, at least partially, from discrimination, in which case they should be noted as matters for future research. In other cases, the disadvantages are helpful in thinking about whether comparable disadvantages experienced by females are the result of discrimination. Some feminists claim that such female disadvantages *are* the product of discrimination. When confronted by comparable disadvantages experienced by males, these feminists must either acknowledge that they too are the product of discrimination or they must revise their views about the extent to which female disadvantage is attributable to discrimination.

Conscription and Combat

When the military is accused of sex discrimination, the purported victims are usually female. This, of course, is part of the broader pattern of seeing females as the sole victims of sex discrimination. The criticism of the military is usually that women who wish to be part of the armed forces are excluded, either entirely or from certain roles, most notably ground combat, but also aviation and warships. It is thus not surprising that those who defend the exclusion of women from combat similarly focus on volunteer women, arguing that those women who want to serve should be prohibited from doing so. Most proponents and opponents of integrating women into all aspects of the military tend not to expend much time or energy arguing for or against the conscription of females, and especially conscription into combat roles. The prevailing assumption is that where conscription is necessary, it is only men who should be conscripted and, similarly, that only males should be forced into combat.

This, I shall argue, is a sexist assumption. The disadvantages men suffer in being conscripted and forced into combat are the products of wrongful discrimination. While those women who are desirous of combat positions are sometimes discriminated against in being excluded from these, many more men who would like to avoid such positions are discriminated against by being forced into them. Put another way, some women are *excluded* from combat, but many more women are *exempt*. While some men are excluded from combat (because they fail the relevant tests), many more are pressured or forced into combat (and the military more generally).

It is absolutely clear that the burdens of conscription and combat are substantial, as I argued in Chapter 2. It is equally clear, as I also showed, that these burdens are distributed on the basis of sex. The question before us now is whether there is adequate justification for this distribution of burdens. If there were adequate justification, then the discrimination would not be wrongful and thus not sexist. I shall argue, however, that the imposition of those burdens on males alone cannot be justified. To make this case I shall consider a number of arguments that seek to defend female exemption or exclusion from conscription and combat and I shall argue that they fail. Most of these arguments appeal to biologically based differences between males and females – differences that, it is said, cannot be eliminated by social means. A notable proponent of this position is Kingsley Browne.[1] His is the most compelling and fully developed argument against women being sent into combat and thus I shall consider it in some detail.[2]

Kingsley Browne's basic argument

Professor Browne argues that there are a number of physical and mental differences between men and women that make it problematic to integrate women into combat activities.[3] Men are physically stronger than women, they can run faster, throw further and more accurately. He argues that these differences cannot be overcome through training. Women, he argues, are also more prone to training injuries.

Turning to mental differences, he says that men are more inclined to take risks, are less fearful (and they fear cowardice more than injury or death[4]), are more aggressive and dominant, less nurturant and empathetic and have a higher tolerance for pain. He also argues that "men love war."[5]

He denies that these differences are mostly attributable to socialization.[6] Rather, he says, they are the result of hormonal differences between the sexes, which in turn are a product of sexual selection,[7] because different traits are adaptive in men and women.

Professor Browne argues that these differences are very relevant to combat. He rejects the claim that combat has become sufficiently mechanized and computerized that soldiers no longer engage in hand-to-hand combat.[8] When troops find themselves in such close contact with the enemy, physical strength can be the difference between life and death. This, he says, is true not only in fighting but also in removing the wounded from the battlefield. Women are much less likely to be able to carry much larger, wounded male soldiers from the combat zone.[9] Strength can also be required in aviation if a pilot is to bring a damaged aircraft under control[10] or to operate the lever on a jet's ejector seat.[11] It can also be required for tasks such as lifting heavy artillery shells and carrying machine guns.[12] He says that many women are also unable to throw a grenade sufficiently far to avoid blowing themselves up.[13]

The psychological differences between the sexes are also relevant, he says. For example, combat requires a greater willingness to take risks, because without soldiers taking risks, battles and wars cannot be won. Because war is dangerous, combatants are more inclined to take effective action if they are less fearful of injury and death. Combat is an aggressive activity, and thus combat troops need to have greater levels of aggression. Soldiers who have a higher tolerance for pain will be more likely to be able to continue fighting if they are wounded.

For these reasons, he says, women are less likely to be good soldiers. Because he thinks that "military effectiveness must be the touchstone of military manpower policy,"[14] females should not be sent into combat.

Professor Browne's argument so far can be formalized as follows:

(1) There are physical and psychological differences between men and women.
(2) These differences are not primarily a product of socialization, but rather substantially the product of biology.
(3) The attributes females have (and the attributes they lack) make them less likely to be good soldiers.
(4) The guiding consideration in determining who performs which tasks in the military should be military effectiveness.
(5) Military effectiveness requires sending into combat those troops who are most likely to do the job well.
(6) Therefore, females should not be sent into combat.

Professor Browne develops his argument further, but before considering those additional components of his argument, we should understand the problems with the basic argument.

"Slippage"

The first of these problems concerns the differences between men and women. The existence of these differences, to which Professor Browne repeatedly refers, is obviously central to his case. Why, however, does he include the second premise – that these differences are, to a significant degree, attributable to biology? He clearly thinks it is an important step in his argument, for otherwise he would not devote as much attention as he does to defending this claim. Perhaps the assumption is that whereas products of socialization are alterable, there is nothing that we can do about differences that are attributable to biology. In Chapter 3 I argued that this is not always true. However, for the sake of argument, we can temporarily assume otherwise.

Now imagine that although there were the stated differences between men and women, they were primarily a product of socialization. Under such circumstances it might be argued that these sex differences, even if the result of socialization alone, would surely be relevant to a policy decision about whether to conscript only men or also women. In other words, it might be said that if men tend to have attributes that make them better suited than women to combat, then it is not unfairly discriminatory to force only men into combat, irrespective of how men came to have those attributes.

The strength of this argument depends on considerations to which I referred in Chapter 3 and to which I shall return shortly. However, it is worth noting that even if discrimination at the policy-making level were not unfair, it would still be unfair discrimination to socialize males in a way that made them alone liable to the considerable costs associated with conscription and combat.[15] This is why Professor Browne requires (or may be purported to require) the second premise. Without it, the charge of upstream wrongful discrimination can be leveled and it can be argued that we should begin to socialize boys and girls differently from the way they are currently socialized.

However, if the second premise is necessary then the problem is that there is some slippage in Professor Browne's argument. He describes many more differences between the sexes than he demonstrates are attributable to biology. Moreover, even when he does provide evidence that a given difference is partly biological, it is often unclear how much of the difference is attributable to biology. He thus slips from claims about differences between the sexes to claims that these differences are (significantly) attributable to biology, but the evidence for the former does not always support the (full extent of) the latter.

Consider, for example, the claim that men fear cowardice[16] or that men love war.[17] Insofar as these are true of men but not women, Professor Browne does not provide evidence that these differences are biologically based. This is a problem because it is not sufficient merely to point to numerous current differences between the sexes. Such differences could be substantially due to socialization, in which case the socialization itself may be discriminatory. Therefore, it is essential to the argument that these differences instead be shown to be substantially biological, and even then that they are not remediable by socialization (without unacceptable costs) if the biological differences are undesirable.

The difference in strength between men and women *is* primarily attributable to biology (even if social factors can make some relatively small contribution). However, in the case of other attributes, it is far from clear *how much* of the difference is caused by biological differences. For example, Professor Browne refers to the masculinizing effects of *in utero* androgen exposure. Although he notes that "testosterone is most often linked in the public mind with aggression," a link he seems to accept, he cites no specific evidence of this link.[18] He also acknowledges that the "relationship between circulating testosterone and aggression is not a simple one."[19] In humans there is, he says, no linear correlation, as there is in mice, between levels of testosterone and levels of aggression. Rather, he says, testosterone levels increase when a man is presented with a challenge, such as sexual opportunity or a competitive challenge from another male.[20] He also notes that testosterone levels "have been found to be positively correlated with the trait of 'sensation-seeking' in some studies." And he says that "in nonhuman animals – and potentially in humans – low levels of testosterone are associated with fear,"[21] the cited evidence for which is a study on rats.

If we accept that this evidence supports the claim that there is a biological basis for the stated differences between the sexes, the evidence hardly shows that the differences we see between the sexes are *fully* or even *substantially* explained by these biological considerations. Moreover, there is good reason, as I indicated earlier, to think that basic biologically caused differences would be amplified by societal expectations.

Military effectiveness

A second problem concerns the fourth premise in (my construction of) Professor Browne's argument. He says that "military effectiveness must be the touchstone of military manpower policy."[22] At first sight this premise may seem indisputable. Surely various military positions should be staffed by those most suited to performing them, particularly when assigning less suited people could lead to greater costs, especially in lives and injuries (to one's own side). However, there are a number of problems with this assumption.

First there are moral constraints on the invocation of an effectiveness principle. While all militaries may believe that they are engaged in just war, at least one side in any conflict must be wrong. And if we consider only the initiation of wars, such decisions must surely be wrong much more often than they are right. If one is not justified in waging war, then waging it more effectively may actually be morally worse. Consider, for example, military manpower decisions by the Axis powers in the Second World War. While the military leaders might have thought that their invasion of or attacks on other countries, and subsequently defending themselves against Allied forces, was permissible or even required, they should actually have desisted from starting war. Once begun, they should have surrendered earlier rather than later. The conscription of only males into the armed services of the Axis powers cannot be *objectively justified* by the greater effectiveness of an exclusively male military, even if an exclusively male military were indeed more effective. In other words, Axis power leaders cannot objectively justify their sending only male conscripts into battle on the basis of the military effectiveness principle. The same is true of hundreds of other states and armies in the history of humanity. While there might be disagreement about which states and armies these are, we can agree that there are many such cases.

Even when states are warranted in going to war, they cannot employ a military effectiveness principle without moral constraint. This is because just wars are those that not only have just cause but are also waged in a just way. In other words, meeting the *jus ad bellum* conditions does not eliminate the necessity for *jus in bello*. Sometimes this requires sacrificing a measure of effectiveness, even though the effectiveness should not be abandoned entirely. Professor Browne seems insufficiently sensitive to this. For example, he says that including "women in combat forces might reduce rapes and war atrocities"[23] but then quickly notes, as if to neutralize this point, that some "measures to reduce wartime atrocities might come at the cost of combat effectiveness ... since some psychological traits that cause men to be willing to kill in battle may dispose them in extreme circumstances to overdoing it."[24] The question of what *jus in bello* requires and, more specifically, to what extent moral considerations should constrain a military effectiveness principle is not one I can answer here. And thus I shall not consider whether we should add a condition to the requirements of just war – namely that those forced into combat not be forced on the basis of their sex (or race or creed, and so forth). It would be an unusual condition – one that focuses on justice to one's own conscript troops – and it is a more controversial condition than I require in order to make my case. What should be clear, even if we set such a condition aside, is that an unqualified invocation of the military effectiveness principle is problematic even when a state is fighting a war it is justified in fighting.

It is worth noting that even if, as a matter of fact, no military would (currently) accept particular moral constraints on the principle of military effectiveness, this tells us absolutely nothing about whether they *should*. Abandoning racial discrimination might, at a particular time, not be a live option for a society in the grip of racism, but it simply does not follow from their limited moral vision that they are not engaged in wrongful discrimination. Similarly, Genghis Khan never constrained his military by ethical principles that limit the actions (and thus effectiveness) of some militaries today. It does not follow that Genghis Khan was morally justified in doing what he did. It thus will not do for the advocates of *realpolitik* to lampoon my view as idle speculation of a philosopher detached from the practicalities of the real world. I make no claim about whether states will (now or later) recognize the importance of non-discrimination in conscription. I am making a claim about whether they should.

Professor Browne also seems to underestimate the ways in which respecting the moral constraints on war can sometimes (but obviously not always) *increase* military effectiveness. For example, it is very likely that invading or occupying forces raping locals or inflicting other atrocities on them will cause or exacerbate animosity towards those forces, thereby motivating locals to support resistance or insurgent forces. Or consider the role played by female US soldiers in performing searches on female civilians in Afghanistan and Iraq.[25] If these searches were performed by male soldiers, antipathy to the occupying US forces would be considerably greater, making success much more elusive. But because searches of female civilians are often conducted by patrols that encounter insurgents, the inclusion of women in what often become combat conditions has been essential if female civilians are to be searched by female soldiers. If female soldiers are to be placed in such conditions, it would surely be more effective if they were also suitably trained for combat.

This broader view of effectiveness can also shed light on why those with the "masculine traits" to which Professor Browne refers, might *sometimes* be less effective in battle itself. Although a propensity to risk-taking is sometimes necessary for military effectiveness it is not infrequently a threat to military effectiveness. The Battle of the Somme is but one of many examples where a greater aversion to risk might have saved many thousands of lives that were lost for no military gain. Indeed, it is true in every war (even if not in every battle) in which one side is massacred without achieving its goal. In at least many such cases it would have been better if they had stepped down. The point is that military effectiveness is not always enhanced, even if it sometimes is, by aggressive risk-takers whose greatest fear is cowardice.[26] Thus the question is whether overall, the (hyper)masculine traits unalloyed by a female presence have a beneficial or deleterious effect on military effectiveness. Given the history of pointless carnage consequent to recklessness on the side suffering it, it is very difficult to know the answer. At the very least, the answer is not obvious.

There is a further reason why the inclusion of females in combat troops could sometimes inhibit foolhardy ventures that lead to the massacre of one's own troops without military advantage. Instead of the purportedly greater risk-aversion of females, the mechanism would be the greater valuing of female lives. Professor Browne agrees with me that the norm of valuing female lives more than male lives endures.[27] He thinks that this phenomenon will minimize combat effectiveness for a variety of reasons.[28] For example, he says that enemies will exploit the greater protectiveness that male soldiers feel towards female soldiers. Now, Professor Browne does not explicitly claim that this protectiveness is either substantially biological or immune to social alteration. If it is subject to alteration, then the failure to alter it is indicative of ongoing discrimination against men, even if that discrimination is occurring upstream rather than at the point of deciding who will enter combat. There are at least three directions in which it could be altered. We could encourage greater protectiveness towards males, or less protectiveness towards females or some equalizing combination of the foregoing.

As long as the different levels of protectiveness to the two sexes exist, whether this is primarily social or biological, military leaders will likely be less inclined to dispatch female troops on futile ventures to which they have been *excessively* willing to send male soldiers. If male soldiers were only sent (involuntarily) on missions when female soldiers also were, male soldiers would then enjoy the benefit, now lacking, of having their lives put at risk only when it was really necessary.

Finally, while Professor Browne's primary focus is on the volunteer army, my primary focus is on the conscript army, because that is where the military most overtly and profoundly discriminates against males.[29] A broader view of Professor Browne's military effectiveness condition is relevant here. Sometimes the need for troops outstrips the number of males volunteering. Historically these have been the very circumstances in which conscription (of males) has been imposed. In at least some cases (now and in the future, even if not in the past), having military jobs, including but not only combat positions, open to volunteering women would avoid the need to conscript unwilling men.[30] Even if we assume that men are generally more effective soldiers than women, willing women will, at least in respect of their willingness, be more effective soldiers than unwilling men. Volunteer women will also be self-selective and thus more likely to have other attributes required of a good soldier. This stands in contrast to conscripted men, who will include many men who are below average on the various attributes required of a good soldier. Moreover, because volunteer women would have to prove their fitness to be included, whereas unwilling men would have to prove their unfitness to serve, a volunteer army that includes women could well be preferable to a conscript army of men only. The latter is arguably more likely to include people it should not be including.

Of relevance here is not only effectiveness but also efficiency. Conscript armies have to devote resources to dealing with unwilling conscripts. Whether or not a willing woman is more effective and efficient than an unwilling man might be an open question for those who think that men, all things being equal, are more effective soldiers than women. Nevertheless, it is not a question that can be ignored – or answered glibly.

Dangers of conservatism

We should not reject a conclusion merely because it is a conservative (or reactionary) conclusion. It is likely that at least some traditional views are correct, and thus discarding all received wisdom will come at a cost. At the same time, we should avoid well-known dangers of conservatism. In the realm of sex discrimination, the chief such danger is the assumption that things could not be other than they are or have been. There was a time when the idea of women voting or studying at universities, much less teaching in such institutions, was thought to be ludicrous. People could not imagine that women could be lawyers or engineers or doctors. They thought that society would collapse if women worked outside the home. Consider some examples.

Harvard medical students, in a letter to the (Boston) *Daily Evening Transcript*, objected to the admittance to the medical school of the first female medical student. They wrote that they

> deem it proper both to testify our disapprobation of said measure, and to take such action thereon as may be necessary to preserve the dignity of the school and our own self-respect. Resolved. That no woman of true delicacy would be willing in the presence of men to listen to the discussion of the subjects that necessarily come under the consideration of the student of Medicine. Resolved, That we object to having the company of any female forced upon us, who is disposed to unsex herself, and to sacrifice her modesty, by appearing with men in the medical lecture room.[31]

Justice Bradley, in an 1872 US Supreme Court opinion affirming the State of Illinois' refusal to admit a woman, Myra Bradwell, to the state bar, wrote: "The natural and proper timidity and delicacy which belongs to the female sex evidently unfits it for many of the occupations of civil life."[32]

Arguing against women having a right to vote, Sir Almroth Wright stated that the "woman voter would be pernicious to the State not only because she could not back her vote by physical force, but also by reason of her intellectual defects."[33]

The aim in providing these quotations is not to imply that current conservative arguments about women in combat *are* contemporary analogues of these earlier views. Instead the aim is to show that they *might* be. If people in former times could have held their preposterous views with the conviction they did, it is entirely possible that people today could be making the same mistake. If we are going to countenance a profound form of discrimination – one that subjects some people, but not others, to the horrors of war merely on basis of their sex, we need to be confident that we are not making the same mistake as has been made many times before.

Professor Browne says that we should "guard against the arrogance that convinces us that we are the first society wise enough to recognize that men and women are interchangeable in combat roles."[34] I am suggesting that we should guard equally against the arrogance that convinces us that we are the first society wise enough to avoid making a mistake that has been made a hundred times before. There is a common human tendency to see the current norms as natural, desirable and unavoidable. In some cases the current norms may indeed be correct, but we cannot assume them to be so.

Professor Browne suggests that in determining who bears the burden of proof we need to consider what the costs of error on each side are. As he is primarily concerned with a volunteer force, he says that the "primary cost of erroneous exclusion of women from combat would be to deprive a relatively small number of women of that opportunity,"[35] whereas if women are erroneously included in combat the costs will be human lives and "a reduction in military effectiveness."[36] For this reason he thinks that the burden of proofs lies with those who seek to integrate women into combat.

But the costs of the respective errors are not quite as he suggests, especially if we are speaking about conscription rather than a volunteer force. The primary cost of excluding or exempting women from combat will vary. When permitting women to serve in combat would preclude the necessity of conscripting men, the primary cost of excluding women would be that a *large* number of men will be forced into combat with its attendant risks and costs. Although this has historically been taken very lightly, it ought not to be. It is no small matter.

When permitting women to serve in combat would not preclude the necessity of conscripting men, then conscripting only men would inflict a severe hardship on a large number of men just because of their sex. That may not be as bad as the previous case, because many (even if not all) of those men would have been conscripted anyway, but it is a lot worse than excluding a small number of women from the opportunity to participate in combat, which Professor Browne says is the cost. It is worse for two reasons. First, more men will be affected by conscription than women are affected by prohibitions on their volunteering. Prohibitions on women volunteering affect only those few women who would volunteer if they were permitted to do so. By contrast, when men are conscripted, it is typically many of them who are conscripted. Second, being forced to participate in war is arguably worse than being prevented from participating in it.

But there are further possible costs. As I have indicated, there are a variety of ways in which the exclusion of women could make for a less effective fighting force and thus a force in which more of one's soldiers' lives would be lost. Thus an erroneous exclusion of women from combat, like an erroneous inclusion of women, could increase the number of deaths on one's own side. Moreover, it is at least relevant that the deaths that would result from the erroneous exclusion of women would be exclusively those of a sex whose lives are systematically less valued such that they are already at a disadvantage in terms of life expectancy.

The upshot of all this is that the costs of the two possible errors do not clearly lead to the conclusion that the burden of proof rests on those who would integrate women into combat. There is another principle for assigning the burden of proof. On this alternative principle, the burden of proof lies with those who would discriminate on the basis of race, sex, sexual orientation, religion and other such attributes. Such discrimination is presumptively wrong, and this presumption can be defeated only if there is good reason for the discrimination. Professor Browne might retort that the substantial biologically based differences between men and women provide such reason. However, that is a separate question, which can only be answered by examining his other arguments, as I am doing.

It is possible that I am wrong, but the real test of whether it is Professor Browne or I who is wrong would be to include women and see what happens. As Professor Browne acknowledges,[37] when countries are *in extremis* they have been known to allow women into combat – because, he says, it is better to have an additional fighter, even if of an inferior kind. He denies that women should therefore be included in less dire circumstances. My counter-claim is that it is much better to test the hypothesis that sex integration can work in circumstances that are less dire. If the hypothesis survives, one can be better equipped to fight the wars that do pose an existential threat by knowing that one can conscript and train females as well.

Some will argue that the hypothesis has already been tested, given the extent to which women have been integrated in the US operations in Afghanistan and Iraq. According to media reports the experiment has been a success.[38] Professor Browne has a different reading of events and thinks that the media reports to the contrary can be explained. He asks how we would know whether the inclusion of women in combat has been a mistake. He claims at various points in his book that there is great pressure on members of the military, at least in the United States of America, to endorse the integration of women. For example, he says that although "military leaders were initially resistant to sexual integration, decades of political pressures and inculcation into the officer corps of the lesson that failure to support sexual integration will kill their careers have left a military leadership unwilling to admit that the emperor has no clothes."[39]

We cannot exclude the possibility that soldiers and military leaders feel pressure, when they speak to journalists and others, to endorse the inclusion of women in the military and in combat. This is one of the many dangers of political correctness. It stifles discussion and prevents people speaking their minds. However, we need to be cautious about the argument that military endorsement of female participation is a consequence of such pressure.

First, the United States military seems to have been proactive, by circum-venting regulations limiting the integration of women. There is still a regula-tory prohibition on assigning women to combat units (below the level of brigade). The military has *de facto* bypassed this prohibition by "attaching" women to combat units rather than "assigning" them to such units. It is hard to see why the military leadership would bypass policies that prohibit what the military leadership purportedly really want prohibited. It is possi-ble, of course, that the military leaders have concerns about the inclusion of women but see it as a (temporary) necessity. (For example, they need female troops to search female civilians in Iraq and Afghanistan.) But that itself would be a military decision, even if it is a reluctant or begrudging one, about all-things-considered effectiveness rather than a consequence of political pressure.

Second, one wonders how cowardly a military leader would have to be to parrot the purportedly politically correct views of his civilian bosses if that reduced military readiness. Military leaders (in liberal democracies) are appropriately bound to follow the orders of the country's political leadership, but following orders and explicitly endorsing the underlying views or the political leadership are quite different matters. It is hard to reconcile the bravery required to sacrifice one's life with the utter spinelessness of not contradicting views that seriously compromise the military's effectiveness. This does not prove, of course, that military leaders are not acting in a cowardly manner, but if they are acting in such a way they bear a responsibility to find the courage to speak out.[40]

Finally, if the statements of military personnel are not to be trusted because they are suspected to be the result of political pressure, then the most reliable way to determine their actual views would be via an anonymous survey, preferably one that examined the views of people of various ranks and serving in different branches of the armed services. It would be interesting to see the results of such a survey.

Let us assume, however, that the results of such a survey would show that military personnel think that sex integration had failed. It would not follow that they were correct. It could be that the survey was detecting early prejudicial resistance to integration, which is hardly an uncommon phenomenon. More objective ways of assessing the success or failure of sex integration are required to determine whether it really has worked.

Statistical differences

Consider next an objection that Professor Browne anticipates. This fourth objection notes that the relevant differences between men and women are statistical rather than categorical. For example, it is not the case that all men are stronger than all women, but rather that men *tend* to be stronger than women. Thus, it might be argued, we should choose for combat those individuals, irrespective of their sex, who have the attributes that are most suited to combat. This might lead to a disproportionate number of men being sent to battle, but, the objection goes, it would be preferable to using sex as a proxy for the relevant attributes when determining who would make the best combat soldiers.

Indeed, as we saw in the previous chapter, armed forces have been notoriously undiscriminating with regard to which males it will enlist. It has not been unusual for *boys* to be enlisted. Whatever the differences between the average (young) woman and the average (young) man might be, the differences between the average young woman and the average boy are less marked.

Professor Browne anticipates this objection and has at least three kinds of response to it. The first is that the use of sex as a proxy is, contrary to the objection, indeed preferable. While the strength of individuals and their ability to throw could relatively easily and cheaply be screened, many of the other attributes do not lend themselves to easy measurement. He says that "one never knows who is going to be an effective soldier until the shooting starts, and the identity of the good fighters often turns out to be a surprise."[41] The implicit assumption here is that while some females could turn out to be surprisingly good fighters, one is more likely to get more good fighters if only men are sent into combat.

There are a number of problems with this argument. First, and foremost, are moral problems with treating people on the basis of attributes (such as their sex) that are a proxy for the attributes that are actually relevant. It is not that this may *never* be done. However, the less accurate the proxy and the greater the burden imposed on people because they have the proxy attribute, the less warranted is the use of the proxy, all other things being equal. If being male were an extremely reliable way of picking out those people who had the attributes of a good combat soldier, then it would be less problematic than it is given that sex is actually quite a blunt proxy. For example, Professor Browne says that "men love war." If this were true of vast numbers of men, conscription would not be necessary, because enough men would volunteer. This suggests that most men do not love war. There may well be even fewer women who love war, but it remains the case that sex is a very poor proxy for working out who loves war. There will be many men who are less suited than many women to enter the military and combat, even if men on average are better suited to war. Many men who hate war and loathe being in the military more generally will be swept up in the conscription net merely because they are males.

Second, the use of proxies is often just laziness. People presume that the use of a proxy is the only way to attain some goal. Defenders of affirmative action tell us this about the use of race or sex in racial and gender preference policies, and defenders of male-only conscription tell us this about the use of sex in determining who will be forced into the military. But the best test of whether they are correct is to deny them the use of the proxy. Because necessity is the mother of invention, they might then discover previously unimagined ways of attaining the desired goals. This is exactly what happened with the South African National Blood Services, which had maintained that there was no alternative to the use of "race" as one proxy for HIV-tainted blood. Following governmental outrage in the wake of the exposure of this policy, alternatives were soon found.[42] As this case illustrates, the laziness of using proxies is often reinforced by scaremongering. Defenders of male-only conscription use fear as a way of preserving the proxy. They tell us that without the use of the proxy, the armed forces defending us will not function as effectively. There is, of course, a chance that on this one occasion the defenders of a proxy are correct, but we can have no confidence that they are.

Third, even if sex does reliably track the relevant attributes, it is far from clear that the differences between men and women are *sufficiently* attributable to biological factors that they would not be susceptible to significant alteration by social means. Thus even *if* it were not unfairly discriminatory, at a given time, to use sex as a proxy, this would be attributable to upstream discrimination. Therefore, to rely on this from generation to generation without addressing the upstream discrimination would be unfair.

Furthermore, it would not be enough to claim that biological difference explains *part* of any given difference between men and women. Among other things, it would also need to be shown that the biological factors explain a large part of the difference. This could be shown in the case of physical strength, but that is also an attribute easily measurable without recourse to sex as a proxy. When it comes to various psychological attributes it is much less clear that any biological basis explains as much of the difference as Professor Browne seems to think.

Even if women are generally inferior soldiers and this is substantially attributable to biology, willing female fighters, especially if they are trying to prove themselves in the face of male scepticism about their ability, may very well be better fighters than men who resent being forced into combat. Finally, even if female volunteers are generally not as good fighters as unwilling men, I have suggested that the narrow focus on fighting ignores other relevant features of an effective and efficient military.

Professor Browne's second argument against a policy of determining which individuals, irrespective of their sex, have the relevant attributes is that the effectiveness of most combat soldiers depends on their being part of an exclusively male team. One reason for this, he says, is that "one of the greatest fears and most powerful motivators of fighting men" is their "concern about not measuring up as a man."[43] If women, who are not under pressure to prove their womanhood through combat, are part of the fighting force, it is said, such pressure will be reduced. If women become combat soldiers, combat will be seen less as a manly activity and thus men will be less pressured to prove their manliness in combat. A second reason for the greater effectiveness of all-male combat units, he says, is that group cohesion, which is essential to effectiveness, is promoted by male bonding,[44] which, he says, is different from the kind of relationships women form with one another and which men and women form.[45] Men's resistance to the inclusion of women in combat is also likely to be intractable, he says.[46]

Furthermore, men are more likely to follow other men. Part of the reason for this, he says, is that effective combat leaders are those who are more willing to expose themselves to danger, and men are generally more likely to be so willing.[47] Dominance, another trait he says that men exhibit to a greater extent than women, is also crucial to military leadership.[48] Moreover, the type of leadership to which he says men are more inclined – "the autocratic or directive style" – is better suited to military leadership.[49]

My earlier objections pose challenges to this response, too. For example, a man's fear of not "measuring up as a man" and the resistance of male soldiers to the inclusion of women, even if they have a biological basis, have not been shown to be substantially attributable to unalterable biological factors. Thus the slippage objection arises here. So does the concern about the dangers of conservatism. Men have historically been resistant to the inclusion of women in many professions and other areas of activity, yet these attitudes proved amenable to change. Now it is true that male resistance to the inclusion of women in combat has proved to be more intractable than their resistance to the inclusion of women in any other area, but it is not surprising that those occupations most closely associated with male gender roles will be hardest to penetrate. However, we cannot assume that because there has been more enduring resistance to women entering combat that that resistance cannot be overcome, especially given the long track record of error.

The objection about military leadership is an odd one. The inclusion of women in combat does not entail promoting to leadership positions women who are not fit to be military leaders. Professor Browne has provided some indication of what makes a good military leader. Some women will prove themselves good leaders by, for example, exposing themselves to danger. Even if Professor Browne thinks that there will be disproportionately few women who meet these standards, he has provided us with no reason for thinking that those women would not make good leaders. Moreover, insofar as male soldiers are motivated by notions of masculinity, the pressure on them to perform will be heightened when they are led by a *woman* who has proven she can lead.

Perhaps, however, the concern is that there are pressures to promote women even when they have not proved themselves to be capable leaders. Such affirmative action promotion is not unknown, and it might be argued that it will be especially dangerous in the context of combat troops. However, the fitting response to such double standards in promotion is to oppose the double standard rather than to oppose the inclusion of women.

Even if my responses to Professor Browne's objections fail, there is another solution: admit women to combat roles but segregate male and female soldiers into different units (such as platoons, companies, battalions or brigades). Males would still be able to bond within their units. They would be led by other males. When wounded they could be carried away from battle by other men who are more likely to bear that load. Professor Browne considers this possibility, but he rejects it for the following reasons.[50]

First, he wonders whether there would be sufficient women willing to participate in battle without large numbers of men around them. That point is entirely moot in the case of conscripts, who are not afforded the choice. In the case of volunteers, females would at least have the choice.

Professor Browne also wonders whether the public would be willing to send women into combat without males "to protect them." If Professor Browne is correct that this is not currently a political possibility, the very fact that he was correct would support my claim that males are being discriminated against. One cannot invoke the public's prejudice to show that the prejudicial treatment is not prejudicial. Perhaps it will be said in response that people's prejudices need to be taken into account in deciding who ought to be conscripted and sent into combat because the failure to do so will have bad effects. However, that is a separate question, and an affirmative answer is far from obvious. This is because of the many problems with pandering to prejudice. Even if it turns out that we should take people's prejudices into account, it certainly does not follow that the prejudices do not exist or that they should not be undermined in some other way.

A further problem, says Professor Browne, is that while individual weaknesses in females would be masked by large numbers of men in the same unit, a unit of only female soldiers would magnify the deficiencies. He also doubts that "all-female groups would exhibit the same kind of cohesion that men's groups exhibit."[51] The second of these two concerns is more speculative than the first, but even if both are currently reasonable concerns, they make problematic assumptions. If the assumption is that there are biological differences that are immune to social alteration, then the slippage problems, discussed earlier, arise here again. Perhaps, however, the assumption is the more modest one that although the differences are liable to social alteration, they cannot be changed quickly. On this view, the military is in the interim warranted in making decisions based on the current differences. Alternatively (or in addition), the assumption may be that that although the biological differences are liable to social alteration, the costs of such alteration are unreasonable. Neither of these more modest assumptions has been demonstrated. Given the dangers of conservatism, it is quite likely that they may be overestimated.

Professor Browne has a third kind of argument against a sex-neutral method of determining which individuals should be selected for combat. This kind of argument appeals to particular vulnerabilities of women. Women, he says, are more vulnerable to rape, both by fellow soldiers[52] and by the enemy if they are taken captive.[53] Unlike men, women can also become pregnant. Professor Browne says that pregnancy presents many problems.[54] One is that pregnant women cannot be deployed or will need to be withdrawn from a deployment if they become or are found to be pregnant. Among the knock-on effects of this is that women can avoid deployment simply by becoming pregnant. Because men who render themselves medically or otherwise unfit for service are subject to disciplinary action, a double standard is created, which increases resentment towards women. Pregnant women, unless they terminate the pregnancy, become mothers. Many are single parents. Because more custodial parents are female, more problems arise when single mothers try balancing child rearing with the demands of a military career, which can include deployment overseas for long periods.

These sorts of arguments are less convincing than the others. The fitting response to rape of female soldiers by their fellow soldiers is not to ensure that there are no female soldiers but to take action to prevent rape and then prosecute it when it does occur. Female soldiers are more likely than male soldiers to be sexually assaulted and raped when taken captive, although male captives have also frequently been subjected to sexual assault. But the argument that women should therefore be exempt from combat only works if one thinks that sparing women this fate is more important than sparing men from the kind of treatment that is regularly inflicted on male captives. Severe ill-treatment of captives is, sadly, a regular occurrence. This is why we need and have the Geneva Convention, ignored though it often is.

Professor Browne's response to this rebuttal is that "rape is generally considered a more serious imposition than nonsexual assault."[55] Whether or not all those who say this really believe it, it is a claim that is hard to justify. For example, is it worse to be raped or to be tortured? The answer probably depends in part on the individual, but it is far from obvious that rape is worse. There are many people who would prefer to be raped to being tortured (in other ways). Obviously rape is sometimes worse than some non-sexual assault, but it is equally obvious that non-sexual assault is sometimes worse than sexual assault. For example, is fondling a woman's breasts really worse than inflicting excruciating torture on a man? (Anybody who answers this rhetorical question affirmatively should ask whether it would be worse for a woman to have her breasts fondled or to be subjected to excruciating torture. If it is the latter, it needs to be explained why altering the sex of the tortured person is sufficient to make breast fondling worse.) Moreover, torture of male captives is not infrequently sexual.[56] Consider, for example, electric shocks to the genitals, or the sorts of treatment inflicted by US soldiers (including female soldiers) on prisoners in Abu Ghraib prison.[57]

There is disagreement about how many women purposefully become pregnant in order to avoid deployment (or other unwanted tasks). However, pregnancy, whether intentional or otherwise, does considerably reduce the rate at which females are deployed.[58] Professor Browne seems to think that there is nothing that could be done about this. I disagree. We live an age of effective contraception and safe abortion. The former include various long-acting methods, at least some of which could be employed to circumvent the problem of soldiers failing, in the heat of passion, to bother with barrier contraception. The use of long-acting contraception need not prevent female soldiers from becoming mothers. Instead, it can assist in the timing of their pregnancies in a way that would enable the military to plan deployments more reliably. In some cases, a soldier's request to end contraception could be temporarily declined until she has completed her tour of duty. But the relevant regulations could also prohibit the military from endlessly deferring a soldier's pregnancy.

There will be those who will object to compulsory contraception and, *a fortiori*, abortion. The abortion case is harder and thus, although I think that a case might be made for sometimes requiring a pregnant servicewoman to have an abortion, I shall focus for now only on contraception, which is a much less serious intervention. Some will argue that a woman should have control over her body even with regard to contraception. The problem with this argument, however, is that soldiers generally have much less control over their bodies than do civilians. They may, it is thought, be subjected to compulsory medical examinations and medication, as well as being sent involuntarily into harm's way. Insofar as control over one's body is permissibly restricted in the case of other soldiers, it should also be permissible to restrict it for female soldiers.

In a volunteer force, female soldiers could actually consent, while enlisting, to long-lasting contraception and the requirement that pregnancies must be planned and will require military permission. Such consent could be a condition of enlistment. Female conscripts might not consent, but it is hard to see how compulsory contraception is really a more serious violation than compulsory combat. Some people do not see this because, as I have been arguing, males are treated in ways that many people simply would not dream of treating females.

I don't suggest that this will eliminate the pregnancy problem entirely, but it could certainly reduce it to very manageable levels. Men, after all, are also susceptible to unpredictable medical conditions that render them ineligible for deployment. Managing the pregnancy problem in the way I have suggested would very likely bring females to a similar rate.

It would also significantly address the single-mother problem. Professor Browne reports that the United States military will only enlist single parents if they attest that their children are in the full custody of the other parent.[59] The problem, he says, is when enlistees become single parents *after* they join the service. Under my proposal, the military could require those enlistees seeking permission for pregnancy to attest that there are suitable arrangements in place to care for the child (or children) that will result from the pregnancy. Such arrangements may not be foolproof, but they would significantly reduce the problem.

Finally, my proposal would avoid the deployment-evasion double standards problem, whereby women could avoid (or be seen to be avoiding) being deployed by becoming pregnant. Under my proposal, unauthorized pregnancy, unless contraceptive failure or rape could be demonstrated, would be grounds for disciplinary action.[60] Some might wonder how the difference between contraceptive failure and sabotage of contraception (or between rape and consensual sex) could be established, but the very same sorts of problems have not prevented military courts from distinguishing between self-inflicted and enemy-inflicted wounds in male soldiers.

Professor Browne argues that evasion of deployment through pregnancy is not the only double standard that causes problems. Among the double standards he alleges are these.[61] Female soldiers are held to lower physical standards. They are allowed to have showers more often than men while in the field. Some women use "female problems" such as complaints about menstrual cramps to avoid unpleasant duties. Women are more likely to defy authority, and more likely to get away with it. Women can use complaints of sexual harassment (or threats of such complaints) to avoid doing some things that they would rather not do. Women who are engaged in sexual misconduct are less likely to be investigated and disciplined than are males who engage in such behavior. The perception of these double standards creates resentment and thus compromises the necessary group cohesion.

It is unclear to what extent these perceptions are accurate and to what extent they are mistaken. The case of physical standards is straightforward. The requirements for women are lower than those for men, given the physical differences between the sexes. This does not mean that there is no unfairness here. Even the physical differences are statistical and thus there are a small number of men who are less capable than a small number of women of meeting the male standards. If the physical differences are what explain the differential standards, it seems unfair that the standards should be set on the basis of one's sex rather than one's ability. In other words, it is hard to see why two people, both of whom are physically incapable through no fault of their own of meeting particular standards, should either nonetheless be held to those standards or held to lower standards depending only on their sex.

There is a sliding scale of possible standards to be set. The higher the standards are set the fewer women, and the fewer men, will be able to meet them. While there is no specific level at which the standards must be set, there are obvious constraints. They must not be set so high that an insufficient number of people could meet them, but they should also not be set so low that many people meeting them are unable to do things they will need to be able to do. Nor need there be only a single standard. It is possible to stream people. The military already has units that are more and less elite. It is hard to see how those meeting higher standards will resent those meeting lower standards if the higher achievement is also recognized with greater prestige. If more men meet the higher standards, then women will be under-represented in the more elite units, but that is something we should accept, for reasons I shall amplify in Chapter 6.

The other double standards to which Professor Browne refers are both harder to prove and more worrying if they do occur. If they do occur, there is a further question about how pervasive they are. To the extent that they do exist they are further examples of the second sexism. Professor Browne's and my responses to this are quite different. He sees the problem of double standards *within* the military as intractable and thus avoidable only by excluding women from combat – or from the military more generally. My response is to condemn the differential standard, as I think we should in every other instance of the second sexism, including the exemption of women *from* the military, and to hold men and women to the same standards in all cases, except where there is good reason not to do so.

Final thoughts on combat and conscription

In Chapter 2 I described the many disadvantages males have experienced and continue to experience with regard to conscription and combat. These disadvantages are a consequence of discrimination. People have different beliefs about men and women. As a result men and women are treated differently. If this discrimination is wrong, then men are the victims of sexism.

The most promising argument that the discrimination is not unfair is one that would show that there are relevant differences between men and women that fully justify the different treatment. I have now examined what I take to be the most comprehensive and careful defense of the view that women ought to be excluded and exempt from combat because of the differences between men and women. In rejecting this argument I have not claimed that there are no differences between the sexes (beyond the obvious anatomical and physiological ones). Nor have I claimed, as the social constructionists do, that none of the differences are attributable to biological variation between the sexes. If that were true, it would be easier to argue that the discrimination is unfair. Instead, I have made the harder case. I have argued that even if there are some biologically based differences between the sexes, conscripting and sending into combat only males is unfair discrimination.

I have not argued that the differential military burdens of males and females are *fully* explained by unfair discrimination. Some of the difference may be explained, for example, by relatively free choices. It is the case, however, that unfair discrimination is rampant in this area. Moreover, even if

Professor Browne's argument were sound, it would not warrant the exemption of women from conscription into some national service other than combat. And if, as I have argued is the case, his argument is unsound, the wrong extends far beyond that to the burdens of combat which only men are forced into. Moreover, the use of gender stereotypes to pressure men into volunteering is also morally problematic. This is because such stereotypes go beyond whatever biological differences there might be between the sexes. They coerce men to do what they would otherwise not elect to do. After all, there would be no need to pressure men into enlisting and fighting if they would do it anyway.

Being pressured or forced into combat is among the most severe disadvantages that men suffer. Yet I have had to argue at some length to show that the imposition of these disadvantages is unfairly discriminatory. This is because weighty matters lie in the balance. If incorporating women in combat is as threatening to military effectiveness as Kingsley Browne suggests, then it is a move that may not be undertaken lightly, where the war being waged is a just one. By contrast, no such important matters countervail the other disadvantages that men and boys experience. Accordingly, it is easier to show that these disadvantages are wrongfully inflicted.

Violence

Men, we saw in Chapter 2, are much more often the victims of violence than are women. Men constitute the majority of victims of violent crime. In times of conflict, (non-combatant) men are often killed in much greater numbers than women.

Given men's elevated risk of suffering violence, it is ironic that the phrase "gender violence" is so often treated as synonymous with "violence against women (and girls)." The term "gender violence," or its variant, "gender-based violence," is unclear. Some people have suggested that *all* violence is gender violence.[62] On that view, it clearly cannot be the case that only violence against females is gender violence. However, if all violence is gender violence then the term "gender violence" is a redundancy. It thus seems best to understand gender violence as a subset of violence. One could, of course, simply stipulate that the relevant subset is "violence against women," but that seems arbitrary and, insofar as gender violence arouses special concern, also sexist. Clearly gender violence must have something to do with gender or sex. One reasonable view is that it is violence that is caused or legitimated by (either conscious or subconscious) ideas about gender. Alternatively, it might be understood as violence that disproportionately affects one sex. However, "male" is also a gender or sex and thus it is hard to see how at least some violence against males is not also gender violence.

Why then is the phrase "gender violence" typically used in a way that excludes the gender that is most affected by violence? Why do we hear frequent public calls for an end to "violence against women" (or "women and children") but not for an end to "violence against men"? And if a call for an end to "violence against men" sounds a little too concerned with one sex (in the way that similar calls for an end to violence against women does not to many ears), why are the calls not instead for an end to violence against anybody? Why might it be thought that targeting males for violence is not unfairly discriminatory?

"The perpetrators are men"

One possible answer is that men constitute the majority of perpetrators of violence against both men and women. That, it might be said, is why the calls to end violence, are addressed to men. Violence, it might be said, is a male problem, even if the victims are both male and female. But one problem with this response is that the call is for an end of violence *against women*, rather than for an end to violence *by men*. Its focus is on the victim and not the perpetrator. If males are more commonly the victims, then the focus only on the female minority of victims is inappropriate. Moreover, even if one does focus on perpetrators, it is strange to ignore female perpetrators, of whom there are a significant number. Indeed, in the case of violence against children women constitute a substantial proportion if not a majority of the perpetrators.

In any event, when men (or women) are the victims of violence, it does not really matter whether the perpetrator is of the same sex or a different sex. What matters is that they have been attacked. The suggestion that it is other men who have attacked them can be seen to minimize the wrong only if we (inappropriately) blur the distinction between the identities of the particular men, failing to distinguish between the perpetrator and the victim, and instead identifying them both simply as "men." This is really no better than the person who minimizes the violence suffered by blacks in American inner cities or South African townships, for example, by saying that it is perpetrated by "other blacks". [63] Indeed, if there were frequent and exclusive calls for the end of violence against whites in such places where blacks are disproportionately the victims of violence, the prejudicial character of this thinking would be abundantly clear.

To this last point, some will respond that whereas blacks have a long history of being discriminated against, the same is not true of men. For this reason, it might be said, a special concern about violence against whites would be worse than a special concern about violence against women. There are a least four problems with this response.

First, there is a much longer and more damaging history of violence against men than there is against women and thus in this limited regard focusing on violence against women is like focusing on violence against whites. Second, discrimination against males is not restricted to their being disproportionately the victims of violence. There are, as I am arguing, numerous other instances of discrimination against males. Third, even if one thinks that there are other ways in which women are worse off than men, or blacks are worse off than whites, it is true that men are like blacks (in the relevant contexts), in being the greater victims *of violence*. Finally, even if a special concern with violence against whites were worse than a special concern with violence against women, it does not follow that focusing on violence against women at the cost of attention to violence against men is at all acceptable. Thus, at the very least the imagined example of a special concern about violence against whites can be seen as an (exaggerated) analogy to highlight the problem with attending only to violence against women.

"Men are better able to defend themselves"

There is another possible answer to the question about why there is more attention to violence against women than there is to the problem of violence against men. According to this answer, men are better able to defend themselves. They are less vulnerable, it might be said, and thus in less need of protection. Among the errors in this response is the slippage to which I referred earlier. Let us assume that men are, in general, bigger and stronger than women. We can even assume that they are not only more able but also more willing to defend themselves. It is a massive inferential leap from here to the claim that men are sufficiently more able than women that they can *successfully* defend themselves against the actual attacks on them. Indeed, the fact that so many more men are the victims of murder, for example, is an indication that men (on average) are not sufficiently capable to defending themselves against murder.

Consider an analogy. Let us imagine that dogs are attacked, maimed and killed more often than rabbits. Somebody notes that dogs are subjected to more abuse than rabbits and asks why there is so much attention to "violence against rabbits" and none to "violence against dogs." Supporters of the rabbits reply that dogs are better able to defend themselves than are rabbits. That claim might be true, but it is still the case (in my supposed example) that neither dogs nor rabbits are able to defend themselves against the sorts of assaults from which dogs are disproportionately the victims. The greater capacity of dogs to defend themselves is thus entirely beside the point.

It might be suggested, in response, that while men may not be able to defend themselves against male perpetrators, they are at least able to defend themselves against their wives in the domestic context, which is often the focus of campaigns to end violence against women. This suggestion is also flawed. First, violence is no more acceptable just because the victim has some capacity to defend himself. Second, contrary to the stereotype, men are not always able to protect themselves against female assailants, particularly if the latter are using some kind of weapon. Third, why should domestic violence receive greater attention than other forms of violence that are often more serious? (Sometimes domestic violence leads to death, but murder outside the domestic context is much more common and males are the main victims of murder.)

Given that there is already a norm discouraging violence against women, it is actually men who, all things considered, are more vulnerable to violence. This is because one's vulnerability is a function not only of one's defensive capacity but also of the likelihood that one will be attacked.

There is, to be sure, *some* violence against men that is justified (just as there is some violence against women that is justified). If one is attacked, for example, it is permissible to defend oneself, violently if necessary. If more men are perpetrators of violence, more of those who suffer violence at the hands of defenders will likely be male too. But this surely accounts for a relatively small proportion of all victims of violence. More often than not, aggressors prevail over their victims and do not suffer from violent self-defense by their victims.

Insofar as a violent attack is not warranted, the victim is wronged by the violence. It is no coincidence that males constitute the majority of victims of violence. It is because there are stronger social norms discouraging violence against women. Even if one thought that females were less capable of defending themselves and thus required some additional social protection, it is still the case that the social norms more than compensate women for any defense disadvantage they might have. The net effect is that men are unfairly disadvantaged. There is no good reason for this sexist feature of society.

"Men pose a greater threat"

There is a third line of argument that seeks to deny that the disproportionate amount of violence to which men are subjected is inappropriately discriminatory. This particular argument can apply only in some situations in which men are the primary victims of violence. The argument says that because males pose a greater threat to opposing forces in a conflict, they are legitimate targets. More specifically, men of fighting age, even if they are not combatants or not known to be combatants, might in reality be combatants or they are potential combatants. There is, it is said, thus a rational basis for targeting and killing them in what is said to constitute a pre-emptive strike.

There are many problems with this line of argument. While there might be some cases in which young males are potential enemy combatants, this cannot explain anything like the full extent of situations in which males are singled out for violent treatment. Most obviously, it does not apply to most cases where men are the victims of ordinary violent crime. In such cases the victims are not potential enemy combatants. The possible exceptions to this are those male victims who are themselves gang members and thus pose an implicit threat to members of opposing gangs.

The argument's clearest application is to non-combatant male victims of violence in situations of war and similar conflicts. But even in such cases, the category of "young men of fighting age" is often treated very elastically. Older men are also killed, even when it is clear that they are no longer capable of combat,[64] and boys are killed because they will become young men of fighting age.[65] Sometimes even neonatal boys are not exempt. Consider, for example, the Rwandan genocide of 1994, in which Hutus "were determined to seek out and murder Tutsi boys ... They examined very young infants, even new-borns, to see if they were boys or girls. Little boys were executed on the spot."[66] Older boys were also "relentlessly hunted down. Many mothers dressed their little boys as girls in the hope – too often the vain hope – of deceiving the killers. The terrified boys knew exactly what was happening."[67] This is not to deny the many female deaths in the Rwandan genocide, but only to note that males were most at risk.

Young men, although of fighting age, are killed even if it should be clear to their killers that they do not pose a threat or, at least, not a sufficiently imminent or likely threat to warrant killing them. The OSCE report on Kosovo, for example, noted that in most cases young men "seem to have been killed simply because they were male and young enough to join" the Kosovo Liberation Army.[68]

Moreover, there are conditions when selecting out young males for killing is wrong even when they *are* more likely to be (potential) enemy combatants. These are conditions in which the threat young males pose can often be neutralized by taking them captive rather than killing them. Unarmed civilians who are merely potential combatants can easily be captured instead of being summarily executed. Indeed, they often are executed immediately after being apprehended, which shows that capture was possible. Execution need not follow. And even in those very rare circumstances where killing a civilian is the only way to neutralize the threat he poses as a potential enemy combatant, it is not necessary also to torture him prior to killing him.

In any event, many potential enemy combatants would be justified in taking up arms because one's own aggression against them is unjust. In such cases, it would be wrong to kill them. For example, when armed resistance commenced against the 1971 Bengali genocide, the Pakistan army began to

seek out those especially likely to join the resistance – young boys. Sweeps were conducted of young men who were never seen again. Bodies of youths would be found in fields, floating down rivers, or near army camps. As can be imagined, this terrorized all young men and their families within reach of the army. Most between the ages of fifteen and twenty-five began to flee from one village to another and toward India. Many of those reluctant to leave their homes were forced to flee by mothers and sisters concerned for their safety.[69]

There is clearly no (objective moral) justification for first targeting males in genocidal assaults on the grounds that they might be more inclined to resist.

Finally, it is worth noting the "snowball effect" of male disadvantage. Being male is first grounds for being forced or pressured into combat. It thereby becomes grounds for being singled out as a potential combatant. There are, of course, comparable cases of a snowball effect of female disadvantage, but whereas some feminists make much of these cases, they ignore the male cases. Yet there is no less reason to attend to the cascading of male disadvantage.

Two kinds of discrimination

None of the reasons usually proffered to explain the greater concern about violence against women can explain why so little attention is given to the problem of violence against males. Given that the great majority of victims of violence are males and that violence against males is (at least usually) no more justified than violence against females, we should conclude that the almost exclusive attention to violence against women is inappropriate.

There is a difference between one sex suffering the bulk of some evil and this being the product of unfair *sex* discrimination. Sometimes it is not a person's sex itself that makes him or her more susceptible to some evil. Instead, it is some other attribute that is shared disproportionately with others of his sex. Thus, Adam Jones notes that while males were the majority of victims of the Stalinist purges, they were not singled out because they were male, but rather for other attributes.[70] It just so happened that the overwhelming majority of those with those attributes were male. This does not mean that the purges were not "gendered," and he suggests that that aspect of the mass killings is worthy of attention. It means only that there was no targeting of males *qua* males. Insofar as we do not treat such cases as cases of sex discrimination, we should offer equivalent judgments of those cases where although females constitute the majority of victims of some evil this is not because they are female.

That said, there are very many cases where males are selected for, or not protected from, violence because they are male, and these cases are sufficient to demonstrate that males suffer sex discrimination in this area. In other words, even if some of the violence males suffer is not because they are males, much of it is.

There are actually two interrelated forms of discrimination here (and in some of the other instances of disadvantage). First, people are less inhibited from committing acts of violence against males than against females. Second, when violence is inflicted on males, other people take it less seriously. The latter partly explains the former. In other words, it is partly because violence against males is taken less seriously that some people are more inclined to perpetrate violence against males, and other people are less inclined to prevent it. But the failure to take violence against males seriously not only contributes to the greater violence against males but also constitutes a further harm in itself. Being discriminated against is bad enough. Not having the fact of this discrimination recognized compounds the wrong and may constitute a further form of discrimination.

Corporal Punishment

Corporal punishment is an increasingly controversial practice. As we saw in Chapter 2, it has historically been inflicted by the military on soldiers and sailors, by the courts on criminals, by schools on pupils and by parents on their children. In some countries it continues in all these contexts, while in others it has been banned in all situations. In most places, however, it is legally permissible in some but not other contexts. The question whether it is legally permissible is not the same as the question whether it is morally permissible. Those who think that corporal punishment is always wrong (or even always wrong in a given context) will be committed to saying that inflicting it on males (in the relevant context) is also wrong. If a wrong is systematically inflicted on one sex but not another, then those on whom it is inflicted are the victims of sex discrimination. That is all that need be said to prove to categorical opponents of corporal punishment that its infliction on males but not females, or its greater infliction on males, is wrongful discrimination.

But what about those who think that corporal punishment is *sometimes* morally permissible?[71] Is there any justification, according to such a view, for the disadvantages that males suffer with regard to corporal punishment? A few arguments have been advanced in support of an affirmative answer, but none is satisfactory.

"Males are more badly behaved"

One of these arguments is that boys and men are more badly behaved than girls and women, and thus deserve the higher rates of corporal punishment that they experience.[72]

Even if we assume the truth of the premise, this claim fails to justify all the sex differences in the administration of physical punishment. It might explain why boys and men are subject to more corporal punishment even when it is permitted for both sexes. However, it does not explain why there is a prohibition on the physical punishment of females in some places. If females commit fewer acts that are thought to be deserving of physical punishment, then the implication is that they would receive such punishment less often. The implication is not that they would never receive it. Put another way, the claim that males are more badly behaved is insufficient to explain why physical punishment of females is sometimes prohibited where it is permissibly inflicted on males. Even if, contrary to fact, females *never* did those things for which males are physically punished, a prohibition on corporal punishment of females would not be warranted. There is no need to prohibit a form of punishment that females would never do anything to do deserve.

Where physical punishment of females is permitted, the argument that males are more badly behaved than females does not explain why females receive physical punishment less often even when they commit the same offenses as males. And it does not explain why the corporal punishment females do receive is often milder than that meted out to males for the same offenses.

A further problem is that, as we saw in Chapter 2, boys often have been physically punished for "violations" such as making spelling or mathematical mistakes, which cannot plausibly be thought to deserve punishment of any kind and certainly not corporal punishment. Much of the physical punishment inflicted on boys cannot be explained by their worse behavior. Instead it is explained by the alacrity with which people resort to hitting boys.

Finally, it is entirely possible that inappropriately hitting boys actually encourages some of the bad behavior for which boys are physically punished. In saying this I am not offering the common argument often advanced against all corporal punishment – that "violence breeds violence." Instead of saying that physical punishment always causes inappropriate conduct in those punished, I am suggesting that inflicting physical punishment too frequently or too harshly can have counterproductive effects. This claim is much more plausible than the more extensive claim that corporal punishment always has such effects. As it happens there is some preliminary (although not conclusive) evidence that harsh discipline does explain some poor conduct in boys.[73]

"Corporal punishment is not as damaging to males"

A second justification sometimes advanced for inflicting corporal punishment more readily or only on males is that it is said to be less damaging to them than it is to females. For example, it might be claimed that males have a higher pain threshold or can tolerate more pain or that they are less psychologically hurt by physical punishment. Boys (and men), it might be said, can take corporal punishment better than girls (and women).

To reject this argument, it is not necessary, as some think, to deny that there are differences between the sexes. There is evidence of male and female sex hormones leading to sex differences in pain, with females being more sensitive to it.[74] The problem with invoking this evidence to support the conclusion that corporal punishment should be inflicted exclusively or disproportionately on males is that this involves over-interpreting the evidence and making inferential leaps.

Whatever differences in pain there are between the sexes they are statistical rather than categorical. It is not the case that every female is more sensitive to pain than every male. The claim is a generalization rather than a universalization. To inflict corporal punishment on the basis of a person's sex is thus to treat him as a member of the sex to which he belongs rather than as the individual he is. Those concerned about unfair treatment *of women* certainly are, or should be, allergic to treating people on the basis of generalizations about their sex. This is not only because it is unjust but also because treating people this way will often be to the disadvantage of females. Jobs requiring greater height and strength, for example, could be restricted to males because "females are shorter and weaker than males." Even many conservatives recognize that treating people on the basis of characteristics of their group can, at least sometimes, be wrong. They might think that there are select cases where discrimination on the basis of group characteristics is permissible. However, because they think that there are other cases in which it is not permissible, it is insufficient simply to point to generalizations in order to justify treating all members of one group differently from all members of another group.

Moreover, the differences in pain thresholds and tolerance that we see between the sexes are not fully attributable to biology. Even those who recognize that there are biological differences also acknowledge that socialization plays a role.[75] Boys are discouraged more than girls from complaining about pain. Reports of pain are often seen to be "unmanly," whereas there is no comparable disincentive to females complaining of pain. This means that the differences in pain reports probably exaggerate the differences in the perception of and sensitivity to pain. The extent to which boys and men underplay the pain is not a reliable indicator of how much less it affects them than it does girls and women.

Next, whatever biological differences there may be in pain perception and reactivity, these are *relatively* minor. In other words, it is not the case that girls do feel pain but boys do not. Nor is it the case that stimuli that are very painful to girls are *much* less painful to boys (if they are less painful at all). The differences appear to be relatively modest. Both males and females feel pain. Moreover, there is much that we do not (yet) know about sex differences in pain. For example, we do not know for sure whether the differences are linear – that at every level of increasingly noxious stimuli females feel more pain. What we do know is suggestive that the differences actually diminish as the pain becomes more severe.[76] This is obviously relevant to the severe pain that can be inflicted by at least some forms of corporal punishment.

For these sorts of reasons it is a mistake to infer from the fact that there are some sex differences in pain that it is acceptable to inflict pain on males but not on females. Those who cannot see the mistake should consider the following. Although females are generally more sensitive to pain, their "pain thresholds increase throughout late pregnancy and abruptly just prior to parturition."[77] Does this fact justify the withholding of analgesia from women in childbirth? Those who make inferential leaps from biological generalizations about differences in pain perception might be committed to the affirmative answer they probably do not wish to give. But an affirmative answer is absurd. Women giving birth might feel less pain than they otherwise would if they had not undergone the hormonal changes in late pregnancy, but it certainly does not follow that they are not experiencing considerable pain in parturition. The same logic applies to the pain experienced by males in corporal punishment.

It is also worth noting that pain, along with psychological distress, is not the only negative feature of some corporal punishment. Flesh-lacerating canings and whippings, for example, are physically very damaging. I do not know of any evidence that male flesh is less prone to laceration, but even if it were, any beating that is severe enough to have this effect exceeds whatever protective effect there might have been.

A common assumption is that if inferences about the acceptability of corporal punishment can be made from sex differences (whether biological or social), the conclusion is that it is boys and not girls on whom it may be inflicted. But if one is drawing conclusions, there is a case to be made for drawing the opposite one. One of the problems with inflicting corporal punishment on boys or men, particularly in environments where there is pressure for them to prove their manliness, is that a macho attitude can be developed towards physical punishment. It has not been uncommon for schoolboys and soldiers to brag about their capacity to bear canings or lashings.[78] One important consequence of this is that corporal punishment's deterrent capacity for males can sometimes be diminished. Insofar as this dynamic is not operative with girls and women and they fear corporal punishment both more than other punishment and more than boys fear corporal punishment, it may actually be preferable to inflict it on females rather than on males. Its deterrent effect on females may be greater. It is, of course, also possible that inflicting it equally on females and males could have the effect of making it a less macho punishment and thus increasing its deterrent effect on males. However, the macho attitude could still creep in if girls acted more fearful of and pained by being hit, because there would then still be pressure on males not to act like girls and women.

That said, inflicting corporal punishment in a gender-blind way would go some way to breaking down stereotypes about males and females. By treating males and females equally it would reject an exaggeration of whatever average sex differences there might be.

Sexual Assault

Whereas many people think that it is permissible or even desirable to inflict corporal punishment on boys and men, almost nobody thinks that sexual assault of males is acceptable.[79] Thus, the question before us now is not whether sexual assault on males is acceptable, but rather whether male disadvantage in this regard constitutes unfair sex discrimination.

We saw in the Introduction that a practice can be discriminatory even if it is wrong (primarily) on other grounds. Sexual assault – along with the failure to take it seriously – is wrong for a variety of reasons that have nothing to do with discrimination. However, this does not mean that discrimination does not add a further component of wrong. It is about this additional wrong that I inquire in asking whether males are the victims of wrongful sex discrimination.

In defense of a negative answer some people might say that of the two sexes, it is females who constitute the majority of sexual assault victims. This is not a coincidence. Females are more vulnerable to sexual assault because they are females. In accordance with this view, it is females and not males who are the victims of sex discrimination in the realm of sexual assault. Although there are males who are victims of sexual assault, this is less common. According to this argument, sexual assault of males is wrong, but it is not sex discrimination.

The first thing to notice about this argument is that those who advance it, at least in this unqualified form, will have to recognize its implications for the case of violence considered earlier. More specifically they will have to concede that it is males *and not females* who are the victims of sex discrimination with regard to violence. This is because, as we have seen, males constitute the majority of victims of violence, and the argument claims that only the sex that constitutes the majority of victims of a particular kind of wrong can be the victims of sex discrimination.

Yet it seems that women could be the victims of sex discrimination in being the main victims of some kinds of violence, even if males are the victims of sex discrimination in being the main victims of violence overall. But if we are to draw that distinction, then the way is open to recognizing that both males and females could be victims of sex discrimination in the context of sexual assault. That is to say, we could note, as I did in Chapter 2, that while females are the majority of victims of sexual assault, there are other ways in which males suffer discrimination regarding sexual assault. Such assault of males is under-diagnosed and taken less seriously. Victims of it receive less sympathy and are more often thought to have invited or enjoyed it. Thus, while fewer males are victims of sexual assault, the difference in incidence is not as marked as is generally thought. And those males who are sexually assaulted must deal not only with the assault but also with the other disadvantages just mentioned. Because these additional disadvantages are experienced as a result of prejudices about males, the case for thinking that this constitutes sex discrimination is very strong.

Some people might be troubled by the idea that both males and females could be the victims of sex discrimination in the context of any given wrong, such as sexual assault or violence. However, there are two ways of responding to this, the first less satisfactory than the second.

First, it might be said that the sex of the victim is often crucial in the assailant's decision to perform the assault. In other words, where the perpetrator sought out a person of a particular sex and would not have sexually assaulted a person of the opposite sex, then the perpetrator was discriminating on the basis of the victim's sex. On this account it is possible that both males and females could be assaulted because of their sex and thus both could be the victims of sex discrimination. Of course, it is not always the case that a perpetrator seeks out a person of a particular sex. For example, most prison inmates who rape other inmates rape people of the same sex only because that is all that is available to them. In such cases the victim's sex is incidental, and the assault, on the view being discussed, would not constitute sex discrimination.

If this is viewed as a complete account of sex discrimination then it is too restrictive an account. Sex discrimination is not simply about what individuals do. It can also be the product of systems and structures. If systemic factors inappropriately favor one sex over another, even unwittingly, we should say that they are unfairly discriminatory. But once we agree to this we require a broader account of how both male and female victims of a given wrong could be suffering from sex discrimination.

This brings us to a second account, one that proposes a distinction between different subspecies of wrongs. If one sees "sexual assault" as a single wrong, then there may be a problem with seeing both males and females who suffer that wrong as victims of sex discrimination. How can both males and females be disadvantaged – by one and the same kind of wrong – relative to the other sex? However, if we distinguish between different aspects of sexual assault, then it could be that females are discriminated against in some ways and males are discriminated against in others. We can say that women are the victims of sex discrimination because they are more likely to be the victims of sexual assault; and we can say that men are the victims of sex discrimination because sexual assault of them is more likely not to be taken seriously.

Circumcision

We saw in the previous chapter that some of the disadvantages of circumcision are unavoidable if one is to reap the (modest) benefits of being circumcised. If the condition of being circumcised has medical benefits, one cannot enjoy those benefits unless circumcision is performed. Accordingly, I do not claim that these disadvantages are instances of discrimination.

However, we also saw that there are some avoidable disadvantages of circumcision. In the western world the most common of these is the failure to use anesthetic if the procedure is performed in the neonatal period. In those cultures where circumcision is not performed under aseptic conditions, the disadvantages are still more serious. They include elevated risk of infection and the consequence danger of losing the penis or even of death. These disadvantages, I suggest, are wrongfully discriminatory in addition to the more basic wrong of treating *anybody* like this.

We have already encountered some ways of denying this and found them to be wanting. First, it cannot be denied, in the case of infant circumcision, that the boy feels no pain. The scientific evidence simply does not support this. A *fortiori* one cannot deny that older boys feel pain. Nor can one justify the infliction of this severe pain on the grounds that boys are better able to bear pain. Even if somebody is better able to endure pain, it does not mean that one is entitled to inflict pain, especially severe pain, when one could easily avoid doing so.

The practice of circumcising boys without anesthesia stands in contrast, I noted in Chapter 2, to the outright prohibition on cutting the genitals of girls. I argued that one could consistently permit male circumcision while prohibiting female genital cutting as it is typically practiced. This is because the latter is usually a much more radical procedure. However, the same cannot be said of the mildest forms of female genital cutting, which involve only the drawing of blood without the removal of any genital tissue. I suggested in Chapter 2 that it is not consistent to prohibit this, as some western societies do, while permitting the more radical and painful procedure of removing the male foreskin.

I shall now consider an argument advanced by some feminists which seeks to show that there is no inconsistency here. They wish to say that even if male circumcision is permissible, no form of female genital cutting is. According to this argument, the cultural meanings of male and female genital cuttings are very different. Male circumcision, the argument goes, is affirming of a male. In the relevant cultures it is a badge of honor – a positive symbol. By contrast, it is said, female genital cutting is demeaning to women. It is a mechanism for controlling their sexuality. In excising the clitoris, it is said, an important source of sexual pleasure is removed. In infibulating a girl – sewing together what remains of the labia majori – infidelity is prevented.

The problem with this argument is that even if one thinks that these more radical forms of female genital cutting treat women as sexual objects to be controlled by their men-folk, it is hard to see how this could also be true of the milder forms of female genital cutting. This is so for a few reasons.

First, while removing the clitoris, an organ of sexual pleasure, or sewing up the (remnants of the excised) vulva, can very plausibly be thought to be controlling of female sexuality, the same simply cannot be said of merely nicking the clitoral prepuce. Second, even if one does more than nick the clitoral hood, but actually excises it, one would need evidence that this diminishes sexual pleasure, and I am not aware of any such evidence. Third, even if there were such evidence, removal of the clitoral prepuce could only be distinguished from male circumcision if removal of the male foreskin did not have a similar effect.[80] It is hard to see how reduction of female but not male sexual pleasure could be thought wrong. Finally, it is implausible to think that the milder forms of female genital cutting are tainted by association with the more severe forms. This is because the meaning of cultural practices can and does change, and thus it cannot be assumed that because a cultural practice was once demeaning it, especially in a modified form, remains so. To claim that female genital cutting is demeaning but male circumcision is not, irrespective how mild or severe each practice is and irrespective of the meaning that is actually attached to them at a given time, is to treat the claim as a dogma rather than as one that is testable.

Education

In Chapter 2 I showed that males suffer significant educational disadvantage. Boys drop out from school at higher rates than girls, fewer young men than women go on to tertiary educational institutions and fewer males than females earn degrees.

Unlike many other cases of male disadvantage I have discussed and shall still discuss, it is hard to prove that male disadvantages in the educational realm are the result of discrimination. This is because there are other possible causes of these particular disadvantages. For example, it could be that males and females do not have the same distributions of ability. Some have suggested that there is greater variance in the distribution of male talent, with the result that there are more males at the extremes of cognitive capacity. Using a memorable phrase, Helena Cronin suggests that there are more male "Dumbbells and Nobels."[81] It could be, therefore, that more males than females lack the cognitive capacity to succeed educationally, which would explain why males drop out at higher rates and, in the absence of discrimination against women, why males earn fewer degrees.

This does not preclude the possibility that social factors may also be playing a role. Perhaps struggling boys are not encouraged as much as struggling girls. Perhaps they are treated more harshly. Perhaps people care less when they drop out. I would be surprised if sex roles played no part at all, but it is notoriously difficult to demonstrate what, if any, part discriminatory attitudes and practices play.

For that reason, I intend to make only a limited, but nonetheless important point about whether male educational disadvantage is a product of discrimination. Some feminists leap from the fact of female disadvantage to the conclusion that females are being discriminated against. However, the former does not entail the latter. Sometimes there are alternative explanations.

Consider the following case. As we saw in Chapter 2, while boys are disadvantaged in other ways, they tend to do better on science and mathematics tests. Some feminists have assumed that this must be the product of discrimination. They have noted that while boys do better on the standardized tests in these subjects, girls do better than boys in class assessments. Thus it has been suggested that the differential is explained by gender bias in the standardized tests. That is one possible explanation, but we cannot assume that it is the correct one. It could as easily be the case that girls are being favored in class assessments, and that when they come to write fairer, standardized tests, that bias is eliminated.

There is some reason to think that the problem does not lie with a gender bias in the standardized tests. Christina Hoff Sommers has argued that because Taiwanese and Korean girls score much higher than American boys on the same standardized tests, it would seem that the gender-biased explanation of the standardized tests is not entirely satisfactory.[82] Moreover, the higher drop-out rate for boys may partially explain the better average performance by boys on standardized tests. The academically weakest boys tend not to write.[83]

We see, therefore, that one cannot leap to the conclusion that there is educational discrimination (either against girls or against boys). To show that there is discrimination, one needs to demonstrate that the disadvantage is a product of people being treated differently without good cause. If feminists recognize this, then some of them may need to withdraw *some* claims they make about discrimination against women.[84] And if they do not recognize it, then they may be forced to say that males (in some parts of the world today) are also being discriminated against just because they suffer more educational disadvantage.

Discrimination is not always obvious. Sometimes it is subtle. Sometimes it is hidden in systemic and structural phenomena that camouflage it. Thus my claim is not that if we cannot prove discrimination it does not exist. Instead my claim is a more modest one. We need to distinguish between those cases where there is clear evidence of discrimination and those cases that are more complicated and less clear. There may well be discrimination in the latter cases, but to assume that there is discrimination and to proclaim it without qualification is to exceed what the evidence permits us to say. We can speculate and hypothesize, but we need to be clear that that is what we are doing.

It is hard to know what to do in those cases where it is unclear whether there is discrimination. If there is discrimination we want to do something about it, but if there is not then attempting to rectify non-existent discrimination by means of an affirmative action program that favors some people on the basis of their sex may actually increase injustice. This is not to suggest that other means might not be employed to compensate for disadvantage. These are complicated matters, to which I shall return in Chapter 6.

Family and Other Relationships

Of the disadvantages males suffer in the family and other relationships, some are quite clearly the products of discrimination, while others are less clearly or less exclusively so. When laws target male homosexuals but not lesbians, there is clear discrimination. When male homosexuals are more likely to be the victims of hate crimes than lesbians, that too is a product of discrimination. Male homosexuals are being targeted. Obviously they are being targeted partly on the basis of their sexual orientation, but because lesbians are not targeted to the same degree, male homosexuals are also being targeted on the basis of their sex. Feminists often note that discrimination on the basis of sex, class and race can interact. There is no reason to think that discrimination on the basis of sex and discrimination on the basis of sexual orientation do not also interact, or that discrimination on the basis of sex cannot interact with other discrimination on the basis of other attributes if the sex in question is male.

The custody of children following divorce is more complicated than the case of discrimination against male homosexuals. When males seek custody of their children, they are less likely than females to obtain custody. It is hard to prove that this is a product of discrimination without looking at individual custody decisions and comparing them. It is *possible*, after all, that fewer males are suited to caring for children than their ex-wives and that the courts are appropriately awarding custody on the basis of the children's best interests.[85] While this is possible, it is also extremely unlikely that this explains the full differential in rates of custody success between men and women.[86] Moreover, given the stereotypes of women as child-carers and men as being less caring and nurturing, it is very likely that this plays at least some part, perhaps even a substantial part, in custody decisions made by the court. But it is discrimination to decide on the basis of a person's sex whether he or she would be a worse or better parent. Moreover, it is clearly unfair to withhold custody from a man if he would be a better custodial parent than his ex-wife.

Matters are murkier when fathers do not request custody. It is easy to attribute such cases to a choice on the part of the fathers and thus to deny that this component of the custody disparity is a product of discrimination. However, if one makes that move, one would have to attribute many female disadvantages to choice, too. I shall discuss this matter further in Chapter 6. For now, I note that choices (by both males and females) can be made in discriminatory contexts. Thus, if fathers know that they have very little chance of winning custody, they may be less inclined to try.[87] There is some evidence that this is exactly what happens.[88] Choices can also be made under the influence of gender roles and stereotypes. For example, if fathers are susceptible to gender stereotypes and roles, they might defer to their ex-wives on the custody issue and thus not even contemplate seeking custody themselves. Where choices are made in discriminatory contexts or are influenced by prejudicial ideas, then discrimination has played a role, even if a more indirect one.

Consider next the matters pertaining to paternity. I already indicated in Chapter 2 that the basic disadvantage a man has of being less sure than a woman whether a child is his own is something that could not be avoided until reliable paternity testing became a possibility, and was thus in itself not a product of discrimination. Today paternity testing is possible, but I noted that it might often be difficult for a man in a relationship with a woman to make use of the technologies that would either confirm his paternity of a child or show him not to be the genetic father. Again, it might be said that a man's failure to take advantage of technologies that would remove his disadvantage are the products of choice. That may be so, but choices can be constrained. If a man requests a paternity test when he has no evidence to be suspicious, he would cast aspersions on his wife and could very well damage the relationship. Widespread male suspicion and demands for paternity testing would be an affront to women. Given this, we should realize that there are constraints on men securing paternity tests. The point is not that this makes the uncertainty about paternity discriminatory. Instead, the point is that given male uncertainty and the constraints on overcoming it, exploiting the uncertainty would be discriminatory. Whether that discrimination is unfair depends on the circumstances. If, for example, a woman was raped and disclosing this to her husband, with the implication that the child may not be his, would lead her husband to beat her, then it seems fair that she not make the disclosure. In other circumstances, where the wife has an affair and then cuckolds her devoted and unsuspecting husband, she has treated him unfairly.

The law also discriminates against males as a consequence of paternity uncertainty. We saw how United States law has a different standard for treating the offspring of a male US citizen and a foreigner in comparison with the offspring of a female US citizen and a foreign national. This is an odd kind of sex discrimination, because it makes no difference whether the offspring are males or females and thus the burdens or benefits can be experienced by both male and female offspring. The sex discrimination is against a secondary victim – the parent of the offspring. United States law discriminates against male citizens in denying their offspring automatic citizenship. The law had a more compelling rationale before the advent of reliable paternity tests and thus the discrimination may not have been wrong in the past. However, now that reliable paternity tests are available the law's discrimination has become unreasonable and thus wrong.

The law also discriminates unfairly in the assignment of paternal responsibilities. I noted in Chapter 2 that whereas a (conscious and minimally competent) woman cannot gestate and bear a child without knowing that she has become a genetic or gestational mother, a man might not know that he has become a genetic father. This could happen following a brief sexual encounter where the woman does not subsequently inform the man that she has become pregnant. Even when a woman does tell a man that she is carrying his child, he typically lacks the choice at that stage whether he will become a father. The woman, however, often retains the choice. For example, where abortion is legal or at least available, women may or can still choose whether to become mothers. Alternatively the woman could put the child up for adoption. The upshot of this is that whereas both a man and a woman can choose whether to have sex, once a woman is pregnant, she has choices that the father of the fetus does not.

I am not suggesting that this itself is unfairly discriminatory. To require that a woman obtain the consent of her partner for an abortion or to force an abortion on her if the partner does not want to become a father is to impose too great a burden on her. We have to recognize that the biological differences are relevant here. However, the law may sometimes be wrongfully discriminatory when it then imposes paternal responsibilities on men who explicitly do not want to become fathers or who do not even know that they have become fathers. In other words, it seems reasonable to say that whereas a woman has the right to choose whether or not to carry a fetus to term, this right should not always impose paternal duties on the genetic father. She may decide whether to become a mother and to assume maternal duties. If the father may not decide whether he will become a genetic father, he should in some circumstances preserve the right to decide whether or not he will assume paternal duties.[89]

Some feminists disagree with this. They want the woman to decide whether she will become a mother and also to decide whether the genetic father will acquire paternal responsibilities, such as financial support. I agree that this view is defensible in some circumstances. However, there are other situations where this seems manifestly unfair.[90]

Consider, for example, pregnancies that result from statutory rape of a male minor (or an offense approximating that). The courts, at least in the United States, have held minor boys responsible for child support, even though they became fathers through statutory rape or sexual assault by an older woman.[91]

Or consider cases of what Donald Hubin calls "purloined sperm" – where a woman obtains sperm from a man while he is unconscious or under false pretences, and does so for the purposes of conceiving a child without his knowledge or consent.[92] In one case a man had passed out drunk. A woman, who said she would care for him, seems to have partially undressed him and copulated with him without his awareness. She became pregnant as a result and then sued him for child support. The court ruled that he was liable for such support.[93] Although this is a case of stolen sperm, it is also a case of rape, because the man did not give consent to sexual intercourse. It is hard to imagine an analogous case in which a man raped an intoxicated woman, then, having gained custody of the resultant child, successfully sues the woman for child support.

A clearer case of purloined sperm, uncomplicated by the specter of rape, is that of a woman who offered to fellate a man if he wore a condom. She then seems to have inseminated herself with the contents of the condom. The genetic father of the resultant child was then sued for child support. The court found for the plaintiff.[94]

It has been argued that while the father is a victim in each of these cases, the offspring is still more vulnerable and that is why the father must be liable for child support. That argument lacks force when the mother can provide all the necessary financial support. In such cases, the baby can be supported without the contributions of the victim of rape or stolen sperm. It is thus unfair to require the male victims to alleviate the female assailants of duties those assailants could discharge unaided.

But what of cases where the mother is unable to provide all the financial resources necessary? Here the reasoning of the courts is more compelling. Even if it is unfair to force an unwilling father to provide child support it would arguably be more unfair to deny an innocent child of the support it requires. A dissenting judicial opinion in one of the aforementioned cases wisely recommended that the father should be ordered "to support the child only to the extent that the mother's earning ability was insufficient to support the child."[95] That is to say, instead of requiring him to pay half the costs, he should be obligated only to pay the difference between what the mother could earn and what the child needed for support.[96]

It should be noted, however, that if one thinks that the case for child support works in such cases, then one must make a parallel claim about, for example, young girls who bear children as a result of statutory rape. If those men with whom they assent to have sex are unable to provide all the necessary financial support, then the girls who bore the children should, according to this argument, be held liable for the remainder. If that conclusion is rejected, the parallel one about male victims of statutory rape should also be rejected.

It is not only via abortion that women are able to avoid assuming parental responsibilities. Once a child is born, the mother can put the child up for adoption. If the child is adopted,[97] she can absolve herself of parental responsibilities. If, by contrast, she wants to keep the baby, the child's father cannot avoid his legal responsibilities of at least providing financially for the child.

Do differential paternity and maternity leave benefits unfairly discriminate against fathers? Some conservatives and some feminists will deny that they do, albeit for different reasons. Gender-role conservatives will argue that mothers are more important to infants and thus that maternity leave guarantees may reasonably exceed the paternity leave benefits. This claim might be filled out in different ways. One is that since it is mothers who lactate, it is more important that they have time off from work to breastfeed their babies. An even less defensible claim would appeal not to female biology but to a maternal role as nurturer of young children. Feminists would rightly object to both these versions of this conservative argument. Underlying their objections would be a rejection of the idea that it is mothers who must bear primary responsibility for caring for infants. Fathers, they would say, should share this responsibility. There is no reason why the party who gestates the child must also care for it after it is born. Although human gestators are also the lactators, lactating mothers could, for example, express milk that is later bottle-fed to their babies while they are at work.

These sorts of answers would suggest that feminists should be friendly to equalizing maternity and paternity leave benefits. At the very least, doing so would upset the presumption that it is mothers who should take time off from work to care for infants. That said, some feminists might still deny that *fathers* are the victims of wrongful discrimination when there is no parity between maternity and paternity leave benefits. In defense of this they might argue that because the differential leave benefits results in *mothers* carrying the greater load of infant care, it is they rather than the fathers who are the victims of wrongful discrimination. I think that there is merit to this argument, but I deny that it captures the full picture. It is true that the differential parental leave allowances will result in more mothers than fathers being pressured into taking parental leave. However, focusing only on this ignores those fathers who either want to or need to care for their infants or to share equally in such care. They are denied the same benefits guaranteed to mothers. Even if such fathers are in a minority, it is nonetheless unfair to them.

Bodily Privacy

We saw evidence in Chapter 2 that males are disadvantaged in significant ways by the lesser respect for their bodily privacy than for that of females. For example, we saw that the courts in the United States have given much more weight to the interests of female prisoners in not being searched or viewed naked by male guards than they have to the interests of male prisoners in not being searched or viewed naked by female guards. International guidelines on the minimum standards for treating prisoners prohibit female prisoners being supervised by male guards, but are silent about male prisoners under female guard. We saw that the privacy of male conscripts was invaded in ways that would be unimaginable if they were female. And we saw that male public toilets are structured to give urinating men less privacy than urinating women.

It is clear that males and females are being treated differently. Can these differences be justified objectively? In other words, are the disadvantages that males experience with regard to bodily privacy the product of unfair discrimination or can they be explained in other ways?

Most of the time, the discrepant treatment of males and females in this area is not even noticed. When this is the case no attempt is made to defend it. However, some (but not all) of the courts that have ruled on the question of cross-gender prison supervision have attempted to argue that there is no inconsistency. Only some of these arguments could also be employed with reference to other contexts in which male privacy seems to be less respected. I shall consider the various arguments and their possible applications. In doing so, I shall show that they all fail. Indeed, the arguments of the courts seem like rationalizations of an antecedent prejudice about the variable importance of female and male bodily privacy.

My aim is not to conduct a legal analysis – to determine which courts have provided the correct legal interpretation. Unlike the courts, I am not interested in whether their reasoning is legally sound. Even when judges accurately interpret the Constitution and legislation and follow precedent, their arguments show only what the law says. It does not tell us whether the law should be that way. Thus, it is possible that males have a weaker *legal* claim to privacy than females. However, that carries no more weight than the fact that women had no legal claim to vote before they were enfranchised. Instead I am interested in whether there is a moral, rather than a legal justification for the differential treatment of males and females. My aim, in examining the courts' arguments, is to determine whether they could be used to show that there is a moral justification for the different treatment.

"Women have a greater interest in bodily privacy than do men"

It should come as no surprise that some people have tried to defend the different treatment by arguing that women have a greater interest than men in bodily privacy. This argument has application to all the contexts I have mentioned, but it has been discussed explicitly in the context of cross-gender prison supervision. For example, in *Jordan v. Gardner*, the Court of Appeals, following the District Court, stated that "physical, emotional and psychological differences between men and women may 'well cause women, and especially physically and sexually abused women, to react differently to [pat-down] searches ... than would male inmates subjected to similar searches by women'."[98]

This argument suffers from a number of problems that should by now be familiar. At the outset it hardly seems sufficient, in justifying quite serious invasions of a man's privacy, to claim that women "may well" be more adversely affected by such invasions. Speculation is not sufficient. One requires evidence. Nor can we take the outward reactions of males and females as decisive evidence of the actual effect on them. This is because we know that males are encouraged to exhibit greater toughness and to be sexually less reticent. There are thus pressures on males not to reveal how they feel about invasions of their bodily privacy. It is remarkable that notwithstanding this, so many men have lodged complaints. Yet when men have complained, the courts have been less likely to take them seriously, claiming in one case that the male "inmates had not shown sufficient evidence of pain."[99] It seems that unless men show their pain in the way women do, their legal complaints that they are suffering extreme psychological distress are simply not taken seriously – and even then they may not be.

However, let us assume, for the sake of argument, that women would be more adversely affected by cross-gender searches and observations while naked. That is a generalization. Even if more women than men would be especially badly affected, there will be some men who will be more adversely affected than some women. Indeed, there is good reason to think that at least some of the men bringing these cases fall into this category. Now, perhaps it will be suggested that the courts find it reasonable to treat men and women on the basis of generalizations about each sex. However, it is clear that they find this reasonable only when it redounds to female advantage or male disadvantage. When females are disadvantaged by generalizations about their sex, the courts are explicit in rejecting this reasoning. For example, in finding for female guards in an equal opportunity suit in which they sought access to a fuller range of positions, the Court in *Griffin v. Michigan Department of Corrections* asserted that a "woman should be evaluated and treated by an employer on the basis of her individual qualifications and not on the basis of any assumptions regarding the characteristics and qualifications of women as a group."[100]

The foregoing is also relevant to considering those prisoners who have been victims of sexual abuse. It is entirely plausible that they could be more adversely affected by pat-down searches and strip searches. And it could well be that there are disproportionately more victims of sexual abuse among female prisoners than among the female population in general. The same could well be true of males. Imprisoned males may be disproportionately likely to have been sexually abused (if not before they came to prison, then since they were incarcerated).

Now it is true that more female than male victims of sexual abuse are abused by people of the opposite sex (even though the differential, as we saw in Chapter 2, is not as great as is commonly thought). However, it does not follow that all women should be treated on the basis of how a subset would be affected. Moreover, it is curious that the courts give absolutely no thought whatsoever to the possible effects of strip searches and body cavity searches by male guards on those male prisoners who were victims of homosexual sexual abuse. Such searches are sometimes a security necessity, but probably not as often as they are actually performed. In addition, the way that they are conducted can be more or less sensitive to male prisoners, especially those who are the victims of sexual assault, yet the courts have been rather cavalier in defending the performance of these searches in full view of other prisoners, for example.[101] Nor can we assume that the heightened effects of invasive searches on male victims of homosexual assault are present only when the guard performing the search is male. The court never considers the possibility that male victims of homosexual assault, having been "feminized" by male assailants, may feel even worse for now undergoing comparable treatment by a female. It is an open question whether there is any such effect, but the failure to consider the possibility stands in stark contrast to the sensitivity the courts show to female victims of sexual assault.

Even if it we assume both (a) that women are more adversely affected by being searched and viewed naked by guards of the opposite sex; and (b) that it is appropriate to treat men and women on the basis of generalizations about their sex, it still would not follow that the invasions of privacy are permissible for male prisoners but not for female prisoners. It could be insufficiently bad for female prisoners to warrant ruling in their favor, even though it would be worse for them than for male prisoners. Alternatively, and more plausibly, it could be sufficiently bad for male prisoners to justify ruling in their favor, even though it were not as bad as for female prisoners.

"The conditions are different"

The justifications that the courts have provided for their judgments concerning bodily privacy of male and female prisoners and equal opportunity employment for male and female guards often appeal to specifics of the case at hand. This is meant to explain why the courts reached the particular judgments they did. The implicit claim is that the case at hand differs from other cases (where the prisoners or guards are of a different sex) and thus apparent inconsistencies are not real ones. On rare occasions the courts have explicitly attempted to explain away those apparent inconsistencies. When we look at the particular arguments that have been advanced, however, we see that they are inadequate. They appear to be rationalizations rather than unprejudiced reasoning.

Two cases are very rarely, if ever, alike in every relevant way. Judgments should be made on the full constellation of facts in a given case. Thus, showing that two cases with a common variable were decided in two different ways leaves open the possibility that other variables in the cases account for the difference. However, a trend emerges when we examine each of the variables that the courts have stated were relevant in their decisions.

One variable that the courts have cited as relevant in judgments concerning fully clothed cross-gender pat-down searches is the degree of intrusion into bodily privacy that the search incurs. Thus, in justifying its finding against male inmates objecting to such searches, the court in *Smith v. Fairman* cited the fact that the genital area was excluded in the searches under review.[102] However, in other cases, when female guards did conduct pat-down searches that included the groin area, the courts still ruled against the male inmates.[103] And when male searches of female inmates included the groin area then the court found in favor of the inmates.[104] Now it is true that in one of the cases involving male plaintiffs the touching of the groin and anal areas was said by the court to be only "brief and incidental" whereas in the case of female plaintiffs the search was said to be more intrusive than this. However, in another case involving male plaintiffs the court makes no mention of how much contact was made with the groin area. This leaves one wondering whether the greater contact with female genitalia (through the clothes) was highlighted but similar contact with male genitalia was simply glossed over. At the very least, one wonders why the specific degree of contact with the male genitalia was either not considered or not thought worthy of mention.

The inconsistencies become clearer if we shift from fully clothed pat-down searches to strip searches and inmates being viewed naked by guards of the opposite sex. Very often courts are not even asked to rule on strip searches of female inmates by male guards because prison policy already precludes it.[105] And sometimes prisons already have mechanisms in place to protect female prisoners from being viewed naked by male guards.[106] Thus, when the courts find that male inmates being viewed naked by female guards is acceptable because it is infrequent and casual, from a distance, or only via purportedly indistinct images on a monitor,[107] male inmates are already being discriminated against, even if not by the courts alone. And where the courts have been asked to rule on prison policies that do not protect female inmates in this way (or do not do so as much as they could), they have tended to impose protections on the privacy of female inmates.[108]

As it happens, however, whether males are being viewed infrequently, casually, from a distance or via indistinct monitors actually makes no difference to whether the courts rule in their favor. Even when male inmates are (regularly) strip searched or body cavity searched by female guards, the courts have ruled against the male inmates.[109]

Thus, female inmates are protected from even incidental and brief observation by male guards while they are naked, while the courts refused to protect male inmates from being subjected to regular strip and body cavity searches by female guards.

In justifying the practice of female guards searching male prisoners, the courts have sometimes referred to the professionalism of the female guards.[110] The professionalism of male guards is rarely mentioned, but when it is, it is only to say that it is insufficient to justify a search of a female prisoner (even if she is fully clothed).[111]

Nor does distinctly *un*professional conduct by female guards lead the courts to find in favor of male inmates. Keith Somers sued female guards who, in violation of prison policy, conducted regular visual body cavity searches on him. He alleged that during these searches and when they monitored him while he showered, they pointed at him and made jokes among themselves.[112] A magistrate judge and then the District Court denied the guards qualified immunity from the suit. The guards appealed this decision and the Court of Appeals reversed the judgment. That is to say, it ruled in favor of the female guards and against the male prisoner. This decision was based not on an alternative finding of the facts, which do not seem to have been in question, but rather on a point of law. The Court of Appeals construed the question before it narrowly – whether "at the time of the alleged conduct, a male inmate had clearly established Fourth or Eighth Amendment rights to be free from routine visual body cavity searches and shower viewing by female guards."[113] The Court concluded that he did not.

This is odd. The Fourth Amendment right protects against "unreasonable searches." It is hard to see how a search prohibited by prison policy could be deemed a reasonable search, particularly given that the policy prohibiting female guards from performing routine visual body cavity searches on male prisoners is a reasonable one. The Eighth Amendment protects against cruel and unusual punishment. The courts have regularly found that female inmates have an Eighth Amendment right against much lesser invasions. It thus appears discriminatory to deny males protection against much more severe invasions. The Court was aware of this and thus explicitly attempted to show that, contrary to appearances, there was no real inconsistency. However, the arguments it raised to this end are ones that I have considered above and rejected.[114]

Another way in which United States courts have attempted to justify the judgments they make in particular cases is by appealing to the level of security required in a given prison context. The rationale here is that the greater the security need for a search the more it would take to show that a particular search is unreasonable.

There is, of course, a distinction between whether a given kind of search is reasonable and whether the same search conducted by somebody of the opposite sex is reasonable. Given that the security requirements themselves could be met fully if cross-gender supervision were not permitted, appealing to security needs in order to justify cross-gender searches requires also explaining why the security needs should be met by cross-gender supervision. This is typically done by appealing to equal employment opportunities. I shall consider that argument later.

For now it is noteworthy that the courts invoke the security consideration selectively. Where there are greater security issues in cases involving male prisoners, then this is invoked to justify the greater invasion of privacy.[115] Similarly, when there are lesser security issues in cases involving female prisoners, then the courts appeal to this to show that the invasions of privacy are unreasonable.

However, when the courts have considered cases including female maximum security prisoners, they have not invoked security considerations to justify greater invasions of female privacy by male guards.[116] Similarly, in the case of a male who had not yet even been convicted of a crime, and was instead a pre-trial detainee, the court failed to rule in his favor against being viewed naked by female guards.[117] Because one is legally innocent until proven guilty, the court failed to protect an innocent man who complained about being viewed naked by female guards.

There is an even more glaring inconsistency in judicial reasoning about the bodily privacy of male and female inmates. As noted before, female prisons, even before matters come to court, tend to have at least some mechanisms in place to protect the inmates from the view of male guards while the prisoners are in states of undress or using the toilet. For example, they are permitted to cover the windows on their cell doors for fifteen minutes while using the toilet or changing. Translucent screens protect them from male view while showering.[118] Although male prisoners are occasionally afforded such protections, typically they are not. They are not entitled to cover their cell windows and are not given screens or curtains to protect them from the view of female guards. Yet, in offering their judgments against affording males the same protections as females the courts are quick to remark that male prisoners who are concerned about their modesty could protect themselves "by adjustment of their own habits."[119] More specifically: "The use of a covering towel while using the toilet or while dressing and body positioning while showering or using a urinal allow the more modest inmates to minimize invasions of their privacy."[120] But it should be obvious that such mechanisms are as open to female inmates as to male ones. Of course, they do not protect males from strip searches and body cavity searches, which simply cannot be undertaken without violating the bodily privacy of the prisoner. However, if the suggested measures are adequate for males, then they should be so for females, too. And if they are not adequate for females there is no reason to think that they are adequate for males. When the courts make these suggestions to males while they add to the formal protections female inmates have, they unfairly discriminate against males.

Equal employment opportunity

A recurring theme in legal cases concerning cross-gender prison supervision is that of equal employment opportunities. Both male and female guards have argued that excluding them from positions and tasks that compromise the privacy of opposite sex inmates limits their own equality of employment opportunities. The courts have tended to sacrifice the privacy interests of male inmates to protect the employment opportunities of female guards. However, they have tended to rule in favor of male guards' equal employment interests only insofar as these are compatible with preserving the privacy interests of female inmates.

Most courts have at least recognized that there is a conflict between the privacy interests of inmates and the employment opportunity interests of guards. However, one court in finding for female guards rejected the male inmates' arguments that their privacy be respected, because the latter view was "based on stereotypical sexual characterization that a viewing of an inmate while nude or performing bodily functions, by a member of the opposite sex, is intrinsically more odious than the viewing by a member of one's own sex."[121] The court claimed that this assumption cannot withstand scrutiny.

If this claim where applied consistently, it would apply as much to female inmates being viewed, strip searched and body cavity searched by male guards as it applies to naked male inmates being viewed and searched by female guards. Yet the courts do not make the claim that there is no difference between female inmates being viewed naked by male or by female guards. They always take the viewing by male guards to be worse. Thus, to say that cross-gender viewing is no more odious than same-gender viewing only when it is naked males who are being viewed is another manifestation of male bodily privacy being taken less seriously. It is also evidence for my earlier claim that the courts are engaged in rationalization of prejudice rather than in honest reasoning.

The fact that the courts are inconsistent on this matter tells us nothing about how the inconsistency should be fixed. There are at least two options. One could agree that being viewed naked by non-intimates of the opposite sex (without one's permission) is no worse than being viewed by non-intimates of the same sex, and then apply this equally to males and females. Alternatively, one could claim that the cross-gender viewing is worse and then apply that equally to males and females. Which is correct?

Any viewing of a person in a state of undress without that person's consent is an invasion of bodily privacy. This is true irrespective of whether the observer is the same or another sex. The severity of the invasion varies depending on a number of factors including the degree of undress, the duration of the exposure, the number of people who observe the exposure and the sensitivity of the exposed person to being exposed. With regard to the last-mentioned, the shyer somebody is about being exposed, the worse the exposure is. Most people are shyer about being naked in the presence of (non-intimates) of the opposite sex. Thus, at the very least, most people will experience cross-gender exposure as worse. That should certainly be something the courts – and the rest of us – consider. But how much weight is given to this should depend both on how reasonable it is to be shyer about being exposed to people of the opposite sex and on the extent to which even unreasonable preferences should be considered.

In general (but not without exception) it is reasonable to be shyer about being bodily exposed to people of the opposite sex. This is because bodily modesty is partly a function of how others will perceive one's exposure, and of how one imagines that they will perceive it. If the viewer has a sexual interest, whether psychological or physiological,[122] the invasion is greater than if the viewer has no such response. The chances that somebody of the opposite sex will have a sexual interest of some kind are much greater than the chances that somebody of the same sex will. Even where people of the opposite sex have an outwardly professional response to one's exposure, one might wonder whether they have some sexual interest or arousal in addition. This is because the presence of a professional interest and demeanor is not incompatible with other interests. Thus, as a generalization, cross-gender exposure is worse.

It is a generalization because sexual interest is obviously not always heterosexual. In a significant minority of cases, the sexual interest is homosexual. In such cases, the severity of the exposure to somebody of the same sex is comparable to that of exposure to people of the opposite sex. It is interesting that even though we are today much more aware of the prevalence of homosexuality and of the fact that somebody's being homosexual may not be visible to others, the implications of this are suppressed. For example, if bodily exposure to homosexuals of the same sex as oneself is comparable to exposure to heterosexuals of another sex, one should presumably want comparable protections of bodily privacy from exposure to each.[123] Yet single-sex toilets and change rooms make no such accommodation, and most people do not seem to be perturbed by this. Instead, they seem to be in denial that some of those sharing these toilets and change rooms with them may be viewing them in the same way that a heterosexual member of the opposite sex would.[124] It is not clear to what extent we should consider this irrational denial and to what extent we should ignore it.

Sexual interest might not be the only relevant factor making cross-gender exposure more troubling. I leave open the question whether exposure of body parts not possessed by the person viewing them justifies greater shyness.

We should conclude that exposure to somebody of the opposite sex is generally worse. Part of this is attributable to the fact that exposure to people of the opposite sex *feels* worse to most people. It is worse in that way, even if the perception is not as accurate as it could be. The sex of the viewer is, at least in part, taken as a proxy for his or her sexual orientation. The perception would be more accurate if it also took sexual orientation into account.[125] But the use of a person's sex is still a more accurate guide to the level of invasion than is a policy of ignoring the sex of the person viewing the nudity of others.

Having concluded that being viewed naked by people of the opposite sex is *generally* worse than being viewed by people of the same sex, we need to determine how this should be weighed against the interest of guards (and potential guards) in employment opportunities. More specifically, have the courts been justified in prioritizing the employment opportunities of female guards over the privacy interests of male prisoners, even though they have not prioritized the employment interests of male guards over the privacy interests of female inmates?

One important argument defending the apparent inconsistency is this. Most prisoners are male. If women were to be restricted to guarding female inmates only, they would have many fewer opportunities than would male guards. In other words, respecting the privacy interests of male prisoners impacts more on female guards than respecting the privacy interests of female prisoners impacts on male guards.

One way of challenging this argument would be to compare the proportion of female prisoners to the proportion of females who are or want to become prison guards. If females are equally under-represented in both categories, then female and male guards may have equal, even if different opportunities. If that were the case, the argument would not get off the starting blocks. However, let us assume for the sake of argument that the opportunities for female guards would be more limited than the opportunities for male guards if cross-gender supervision were prohibited or restricted. There are a few reasons why it would still be unclear that males and females may be treated differently.

First, while female guards would bear a greater cost in employment opportunities than would male guards if cross-gender supervision were prohibited or restricted, male prisoners bear a greater privacy cost than female prisoners if cross-gender supervision is permitted. In other words, each policy has a disproportionate impact on one or other sex. Some might suggest that the rights of guards should be prioritized over the rights of prisoners because the prisoners are being punished. If hardships are to be borne, they should be borne by those who are being punished.

But this brings us to additional problems with the asymmetrical treatment of male and female guards and prisoners. It does not explain why pre-trial male detainees have had their privacy interests sacrificed for the sake of the employment opportunities of female guards. Moreover, while convicted prisoners forgo some of their privacy rights in being convicted of an imprisonable offense, they still retain a truncated right. (The courts have recognized this, although they tend to protect a truncated right to privacy only if the inmates are female.[126]) Being viewed by a guard of the opposite sex is made no less intrusive just because that guard's employment opportunities would be restricted if she were prevented from viewing the prisoner naked. If a prisoner has a right not to be viewed naked by a guard of the opposite sex, then the right to equal employment opportunity is simply moot. Nobody has a right to employment that violates the rights of others. Thus, the prior question is whether the prisoner has a right not to be viewed naked by guards of the opposite sex. If he does, then the guard does not have a right to a job that involves viewing him naked, even if that restricts her employment opportunities.

However, what if one rejected this reasoning and claimed that whether or not a prisoner has a right not to be seen naked by a female guard depends in part on her employment opportunities? First, one would need to realize that the same would have to be said of female prisoners if it turned out that the employment opportunities of male guards were negatively affected. I doubt very much that, faced with such a situation, the courts, given their current bias, really would sacrifice the bodily privacy of female inmates. It is easy for them or their defenders to say that they would rule differently, but we see nothing in their reasoning that would lead us to think that this is true.

For example, privacy interests of prisoners and employment opportunity interests of guards are not always in conflict. As we saw earlier, the courts have found ways to protect the privacy of female prisoners while not significantly compromising the employment opportunities of male guards. However, they have made no such efforts on behalf of male prisoners. The overwhelming evidence is that the privacy of male prisoners is taken less seriously and regarded as less important. Indeed, those who countenance the greater invasions of male privacy often say as much. They think their view can be justified, but I showed earlier that it cannot be.

If the tables were turned and males were protected from unwanted invasions of bodily privacy in the way that females now are, and females were as unprotected as males currently are, we can be sure that feminists would be denouncing this as another manifestation of sexism against females. They would be right to do so. But, given the way things actually are, we should conclude that the failure to have due regard for the bodily privacy of males is unfairly discriminatory.

Life Expectancy

The shorter life expectancy of men is a disadvantage. We need not claim that all of the difference in length of life between the sexes is attributable to discrimination in order to think that some of it is. It is not currently possible – and it may never be possible – to work out what proportion of the difference is the consequence of discrimination. However, determining the precise proportion is not necessary in order to show that males' shorter life span is partly the consequence of discriminatory treatment. We have already seen that the lethal violence to which men are disproportionately subjected is often the product of discrimination, and thus we can conclude that this contributory factor to males' reduced life expectancy must be the product of discrimination. However, there are other contributory factors that are also the result of discrimination.

When the life expectancy of women is shorter than that of men, some feminists take this to be evidence for discrimination against females. This is the case even when greater female mortality is attributable to such biological phenomena as peripartum mortality. Feminists are not wrong in saying this. Although only women can become pregnant and thus only women are susceptible to the risks of pregnancy and childbirth, social factors influence how often women become pregnant, what control women have over whether and when they become pregnant and what medical resources are available to them when they do gestate and give birth to a child. But parallel claims can be made about those biological conditions to which men are more prone. For example, whether resources are directed to research on and treatment of conditions to which males are more likely to succumb is often a matter for social choice. The choices are often made in ways that do not protect males.

For example, some medical research funding disparities favor women. In 1993, for instance, the National Cancer Institute (in the USA) "budgeted $273 million for research on cancers specific to women, including breast, cervical, ovarian, and uterine cancers, and $41 million for research on cancers specific to men, including prostate and testicular cancers."[127] While these specifically male cancers kill fewer people than the female cancers kill, it is noteworthy that the National Cancer Institute's research expenditure on breast cancer, which kills 46 000 women a year in the US, exceeds the amount spent on research into lung cancer, a disease which kills 93 000 men and 56 000 women annually.[128]

The claim that some medical research funding disparities favor women does not preclude the possibility that others favor men. There was a widespread perception that more trials in the United States were being performed on men.[129] This led to special measures to rectify this perceived problem. Others have found that women were not under-represented even before the aforementioned rectificatory measures were introduced, and that the perception was based on misunderstanding.[130] However, even if there are some research disparities favoring men, this would not undermine the claim that there are (also other) ways in which women are favored by current research practices. These might partially explain the life-expectancy differentials of males and females. That is to say, if women were not favored in some ways then the life-expectancy differentials might be smaller than they currently are.

One cannot conclude that there is a *net* favoring of females over males in medical research. To make any such claim one would need a careful investigation of all such research. I know of no such studies. However, in the absence of such studies one also lacks the evidence to claim that there is net discrimination *against* females. Thus, if instances of purported bias against females in medical research are thought relevant, then instances of bias against males, the sex with the shorter life expectancy, are at least as relevant.

We saw in Chapter 2 that men are at greater risk of suicide. Some might suggest that because suicide is something one does to oneself, males are not being discriminated against. This is, at most, only partly true. Although some suicides are rational, many are not. When they are the product of psychopathology they are not the result of free and informed choice. While the relevant pathology may have no social contribution, it is also quite possible that it does. This is supported by the fact that rates of suicide vary geographically and historically and that there is at least one place – China (and especially rural China) – where, as we saw in Chapter 2, the female rate of suicide is higher than that of males. There are a number of possible social factors that might contribute to the higher rates of suicide in men. For example, men may be under greater stress. Their gender role might incline them to greater lethality in their suicide attempts. Indeed, these factors may obtain even in cases where suicide is not irrational. I am not claiming that it is certainly the case that discriminatory social factors influence the rate of male suicide. Instead, I am claiming that they might do. It is a question that requires further study.

Another contributory factor to the shorter life expectancy of males is the disproportionate number of males among workplace fatalities. Now, some might argue that men constitute a greater number of workplace fatalities because men constitute a disproportionate number of those employed in more dangerous occupations. Because men choose such occupations, it might be said, they are not being discriminated against.

If this argument is intended to show that workplace fatalities involve no discrimination against men, then it fails. First, although the results of different studies have not been consistent, at least some studies have found that the rate of fatal accidents among males is greater than that of females even in the same occupations.[131] To this it might be responded that this is because men choose to take greater risks. However, even if we grant that men do take greater risks, this does not preclude the possibility of discrimination. Men might be pressured, for example, to assume such risks. The pressure might be explicit or it might be implicit in their gender role. Again, I am not asserting that this is the case, but only that it could be. If it is thought that women's choices can be pressured or that women choose under the influence of discriminatory gender roles, then there is no reason why the same could not be true of males.

Something similar might be said even if it is only the case that men suffer more work fatalities because there are more men in dangerous occupations. In many places women are no longer barred from these and other occupations. Thus women are choosing into which occupations they will and will not enter. Either those choices are free or they are not. If they are not free, perhaps because the occupations are highly gendered, then there is no reason to think that males choose freely in entering those occupations. Their choices too are influenced by the gendered nature of the occupations. And if the choices whether or not to enter particular occupations are free, then there are no grounds for complaint that women are under-represented in those occupations from which women are not barred but into which they do not choose to enter. It cannot be the case that women are the victims of discrimination when they are under-represented in desirable positions, but that men are not discriminated against when they are over-represented in undesirable or dangerous ones.

Imprisonment and Capital Punishment

Although about half the human population is male, over 90% of those imprisoned and an even higher proportion of those executed are male. Is this over-representation of males a product, at least in part, of discrimination? Some have suggested that it is not. They have argued that men commit most crime and especially most violent crime, and thus it is unsurprising that most of those imprisoned and executed are males. More specifically those advancing this argument claim (or should claim) that the disproportionate judicial punishment inflicted on males is itself proportionate to the disproportionate amount and severity of crime they commit. For if the punishment differential between the sexes exceeded the crime differential, something other than desert would have to explain the further increment of punishment.

Is that argument sound? For the moment, let us set aside the question whether the proportion of punishment inflicted on males matches the proportion of crime committed by them. Even if that question were answered affirmatively, we would need to ask *why* males are responsible for so much crime. This question would parallel the feminist questions about why women perform so much more child-care and domestic work. Some might be tempted to attribute such phenomena to natural differences between men and women. Such a rationale applies equally, of course, to those cases where the purported natural differences disadvantage women as to cases where they disadvantage men. Accordingly most feminists will be reluctant to embrace this explanation. They are right to be reticent about invoking such an explanation. Even if more males are more disposed towards violent criminal behavior, it is very likely, as we have seen, that there is social reinforcement of the traits that incline them to such behavior. Sometimes the social pressure is explicitly to commit crimes, as when young males seeking acceptance from peers in gangs are encouraged to engage in criminal behavior. More often, however, the social reinforcement is upstream rather than proximate. Males are encouraged to be more aggressive, to protect turf, to provide for and protect women and children, to compete for mates and, in the process, to expose themselves to greater risks. In some circumstances these traits make males particularly disposed to crime. If that is the case, then the male gender role plays a part in male crime. If males (and females) were socialized differently then proportionately less crime would be attributable to men, and then fewer men would experience harsh judicial punishment.

So far I have been assuming, for the sake of argument, that the disproportionate male share of imprisonment and execution matches the disproportionate male share of (serious) crime. As it happens, however, there is good reason to question that assumption.

Many studies have investigated whether females are treated more leniently than males by law enforcement officers and by the judicial process. While some studies have found that females are not treated more leniently,[132] most studies have found that a person's sex does make some difference,[133] although the difference it makes is complicated.

There are various decisional nodes in the criminal justice system. These include decisions whether to arrest, whether to prosecute, whether to allow pre-trial release, whether to accept a plea bargain, whether to convict, what sentence to impose, whether to grant parole and whether to commute a sentence. Most studies have focused on sentencing, but there has been some investigation into other stages.

For example, one study found that, controlling for relevant legal variables, female offenders were 28% less likely than males to be arrested for kidnapping, 48% less likely to be arrested for forcible fondling, 9% for simple assault and 27% for intimidation.[134] However, the same study found that females had a 5% higher chance of being arrested for aggravated assault.[135]

Another study found that while "legal factors are the strongest determinants of whether a defendant is released or detained ... female defendants are significantly less likely to be detained than male defendants, controlling for important extralegal, legal, and contextual factors."[136] Indeed, the chance of pre-trial detention was found to be about 37% less for female than for male defendants.[137] Upon further analysis, it was found that females were advantaged at every stage of decision about pre-trial release. They were less likely to receive preventive detention, less likely to have financial conditions placed on their release, had smaller bail amounts imposed when financial conditions were placed and were less likely to be held on bail.[138] Other studies have also found that females are treated more leniently in pre-trial release decisions.[139]

Many studies have found that females are likely to be treated more leniently than males at sentencing, even after controlling for relevant variables pertaining to such matters as the severity of crime and prior offenses.[140]

The results in all studies showing leniency on females are complicated, however. Some studies have found that the sex of the victim also makes a difference. Where the victim is female the offender is more likely to be arrested. In one study, it was found that when "a female was the crime victim, the odds of arrest were elevated by 69 percent for kidnapping, 26 percent for forcible fondling, 13 percent for aggravated assault, 25 percent for simple assault, and by 15 percent for intimidation."[141] Many studies have found that the gender effects become more pronounced when they interact with race or ethnicity as well as age.[142] Thus, in the United States, while white males are treated more harshly than females, the greatest differential is between young black or Hispanic males and white females.

While the balance of evidence suggests that females are treated more leniently in the criminal justice system, there is considerable disagreement about what explains this phenomenon. One popular hypothesis has been the so-called chivalry explanation, according to which the benevolent and protective societal attitudes towards women explain why they are treated more leniently. A variant on the chivalry hypothesis claims that the lenient treatment is accorded only those females who comply with traditional gender role attributes and behaviors.[143] A related hypothesis says that family status (including marriage and care-taking of dependents) that makes a difference. These theories are usually advanced, even if only implicitly, as full explanations of why females are treated more leniently. However, if none of them constitutes a full explanation for the discrepancy, it may very well be the case that some permutation or combination of them correctly explains why females tend to be treated more leniently. Moreover, while it makes some difference what the correct explanation is, it is not clear that, for the purposes of my argument, it makes that *much* difference. There is good reason to think that some form of discrimination is taking place irrespective of what the precise explanation is.

If the chivalry hypothesis is a complete or partial explanation of the greater leniency accorded females, then women enjoy a benefit that men do not. If a more selective chivalry explanation plays a role, then those women who deviate from their gender role are not treated leniently. However, that does not mean that sex discrimination is not taking place. When all women are unfairly disadvantaged and only some men are advantaged, feminists routinely take this to be sexism. They are quite correct that there is no reason to think that sex discrimination must favor every member of one sex and disfavor every member of another sex. If that is the case then males are discriminated against in the current case. They have no chance of receiving the benefit of chivalrous treatment in the judicial system, while women do stand such a chance.

Some have suggested that if the family hypothesis accounts for at least some of the more lenient treatment of women then females are being advantaged not because they are female but because they perform more care-taking work than do men.[144] But this too does not mean that sex discrimination is not taking place. Feminists correctly note, in other contexts, that rules and practices that are formally gender neutral can have a disparate effect on men and women. For example, inflexible working hours are sometimes said to have a disparate impact. Because women bear the greatest burden of child caring, inflexible working hours make it more difficult for them than for men to comply with the required working hours, even though the requirement applies, on the face of it, equally to both sexes. Where a policy or practice has such a disparate impact, feminists tend to take the policy or practice to be unfairly discriminatory. But if that is the case, then we should say the same about the disparate impact of phenomena that disadvantage males. More specifically, it is discriminatory that the courts favor the child-caring contribution that women make over the economic contribution that men make.

Now it might be suggested that there is a difference between the two cases because women are pressured into their child-caring roles, and thus to disadvantage them on the basis of that role is unfair. By contrast, the argument goes, it is not unfair to disadvantage men because they fail to perform a role into which women are pressured. There are a few problems with this argument, however. First, it is unclear that women are any more pressured into their child-caring roles than men are pressured into their breadwinner roles. (I shall say more about this later, for those who doubt this.) Thus for men to be disadvantaged by a role into which they are pressured is as unfair as it is for women to be disadvantaged by a role into they are pressured. Second, even if women are more pressured into their roles, it is still unfair for the courts to favor them on that basis. Those who are accused of crimes and those who are convicted should be treated equally. To favor some people because they play a particular social role, even if they are pressured into that role, is to treat people unequally.[145] Imagine, for example, that soldiers found guilty of committing rape during war were treated more leniently because they were pressured or even forced into combat. Feminists would rightly object to that. However, those feminists should then concede that punishment should be distributed without regard to gender roles.

Others who are uncomfortable with conceding that the more lenient treatment of females constitutes discrimination against males have suggested that this repeated finding is an artifact of an inadequate methodology. One pair of authors, for example, suggested that if "male crack dealers typically dealt in larger quantities than female dealers" or "if men typically held higher positions in [drug] distribution networks,"[146] and research failed to control for this, it might appear as though women were being treated more leniently, even though that would not be the case.

That is indeed a possibility. However, in the same paper, these authors state that sample-selection bias might lead to an underestimation of the impact that an offender's race has on how he is treated by the criminal justice system. Thus, it is noted that if "prosecutors screened out more of the less serious white than black robbery cases" a "finding of 'no race effects' at sentencing ... might be interpreted as indicating that black and white cases were treated the same, yet it does not reflect the cumulative advantage accorded whites."[147] It is curious, however, that these authors did not consider the possibility that this latter hazard might account for the sex effect appearing to be less than it really is.

Why did they not state this possibility? The most plausible answer is that the actual findings of the various studies do not fit their preconceptions.

Thus, while it is possible that the sex effect is smaller than it appears, it is also possible that it is greater than it appears. We cannot be certain about what the precise effect is, but the balance of evidence currently suggests that females are treated more leniently even after one controls for the relevant variables pertaining to the crime and the offender's prior record.

Sometimes the differential treatment of males and females in the criminal justice system is explicit. Consider for example, the South African Constitutional Court case *President of the Republic of South Africa and Another v. Hugo*.[148] On June 27, 1994 then newly elected President Nelson Mandela had, via a Presidential Act, granted a remission of sentence and thus release from prison of three categories of prisoner, including "all mothers in prison on 10 May 1994, with minor children under the age of twelve years."[149] John Phillip Peter Hugo, a father with a minor child under the age of 12 years, sought a judicial order to declare the Presidential Act unconstitutional on the grounds that it unfairly discriminated against him on the grounds of his sex – that he was a father rather than a mother. The case was heard in the Local Division of the Supreme Court, which found in favor of the applicant. The President and Minister of Correctional Services took this on appeal to the Constitutional Court, which reversed the lower court's judgment.

Judge Richard Goldstone, writing for the majority, offered the following justification for the Court's decision. First, the President, according to an affidavit he had submitted, "was motivated predominantly by a concern for children who had been deprived of the nurturing care which their mothers would ordinarily have provided."[150] The Court was of the view that women do, as a matter of fact, bear a disproportionate burden of the care of children and thus remitting the sentences of only mothers was a reasonable way of achieving the goal. Second, the Court recognized that the claim that mothers do most child caring is a generalization, but noted that the small minority of fathers who provided such caring were not precluded from applying on an individual basis. Third, because the remission of sentence was not something to which any of the prisoners were entitled, the Presidential Act "did not restrict or limit ... [the fathers'] rights or obligations ... in any permanent manner."[151] Fourth, it would have been "well-nigh impossible," without raising a public outcry and bringing the administration of justice into disrepute, to release all male parents of minor children under the age of 12 years, given the much greater number of male than female prisoners who would thereby have been released.

This argument, like the ones we saw in the United States courts justifying the violations of male inmates' bodily privacy, seems like a rationalization of prejudicial views about males. Imagine a scenario in which the President had decided to release only fathers because he had been motivated to restore breadwinners to families, perhaps on the assumption that care-givers for children can be found in extended families (or hired with money earned by the breadwinner) but that in impoverished families there was no substitute for the (additional) income of a breadwinner.[152] How likely is it that the Court would have found that because fathers as a matter of fact constitute the majority of breadwinners that the discriminatory remission of sentence was fair? Similarly, how likely is it that the Court would have argued that those women who are breadwinners could apply individually on the strength of their circumstances? And how likely is it that the Court would have argued that since none of the prisoners were entitled to remission of their sentences, the female prisoners were not the victims of unfair discrimination? I suspect that it is not very likely at all.

Perhaps it will be suggested, in response, that the difference is that women are "relegated" to child-caring roles and excluded from breadwinner roles, and thus discriminating on this basis would be unfair to them in my imaginary case. Indeed, the Court claimed that women's disproportionate role in child caring is a result of discrimination against them.

However, if prior discrimination is thought to be relevant here, then one wonders why prior discrimination against males is not thought relevant. Judge Kriegler, in his dissenting option, wrote:

> From the fact that women have suffered discrimination *generally* it cannot be argued that they deserve compensatory benefits in *any* context. I suggest that the relevant context in this case is the penal one, for the effect of the Presidential Act is felt by prisoners. It has not been suggested that women have suffered systematic discrimination in the penal context.[153]

Thus there are two possible realms of discrimination on which the Court could have focused – that in which females are the primary victims and that in which males are. There is better reason for adopting the latter focus. It is true that the motivation for the Presidential Act was the welfare of children rather than the relief of prisoners, and thus it might be suggested that the past discrimination against men is not relevant. However we should be cautious about deferring to the motivation when the impact is discriminatory. Feminists regularly (and rightly) frown on policies that may be devoid of bad intentions (or are even based on good ones), but which have an unfairly discrepant impact on the sexes. Because the Court was of the view that discrimination on the basis of sex is presumptively wrong and requires adequate justification to avoid being unfair, the burden of proof is on those who would perpetrate or uphold sex discrimination. That burden has not been met.

Consider next the Court's fourth argument – that it would have been "well-nigh impossible" to release fathers in addition to mothers, given how many more prisoners would then have qualified for release. This, it was said, would have brought the administration of justice into disrepute and caused a public outcry. The Court noted that the President had not taken his decision lightly. In his affidavit the President had written:

> 5.1   I believe it is important that due regard be had to the integrity of the judicial system and the administration of justice. Whenever remission of sentence is considered, it is necessary to bear in mind that incarceration has followed a judicial process and that sentences have been duly imposed after conviction. A random or arbitrary grant of the remission of sentences may have the effect of bringing the administration of justice into disrepute.
>
> 5.2   I believe further that it is of considerable importance to take into account the legitimate concerns of members of the public about the release of convicted prisoners. I am conscious of the fact that the level of crime is a matter of concern to the public at large and that there may well be anxiety about the release of persons who have not completed their sentences.[154]

The Court was remarkably deferential to this reasoning. The above considerations offered by the President, insofar as they deal with legitimate public concerns, apply equally to male and female prisoners (if the crimes are comparable[155]). Remitting the sentences of convicted females has the same per capita effect on the repute of the justice system. Insofar as there is proportionally less of a public outcry, this is because the public is less outraged by the release of female prisoners rather than male ones, but such prejudices are not a legitimate concern. Great caution should be exercised in appealing to prejudicial views in order to justify discriminatory treatment of those against whom the prejudice is held.

Perhaps it will be suggested that the public outcry would have been not to the release of male prisoners, but to the greater number of prisoners. This line of argument also fails. First, the release, by remission of sentence, of any convicted prisoners subverts the judicial decisions. Obviously more of it is worse than less of it, but the principle applies even to occasional cases. Second, and more importantly, there are other ways in which the number of prisoners released could have been reduced without resorting to sex discrimination. The age of the children could have been reduced from 12 to, perhaps, 8 or 6. Alternatively, only those parents who did not have a spouse caring for a child could have been released. The latter mechanism would have better satisfied the aim of the Act. It is surely more important that a child has at least one parent caring for it than that a child who already has a father caring for it should also have a mother caring for it. The Court seems to have contorted itself to uphold an Act that discriminated against male prisoners.

If women tend to be treated more leniently than men at various stages in the criminal justice process and with regard to whether they are incarcerated and for how long, it would be surprising if females were not also treated more leniently with regard to capital punishment. Indeed, assumptions about women being less dangerous, combined with the lesser regard for male life, would suggest a greater reluctance to execute females.

In a few countries females are exempt from capital punishment. In such countries females may not be executed even if their crimes and criminal records are indistinguishable from those of males who are executed. This is clearly unfair *de jure* discrimination on the basis of sex. Those countries that commute the death sentences of pregnant women also engage in unfair sex discrimination. Although *some* women are not thereby exempt from capital punishment, *no* men are. If some men but no women were exempt from capital punishment feminists would rightly complain that this constituted sex discrimination. To be consistent, we must say the same about countries that exempt some women but no men.[156]

What about those countries that do not (officially) exempt women, or even pregnant women, from execution? Some are nonetheless conflicted about executing women. India considered whether to exempt women from capital punishment. The Law Commission stated:

> While we appreciate that it would be a natural desire to avoid the death sentence on females in most cases, *we do not think that a general exemption is called for*.[157]

The Commission concluded that "if there were a valid case for the retention of capital punishment, it must apply to women as well as men, 'although possibly not to an equal degree'."[158]

Even where there are no formal bars on executing women and ambivalence about executing women is not explicitly expressed, it is quite likely that the discrimination that we saw exists elsewhere in the criminal justice system also influences which people are executed.[159] It is difficult to prove this, but there are strong grounds for a presumption that discrimination is operative. In the United States, for example, Virginia is one of the leading capital punishment states. Only Texas now executes more people than Virginia. Virginia has also executed more women throughout American history than any other state. Yet no woman has been sentenced to death in Virginia since 1973 and no woman has been executed in that state since 1912.[160] Ohio, which was previously one of the leading states in sentencing women to death, has not sentenced a woman to death since 1989 and last executed a woman in 1954.[161] There are also 16 states (in the northwest of the United States) that have never executed a woman.[162] While some of these have executed only very few men, others "generally have had functioning death penalty systems during their state histories, but they have totally excluded female offenders from this punishment."[163]

It strains credulity to think that since 1912 in Virginia and since 1954 in Ohio no woman has committed a crime that is as serious as those for which men have been executed. It is similarly unbelievable that no woman has *ever* committed such a crime in the 16 states that have never executed a woman.

Women may commit less violent crime than men and it may well be that an even smaller proportion of the worst crimes are committed by women. However, it is extremely unlikely that this fully explains the disparity in the numbers of men and women executed. It is much more likely that sex discrimination plays a role.

Conclusion

The arguments I have advanced in this chapter show that many of the disadvantages previously outlined are the consequence of unfair sex discrimination. In some cases, the discrimination is explicit: men but not women are forced into the military or into combat; the law permits the hitting of boys but not girls; males are overtly targeted for violence but females are spared. Sometimes, however, the contribution that discrimination makes to disadvantage is less direct or less explicit. For example, people hold various prejudices about men, including the sorts of beliefs that were outlined in Chapter 3. Sometimes these prejudices are held unconsciously. Nevertheless, they contribute to treating men in ways that cause disadvantage. Or males may be reared to have certain traits (or to have certain traits reinforced), and these traits are disadvantageous in important ways.

I have acknowledged that in some cases the connection between the disadvantage and possible discrimination is so unclear that we cannot be sure it exists, but then the same must be said when the connections between female disadvantage and possible discrimination are as unclear. Thus the uncertain cases of discrimination against men raise a challenge for those feminists who deny that there is a second sexism, or who deny its full extent. Either they must concede that some female disadvantage is not the product of discrimination or they must concede that comparable forms of male disadvantage *are* the result of discrimination. I am unsure about which specific cases warrant each response. However, it is clear that the common practice of attributing to sex discrimination all the disadvantages experienced by females and none of the disadvantages experienced by males cannot be supported by the available evidence and arguments.

Notes

1   Kingsley Browne, *Co-Ed Combat: The New Evidence That Women Shouldn't Fight the Nation's Wars*, New York: Sentinel, 2007.
2   While this argument is worthy of detailed consideration, another argument is so weak that it is worthy of mention in this footnote only because it has actually been advanced. Tom Digby has denied that males are unfairly disadvantaged by

"the warrior role and all that follows from it" because "the overall pattern of men being assigned to combat was advantageous to most societies, in many cases even crucial to their survival" (Tom Digby, "Male trouble: are men victims of sexism?" *Social Theory and Practice*, 29(2), 2003, p. 259). The upshot of this, he claims, is that men too have benefited from the warrior role, by living in societies that have benefited from it. This argument is a stunning rationalization. Following this line of reasoning, women are not discriminated against when, for example, they are excluded from the military, so long as some benefit from this exclusion could be ascribed to them. Professor Digby thinks that males have other benefits, too. He says that "the power that has accrued to men by virtue of their ability to manifest the qualities of the warrior has given men control over important institutions like government and religion, and control over resources in general" (p. 260). Two points may be made in response to this. First, men can manifest the qualities of warrior without actually being a warrior and thus it is not clear why being forced to be a warrior is a benefit. Second, and more importantly, Professor Digby fails to distinguish between those men who pay the cost of being a soldier, and especially the highest cost (namely death), and those (other) men who gain access to power. In other words, he sees only men and women as groups, rather than individual men. One man's benefit does not negate the harm suffered by another man.

3   Kingsley Browne, *Co-Ed Combat*, pp. 19–37.
4   Ibid., pp. 97–99.
5   Ibid., pp. 113–126. "Why men love war" is the title of the relevant chapter. The chapter itself makes a more modest claim – that some men find rewards in war.
6   Ibid., pp. 38–47.
7   Ibid., pp. 48–53.
8   Ibid., pp. 60–63.
9   Ibid., implicitly; and pp. 66, 70, 295.
10 Ibid., pp. 75–78.
11 Ibid., p. 65.
12 Ibid.
13 Ibid., p. 63.
14 Ibid. p. 11.
15 This parallels claims that many feminists have made about upstream discrimination against females. For example, it has been suggested that if girls are socialized to be less competitive than boys and this (partially) explains why fewer women are to be found in leadership positions, the socialization constitutes unfair discrimination even if those making the appointments to senior positions are not discriminating against women because there are fewer competitive women from whom to choose.
16 Kingsley Browne, *Co-Ed Combat*, pp. 97–99.
17 Ibid., pp. 113ff.
18 The evidence he cites is of masculinizing effects more generally. See ibid., pp. 44–45.
19 Ibid., p. 45.
20 Ibid.
21 Ibid.

22 Ibid., p. 11.
23 Ibid., p. 94. He correctly notes that the presence of women need not always have this effect.
24 Ibid., p. 94.
25 Professor Browne recognizes this benefit, but he underestimates its importance.
26 As it happens, even purportedly risk-taking men know when the risks are excessive, and under such conditions the fear of cowardice is not sufficient to keep many of them from undertaking those risks. That is why military leaders have not infrequently motivated soldiers by imposing the fear of a still greater likelihood of death if they fled the battle. Professor Browne himself recognizes this when he notes that during the Second World War, "Soviet officers were authorized to shoot their men on the spot" if they retreated. He also cites reports from Iraqi soldiers who feared the death squads of the Baath Party behind them more than the coalition forces ahead of them (ibid., p. 134).
27 Ibid., pp. 186–189.
28 Ibid., pp. 189–193.
29 I refer here specifically to his and my primary foci, because both of us consider the other case.
30 Within such a volunteer force, one might find that a disproportionate number of men are attracted to combat positions (whether for biological or social reasons). Nevertheless, the presence of significant numbers of women even in the support positions might preclude the need for males to be conscripted into those positions. Currently 15% of the US military is female. It is conceivable that this proportion will increase at least somewhat – say to 20 or 25% – in the coming decades. Absent those volunteers it might have been necessary to conscript some males, at least to serve in the support positions that many female soldiers occupy.
31 Writing under the pseudonym "Scalpel," "The Female Medical Pupil," *Daily Evening Transcript*, January 3, 1851, p. 2.
32 *Bradwell v. The State (Illinois)*, 83 US 16 Wall, p. 141.
33 Almroth E. Wright, *The Unexpurgated Case against Woman Suffrage*, New York: Paul Hoeber, 1913, p. 88.
34 Kingsley Browne, *Co-Ed Combat*, p. 288.
35 Ibid., p. 290.
36 Ibid. The appeal to fear is another common technique used to support conservative conclusions.
37 Ibid., p. 93.
38 See, for example: Lizette Alvarez, "G.I. Jane Breaks the Combat Barrier as War Evolves," *New York Times*, August 16, 2009; Steven Lee Myers, "Living and Fighting alongside Men, and Fitting In," *New York Times*, August 17, 2009.
39 Kingsley Browne, *Co-Ed Combat*, pp. 1–2.
40 Both Iddo Landau and Don Hubin have reminded me that members of the US military have spoken out, in opposition to some of their civilian bosses, against the inclusion of openly gay people in the military. This suggests that at least some military leaders do have the courage to speak their minds.
41 Kingsley Browne, *Co-Ed Combat*, p. 111.

42   Chris Bateman, "Blood service adjusts after 'racist' claims," *South African Medical Journal*, 95, 2005, pp. 728–730.

43   Ibid., p. 88.

44   Ibid., pp. 135–146. Michael Levin says that the "brawling, drinking, athletic, rough-house, vulgarity, and sexual braggadocio of young men in groups incomprehensible to most women, are the rituals that cement the male bond" (*Feminism and Freedom*, New Brunswick, NJ: Transaction Books, 1988, p. 244). What Professor Levin does not recognize is how many *men* find that sort of behavior incomprehensible.

45   Kingsley Browne, *Co-Ed Combat*, pp. 136–137, 164–169.

46   Ibid., pp. 169–175.

47   Ibid., p. 150–160, esp. p. 153.

48   Ibid., p. 154.

49   Ibid., pp. 154–155.

50   Ibid., pp. 279–280.

51   Ibid., p. 279.

52   Ibid., pp. 199–200.

53   Ibid., pp. 235–241.

54   Ibid., pp. 243ff.

55   Ibid., p. 239.

56   See, for example, Joanna Bourke, *Rape: A History from 1860 to the Present Day*, London: Virago, 2007, p. 362.

57   There is also plenty of evidence of sexual assault on males in other conflict situations. See, for example: Pauline Oosterhoff, Prisca Zwanikken and Evert Ketting, "Sexual torture of men in Croatia and other conflict situations: an open secret," *Reproductive Health Matters*, 12, 2004, pp. 68–77; Eric Stener Carlson, "The hidden prevalence of male sexual assault during war," *British Journal of Criminology*, 46, 2006, pp. 16–25; Kirsten Johnson, Jana Asher, Stephanie Rosborough *et al.*, "Association of combatant status and sexual violence with health and mental health outcomes in postconflict Liberia," *Journal of the American Medical Association*, 300(6), August 13, 2008, pp. 676–690.

58   Presidential Commission on the Assignment of Women in the Armed Forces, *Women in Combat: Report to the President*, McLean, VA: Brassey's (US), 1992, p. 20.

59   Kingsley Browne, *Co-Ed Combat*, p. 254.

60   After I wrote this, a US general in Iraq issued a policy that would make pregnancy an offense for which a female battlefield soldier and the male soldier who impregnated her could be court-martialled ("Pregnant G.I.s Could Be Punished," *New York Times*, December 20, 2009). Curiously he subsequently said that "he would never actually seek to jail someone over pregnancy" ("U.S. General Backs Off Pregnancy Policy," *New York Times*, December 23, 2009). Just days later, his superior, the top US commander in Iraq, indicated that he would rescind the policy ("Commander to Rescind a Provision on Pregnancy," *New York Times*, December 26, 2009). This lends some support to Professor Browne's claims about double standards, but the fitting response to such double standards, as I indicated before, is not to accept them but rather to eliminate them.

61   Kingsley Browne, *Co-Ed Combat*, pp. 208–220.

62 See, for example, Fiona Leach and Sara Humphreys, "Gender violence in schools: taking the 'girls-as-victims' discourse forward," in Geraldine Terry with Joanna Hoare (eds), *Gender-Based Violence*, Oxford: Oxfam, 2007, p. 108.

63 Adam Jones makes a similar point: Adam Jones, "Gendercide and genocide," *Journal of Genocide Research*, 2(2), 2000, pp. 205–206.

64 Consider, for example, the massacre of old men along with younger men in Srebrenica. See David Rohde, *Endgame: The Betrayal and Fall of Srebrenica, Europe's Worst Massacre Since World War II*, Boulder, CO: Westview Press, 1997, and esp. pp. 207, 216 and 229.

65 Ibid., and esp. pp. 205 and 230; African Rights, *Rwanda: Not So Innocent – When Women Become Killers*, London: African Rights, 1995, pp. 58 and 59.

66 African Rights, *Rwanda: Death, Despair and Defiance*, rev. edn, London: African Rights, 1995, p. 815.

67 Ibid. See also, African Rights, *Rwanda: Not So Innocent*, p. 81.

68 Organization for Security and Co-operation in Europe, *Kosovo: As Seen, As Told: An Analysis of the Human Rights Findings of the OSCE Kosovo Verification Missions, October 1998 to June 1999*, Warsaw: OSCE, Office for Democratic Institutions and Human Rights, 1999, p. 196.

69 R.J. Rummel, *Death by Government*, New Brunswick, NJ: Transaction Books, 1994, p. 329.

70 Adam Jones, "Gendercide and genocide," p. 207, n. 13.

71 My own view is that although most instances of corporal punishment are wrong, physical punishment may sometimes be permissible – or at least that the arguments that it is *always* wrong fail to establish that conclusion. (See David Benatar, "Corporal punishment," *Social Theory and Practice*, 24(2), Summer 1998, pp. 237–260.)

72 Among those who claim this are Myra and David Sadker, *Failing at Fairness: How America's Schools Cheat Girls*, New York: Charles Scribner's Sons, 1994. They say: "In most cases when boys get tougher discipline, however, it is because they deserve it" (p. 201).

73 Madeline H. Meier, Wendy S. Slutske, Andrew C. Heath and Nicholas G. Martin, "The role of harsh discipline in explaining sex differences in conduct disorder: a study of opposite-sex twin pairs," *Journal of Abnormal Psychology*, 37, 2009, pp. 653–664.

74 See, for example, Anna Maria Aloisi and Marco Bonifazi, "Sex hormones, central nervous system and pain," *Hormones and Behavior*, 50, 2006, pp. 1–7; and Roger Fillingim, "Sex-related influences on pain: a review of mechanisms and clinical implications," *Rehabilitation Psychology*, 48(3), 2003, pp. 165–174.

75 Anna Maria Aloisi and Marco Bonifazi, "Sex hormones, central nervous system and pain," p. 1; Roger Fillingim, "Sex-related influences on pain," p. 169.

76 Roger Fillingim, "Sex-related influences on pain," p. 166.

77 Rebecca M. Craft, Jeffrey S. Mogil and Anna Maria Aloisi, "Sex differences in pain and analgesia: the role of gonadal hormones," *European Journal of Pain*, 8, 2004, p. 407.

78 See, for example: Scott Claver, *Under the Lash: A History of Corporal Punishment in the British Armed Forces*, London: Torchstream Books, 1954, p. 63; Joseph A. Mercurio, *Caning: Educational Rite and Tradition*, Syracuse,

NY: Syracuse University Division of Special Education and Rehabilitation and the Center on Human Policy, 1972, p. 90.

79   Almost nobody, that is, other than perpetrators.

80   Some Jewish authorities have made precisely this claim *in defense* of circumcision. See Moses Maimonides, *The Guide for the Perplexed*, 2nd edn, trans. M. Friedländer, New York: Dover Publications, 1956, p. 378.

81   Helena Cronin, "Mind the (Gender) Gap: It's More Than Cultural," *Cape Times*, August 29, 2008, p. 11. See also: http://www.edge.org/q2008/q08_10.html (accessed January 11, 2010).

82   Christina Hoff Sommers, *Who Stole Feminism?*, New York: Simon & Schuster, 1994, pp. 162–163.

83   Christina Hoff Sommers, "The War against Boys," *Atlantic Monthly*, May 2000, pp. 59–74, at p. 61.

84   Here is one possible example. We saw earlier that feminists note that girls receive less teacher attention than do boys. They assume that this indicates discrimination. However, there is at least some evidence that the rate at which teachers call on boys is not disproportionate to the rate at which boys volunteer to be called on. See Ellen Rydell Altermatt, Jasna Jovanovic and Michelle Perry, "Bias or responsivity? Sex and achievement-level effects on teachers' classroom questioning practices," *Journal of Educational Psychology*, 90(3), 1998, pp. 516–527.

85   Donald Hubin correctly notes that the "phrase 'award custody' constitutes a strange twisting of reality in the context of divorce, dissolution and most other conflicts over custody between natural and adoptive parents." This, he says, is because "such parents typically appear before the court at the outset each with full parental rights. No one is *awarded* rights; one parent is *deprived* of rights" (Donald C. Hubin, "Parental rights and due process," *Journal of Law and Family Studies*, 1(2), 1999, pp. 123–150, at p. 136.

86   Interestingly, one study found that both mothers and fathers perceived the legal system (in Arizona) to be slanted towards mothers rather than fathers, even though they did not agree on the extent of that slant. See Sanford L. Braver, *Divorced Dads: Shattering the Myths*, New York: Jeremy P. Tarcher/Putnam, 1998, p. 104.

87   See Robert H. Mnookin and Lewis Kornhauser, "Bargaining in the shadow of the law: the case of divorce," *Yale Law Journal*, 88(5), April 1979, pp. 950–997.

88   See Paul Millar and Sheldon Goldenberg, "Explaining child custody determinations in Canada," *Canadian Journal of Law and Society*, 13, 1998, pp. 209–225, esp. p. 215; Paul Millar, *The Best Interests of Children: An Evidence-Based Approach*, Toronto: University of Toronto Press, 2009.

89   For a defense of this view see Steven D. Hales, "Abortion and fathers' rights," and "More on fathers' rights," in James M. Humber and Robert F. Almeder (eds), *Reproduction, Technology, and Rights*, Totowa, NJ: Humana Press, 1996, pp. 5–26 and pp. 43–49; Elizabeth Brake, "Fatherhood and child support: do men have a right to choose?" *Journal of Applied Philosophy*, 22(1), 2005, pp. 55–73.

90   The following circumstances are discussed by Donald C. Hubin, "Daddy dilemmas: untangling the puzzles of paternity," *Cornell Journal of Law and Public Policy*, 13, pp. 29–80.

91 See, for example: *Mercer County Dept. of Social Services on Behalf of Imogene T. v. Alf M.*, 155 Misc.2d 703, 589 N.Y.S.2d 288; *State of Kansas* ex rel. *Hermesmann v. Seyer*, 252 Kan. 646, 847 P.2d 1273; *Jevning v. Cichos*, 499 N.W.2d 515; *County of San Luis Obispo v. Nathaniel J.*, 50 Cal.App.4th 842, 57 Cal.Rptr.2d 843.

92 Donald C. Hubin, "Daddy dilemmas."

93 *S.F. v. State* ex rel. *T.M.*, 695 So.2d 1186.

94 *Louisiana and Rojas v. Frisard*, 694 So.2d 1032, 96-368 (La.App. 5th Cir. 4/29/97).

95 *S.F. v. State* ex rel. *T.M.*, at p. 1191.

96 This could be more than half.

97 In some places, such as various states in the US, as well as in Germany and Japan, successful adoption is not even necessary. So-called "Safe Haven Laws" enable women to deposit babies at designated places without legal penalty. If the babies are not adopted they will be wards of the state.

98 *Jordan v. Gardner*, 986 F.2d 1521 (9th Cir. 1993), p. 1525.

99 *Somers v. Thurman*, 109 F.3d 614 (9th Cir. 1997), at p. 623, citing that court's earlier decision in *Grummett v. Rushen*, 779 F.2d 491 (9th Cir. 1985), p. 493.

100 *Griffin v. Michigan Dept. of Corrections*, 654 F.Supp. 690 (E.D.Mich.1982), p. 701.

101 *Michenfelder v. Sumner*, 860 F.2d 328 (9th Cir. 1988).

102 *Smith v. Fairman*, 678 F.2d 52 (7th Cir. 1982).

103 *Timm v. Gunter*, 917 F.2d 1093 (8th Cir. 1990); *Grummett v. Rushen*.

104 *Jordan v. Gardner*.

105 *Torres v. Wisconsin Department of Health & Social Services*, 838 F.2d 944 (7th Cir. 1988).

106 Ibid.

107 *Grummett v. Rushen*; *Michenfelder v. Sumner*.

108 *Forts v. Ward*, 621 F.2d 1210 (2nd Cir. 1980), *Robino v. Iranon*, 145 F.3d 1109 (9th Cir. 1998).

109 *Oliver v. Scott*, 276 F.3d 736 (5th Cir. 2002); *Somers v. Thurman*.

110 *Timm v. Gunter*; *Griffin v. Michigan Dept. of Corrections*; *Grummett v. Rushen*.

111 *Jordan v. Gardner*.

112 *Somers v. Thurman*.

113 Ibid., p. 617. Note that the question was construed in gender-specific terms. Thus, at the outset, the Court assumed that male inmates might not enjoy such rights even if female inmates do.

114 For example, the Court claimed that women are more likely to be more adversely affected by cross-gender searches.

115 *Oliver v. Scott*; *Michenfelder v. Sumner*.

116 *Jordan v. Gardner* included minimum, medium and maximum security female prisoners, but the judgment in that case made no reference to the different levels in determining whether the fully clothed searches by male guards were reasonable.

117 *Johnson v. Phelan*, 69 F.3d 144 (7th Cir. 1995). Judge Posner, in his dissenting opinion, noted that the Court does not even know with what crime Albert

Johnson was charged. "It would be nice," he wrote, "to know a little more about the facts before making a judgment that condones barbarism" (p. 156).

118 See *Forts v. Ward.*

119 *Bagley v. Watson*, 579 F.Supp. 1099 (D.Or.1983), p. 1104.

120 *Timm v. Gunter*, p.1102.

121 *Griffin v. Michigan Dept. of Corrections*, p. 701.

122 This distinction is important because physiological arousal is possible in the absence of psychological arousal (as we saw in Chapter 2), and vice versa. Yet either might be thought to be relevant.

123 There might also be less reason to be concerned about bodily exposure to homosexual members of the opposite sex than to homosexual members of the same sex as oneself.

124 For more on this see, David Benatar, "Same-sex marriage and sex discrimination," in *American Philosophical Association Newsletter on Philosophy and Law*, 97 (1), Fall 1997, pp. 71–74. There I suggest that the solution to the problem of single-sex toilets (and change rooms) would be unisex ones in which every individual has a high level of privacy from every other individual – much as one has in the toilets people have in their homes.

125 There are possible mechanisms for considering not only a potential guard's sex but also his or her sexual orientation in determining how extensive an invasion he or she would pose to prisoner privacy, but I shall not discuss them here.

126 See *Johnson v. Phelan* and *Robino v. Iranon*, as contrasted with *Griffin v. Michigan Dept. of Corrections*.

127 Ace Allen, "Women's health," *New England Journal of Medicine*, 329 (9) December 1993, p. 1816.

128 Ibid.

129 See, for example, Nanette K. Wenger, Leon Speroff and Barbara Packard, "Cardiovascular health and disease in women," *New England Journal of Medicine*, 329, July 22, 1993, pp. 247–256; Ruth B. Merkatz, Robert Temple, Solomon Sobel *et al.*, "Women in clinical trials of new drugs: a change in Food and Drug Administration policy," *New England Journal of Medicine*, 329, July 22, 1993, pp. 292–296; Marcia Angell, "Caring for women's health: what is the problem?" *New England Journal of Medicine*, 329, July 22, 1993, pp. 271–272.

130 Curtis L. Meinert, Adele Kaplan Gilpin, Aynur Unalp and Christopher Dawson, "Gender representation in trials," *Controlled Clinical Trials*, 21, 2000, pp. 462–475.

131 See, for example, Yen-Hui Lin, Chih-Yong Chen and Jin-Lan Luo, "Gender and age distribution of occupational fatalities in Taiwan," *Accident Analysis and Prevention*, 40, 2008, pp. 1604, 1607.

132 Imogene. L. Moyer, "Demeanor, sex, and race in police processing," *Journal of Criminal Justice*, 9, 1981, pp. 235–246; and Debra A. Curan, "Judicial discretion and defendant's sex," *Criminology*, 21(1), February 1983, pp. 41–58. It should be noted, however, that while the author of the latter study claims that her study shows that investigations show no sex effect, this is only partly true. The results were somewhat mixed. In her paper, she notes that at "the sentencing stage ... results using the total sample showed that females were treated

more leniently than males. When the data were analyzed for each of the three time periods this finding of leniency was shown to be specific to the two most recent periods" covered in the study (p. 54). It was in "negotiations, prosecution and conviction" that no sex effect was found.

133 I shall discuss some of this literature below, but for a broader review and the claim that most studies show that the offender's sex makes a difference, see Darrell Steffensmeier, John Kramer and Cathy Streifel, "Gender and imprisonment decisions," *Criminology*, 31(3), 1993, pp. 411–446.

134 Lisa Stolzenberg and Stewart J. D'Alessio, "Sex differences in the likelihood of arrest," *Journal of Criminal Justice*, 32, 2004, pp. 443–454.

135 However, the authors of the study say that the last-mentioned "relationship was relatively weak given the large sample size." Ibid., p. 449. (A weak correlation in a large sample size constitutes weak evidence.)

136 Stephen Demuth and Darrell Steffensmeier, "The impact of gender and race-ethnicity in the pretrial release process," *Social Problems*, 51(2), 2004, pp. 222–242, at p. 233.

137 Ibid.

138 Ibid.

139 See, for example, Kathleen Daly, "Discrimination in criminal courts: family, gender, and the problem of equal treatment," *Social Forces*, 66(1), 1987, pp. 152–175.

140 See, for example, Patricia Godeke Tjaden and Claus D. Tjaden, "Differential treatment of the female felon: myth or reality?" in M.Q. Warren (ed.), *Comparing Female and Male Offenders*, London: Sage Publications, 1981, pp. 73–88; Kathleen Daly, "Discrimination in criminal courts"; Gayle S. Bickle and Ruth D. Peterson, "The impact of gender-based family roles on criminal sentencing," *Social Problems*, 38(3), 1991, pp. 372–394; Carol Hedderman and Mike Hough, "Does the Criminal Justice System Treat Men and Women Differently?" Research Findings 10, Home Office Research and Statistics Department, May 1994; Darrel Steffensmeier, Jeffrey Ulmer and John Kramer, "The interaction of race, gender and age in criminal sentencing: the punishment cost of being young, black and male," *Criminology*, 36(4), 1998, pp. 763–798; Cassia Spohn and Dawn Beichner, "Is preferential treatment of female offenders a thing of the past? A multisite study of gender, race, and imprisonment," *Criminal Justice Policy Review*, 11(2), 2000, pp. 149–184.

141 Lisa Stolzenberg and Stewart J. D'Alessio, "Sex differences in the likelihood of arrest," pp. 449–450.

142 Darrel Steffensmeier, Jeffrey Ulmer and John Kramer, "The interaction of race, gender and age in criminal sentencing"; Stephen Demuth and Darrell Steffensmeier, "The impact of gender and race-ethnicity." There is also some support in Lisa Stolzenberg and Stewart J. D'Alessio, "Sex differences in the likelihood of arrest."

143 See, for example, Christy A. Visher, "Gender, police arrest decisions, and notions of chivalry," *Criminology*, 21(1), February 1983, pp. 5–28.

144 Kathleen Daly, "Discrimination in the criminal courts."

145 Nor can it be argued that although it is unfair to treat female offenders more leniently than male ones, it is nonetheless justifiable to be more reluctant to

sentence child-caring mothers to prison on account of the secondary effects that imprisonment would have on their children. Sentencing breadwinning fathers to prison could also have secondary effects on the children and it is not clear that these are typically worse for the child. A child whose mother is imprisoned will likely be placed in the care of others. While less than ideal, it is not clearly worse than staying in the care of a mother who is less able to provide for the child's material needs.

146 Kathleen Daly and Michael Tonry, "Gender, race and sentencing," *Crime and Justice*, 22, 1997, pp. 201–252, at p. 231.
147 Ibid., p. 230.
148 *President of the Republic of South Africa v. Hugo*, 1997 (4) SA 1 (CC).
149 The other two categories were all children under the age of 18 and all disabled prisoners who were in prison on May 10, 1994.
150 Affidavit of President Nelson Mandela, quoted by Richard Goldstone in *President of the Republic of South Africa v. Hugo*, p. 38.
151 Ibid., p. 26.
152 Some might argue that women are breadwinners in many single-parent families. Even if this is true, imagine a scenario in which it were not, because it seems unlikely that even then the Court would have reasoned in a way parallel to the way it reasoned in *Hugo*.
153 *President of the Republic of South Africa v. Hugo*, p. 38.
154 Ibid., p. 25.
155 Here it is relevant that neither the Presidential Act nor the Court's opinion was concerned with the severity of the crimes committed. That, rather than the sex of the prisoners, may well be relevant.
156 Roger Hood and Carolyn Hoyle refer to a case of a woman in Vietnam who in 2000 was spared after she became pregnant in prison, while the others in her gang were all executed. See their book, *The Death Penalty: A Worldwide Perspective*, 4th edn, Oxford: Oxford University Press, 2008, p. 195.
157 Quoted by Subhash C. Gupta, *Capital Punishment in India*, New Dehli: Deep & Deep Publications, 1986, p. 151.
158 Ibid.
159 G. Scott, *The History of Capital Punishment*, London: Torchstream Books, 1950. David C. Baldus, George Woodworth and Charles A. Pulaski, Jr., *Equal Justice and the Death Penalty: A Legal and Empirical Analysis*, Boston: Northeastern University Press, 1990, p. 159.
160 Victor L. Streib, "Gendering the death penalty: countering sex bias in a masculine sanctuary," *Ohio State Law Journal*, 63, p. 441.
161 Ibid.
162 Ibid., p. 448.
163 Ibid., p. 449.

5

Responding to Objections

Women have always been the primary victims of war. Women lose their husbands, their fathers, their sons in combat.

Hillary Rodham Clinton, speech at First Ladies' Conference on Domestic Violence, El Salvador, November 17, 1998.

The evidence provided in previous chapters demonstrates that males suffer considerable disadvantage and that much of this, like much of the disadvantage suffered by females, is a consequence of unfairly discriminatory attitudes and practices. It is hard to imagine why, in the light of this, some people are so resistant to recognizing that males can be the victims of sexism.

Such people employ a number of strategies to make their case. The failure of some of these strategies should already be clear. There is no point, for example, in trying to deny that males suffer serious disadvantage. The evidence outlined in Chapter 2 proves otherwise.

Other second sexism denialists might seek to defend traditional gender roles. Some of what I said in Chapter 3 responds to such a view. I shall not say more in criticism of such a view. Feminists have written volumes effectively refuting defenses of traditional gender roles. There is little point in rehearsing those arguments. While obviously there are many people in very traditional societies who embrace deeply differentiated gender roles, they are unlikely to be readers of this book. In western societies, those who defend gender roles often forget how untraditional their particular conception of gender roles is. Few if any gender-role conservatives in Australia, Britain, Canada, France, Germany, Italy, New Zealand and the United States, for example, believe that women should be barred from higher education, denied the vote or the right to enter into contracts. They are conservative only in seeking to conserve residual gender

The Second Sexism: Discrimination Against Men and Boys, First Edition. David Benatar.
© 2012 John Wiley & Sons, Inc. Published 2012 by John Wiley & Sons, Inc.

differentiation. They are not (very) reactionary, and are not seeking a return to the more traditional gender roles common even a century or two ago.[1] The arguments I have already advanced do address the views of the contemporary western gender-role conservatives, sometimes explicitly and sometimes implicitly.

In this chapter, I plan to consider a number of arguments advanced mostly by those feminists who seek to deny that there is a second sexism. I shall categorize these arguments and I shall consider both their form and, where appropriate, particular examples. In distinguishing the different arguments I do not mean to suggest that they are mutually exclusive. Indeed, they are often inter-related.

The Inversion Argument

By the "inversion argument," I mean the argument that instances of discrimination against men are *instead* forms of discrimination against women. On this view, what I have called the second sexism is instead just another form of discrimination against women. Sometimes the inversion argument or technique applies to a phenomenon that discriminates both against men and against women, but it presents the situation as discriminating only against women. We might call this a *hemi-inversion* argument. It inverts only that aspect that discriminates against men, thus presenting the phenomenon as disadvantaging only women. Another variant of the inversion argument is what we might call *semi-inversion*. In this version, discrimination against males is partially recognized, but it is either partly eclipsed or it is minimized by focusing on discrimination against females.

Rarely are inversion arguments explicitly presented.[2] That is to say, those employing this sort of argument do not usually argue (although they sometimes do) that defenders of the second sexism have things backwards. Rather they usually simply invert, by presenting the issues as instances of anti-female bias. To this extent, my characterization of inversion as an argument is a construction of an argument out of a practice. The infrequency of an explicit argument for inversion is understandable. Were an argument for inversion explicitly presented, its weakness would be much more apparent.

The inversion argument is perhaps the most common objection to the claim that there is a second sexism, and it will thus receive the bulk of my attention in this chapter. Before I present a number of examples of inversion and show why these attempts are unable to disprove that there is a substantial second sexism, it is worth noting that there is a kernel of truth in the inversion argument. It is this: wrongful discrimination against females is closely (albeit contingently) related to wrongful discrimination against males. It should be clear why this is the case. Gender roles, for example, designate some traits, activities and occupations as masculine and others as feminine. Males without designated masculine traits and seeking to avoid activities and occupations designated by gender-role conventions as male will be a disadvantaged. Similarly, females with designated masculine traits or seeking to pursue activities and occupations designated as male will also be disadvantaged. Insofar as males are forced into some activities and females are barred from them the disadvantage will cut two ways. The same, of course, is true of females who are forced into purportedly feminine activities and occupations and males barred from them.

I said that wrongful discrimination against females is *contingently* related to wrongful discrimination against males. There is no necessary connection between the two. Gender roles might constrain one sex but not the other. We can imagine a society in which females were permitted to have any traits and engage in any occupations and activities, but men were restricted. In such a society, members of one sex but not the other would be the victims of discrimination.

This might partially explain why the relation between discrimination against males and discrimination against females is obviously not a linear one. That is to say, it is not the case that increasing discrimination against one sex increases discrimination against the other sex at the same rate. The same is true for decreasing discrimination. Indeed, part of my claim is that while great inroads have been made against anti-female sexism in many parts of the world, sexism against males has been far more enduring. Nevertheless, in the actual world (rather than in merely possible worlds) it may be the case that anti-female sexism cannot be *completely* eliminated without also attending to the second sexism. If that is the case, then those feminists who are concerned only with the interests of females (rather than with gender equality) may nonetheless have an interest in attending to the second sexism. The relationship between the first and second sexisms can be made clearer if we look at some examples of inversion.

Conscription and combat

Consider, first, those authors who present attempts at excluding and exempting women from combat as forms of discrimination against women only. They say, for instance, that the military, faced with an increase in the number of women soldiers, "seems to have an exaggerated need to pursue more and more refined measures of sexual difference in order to *keep women in their place*,"[3] noting that western armed forces

> search for a difference which can justify women's continued exclusion from the military's ideological core – combat. If they can find this difference, they can also exclude women from the senior command promotions that are open only to officers who have seen combat.[4]

As I have argued, refusing to send women into combat does indeed discriminate against some women. That it is a minority of women who are disadvantaged – those who seek combat opportunities and the military career benefits that follow from combat experience – does not alter the fact that *these* women are indeed the victims of sex discrimination. But to present the matter exclusively in terms of the negative effects it has on women is to ignore the much greater disadvantage suffered by vast numbers of men who are forced into combat against their wills. When it comes to forcing people into combat, women but not men are exempt. Thus, while the *exclusion* of women from combat discriminates against some women, the *exemption* of women from combat discriminates against more men and in favor of more women. It is well and good to note, as I have done, how an instance of sex discrimination can cut both ways. It is quite another to present everything as discrimination against only women.

A number of those who advance the inversion argument in the context of conscription and combat ignore the distinction between exemption and exclusion, even when that distinction is made explicit.[5] However, it should be clear that I have not denied that the exclusion of women from combat discriminates against (some) women. My claim concerns the *exemption* of women from combat.

James Sterba facilitates his inversion by taking as his paradigmatic case, those countries (such as the United States and United Kingdom today) in which there is no conscription. He notes that in such societies men are free to choose whether or not they wish to enter the military or combat. Obviously the discrimination of male-only conscription is not evident in *these* societies. To focus on such societies in an attempt to rebut my claim is like responding to the claim that female genital excision is discriminatory by saying that in Austria, Japan, Scotland and Zimbabwe, for example, women are not subject to excision.[6] It is plainly obvious that those men who *are* conscripted merely on account of their sex do suffer a disadvantage relative to women who are exempt.

Some people will not concede even this. In justifying a focus on the United States and the United Kingdom (rather than those countries where conscription does exist), it has been said that if women

> have managed to fashion the military to serve their interests, surely they must have succeeded in doing so in countries that are most strongly committed to enhancing the cause of women and where there is a fairly strong likelihood that members of the military of those countries would engage in combat.[7]

But this argument imputes to those who recognize that there is a second sexism a view that they need not hold. More specifically, those who recognize the existence of a second sexism need not claim that women "fashion" society to their benefit, a claim that suggests that the social order is *designed*. Instead, it need only be claimed that there are ways in which society favors women, often unconsciously and indirectly.

Some inverters believe it relevant that there are (purportedly) very few men today who are conscripted into combat (although apparently they do not think it relevant that relatively few women are disadvantaged by a combat *exclusion* – namely those women who want access to combat). It has been asked, rhetorically: "where today are the vast numbers of men who are forced into combat against their wills, especially in contemporary liberal democracies?"[8] This ignores a number of important considerations. First, even if there were currently *no* men conscripted into combat, there have been millions of such men in living history, and many of those who were not killed during service are still alive. Surely such veterans are as worthy of consideration as are survivors of other severe discrimination and ill-treatment.

It is true that, at the very moment I write this, a small proportion of conscripts are engaged in combat. However, if human history is any indication of what is to come, we know that there will be both a steady stream and occasional torrent of hostilities into which soldiers will be conscripted. Men will overwhelmingly bear this burden unless the second sexism is addressed.

Some people have assumed that the only conscription worthy of consideration is conscription *into combat*.[9] But this ignores the numerous other disadvantages of conscription even in the absence of combat. These include the infringement on freedom, the invasions of privacy, lost time, interrupted careers, separation from family, and the demeaning treatment associated particularly (but not only) with basic training. *Millions* of men in dozens of countries where conscription exists are subjected to such disadvantages, while their sisters are exempt.[10] It is entirely too glib to overlook all this.

My concerns are with those men who are forced (by conscription or the threat of ostracism) into the military or combat. However, the disproportionate number of male volunteers, even in the absence of explicit coercion, should raise some questions for those feminists who have concerns about females volunteering to be porn stars, prostitutes and strippers. Some feminists, to be sure, are prepared to accept the choices of at least some such women as fully voluntary, but others deny that such decisions are truly free. Those who adopt this latter view should be equally concerned about the subtle pressures and gender roles that very likely (at least partially) explain why disproportionate numbers of males volunteer for the military. If female prostitutes are not taken to choose freely despite their apparent consent and the (sometimes) lucrative benefits of their profession, then we have equal reason for thinking that males who volunteer for combat may not be choosing freely, notwithstanding any benefits they may have. And if all these males do choose freely, then so do the prostitutes.

Some people are willing to accept the choices that men and women make under the influence of gender roles.[11] They then deny that large numbers of men are forced into the military and combat, because, they say, even in the absence of conscription "many men would continue to enlist in the military and fight voluntarily."[12] I grant the obvious fact that in the absence of conscription and coercion many more men than women (currently) volunteer for the military. However, from the claim that (a) many men voluntarily join the military, some falsely infer that (b) not many men are forced into the military by conscription.[13] That is like inferring from the fact that there are many female prostitutes that there are not large numbers of women who do not want to be prostitutes.

Even those with a more balanced approach tend to make much more of the negative impact on women than of those discriminatory practices whose primary victims are men. Thus, one author who notes that war is "often awful and meaningless,"[14] observes that there are advantages which combatants enjoy. She cites a prisoner of war graffito "freedom – a feeling the protected will never know"[15] and "the feelings of unity, sacrifice and even ecstasy experienced by the combatant."[16] Moreover, she notes that women "who remain civilians will not receive the post-war benefits of veterans, and those [women] who don uniforms will be a protected, exempt-from-combat subset of the military. Their accomplishments will likely be forgotten."[17]

Although true, the significance of these advantages is overdone – even to the point of depravity. Certainly, many of those who never experience its loss may not have the same acute appreciation of freedom, but that acute appreciation is, at most, a positive side effect of an immensely traumatic and damaging experience. Imagine how we would greet the observation that although paraplegia is "often awful and meaningless" it is only those who have lost the use of some limbs who can truly appreciate the value of having those limbs functional.

Next, although veterans do have benefits denied to others, this is a form of compensation for sacrifice made. It is hardly unfair that compensation is not given to those to whom no compensation is due. People should be free, of course, to decide whether they want to accept the sacrifices of joining the military and the compensation that goes with it, but the absence of that choice is the disadvantage rather than the mere absence of the compensation.

Finally, while the tasks of non-combatants are indeed less likely to be remembered, this observation grossly underplays the extent to which the tasks and sacrifices of most *combatants* are unremembered. Many of these who die in battle lie in unmarked graves or are memorialized in monuments to the "Unknown Soldier." In exceptional cases, as with the Vietnam War memorial, a deceased combatant's memorial consists of an engraving of his name, along with thousands of others – hardly a remembrance proportionate to the sacrifice.

Violence

The use of the term "gender violence" to refer exclusively to violence against women is another example of inversion. Although men are the sex most targeted by violence, "gender violence" is used synonymously with "violence against females." Of course, men are not the sole victims. Women are sometimes also targeted, but with the exception of sexual violence, females are a minority of those targeted on account of their sex. This is not to deny that violence against women is worthy of attention. Instead, it is to deny only that it is *more* worthy of attention than is violence against males.

The way terms like "gender violence" are used does not amount to an explicit denial of discrimination against males. However, it is an implicit denial. It hides the fact that such discrimination takes place. Nor are such implicit denials limited to the usage of such phrases. They are pervasive. Adam Jones has noted and documented many such cases where people ignore, often willfully, violent discrimination against males. He observes, for example, that although men are regularly targeted for killing, it is women who have received special attention for refugee status by the Canadian Immigration and Review Board.[18]

Professor Jones also relates that he conveyed his concerns about gender bias to the president of the International Center for Human Rights and Democratic Development (ICHRDD). He "received a three-sentence response" from an assistant, thanking him for his letter but saying that these issues were not part of their mandate. The Srebrenica massacre occurred eight months later. The following year "the ICHRDD founded an international Coalition on *Women's* Human Rights in Conflict Situations."[19]

Professor Jones also draws attention to "The Edmonton Resolution: A Blueprint for Peace, Justice, and Freedom," which called "upon all states to promote and protect the human rights of all citizens, and especially those of women [and] girl children."[20]

He shows how Amnesty International failed, during the Kosovo conflict, to "devote meaningful attention to the pattern of gender-selective mass executions" and other serious human rights violations.[21] By contrast Amnesty International *did* highlight human rights violations against *women*, claiming that they are "particularly vulnerable to human rights violations."[22] Among other instances of such hyperbole to which he refers is the case of the "UN special rapporteur on Rwanda, René Degni-Ségui, who stated in January 1996 that women 'may even be regarded as the main victims of the massacres'" in Rwanda.[23]

Consider, too, the following exaggeration and the odd reasoning offered in support of it. Ronit Lentin has claimed that since "the female-to-male ratio is 1, or just over 1, this means that half of the casualties of what is termed 'catastrophe' by organizations such as the International Federation of Red Cross and Red Crescent Societies, are women."[24] This argument makes the assumption that catastrophe is equally distributed between the sexes. Yet this assumption is no more true of mass killing than it is of rape. Males are not half the victims of rape even though, worldwide, they are about half of the human population. Similarly, women are not half of victims of mass killings merely because they constitute about half of the world's human population.

Sometimes officials of human rights organizations are aware of the bias, but this has not resulted in correction. For example, Charli Carpenter quotes an official from the Office of the United Nations High Commissioner for Refugees (UNHCR) as follows:

> In the media women and children are often mentioned, especially if there are casualties. ... In UNHCR we often do use it as well. And I think it is linked to the way in which within the organization we are struggling to mainstream gender in our operations; and it's also linked to the fact that a lot of HCR members, and a lot of donors are really pushing women and children all the time, and NGOs say we are still not doing enough for women and children.[25]

Nor is this an isolated case. Professor Carpenter quotes many other officials to whom she has spoken who have also recognized "the use of gender stereotypes, and particularly the neglect of civilian men as a problem."[26]

Consider, next, an example of hemi-inversion of the facts about domestic violence. Deborah Rhode, taking issue with the widespread finding that rates of domestic violence by husbands and wives are comparable, says that they rely on a "widely discredited survey technique."[27] She objects that the surveys "conspicuously omit certain abuses that wives almost never commit, such as sexual abuse or stalking" and "inquiries about context and consequences."[28] She says that

> women are about six times more likely than men to suffer serious injuries, and are far more likely to act in self-defense. In cases reaching the criminal justice system, women account for 90 to 95 percent of those brutalized by a partner.[29]

This kind of response to male disadvantage is typical of many. It involves both selectivity[30] and rationalization. For example, stalking is not itself violent (even if it causes a fear of violence), and thus although it is worthy of investigation, it is not clear that that its omission affects the findings about domestic *violence*. In any event, we really do not know that wives "almost never" stalk until research is done that yields this finding. Perhaps it is true, but perhaps it is not. Given how unreliable ordinary views about spousal abuse are, we can hardly be confident that our untested views on this matter are reliable. Indeed, one study that did inquire about stalking found that some husbands had been stalked.[31]

The reference to sexual abuse also diverts our attention from (other) domestic violence. It may well be the case that more wives than husbands are sexually assaulted by their spouses. However, it is unclear how this is relevant. Sexual assault is often distinguished from (other) physical assault. It is thus not unreasonable to say that while more wives are sexually assaulted by their husbands than vice versa, the rate of (other) physical assault is comparable for each sex. The attempt to bundle sexual assault into the physical violence category in order to deny that husbands are assaulted as often as wives is disingenuous. It is like trying to bundle sexual assault into assault more generally in order to minimize the salience of women as the major victims of sexual assault.

The claim that when women assault their husbands or partners they are far more likely to be acting in self-defence, as we saw in Chapter 2, is not supported by the facts. Women initiate violence against their male partners at least as often as men initiate violence against their female partners.

The claim that women are more likely to suffer serious injuries is also not supported by the available evidence. The evidence on this question, we saw, is mixed. Some studies have found that men are more likely to inflict serious injuries on women, but other studies have found the reverse, and the remaining studies have found no difference. The claim that women are more likely to suffer injuries is thus highly selective.

However, even if it is established that females are more likely than males to suffer serious injury at the hands of intimate partners, it certainly does not follow that violence against males should not be taken seriously. To suggest otherwise would entail that the less injurious violence against women also need not be taken seriously. This is because it would be inconsistent to take moderate and minor injuries of females seriously without also taking moderate and minor injuries of males seriously. Since only a minute proportion of all domestic violence causes severe injury, the implication would be that most domestic violence against women need not be taken seriously. That is surely a conclusion we should reject.

Referring to the proportion of cases reaching the criminal justice system is also disingenuous. The assumption underlying this move is that it is the more serious cases that reach the criminal justice. This, however, would imply that those rapes that do not reach the criminal justice system are uniformly less serious than those that do. It is hard to imagine feminists accepting that conclusion. Indeed feminists commonly note that rape is under-reported.[32] Yet we have very good reason to think that assaults on husbands are under-reported. It is very likely that men are less likely than women to press charges for domestic abuse even when they suffer comparable injuries. They may be more ashamed of not being able to defend themselves. They may also be less likely to be believed and they may know it. Indeed, the denial by Professor Rhode and others that husbands are abused at least as often as wives is evidence that husbands are less likely to be believed.

Females are the victims of domestic violence but the evidence does not support the claim that they constitute the majority of victims of such violence. When we look at violence more generally, we find, as I demonstrated in Chapter 2, that most victims are males. This fact is inverted so often that popular wisdom has it that women are most vulnerable to violence. The inversion is pervasive. The foregoing cases are but a few examples of the thousands of instances that could be cited.

Circumcision

Some feminists have found a way to invert the disadvantages to males of circumcision. Removal of a boy's foreskin without the benefit of anesthesia is a disadvantage. It is also discriminatory if the infliction of comparable pain on a girl in comparable circumstances would not be countenanced. Yet some feminists have inverted matters by ignoring the discrimination against males and portraying circumcision of males as discrimination against females.

Some seem to say that male circumcision itself is discriminatory against girls. Dr. Marjorie Cramer, for example, when asked by her Reform rabbi to enroll in a course to train Jewish ritual circumcisers, initially said "Why would I want do such a sexist thing, a ritual only for boys?"[33] Others focus only on the absence of a neonatal *ceremony* for girls. They claim that girls are deprived of the attention given to newborn boys and have thus introduced neonatal ceremonies for girls. These ceremonies parallel the male ceremony in many ways. The names given to the ceremonies are similar to those given to the ceremony for boys.[34] They sometimes suggest that this ceremony take place on the eighth day of the child's life. The reason given for this timing is the allegedly egalitarian one that this "is the same day on which a ceremony for a boy would be held."[35]

In this way some Jewish feminists take the traditional practices as discriminatory against girls. They think that the discrimination is avoided by the introduction of a ceremony for girls. There is no acknowledgement that circumcision of boys, without anesthesia, is discriminatory. This is curious, because, in seeking to rectify the purported discrimination against girls, these Jewish feminists have not suggested that girls, like boys, should be circumcised. If circumcision of males really were discriminatory against girls, it would seem that the best way to rectify that would be to circumcise girls, too.[36]

A neonatal *ceremony* means nothing to the neonate. An infant boy is unaware that he is the center of attention. He is unaware that others are making a fuss over him and rejoicing at his birth and his induction into a religious covenant. Similarly, an infant girl for whom there is no such ceremony cannot feel deprived of any of this. And if she is given such a ceremony it does her no more good than such a ceremony does an infant boy. Thus the ceremony is more for the benefit of others. While those who give a girl a *batmizvah* ceremony comparable to a boy's may plausibly be thought to be benefiting her, giving an infant girl a neonatal ceremony to parallel a boy's cannot plausibly be said to be benefiting her. What *does* make a difference to an infant is whether its genitals are surgically altered without an anesthetic.[37] Jewish boys do bear this burden, while Jewish girls do not. In other words, the advantage that it is claimed that Jewish boys have – the ceremony – is not a real advantage, whereas the actual disadvantage, which goes unacknowledged by inverters, is a real disadvantage.

If it were Jewish girls who were circumcised and Jewish boys who were not, I suspect that feminists would offer strident arguments that circumcision discriminated against girls and constituted a patriarchal control of female genitals. They would be appalled at a ceremony in which a baby girl's nappies were removed, her legs splayed and her genitals cut, while both males and females observed. Even if the surgery were performed by women, these women would be judged, as they are in cultures that do cut female genitals, to be instruments of patriarchy. If men began to join the ranks of circumcisers, it would not be hailed as the egalitarian advance that the certification of female circumcisers (of male children)[38] – has been in some Jewish feminist circles. Here it has been said that a female circumciser can give a women's touch[39] and that female circumcisers "may have a special ability to relate to mothers who are having anxiety" about the circumcision of their sons.[40] But this sounds like something we would surely not hear from feminists – namely, recommending a male obstetrician because he brings a "man's touch" and can relate to the husband of the woman in labor. And if that is thought to be a poor analogy, then one can make the same point about males entering into the role of circumcising girls (where the circumcision was comparable to male circumcision). It is very unlikely that feminists would view that as an egalitarian improvement.

Education

My discussion of male educational disadvantage in Chapter 2 has already revealed that there are those who claim that it is girls rather than boys who are educationally disadvantaged. I showed that although girls have been educationally more disadvantaged at many times and in many places, in much of the developed world today it is boys who are more disadvantaged. The key metrics available to us, I suggested, are graduation rates from school and tertiary institutions. Because boys drop out at greater rates than girls and men earn fewer degrees than women, it is males who are most educationally disadvantaged in much of the developed world, even if there are some less severe disadvantages that females experience. Given this, the claim that it is females rather than males who are discriminated against educationally (in the developed world) is an inversion of the way things actually are. Females are worse off in some ways, but these disadvantages are diminishing. The inverters, ignoring the serious ways in which males are disadvantaged, present the educational institutions as disadvantaging only girls and women.

There are many ways in which the inversion is attempted. In making the case that it is males who are disadvantaged, I examined some of these in Chapter 2. Here I consider a few other ways.

One technique is to argue that the disadvantages in question have more to do with race than they have to do with sex. For example, it has been said that the "gender gap between white males and white females in college admission is very small – 51 percent are women and 49 percent are men. Yet only 37 percent of black college students are male and 63 percent female."[41] Thus, it was said, this "may be what sociologists call a deceptive distinction – something that looks on aggregate like a gender difference that's actually much more a race and ethnicity difference."[42] This is an attempt to obscure male disadvantage by suggesting that the real disadvantage is attributable to race or ethnicity.

However, while it is correct to note that race and ethnicity are crucial contributors to educational disadvantage in the United States, they are not the only factors. Sex is playing an important a role. Thus within each ethnic group, females are advantaged over males, even if the extent of the advantage differs.[43] When black males do much worse than black females this is obviously not merely a matter of race, because both black males and females are black. Being male is clearly playing an important role. This is the case even if males in other groups are not as badly disadvantaged relative to the females in their groups. What we have is an interaction of race and sex, but such an interaction does not imply that the disadvantage is more attributable to race than to sex. If that were the case then black males would not be (very) disadvantaged relative to black females.

When race and sex interact to female detriment, feminists do not typically argue that the disadvantage is primarily attributable to the former and thus underplay the contribution that being female plays. They should do the same when it is males who are disadvantaged.

Consider one final example of inversion in the educational context. The 1992 report of the American Association of University Women, to which I referred in Chapter 2, notes that boys constitute a significant majority of students in special education classes. This seems to support the view that there are more boys with mental and learning disabilities – an example of male disadvantage (even if not discrimination). However, the report claims that the greater number of boys in these programs is actually evidence of discrimination against girls who, it says, are less likely to be admitted to such programmes even they are equally in need.[44]

However, there is evidence that numerous neurodevelopmental disorders are more likely to be diagnosed in boys than in girls.[45] These include cerebral palsy, attention-deficit / hyperactivity disorder and autism. Some have suggested that rather than indicating that more boys suffer such conditions, it is instead the case that the conditions are being under-diagnosed in girls. In other words, it is claimed that girls are being discriminated against in not being diagnosed with the conditions they have. There is evidence, however, that while girls are under-diagnosed, this does not explain the full differential, because boys are more likely to suffer such conditions. For example it was found that boys are roughly twice as likely to suffer reading disability.[46]

I do not pretend that this is the final word on the matter. Clearly more research is required. What is disturbing, however, is the apparently reflex assumption that whenever boys appear to be disadvantaged it is in fact girls who are actually being discriminated against. These claims are glib, are not made on the basis of compelling evidence and manifest an unfortunate bias that is itself discriminatory against males.

Sexual assault

Next consider a case of what I earlier called *semi-inversion* – a partial acknowledgement of discrimination against males, but one that is either partially eclipsed or minimized by focusing on purported discrimination against females. One author, writing about cross-gender supervision in American prisons, notes that several "states report that the majority of their staff sexual misconduct complaints involve male inmates and female staff."[47] If these states had reported the reverse trend, it is likely that this would be left as evidence that female inmates are the victims of undiluted discrimination. However, when it is male inmates who lodge complaints against female guards, this phenomenon is thought to require explanation. The explanations proffered minimize the discrimination against males and shift the focus to discrimination against women. Thus we are told that the following factors explain the phenomenon:

> First, the fact that the vast majority of prisoners are male naturally leads to more complaints made by men. Second, female staff have relatively low status in correctional settings, and are therefore less likely to receive protection in correctional environments. Third, female staff may experience such harassment and lack of support from their male counterparts that they form alliances with male inmates for protection and support.[48]

It may well be the case that one reason why more male than female inmates complain of cross-gender sexual misconduct by guards is simply that there are more male inmates guarded by females than there are female inmates guarded by males. However, that does not mean that males are suffering less discrimination. Imagine, quite plausibly, that more female patients complain of sexual misconduct by their male gynecologists than male patients complain of sexual misconduct by their female urologists. It is hardly likely that feminists would dampen their complaints about sexual abuse of female patients by noting that there are so many more female patients of male gynecologists.

The second and third factors cited above are even more outrageous. Even if they are true, they would in no way excuse sexual misconduct by female guards. Now it is true that they are not being cited as excusing factors. Nevertheless, the effect of mentioning such factors when males are the victims of discrimination, but not when women are, is to minimize discrimination against males and to present at least some of it as discrimination against females. Yet whatever relatively low status female staff may have in correctional facilities, their status is much greater than that of male inmates. Thus if we are comparing discriminations here, we must certainly prioritize for consideration the discrimination against the most vulnerable parties. In this case, those are the male prisoners rather than the female guards.

Bodily privacy

The inversion argument is also regularly employed to obscure discrimination against men with regard to bodily privacy. Consider, for example, the pair of authors who presented the exclusion of women in the sports media from male locker rooms after matches as an instance of *blatant* discrimination against those women. As they correctly observe, such sportswriters who "cannot get immediate access to athletes after a game ... may miss deadlines and will likely be 'scooped' by the competition."[49] They entirely ignore the other side of the issue, however, and quote with disapproval the coach who stated "I will not allow women to walk in on 50 naked men." Had it been a male sports writer seeking access to a locker room of 50 naked female athletes, we can be sure that a different tone would have been evident in feminist commentary on the matter. There are alternative solutions to such equity issues – such as denying all journalists, both male and female, access to locker rooms. These authors ignore such options, just as they ignore the invasion of privacy that would be experienced by the male athletes, who would surely be discriminated against if their female counterparts were not also subject to such invasions. Instead, the authors view the matter entirely from the perspective of the female sports writers. I am fully aware that for other reasons male sports draw more attention, and that female writers thus lose more in not having access to male locker rooms than male writers do in not having access to female locker rooms. However, if this is used to justify female access to male locker rooms but not male access to female locker rooms, then the intensity of the writer's interest rather than the athlete's privacy is taken to be the determining factor. And if that is so, then male journalists should be allowed to corner female politicians, actors and other public personalities in female-only toilets and locker rooms if that is how they can scoop an important story. If this were not acceptable, then neither is the intrusion by female sports writers on the privacy of male athletes, irrespective of the writers' interests in getting a story.

I previously demonstrated the same phenomenon when I demonstrated the different degrees to which the bodily privacy of male and female prisoners is respected in the United States. If male and female prisoners were afforded the same degree of bodily privacy, then male and female guards would each suffer disadvantage. Yet it is only the disadvantage of female guards that interests the courts. Similarly, if male and female guards were equally unconstrained in cross-gender supervision, then male and female prisoners would each suffer disadvantage. Yet only the disadvantage of female prisoners has concerned the courts. Put another way, the courts have focused on the employment interests of female guards even when this negates the privacy interests of male prisoners, and have focused on the privacy interests of female prisoners even when this negates the employment interests of males. Protecting the privacy of male prisoners and the employment interests of male guards is seen as discrimination against females. Because protecting the privacy of female prisoners and the employment interests of female guards is not viewed as discrimination against males, the courts are guilty of inversion.

The inversion argument also arises with reference to depictions of male and female nudity in cinema. Matters are complicated here because of differences between male and female nudity. I do not mean to deny that there is any discrimination against females. Instead my claim is that this is inappropriately the exclusive focus.

In some societies, the exposure of female breasts is as common as the exposure of male breasts, but this is not the case in western societies. Accordingly, the not-infrequent sight of female breasts in cinema constitutes a higher level of exposure than the more common sight of bare male chests in film.[50] Yet the exposure of even female breasts is commonly regarded as a lesser exposure than is the uncovering of (either female or male) genitalia. A common complaint is that female genitalia are depicted much more often than are male genitalia.

It has been suggested, for instance, that

> we see plenty of R-rated movies where actresses who are paid a fraction of male salaries are obligated to bare all. I figure there must be an alarm that goes off and wakes up [ratings] board members whenever there's a penis sighting at one of their screenings.[51]

Commenting on the pornographic film *Emmanuelle*, Joel Feinberg notes although female nudity is depicted, albeit without "close-up camera work focusing on [female] sex organs," male sex organs are not shown at all.[52] This latter omission, he says, "is typical of the double standard that generally prevails in works of pornography meant to sell to large general audiences."[53]

It is not clear, however, which sex the stated double standard disadvantages. This is because male nudity and female nudity are not analogous. A woman's sexual organs are generally internal, whereas a man's are not. A naked man is thus, at least in one important sense,[54] more exposed than a naked female, particularly if the latter's pubic area is covered with hair. Thus, while it is true that cinematic depictions of female nudity are more common, it is also the case that when frontal or side male nudity *is* depicted – and this may be more common now that it was earlier – the degree of the exposure is greater. Thus we might note that whereas male sex organs are sometimes depicted in (age-restricted) mainstream cinema, analogous female organs (most obviously the clitoris) are not shown at all in such contexts. To suggest, therefore, that the full discrimination is against females is an instance of what I have called hemi-inversion. Only the disadvantage of or discrimination against females is registered. The disadvantage of and discrimination against males passes under the radar.

Custody

Feminist complaints pertaining to divorce are typically not about the benefits of gaining custody, presumably because those benefits are usually enjoyed by mothers. Instead, the focus has been on purported disadvantages of custody. Thus according to popular wisdom divorced men fail, in significant numbers, to pay child support, they drop out of their children's lives, leaving their ex-wives to do all the child rearing. It is also widely believed that women's financial position deteriorates significantly following divorce, whereas men's financial position is said to improve. Thus, the suggestion is that it is women rather than men who are disadvantaged, all things considered. It is said that while they may enjoy the daily contact with their children, fathers are uninterested in such contact. Women are left with all the parental responsibility along with the financial burden. In this way, a disadvantage experienced by fathers is presented instead as a disadvantage of mothers.

Widespread though these beliefs are, they are untrue.[55] Divorced fathers, unlike many fathers who were never married to the child's mother, have significant attachments to their children and are much more likely to pay child support. The precise extent to which they pay child support is uncertain. However, most research conducted on this question has sought data only from custodial mothers, who can hardly be said to be impartial judges. When fathers were also asked, very different answers were provided.[56] Although fathers are as likely to overestimate their compliance as mothers are to underestimate it, the mere fact that much research has consulted only the custodial mothers is evidence of bias.[57] Moreover, when divorced fathers have failed to pay, the single biggest factor was loss of employment. In other words, once those fathers who had been unemployed were excluded, the compliance levels rise to 80% (according to reports of mothers) or to 100% (according to reports of fathers).[58]

There are also discrepancies between mothers' and fathers' reports of how much contact non-custodial fathers have with their children.[59] While some fathers are derelict, other fathers lose contact with their children through no fault of their own. Visiting privileges often restrict their contact. Mothers often block or interfere with visits.[60] Whereas a failure to pay child support now incurs punishment or enforced payment, denial of visitation usually has no legal consequences for the custodial parent.

The suggestion that the financial position of women deteriorates significantly following divorce, whereas that of men increases, is also false. This widespread and oft-cited claim is attributable to a finding of Lenore Weitzman, who claimed that women and their children experienced a 73% drop in their standard of living, whereas the standard of living of the average divorced man increased by 42%.[61] Some scholars were suspicious of these findings and requested access to the original data.[62] When these were eventually made available, it was established that Professor Weitzman had made a mathematical error which, when corrected, suggested that women's decline was 27% and males increase was 10%.[63] Professor Weitzman has evidently conceded this error,[64] but this does not seem to have diminished the influence of her original conclusion. Subsequent research has suggested that her methodology was problematic and that when all relevant variables are controlled, there is no significant difference between the standard of living of men and women following divorce.[65]

Thus, while there are some men who are derelict in making child support payments, the more common disadvantage is that of fathers who have a much smaller chance of gaining custody. This is also more clearly a consequence of unfair discrimination, both direct and indirect.

Life expectancy

Sometimes the inversion is less overt and more sophisticated. Consider, for example, an argument of Amartya Sen and Jean Drèze, who have drawn attention to the number of female lives that have been lost as a result of advantages accorded males. They have spoken about the world's 100 million "missing women."[66] To reach this figure they first observe that everywhere in the world there are around 105 boys born for every 100 girls. However, more males die at every age. For this reason, in Europe, North America and other places where females enjoy basic nutrition and healthcare, the proportion of males and females inverts – around 105 females for every 100 males. Thus, the overall female–male ratio in these societies is 1.05. Amartya Sen and Jean Drèze observe, however, that in many countries the ratio falls to 0.94 or even lower. On this basis, they calculate the number of "missing women" – the number of women who have died because they have received less food or less care than their male counterparts. This is indeed an alarming and unacceptable inequity.

It is interesting, however, that no mention is made of "missing men." The implication is that there are only women who are missing. There are, however, millions of missing men, as should be most obvious from the greater number of men than women who die violently. There are also other, less obvious ways in which men become "missing." To highlight these, consider how the figure of 100 million missing women is reached. Amartya Sen says that if we took an equal number of males and females as the baseline, then "the low ratio of 0.94 women to men in South Asia, West Asia and China would indicate a 6 percent deficit in women."[67] However, he thinks it is inappropriate to set the baseline as an equal number of males and females. He says that "since, in countries where men and women receive similar care the ratio is about 1.05, the real shortfall is about 11 percent."[68] This, he says, amounts to 100 million missing women.

Now, I think it is extremely enlightening that the baseline is set as a female to male ratio of 1.05. Why start from that point rather than from the ratio that obtains at birth? The assumption is that the female–male ratio of 1.05 is the one that obtains in societies in which men and women are treated *equally in the ways relevant to mortality* – and these are taken to be basic nutrition and healthcare. But clearly males are not faring as well as females in those societies, so why not think that there are relevant inequalities, disadvantageous to males, operative in *those* societies?

Some might suggest that the only inequalities are biological ones – that males are biologically more prone than females to early death. However, I cannot see why that would warrant setting the baseline at the female–male ratio of 1.05. Some influential philosophers, writing about distributive justice, have suggested that because natural inequalities are undeserved, we ought to distribute social resources in a way that compensates for those inequalities. For example, John Rawls says that the outcome of the natural lottery "is arbitrary from a moral perspective,"[69] and Ronald Dworkin says that differences "traceable to genetic luck" are unfair.[70]

If males are biologically prone to die earlier, perhaps the ideal distribution is the one whereby the mortality imbalance is equalized (by funding research and medical practice that lowers the male mortality level to the female level).

This certainly seems to be what many feminists would advocate if biology disadvantaged women in the way it does men.

A *fortiori* is this the case if the shorter life expectancy of males is at least partly the product of social inequalities. Indeed, it seems to be the case that social inequalities do explain part of the difference. Although life expectancy has increased in developed countries over the last century, men have consistently lagged behind women. This suggests that the earlier death of males is (or, at least, was) not attributable to a biologically determined life-expectancy ceiling. As social conditions improved, men lived to be older, but never (on average) as old as women. Social factors clearly play an important part in life expectancy and in men's shortfall.

If it were the case that men tended to live longer than women, either because of natural or social inequalities, we would be told that this inequality would need to be addressed by devoting more attention and resources to women's health. If, for instance, 105 girls were born for every 100 boys, but various factors, including parturition, caused more females to die, there would be strong arguments for diverting resources to preventing those deaths. At the very least, the baseline for determining "missing people" would certainly not be thought to be set after the parturition deaths were excluded.

Thus, if we accept the actual sex ratio at birth – 105 males for every 100 females – as a baseline, then at birth there is a female–male ratio of 0.95. From that baseline there are millions of missing men, at least in those societies in which the female–male ratio inverts to 1.05, who go unseen in the Sen–Drèze analysis. This analysis fails to take account of the connection between its baseline ratio and how our health resources are currently distributed. That the Sen–Drèze analysis highlights the missing women of the world but notes nothing about the missing men is extremely revealing. It is a sophisticated form of the view that lost female lives are more noteworthy than lost male lives.

Moreover, by means of the inversion argument, the call for more attention and resources to women's health is exactly what some people offer even though it is in fact men who die earlier. Such claims do not result from a belief that more is spent on the healthcare of men than women. A Canadian study on sex differences in the use of healthcare services showed that the "crude annual per capita use of health care resources (in Canadian dollars) was greater for female subjects ($1164) than for male subjects ($918),"[71] but that expenditures "for health care are similar for male and female subjects after differences in reproductive biology and higher age-specific mortality rates among men have been accounted for."[72]

Accepting that there is indeed an *equal* distribution of healthcare dollars between men and women, one practitioner of the inversion argument suggested that such expenditure was not *equitable*.[73] This, we are told, is because the greater longevity (of females) is "associated with a greater life-time risk of functional disability and chronic illness, including cancer, cardiovascular disease, and dementia, and a greater need for long-term care."[74] I shall assume that that is indeed so. Living longer does carry some costs, but on condition that those costs are not so great as to render the increased longevity a harm rather than a benefit, the infirmities that often accompany advanced age cannot be seen in isolation from the benefit of the longer life span. An equitable distribution of healthcare resources is not obviously the one that both favors a longer life span for one sex and increases the quality of the additional years of that extra increment of life. Such a distribution would constitute a double favoring of one sex. According to one other possible principle, a genuinely equitable distribution would be one that, all things being equal, aimed at parity of life expectancy and the best quality of life for both sexes within that span of life. Whether or not this alternative principle is the correct one, it cannot simply be assumed that it is not. However, the proponents of the inversion argument are unsatisfied with any *perceived* trends that lessen the gap between men and the healthier sex. Thus we are told, disapprovingly, that at "a time when there have been improvements in the health status of men, the health status of women does not appear to be improving."[75]

A number of philosophers have taken issue with the claim that there are "missing men." One philosopher asks how, if we accept that there are missing men, there could be missing women in those countries in which the sex birth ratio matches the sex ratio in the whole population.[76] The answer is simple: a ratio is only a ratio, and tells us nothing about absolute numbers. While it is true that we have independent reason for thinking that there are missing women, my argument shows that we can be less sure about how many (million) missing women there are. This is because we cannot treat the 1.05 to 1 female–male ratio as baseline, given that we know this ratio arises through the deaths of males. More men die violently, both in war and elsewhere, and non-violently in greater numbers and at younger ages. But there is another reason why the 1.05 to 1 female–male ratio cannot be treated as baseline. There may be missing women even in societies with such a ratio (just as there may be missing men in societies where the sex ratio in the general population matches that at birth).

It has also been asked how "we know from a female–male ratio of 1.05 to 1 that *not enough* is being done to maintain the female–male birth ratio."[77] The female–male birth ratio, it will be recalled, is 0.95. A complete answer to this question obviously requires a judgment about "how much is enough" in distributive justice. That is clearly too big a question for me to answer here. However, this is as crucial for those who say that *not enough* is being done only to prevent the loss of women in those countries where the birth ratio is maintained, as it is for those who also notice the missing men.

I do not propose glib answers, and I certainly do not suggest that whatever research biases there may be against women should not be redressed.

On this score, a number of people advancing an inversion argument have exhibited some confusion. One pair of authors has argued that "the *reason* women live longer has nothing to do with healthcare research dollars being thrown their way."[78] But this ignores that there is a difference between spending on health*care*[79] and spending on healthcare *research*.

If we turn now to the question of healthcare *research*, I need not deny that women are or were neglected. All I have claimed is that even if women are neglected in some ways, there are other ways in which men have been neglected. One example I gave in Chapter 4 is the disproportionate amount of money spent on breast cancer research over lung cancer research. In response to this example it has been suggested that "a fair number of *men* are struck by breast cancer."[80] This is an astounding response, because men account for less than 1% of all cases of breast cancer,[81] and thus this point makes utterly no difference to my argument if one takes into account all the figures I provided.

Some people believe that it is impossible for both women and men to be neglected in healthcare and healthcare research. My point, however, is that there are different ways in which each sex can be neglected and disadvantaged. Less might be spent on research into and care for women than men with condition X. However, more might be spent on some female-specific condition, Y, than is spent on some other condition, Z, that affects disproportionately large numbers of men. The net neglect is hard to calculate only by looking at overall expenditure. This is, in part, because a disadvantaging of one sex often does not procure an advantage to the other. For example, additional increments of research funding need not increase benefit. Extra healthcare may sometimes produce no benefit or even induce iatrogenic suffering. These are complex matters. What we do know, however, is that male life expectancy lags behind that of women, even when improved social conditions lead to increases in life expectancy for both sexes. This suggests that the current distribution of (healthcare) resources favors women more than men in those societies where the sex ratio at birth reverses.[82]

Imprisonment

A kind of inversion argument has also been advanced to recast the leniency females experience in the criminal justice system as an advantage to males. According to this argument the "court's more lenient treatment of women reflects the interests of white males."[83] In explanation of this, it is said that if "women were routinely sentenced to prison, the maintenance of white male hegemony would be threatened because unpaid family labor performed by females would be eliminated."[84]

This is entirely implausible. First, even in societies with high imprison-ment rates, and *a fortiori* in those with low imprisonment rates, imprisoning women whenever one would imprison a man for the same crime would not vaguely approach *eliminating* unpaid family labour performed most often by women. It would be only a marginal reduction. It is hard to see how that could really threaten the purported hegemony. Moreover, the argument would have us believe that the "hegemonic white males" would prefer to avoid this marginal reduction in unpaid family work to a comparable reduc-tion in their *own* chances of being incarcerated. To this it might be objected that the most powerful males are much less likely than less powerful males to be imprisoned and thus they can have it both ways. A reduction in their own, already low chance of imprisonment is not as valuable to them as the potential loss of unpaid family labor. But the problem with this argument is that the most powerful males are typically married to more powerful females who themselves are less at risk than poorer women of being imprisoned. It really is hard to believe that the most hegemonic classes are so concerned about the unpaid family labor of disempowered women and what this means to disempowered men.[85]

The inversion argument is a crass form of partiality. It presents *all* sex inequality as disadvantaging primarily or only women. This is unfair to those males who are the primary victims of some forms of sex discrimina-tion. It also strategically compromises the case against those forms of dis-crimination that do in fact disadvantage women more than men. Unfairly presenting the relative disadvantages of different practices leads to one's legitimate claims being taken less seriously.[86]

The Costs-of-Dominance Argument

A second kind of argument suggests that although there may indeed be dis-advantages to being a male, these are the costs of dominance – the costs that come with being the privileged sex.[87] Unlike the inversion argument, the costs-of-dominance argument does not deny that the costs of being a man are *themselves* actually disadvantages. Instead, this argument recognizes that they are indeed costs, but suggests that they should be seen merely as the by-products of a dominant position and thus not evidence of discrimina-tion against males. In the words of one author, it "is a twist of logic to try to argue ... that because there are costs in having power, one does not have power."[88]

James Sterba is one proponent of the costs-of-dominance argument. He is prepared to acknowledge that some men bear greater burdens than others – the "cannon fodder" in a war bear most of the costs, while the "generals" gain, with relatively little cost, the prestige that accrues to members of the military. He denies, however, that those who are "cannon fodder" are discriminated against on the basis of their sex. This, he says, is "because the overall design of a patriarchal society is to benefit men generally."[89]

It is unfortunate that Professor Sterba has used the language of "design," because he clearly cannot mean what this word suggests – namely that world has been consciously planned and molded to the benefit of males. What he does mean is that men and boys are advantaged while women and girls are disadvantaged by the arrangements that have emerged and developed over centuries, in both more and less conscious ways. On this view the overall structure of a patriarchal society is such as to benefit men generally.[90]

The problem, however, is that this assumes that there is a patriarchal state of affairs and that this benefits males. But whether the more liberal societies are patriarchal and whether they benefit males are points of contention. One cannot read the evidence of advantage and disadvantage on the assumption that patriarchy obtains. The claims (or denials) that a society is patriarchal and that it advantages males must be inferred from the evidence. Advocates of the costs-of-dominance argument must demonstrate the existence of patriarchy and that males are advantaged. It is not sufficient simply to assume that these claims are true.

Part of the problem is that it is unclear what exactly is meant by "patriarchy." "Patriarchy" is commonly said to obtain when males hold power. But the claim that "males hold power" is crucially ambiguous between (a) "(all or most of) those who hold power are males" and (b) "(all or most) males hold power (relative to all or most women)." While the former is true,[91] we clearly cannot infer the latter from this. Indeed, it is the latter that may well be false in many societies in the contemporary developed world.

A second problem for advocates of the costs-of-dominance argument is that even though all societies are still patriarchal in the first sense, it does not follow that males cannot be unfairly discriminated against. If some male elite holds power while the vast majority of males are disadvantaged in certain ways, this male disadvantage would be the cost not of these males' own dominance but of some other males' dominance. But that is not the kind of dominance cost that can refute a complaint of second sexism. If "plebeian" males, because they are (plebeian) *males*, bear certain costs of "alpha" males' dominance then they are the victims of discrimination in much the same way that those females who bear other costs of alpha males' dominance are the victims of discrimination. That it is only *plebeian* males who bear these costs does not undermine the point that it is plebeian *males* and not females who bear these particular costs. They are being discriminated against on the basis of their sex *and* class (or some other such factor). Advocates of the costs-of-dominance argument ignore this possibility. This is odd, given how often feminists have noted that discrimination on the grounds of sex and class can intersect, even though they have typically only referred to cases where the sex in question is female.

It might be suggested that I am shifting from claims about discrimination against some men to claims about discrimination against men collectively.[92] However, to make my case that there is a second sexism, at least as I have defined it, all I need to show is that there are (some) men who are wrongly discriminated against because they are men. To make my case that the second sexism is an extensive problem, all I need to show, as I have shown, is that there are *many* men who are the victims of such discrimination. I do not need to claim that all or even most men are the victims of such discrimination, although it may well be true that, at least at some point in their lives, most or all men are. Thus I do not infer from the fact that "Johnny is discriminated against because he is a male" that there "is discrimination against males (collectively)."[93] I infer from the fact that there are millions of Johnnies who are discriminated against in multiple ways because they are male that there is an extensive second sexism.

Underlying the objection against a purported shift from talk about individual men to men collectively may be thought to be an implicit appeal to an alternative conception of sexism that I discussed in the Introduction (and to which I shall return in the concluding chapter). According to this view, sexism is not merely wrongful discrimination but embodies a further element of domination, subordination or oppression. On this view, it might be suggested, it is insufficient to show that males are the victims of wrongful discrimination. One must also show that they are subordinated, dominated or oppressed. The assumption is that this further element is missing in the case of males, but not females.

There are a few things to note about this argument. First are some reminders about work I did in the introductory chapter. There I argued against this alternative conception of sexism. For those who were unconvinced by those arguments, I also noted that very little rests on how we understand sexism. While I think that males *are* the victims of a second sexism, I am much more interested in convincing people that males are the victims of serious wrongful discrimination that is worthy of opposition. To show that I certainly do not need to demonstrate that there is discrimination against males "collectively." Thus, to those who are concerned about the semantics of "sexism," I would urge a focus on the moral issues rather than the semantic ones.

Finally, it is worth noting that the argument about a purported shift from some men to men collectively appeals not only to an alternative conception of sexism, but also to a claim that women are but men are not oppressed, for example. I shall take up that claim in the concluding chapter.

Despite my general rejection of the costs-of-dominance argument, there are some situations in which it would be sound. Where a cost really is inseparable from one's position of power or (overall) advantage, then it is true that the cost is not a cause for complaint *on behalf of* the power-holder, at least if the power is held voluntarily.[94] However, it does not follow from this that all the costs experienced by males really are connected to their having power or privilege. For example, although the exemption-exclusion of women from the military is the result of females' perceived military incapacity, it is hardly obvious that male power would be impossible without this exemption-exclusion. For example, the rich have often succeeded in preserving (or even enhancing) their privilege, while the poor, for various reasons, have endured a disproportionately heavy military burden. Thus, it need not be the case that those with the power in a society must be those who bear arms. Bearing arms is dirty work, and there is no shortage of examples of underdogs being forced or enticed to do the dirty work.[95]

Similarly, it is far from clear that the greater corporal punishment inflicted on males is an inevitable by-product of male power. Boys are not hit because they are dominant or will someday become dominant. It is not a consequence of current or future dominance. Nor is it a cause of dominance. If physical punishment of boys were, in some way, training for the dominant positions they will occupy, then we would expect feminists to clamor for similar treatment of girls. Yet they do not. The same is true for other ways in which pain is inflicted on boys, including circumcising them without anesthetic.

The higher drop-out rates of males from schools and the fact that a smaller proportion of them than women now earn tertiary degrees are not costs of dominance. The males who are dropping out of school are not dropping out because they are dominant. It is not even clear that they are dropping out because other males are dominant.

It is sometimes alleged that the higher rates of male suicide, the tendency of males to die younger than women, the greater chance that men have of being killed, becoming alcoholic and so forth are side effects of the stresses that come with privilege.[96] It might be argued in response that alleged privileges that have these consequences are not real privileges for those who succumb. Although some men may benefit, many others experience only the costs. However, even if it were true that these were costs of genuine privilege, it would not follow that these costs were *inevitable* results. Those with power can divert resources in order to combat such side effects of their power, thereby further improving their position. Insofar as that is the case, the costs are not costs of dominance, but costs of not being dominant enough or of not using one's dominance for one's own benefit.

It might also be suggested that the failure to take sexual assault of males seriously and the lesser tolerance of male homosexuality are both products of patriarchy. More specifically, it might be claimed that because males are dominant they are in denial about their own vulnerability to sexual assault, and they are more intolerant of those males who deviate from the male gender role. However, both these suggestions are implausible.

Dominant groups are often fully aware of their own vulnerabilities and they routinely use their power to protect themselves from those vulnerabilities. That is exactly why power is needed and wanted. Insofar as dominant groups are not aware of their vulnerabilities, the resultant lack of protection is not a cost of dominance, but a cost of either ignorance or self-deception.

It is similarly implausible to think that greater intolerance of male homosexuality is a cost of male dominance. While gay men might depart from gender roles (in their choice of sexual partner, even if not in other ways), they thereby remove themselves from competition with heterosexual males for access to females. They should thus be *less* threatening than lesbians who, in choosing other females as sexual partners, are either in competition for access to females or make themselves sexually inaccessible to dominant males. Heterosexual males could, of course, resort to legal prohibitions on lesbianism or, if that fails, to rape, but that is exactly why it is so surprising that most energy is focused on targeting male homosexuals. And if it is suggested that heterosexual males are fearful that homosexuals will target them, then we should expect homosexual sexual assault to be taken more seriously than it is. In many times and places, homosexual rape has been treated no more seriously than consensual homosexual acts.

Kenneth Clatterbaugh denies that costs of dominance need be "inevitable" or "necessary,"[97] as I have suggested they must be if the costs-of-dominance argument is to work. But the problem for this view is that insofar as these costs are indeed avoidable, one wonders why those with power have not avoided them. If it is indeed within their power to avoid these costs, and they do not, then they are apparently not wielding their power to their own exclusive advantage and the disadvantage of others. This suggests that the male wielding of power is not incompatible with the wielding of power to female advantage. If, by contrast, they do not have the power to avoid the costs, then we must question whether they are as powerful as they are alleged to be – whether they have as much power as they are said to have. Either way, being the victim of discrimination is compatible with wielding (some) power.

A further problem for the costs-of-dominance argument is that it is curious that as male power has surely (and appropriately) diminished in western democracies, the costs of being male have (inappropriately) increased, not decreased. For example, whereas a century or more ago men were almost guaranteed, following divorce, to gain custody of their children, today they are at a distinct disadvantage. Because custody practices were better for men when they really did enjoy more power than they do now, it is clear that the current custody biases are not inevitable by-products of male power. Defenders of the cost-of-dominance argument want to have it both ways. They want to claim that when fathers routinely get custody of their children in highly patriarchal societies, this constitutes discrimination against women.

Yet when male power declines and women routinely gain custody of children after divorce, that the male disadvantage is a product of male
dominance.

Thus, although it is true that the powerful cannot complain about having
to bear the costs of that power, at least if they have chosen to have power, it
does not follow that all disadvantages they suffer are such costs. Even if it is
true that men in our society enjoy overall advantage – and I am not con-
vinced that this is true any longer in the developed world[98] – it can still be
true that they suffer genuine discrimination that is not an inevitable consequence of their privilege.

Now some will ask why those who hold most positions of power in a
society could be the victims of pervasive discrimination. Why would those
with power allow themselves to be treated in this way? There are a number
of possible answers.[99] It is possible that those purported to have power do
not have it. It is possible that males in western democracies simply no longer
have the power that many feminists attribute to them. However, there is an
alternative answer even if we assume, for the sake of argument, that males
do still hold power. Insofar as discrimination is indirect and unintentional,
those who hold positions of power may not recognize it for what it is. They
might take their disadvantage to be inevitable, perhaps because they share
the very prejudices that contribute to their own disadvantage. A captain and
officers clearly hold the powerful positions on a ship. Yet when it sinks and
they adhere to and enforce a policy of saving "women and children" the
social conventions lead them to use their power in a way that advantages
women and disadvantages men (including themselves).

The Distraction Argument

Not all those opposed to highlighting the second sexism will deny that men
are sometimes the victims of wrongful sex discrimination. However, those
who are willing to grant this may argue that attention to the second sexism
will distract us from the much greater discrimination against women. On
this view, until there is parity between the extent of disadvantage suffered by
men and women, we must devote our attention and energies to opposing the
greater discrimination – that experienced by females.

Tom Digby, for example, claims that using the term "sexism" to refer to
the disadvantaging of men, "erases a history of one group exercising control
over another group"[100] and "drains the concept of its political potency for
diminishing or eliminating the historical control of women by men."[101]

The distraction argument presupposes that the position of women is
worse than that of men. I do not deny this, if it is a global or historical claim
that is being made. In most places at most times, women are and have been

generally worse off than men. This is because the traditional gender roles for women are much more restrictive than for men, and most of the world's human population continues to live in societies that are characterized by traditional gender roles. This is not to deny that there are many men who are worse off than many women, even in those societies. Instead, it is to make only a claim about the relative positions of men and women *in general* in those societies.

But what about contemporary liberal democracies, from whose ranks most feminists are drawn and to which substantial (but not exclusive) feminist attention is devoted? In the light of the significant inroads against sexism made in such societies, as well as the examples of the second sexism that I have outlined, are women worse off than men in such countries? I shall address this question in the concluding chapter. However, the question of which sex suffers the greater discrimination is simply irrelevant to the question of whether attention should be given to the second sexism. This brings me to my first response to the distraction argument.

Wrongful sex discrimination is wrong, irrespective of the victim's sex. It is not only the most severe manifestations of injustice that merit our attention. If it were wrong to focus on lesser forms of discrimination when greater forms were still being practiced, then we would have to attend to racial discrimination (and its legacy) rather than sex discrimination, at least in those places in which racial discrimination is worse than sex discrimination.[102] Moreover, where one opposed sex discrimination, one would have to ignore some forms of sex discrimination if one accepted the view that only the most serious injustices deserve our attention. Not all forms of sexism are equally severe. Using the word "man" to refer to people of both sexes, for example, is not as damaging as clitoridectomy or even as unfair as unequal pay. Feminists who think that we should devote our energies only to eliminating the worst forms of sex discrimination would be committed to a very restricted agenda. But if both major and minor forms of discrimination against women deserve attention, why should major forms of discrimination against men not be equally deserving of concern? How can it be acceptable to want an end to purportedly sexist speech while males die because of their sex?

If one is opposed to injustice, then it is injustice that counts, not the sex of the victim. Even if it is the case that in general women are the greater victims of sex discrimination, it is still the case that some men suffer more from sex discrimination than some women. A young man on the *Titanic* who is denied a place in a lifeboat because of his sex is worse off than the young woman whose life is saved because of her sex. A young man conscripted and killed in battle is worse off than his sister who is not. It does not matter here that *had* he survived, the man would have had greater access to higher education or would have earned more. If he is made to lose his life because of his sex and she has her life spared because of her sex, then this man is the greater victim of sex discrimination than this woman. Countering sex discrimination against men will remove some relative advantages that women enjoy, but that is fair in the same way that it is fair that countering sex discrimination against women removes relative advantages that men enjoy.

There is a second important response to the distraction argument. Far from distracting one from those discriminatory practices that disadvantage females, confronting the second sexism can help undo discrimination against women. Earlier I noted that the kernel of truth in the inversion argument is that the first and second sexisms are closely, albeit contingently, related to one another. Opposing discrimination against one sex is similarly related to confronting discrimination against the other sex. The very attitudes which prevent women from being conscripted and from being sent into combat, thereby discriminating against those males and protecting those women who have no wish to be part of the military, also favor those males but disadvantage those females who desire a military career and who do not want to be excluded from combat. Similarly, the stereotypes of men as aggressive and violent and of women as caring and gentle lead to only males being sent into battle but also entail assumptions that it is women who must bear primary responsibility for child care.

Or consider the small proportion of women amongst the victims of gross human rights violations in places like apartheid-era South Africa. This is at least partly attributable to gender roles that discouraged women from engaging in political activity, especially dangerous political activity in which men were encouraged or expected to participate.[103] Although these gender roles had beneficial effects for women in protecting them from the violence of adversaries, these same gender roles disadvantaged women in other regards. The "women-and-children-first" mentality is another, related example. It disadvantages men in life-and-death situations but has obvious disadvantages for women in other circumstances. Women are protected, to be sure, but in the same way and for relics of the same reasons that children are – they are assumed to be weak and to be unable to look after themselves. Similarly, the battered-woman-syndrome defence, under which the criminal law (at least in the United States) allows evidence of abuse of women, but not of men, to constitute an exemption from criminal responsibility, has the effect of reaffirming prejudices about women as lacking the capacity for rational self-control.[104]

A third response to the distraction argument is that it clearly has a political rather than philosophical agenda. It is more concerned about the political potency of recognizing the second sexism than about its philosophical status. Whatever one might think about the political duties of philosophers, these should certainly not override the philosophical tasks of honestly and accurately understanding and representing the issues, even if this is not politically convenient. Truth, and the philosophically sophisticated pursuit of it, should not be sacrificed in the name of a political cause.

Defining Discrimination

A final way to deny the existence of the second sexism is to object to the conceptions of discrimination and sexism that I have employed. In Chapter 1 I defended my understanding of *sexism* against alternatives to which some feminists appeal. Thus I shall here consider objections to my understanding of "discrimination" and connect those with my earlier discussion about the meaning of "sexism."

Kenneth Clatterbaugh suggests that one should not "accomplish by definition what" one needs "to accomplish by argument."[105] Clearly whether some phenomenon constitutes "discrimination" or "sexism" rests on how exactly one understands these terms, but it involves much more – evidence of disadvantage, unfairness and wrongful treatment. It is those offering the definitional objections to the second sexism who could be accused of defining the second sexism out of existence – trying to accomplish by definition what they need to accomplish by argument.

Tom Digby denies not only that men are victims of sexism, but also that they are victims of discrimination. His discussion of what discrimination and sexism are is provided in the context of an evolutionary account of the male sex role. We can accept this account and then agree with him that we should "not assume that a pattern or strategy that has evolved is thereby justified."[106] However, this should make us more reluctant than he is to appeal to the evolutionary context in determining what is and is not discrimination or sexism.[107]

Following Adrian Piper, Professor Digby distinguishes between *cognitive* and *political* discrimination. The former, commendable, form of discrimination is "to distinguish veridically between one property and another, and to respond appropriately to each."[108] The latter is

> what we ordinarily understand by the term "discrimination" in political contexts: A manifest attitude in which a particular property of a person which is irrelevant to judgments of that person's intrinsic value or competence ... is seen as a source of disvalue or incompetence; in general a source of inferiority.[109]

It is cognitive discrimination that Tom Digby thinks is operative when only men are forced to become warriors. This, he says, is because such a policy "responds to the different properties most men and most women have that determine their contributions to reproduction"[110] and recognizes that men are reproductively more expendable. Given this, why would Professor Digby not also judge ways in which women were discriminated against to be merely cognitive discrimination, if these ways of discriminating were rooted in a recognition that women are reproductively less expendable? His answer, it seems, is that in the political context, male advantage substantially outweighs male disadvantage.[111] Males, he says, have power and therefore the ability to distribute benefits. Moreover, manhood, he says, "has been valorized far more than womanhood."[112] This is why he thinks that females, but not males, can be the victims of political discrimination.

Notice, however, that the definition of political discrimination is not uncontroversial. This is partly because of the vagueness surrounding the notions of "disvalue" and "inferiority." Some "political" discrimination presupposes not the inferiority of the group but its alleged superiority – such as superior Jewish business acumen or superior sexual prowess of blacks. If we reconceive these purported attributes as an inferiority of some other kind – say a *moral* inferiority – then the notion of "inferiority" becomes very fluid. Much that Tom Digby would want to rule out as discrimination could then be deemed to be discrimination. For instance, the alleged superior strength and aggression of men, which leads to their being forced into the military, could be deemed to be morally inferior features.[113] By extension one could say that the exclusion of women from the military is not a reflection of perceived inferiority or disvalue, but rather of their perceived superiority and greater (reproductive?) value. Even on a pretty standard sense of "disvalue" we might explain society's greater willingness to expend male lives as a disvaluing of male life. Indeed, even if manhood is valorized more than womanhood, women are arguably valued more than men, at least in some societies.[114]

This may be why Professor Digby is keen to add to Adrian Piper's definition another condition for political discrimination – that "it has the effect of disempowering persons who fall within the target group – and empowering the group perpetrating the discrimination."[115] But the criterion of (dis)empowerment is also both ambiguous and controversial.[116] It is ambiguous between (a) an overall (dis)empowerment and (b) a (dis)empowerment in one respect. Men may not be disempowered overall by being forced into the military, but they are disempowered with respect to whether they enlist.

In response, perhaps it will be insisted that the first interpretation – overall (dis)empowerment – is the correct one. If so, his argument would here intersect with those who deny that males are the victims of sexism even if they *are* the victims of discrimination. There are many such views, but what they have in common is the claim that sexism consists not merely of wrongful discrimination on the grounds of people's sex. It involves something more, such as domination, subordination or oppression. I argued against these views in Chapter 1 and shall not rehearse those arguments here.

If I am correct that women in the contemporary developed world are not oppressed or subordinated, and others are correct that oppression or subordination is a condition for sexism, then, assuming that males are not oppressed or subordinated, neither males nor females are the victims of sexism in those parts of the world. Moreover, if Marilyn Frye is correct that it is a central claim of feminism that women are oppressed, then feminism no longer has an agenda in those parts of the world and should focus exclusively elsewhere. Many feminists are unlikely to agree to either of these points, in which case they must allow the possibility that males can also be the victims of sexism.

Notes

1 I add the qualification "very," because some do seem to want us to step back from some of the most recent developments, but even they do not recommend a return to the arrangements of a century ago.
2 Kenneth Clatterbaugh erroneously attributes to me the claim that the inversion argument is rarely used ("Benatar's alleged second sexism," *Social Theory and Practice*, 29(2), April 2003, p. 212) when, in fact, what I am saying is that such an argument is rarely *explicitly* presented. The *practice* of inversion is common, however.
3 Cynthia Enloe, "Some of the best soldiers wear lipstick," in Alison M. Jaggar (ed.), *Living with Contradictions: Controversies in Feminist Social Ethics*, Boulder, CO: Westview Press, 1994, p. 603; my emphasis.
4 Ibid.
5 I made the distinction explicitly in "The second sexism," *Social Theory and Practice*, 29(2), April 2003, pp. 177–210. Yet my respondents ignored the distinction in order to advance an inversion argument. For example, James Sterba notes how and why women are *excluded* from combat (where there is an all-volunteer force) and then asks how this could possibly be a form of discrimination against men. (James Sterba, "The wolf again in sheep's clothing," *Social Theory and Practice*, 29(2), April 2003, p. 222.) Carol Quinn and Rosemarie Tong also suggest that the "first sexism" explains the *exclusion* of women from combat. (Carol Quinn and Rosemarie Tong, "The consequences of taking the second sexism seriously," *Social Theory and Practice*, 29(2), April 2003, pp. 238, 241.)
6 Professor Sterba unfairly attempts to undermine my genital excision analogy by comparing it not with conscription but with voluntary military service – *involuntary* excisions are compared with *voluntary* enlistment. Professor Sterba also suggests that the analogy breaks down because female genital excision, where it is practiced, is strongly supported by men and this explains why there is female support for it. ("The wolf again in sheep's clothing," pp. 224–225.) These kinds of claims are hard to verify. Those women who support the practice point to many reasons other than being marriageable – including affirmation of the girl herself and her initiation into the (adult) community. I am not suggesting that we

take these claims at face value. I am suggesting only that we be as cautious in our judgments of allegedly male-affirming claims that support male-only conscription and combat. Male support for male-only conscription and combat may be explained (at least in part) by female endorsement of that conception of masculinity that underpins male-only conscription and combat. For more about cultural biases in judgments about female genital cutting, see Michael Benatar and David Benatar, "Between prophylaxis and child abuse: the ethics of neonatal circumcision," *American Journal of Bioethics*, 3(2), Spring 2003, pp. 35–48.

7   James Sterba, "The wolf again in sheep's clothing," p. 223, n. 10. The latter condition, presumably, is to exclude those countries, such as Switzerland, which conscript males but which are unlikely to enter a war.

8   Ibid., p. 223.

9   Kenneth Clatterbaugh, "Benatar's alleged second sexism," pp. 215–216.

10 For further details about which countries still conscript, please see Chapter 2.

11 For example, Carol Quinn and Rosemarie Tong say: "We speculate that, in the same way that many U.S. women, continue to choose to be wives and mothers (full or part-time) despite the fact that they are free to live their lives entirely in the public world … many men would continue to enlist in the military and fight voluntarily even if they were not required to do so." (Carol Quinn and Rosemarie Tong, "The consequences of taking the second sexism seriously," p. 241.)

12 Ibid.

13 Conscription is itself evidence of unwillingness to enlist and fight. If most men would join the military voluntarily, conscription would not be necessary. Men are conscripted because without being forced to join the military, relatively few would. Joshua Goldstein makes this and a related point. (Joshua Goldstein, *War and Gender*, Cambridge: Cambridge University Press, 2001, p. 253.)

14 Judith Hicks Stiehm, "The protected, the protector, the defender," in Alison M. Jaggar (ed.), *Living with Contradictions*, p. 585.

15 Ibid.

16 Ibid.

17 Ibid, p. 583.

18 Adam Jones, *Gender Inclusive*, London: Routledge, 2009, pp. 115–116.

19 Ibid., p. 116.

20 Ibid., p. 117.

21 Ibid., p. 271.

22 Ibid. For more on Amnesty International's gender bias, see also ibid., p. 274; and David Buchanan, "Gendercide and human rights," in Adam Jones (ed.), *Gendercide and Genocide*, Nashville: Vanderbilt University Press, 2004, pp. 145–146, 149.

23 Adam Jones, "Gender and genocide in Rwanda," in Adam Jones (ed.), *Gendercide and Genocide*, p. 112.

24 Ronit Lentin (ed.), *Gender and Catastrophe*, London: Zed Books, 1997, p. 4.

25 Quoted by R. Charli Carpenter, "'Women, children and other vulnerable groups': gender, strategic frames and the protection of civilians as a transnational issue," *International Studies Quarterly*, 49, 2005, pp. 295–334, at p. 323.

26 Ibid., p. 325.

27 Deborah L. Rhode, *Speaking of Sex: The Denial of Gender Inequality*, Cambridge, MA: Harvard University Press, 1997, p. 109.

28 Ibid.

29 Ibid.

30 The irony here is that she accuses those who list examples of discrimination against males as being "highly selective." (Ibid., p. 230.)

31 Denise A. Hines, Jan Brown and Edward Dunning, "Characteristics of callers to the domestic abuse helpline for men," *Journal of Family Violence*, 22, 2007, pp. 63–72. They report that 29.1% of men who were asked responded that they had been stalked by their wives. This study was published a decade after Professor Rhode's book and thus the objection is not that she ignored it, but that she offered untested claims and engaged in rationalizations.

32 Professor Rhode herself later says of sexual violence against and harassment of women that because "only a small number of abuses result in civil or criminal charges" we need in addition to legal proceedings also other strategies. Deborah L. Rhode, *Speaking of Sex*, p. 243.

33 Nadine Brozan, "Religious Circumcision in a Changing World," *New York Times*, October 19, 1998.

34 The ceremony for boys is called *brit mila* (the covenant of circumcision). Among the names given to the female ceremony are *brit bat* (the covenant of a daughter) and *hachnasat bat l'brit* (the entering of a daughter into the covenant). See, for example, "Berit Mila Program of Reform Judaism: Ceremonies for Girls," http://beritmila.org/Ceremonies%20for%20girls.html (accessed August 10, 2005).

35 See, for example, ibid.

36 For more on this see David Benatar, "Why do Jewish egalitarians not circumcise their daughters?" *Jewish Affairs*, 63(3), Chanuka 2008, pp. 21–23.

37 Michael Benatar and I argue that the failure to use an anesthetic is the biggest problem with neonatal circumcision. See our "Between prophylaxis and child abuse."

38 Although there is biblical, talmudic and *halachic* (that is, Jewish legal) foundation for allowing a woman to perform circumcision, tradition has dictated that ritual circumcisers are men.

39 Mike Weiss, "A Woman's Touch: Lillian Schapiro Is Charting New Territory as an Atlanta Mohelet," *Atlanta Jewish Times*, June 8, 2001. Online at http://atlanta.jewish.com/archives/2001/060801cs.htm (accessed August 15, 2005).

40 Ibid.

41 American Association of University Women, *Beyond the "Gender Wars": A Conversation about Girls, Boys, and Education*, Washington, DC: American Association of University Women, 2001, p. 4.

42 Ibid.

43 US Institute of Education Sciences, National Center for Education Statistics, "Fast Facts: What Is the Percentage of Degrees Conferred by Sex and Race?" Online at http://nces.ed.gov/fastfacts/display.asp?id=72 (accessed October 25, 2009).

44 American Association of University Women, *The AAUW Report: How Schools Shortchange Girls*, Washington, DC: American Association of University Women, 1992, pp. 19–20.

45 Paul Nichols and Ta-Chuan Chen, *Minimal Brain Dysfunction: A Prospective Study*, Hillsdale, NJ: Lawrence Erlbaum Associates, 1981.

46 Jacqueline Liederman, Lore Kantrowitz and Kathleen Flannery, "Male vulnerability to reading disability is not likely to be a myth: a call for new data," *Journal of Learning Disabilities*, 38(2), 2005, pp. 109–129.

47 Brenda V. Smith, "Watching me, watching you," *Yale Journal of Law and Feminism*, 15, 2003, p. 230, n. 22.

48 Ibid.

49 Nijole V. Benokraitis and Joe R. Feagin, *Modern Sexism: Blatant, Subtle and Covert Discrimination*, 2nd edn, Englewood Cliffs, NJ: Prentice-Hall, 1995, p. 40.

50 Notice, however, that outside the cinematic context, men are typically required to remove their shirts more often than women are. While the level of exposure is less for males, bodily modest males might feel a greater invasion than bodily immodest females. The asymmetrical expectations about when to uncover will disadvantage some men, just as the asymmetrical expectations to remain covered will disadvantage some females.

51 Jack Matthews, "A system rated NC-17," *Newsday* (Long Island, NY), November 22, 1992, p. 5.

52 Joel Feinberg, *Offense to Others*, New York: Oxford University Press, 1985, p. 134.

53 Ibid.

54 Some might suggest that one sense in which naked women are more exposed is that they are more likely to be raped. Nudity thereby poses a special vulnerability. But that is certainly not true on screen. A woman who is naked on the screen is not vulnerable to rape during her nudity (unless the on-set security is inadequate).

55 For a compelling demonstration of this see Sanford Braver, *Divorced Dads: Shattering the Myths*, New York: Jeremy P. Tarcher/Putnam, 1998.

56 Ibid., pp. 28–33.

57 Sanford Braver relates that a well-known demographer, commenting on his research, had said that "if the mother tells you one thing and the father tells you something else, then the father is a God-damned liar." (Ibid., p. 35.)

58 Ibid., pp. 33–34.

59 Ibid., pp. 42–45.

60 Ibid., pp. 45–53.

61 Lenore Weitzman, *The Divorce Revolution: The Unexpected Social and Economic Consequences for Women and Children in America*, New York: The Free Press, 1985, p. 323.

62 For an account of this, see Sanford Braver, *Divorced Dads*, pp. 59–62.

63 Ibid.

64 Ibid., p. 61.

65 Ibid., pp. 62–86.

66 Jean Drèze and Amartya Sen, *Hunger and Public Action*, Oxford: Clarendon Press, 1989, pp. 50–59; Amartya Sen, "More Than 100 Million Women Are Missing," *New York Review of Books*, December 20, 1990, pp. 61–66. The idea has been used by, amongst others, Martha Nussbaum and Jonathan Glover in

their edited volume *Women, Culture and Development*, Oxford: Clarendon Press, 1995, pp. 3, 33.

67 Amartya Sen, "More Than 100 Million Women Are Missing," p. 61.

68 Ibid.

69 John Rawls, *A Theory of Justice*, Oxford: Oxford University Press, 1973, p. 74.

70 Ronald Dworkin, "What is equality? Part 2: equality of resources," *Philosophy and Public Affairs*, 10(4), 1981, p. 314. Neither Professor Dworkin nor Professor Rawls is talking about inequalities in health or longevity, but their claims apply equally to these.

71 Cameron A. Mustard, Patricia Kaufert, Anita Kozyrskyj and Teresa Mayer, "Sex differences in the use of health care services," *New England Journal of Medicine*, 338, June 4, 1998, p. 1678.

72 Ibid.

73 Jennifer Haas, "The cost of being a woman," *New England Journal of Medicine*, 338, June 4, 1998, pp. 1694–1695.

74 Ibid., p. 1694.

75 Ibid., p. 1695.

76 James Sterba, "The wolf again in sheep's clothing," p. 231.

77 Ibid.; my emphasis.

78 Carol Quinn and Rosemarie Tong, "The consequences of taking the second sexism seriously," p. 242; their emphasis.

79 Professors Quinn and Tong do also consider evidence about ways in which women are neglected in health*care*.

80 Carol Quinn and Rosemarie Tong, "The consequences of taking the second sexism seriously," pp. 242–243

81 This statistic is contained in the source provided by Professors Quinn and Tong: www.cancer.gov/cancerinfo/pdq/treatment/malebreast/patient. Unfortunately, this page no longer exists. However, the same statistic can be found here: National Cancer Institute, "Male Breast Cancer Treatment: Incidence and Mortality," http://www.cancer.gov/cancertopics/pdq/treatment/malebreast/Health Professional (accessed June 15, 2011).

82 Professor Sterba claims that if "more females were dying off in societies that clearly were not discriminating against women" he would be as unperturbed as he is about the current female–male ratio in those countries where it is 1.05 : 1. But this begs the question. He assumes that in these countries the higher male mortality rate is *clearly* not the result of some kind of discrimination against males. But this is the very point of contention. I have argued that there *is* (indirect and unintentional) discrimination. He recognizes discrimination in sex ratios when the victims are female but not when they are male. Therefore, I am not "flailing against an imaginary opponent" (James Sterba, "The wolf again in sheep's clothing," p. 232).

83 This view is mentioned, even if not endorsed, by Gayle S. Bickle and Ruth D. Peterson, "The impact of gender-based family roles on criminal sentencing," *Social Problems*, 38(3), 1991, pp. 372–394, at p. 373.

84 Ibid.

85 While, in the United States, white women are less likely to be incarcerated than black women, white is not equivalent to "empowered" and it is poor and

disempowered whites who are more likely to become entangled with the criminal justice system.

86 Paralleling the little boy who cried "wolf," this is a case of what we might call the little girl who cried "wolf-whistle." (Being under the threat of a wolf is a bad thing, but so is saying one is under such threat when one is not. Being subjected to sexual harassment, exemplified here by the wolf-whistle, is a bad thing, but so is falsely saying that one is or was subjected to such harassment.)

87 This view is taken by Kenneth Clatterbaugh, "Are men oppressed?" in Larry May, Robert Strikwerda and Patrick D. Hopkins (eds), *Rethinking Masculinity: Philosophical Explorations in the Light of Feminism*, 2nd edn, Lanham, MD: Rowman & Littlefield, 1996, pp. 289–305, esp. pp. 299–300.

88 Ibid., p. 300.

89 James Sterba, "The wolf again in sheep's clothing," p. 229.

90 Tom Digby also makes this claim. See Tom Digby, "Male trouble: are men victims of sexism?" *Social Theory and Practice*, 29(2), 2003, pp. 247–273.

91 This is the claim for which Steven Goldberg argues. See his *Why Men Rule: A Theory of Male Dominance*, Chicago: Open Court, 1993, esp. p. 14.

92 Kenneth Clatterbaugh has raised this objection. See his "Benatar's alleged second sexism," pp. 215–217.

93 Ibid., p. 215.

94 An anonymous reviewer (of an earlier article on this topic) has kindly pointed out that this sort of argument might be applied against a view, mentioned earlier, that more healthcare resources should be directed to women in order to improve the quality of the extra years of life they have over men. Since the disadvantage (a lower quality of life in the extra years) is a cost of the advantage (the extra years of life) there is no ground for complaint according to this argument. More generally, insofar as disadvantages of being female are costs of their being protected against the disadvantages of being male, defenders of the costs-of-dominance argument might be forced to accept a comparable costs-of-protection argument. The obvious response is that many women might not want the protection if it comes at that cost, but the same can be said of many men who might want the purported dominance if it carries the costs it is said to carry. This is why the condition of voluntariness is crucial.

95 It is not always *viewed* as dirty work. Sometimes it is valorized and glorified, but one suspects that this may be a means to encouraging people to participate. Moreover, there is a division of labor within the military. In some contexts the officers have been drawn from higher social strata, but it is then the enlisted men rather than the officers who are assigned the worst tasks.

96 Some advocates of this view think that the burden of proof lies with those who would deny such connections. (See Kenneth Clatterbaugh, "Are men oppressed?" p. 300.) My own view is that when it comes to unequal and discriminatory treatment, the burden of proof lies with those who seek to defend or condone such treatment.

97 Kenneth Clatterbaugh, "Benatar's alleged second sexism," p. 218.

98 I shall argue for this in Chapter 7.

99   It will not suffice to say that because patriarchy is not an intentional plan, male dominance can have unintended side-effects. This is because, as I have shown, such purported side-effects, if unidentified, could be countered.

100 Tom Digby, "Male trouble," p. 265.

101 Ibid.

102 Lest it be suggested otherwise, there are at least some places where racial discrimination is worse than sex discrimination. Apartheid-era South Africa was one particularly obvious example. The legacy of racial discrimination is much worse than that of sex discrimination, both in contemporary South Africa and many other countries, including, the United States. On average, blacks in both places have shorter lives, less education and greater poverty than (non-black) women.

103 Truth and Reconciliation Commission of South Africa, *Truth and Reconciliation Commission of South Africa Report*, Cape Town: Truth and Reconciliation Commission, 1998, vol. 4, pp. 289–290.

104 See Anne M. Coughlin, "Excusing women," *California Law Review*, 82(1), January 1994, pp 1–93.

105 Kenneth Clatterbaugh, "Benatar's alleged second sexism," p. 211.

106 Tom Digby, "Male trouble," p. 257. Contrast what he says here with his claim that to "the extent that evolution of the male gender role has taken place on a biological level, the odds that male disadvantage can be ameliorated are greatly reduced (although it becomes all the more clear that the disadvantage is not unfair)" (p. 266). Would he say the same of the female gender role and female disadvantage?

107 He explains, for example, that men "have generally been advantaged relative to other men by being able to suspend their concern for the feelings, health, and lives of those men, but the consequences has been *dis*advantage for men as a group" (ibid., p. 258). But if we accepted this, then we could provide a similar account of how women have been advantaged relative to other women. By adopting the features of the traditional female role, perhaps thereby making themselves more attractive to males, some women have been advantaged relative to others, even though the consequences have been disadvantage for women as a group. Thus I cannot see how the evolutionary context helps us judge male disadvantage not to be the product of sexism if we continue to think that female disadvantage is the result of sexism.

108 Quoted by Tom Digby, "Male trouble," p. 259.

109 Ibid., p. 260. The distinction between cognitive and political discrimination is similar to but not identical with the distinction I drew in Chapter 1 between discrimination and unfair or wrongful discrimination – that is, between discrimination in the non-pejorative sense of differentiating, and the pejorative sense of treating or viewing them unfairly.

110 Ibid., p. 259.

111 This suggests that cognitive discrimination – a veridical discernment between properties – is not incompatible with political discrimination.

112 Tom Digby, "Male trouble," p. 260.

113 Professor Digby might deny that these features are deemed morally inferior by those who value the male gender role. However, at least some who value this

role do not regard it as *morally* better. Those of them who romanticize the female role may actually regard women as morally better – and therefore in need of protection by those who bear the moral risks and get their hands dirty.

114   To then suggest that valorizing rather than valuing is crucial is to make an ad hoc move to rule out some kinds of disadvantage as discrimination.

115   Tom Digby, "Male trouble," p. 260.

116   Laurence Thomas, in a personal communication, has noted that victims of racism (for example) may even be *em*powered in *some* ways by racism. The example he provides is that of a black man who inspires fear in a white woman. This power would be unwanted by many black men but, he says, some black men may revel in it.

6

Affirmative Action

What's good for the goose is good for the gander.

English idiom

When confronted with the suggestion that there is a second sexism, the first reaction of many people who had not previously contemplated that possibility is to suppose that the second sexism is constituted by affirmative action efforts favoring women. They imagine the complaint to be that males are discriminated against by those affirmative action policies and practices that aim to benefit women. Yet, as we have seen, affirmative action for females was not included in the catalogue of discrimination against males that I have presented.

In turning to affirmative action now, and devoting a chapter to discussing it, my aim is not primarily to add another form of discrimination to those already discussed. Instead my goal is to evaluate whether affirmative action is an appropriate response to sexism, whether of the first or second kind. Indeed, considering affirmative action as a response to the second sexism sheds interesting light on the morality of affirmative action policies and practices that favor females. My conclusion will indeed be that affirmative action in most but not all its forms is immoral and sometimes discriminates unfairly against males. Many feminist and other defenders of affirmative action for females will dislike this conclusion. The good news for them is that I similarly think that affirmative action is an inappropriate response to the second sexism and that such affirmative action would sometimes unfairly discriminate against females.

Affirmative action was first conceived as a policy to favor disadvantaged racial groups. However, females from non-disadvantaged racial groups have

The Second Sexism: Discrimination Against Men and Boys, First Edition. David Benatar.

also been the beneficiaries on the grounds that they are disadvantaged as women. While the issues and arguments relevant to race-based and sex-based affirmative action overlap considerably, they are not identical. Most important are the relative degrees of disadvantage. In countries such as the United States and South Africa, where affirmative action policies have been pursued, females of non-disadvantaged racial groups are considerably less disadvantaged than either males or females of disadvantaged racial goups. Indeed, as we have seen, the males of disadvantaged racial groups are often worse off than the females of the advantaged and often also the disadvantaged groups.

It is worth dwelling on this for a moment, because there is something deeply troubling about giving the same preferential treatment to females from privileged racial groups as to members of disadvantaged racial groups.[1] Members of racially disadvantaged groups often (but not always) live in deprived or even squalid social conditions, experiencing the attendant evils of such conditions. They often attend poor and inadequate schools and their parents may be unable to assist them with their homework or to provide the academic support that complements the formal education obtained in the classroom. Females from privileged racial groups, by contrast, usually live in comfortable and sometimes luxurious conditions, attend schools at least as good as their brothers and have parents who can provide the academic support and enrichment that promotes their capacity. These differences explain why, once formal obstacles to equality of opportunity are removed, females from advantaged racial groups are more likely to succeed than most of those from disadvantaged racial groups.

Obviously my focus in this chapter will be on sex-based rather than race-based affirmative action.[2] Sex-based affirmative action has been said to be necessary to correct three purported problems. First, there are disproportionately few females in various desirable professions and disciplines (such as engineering and mathematics). Second, even where women are better represented at the lower levels in some professional areas, they are under-represented at the senior levels. This is true in the most senior corporate positions, in academia and in parliaments throughout the free world. This is attributed to a "glass ceiling" – an invisible but purportedly real barrier to their rising, in significant numbers, to positions of authority. Third, women are, on average, paid less than men.

If the reasons for the first two disparities were, as was once the case, that women were formally prohibited from such pursuits or their numbers were restricted by quotas, then the response would be not affirmative action but rather the abolition of the formal restrictions. Thus affirmative action is a policy that is recommended when females are formally allowed to participate equally and yet their actual participation falls short of their proportion of the population.

Some action to eliminate or at least reduce the gender pay gap has also been proposed. Although this is not typically referred to as "affirmative action," it is nonetheless a form of affirmative action. Because women's lower pay is typically a function of the former two phenomena, the solution is usually thought to be via a response to them. For this reason, my focus will be on affirmative action as a response to the under-representation of women, both in certain professions and at senior levels. However, I shall also consider the application of this to the pay gap.

Both the under-representation of women in specific areas or positions and the pay gap give rise to two broad kinds of justification for affirmative action. The first is an argument about rectificatory justice. The idea is that although women may not be formally discriminated against any longer, they once were. It is also said that their under-representation in certain areas, and their lower pay, are an indication that they are being discriminated against in more subtle ways and that affirmative action is the way to rectify this. The second kind of argument is consequentialist. According to this argument, increasing the number of women in the relevant positions and increasing women's pay will have beneficial effects. Thus, irrespective of whether the current under-representation and lower pay are products of discrimination, we should employ measures to increase the number of females in those endeavors in which they are a minority and to reduce the pay gap. I shall examine each of these rationales in turn, but first it will be helpful to clarify what is meant by "affirmative action."

The phrase "affirmative action" is ambiguous. It can refer to a variety of different kinds of policy or practice. Its mildest form is what we might call "equal opportunity affirmative action." This form of affirmative action involves no preferential treatment. Women are not favored over men. Instead equal opportunity affirmative action aims to ensure that opportunities genuinely are equal and that any hidden and subtle obstacles to equality are exposed and removed.

One such impediment, it is said, results from traditional notions of what constitutes "being qualified." Defenders of affirmative action often argue that not only are these prejudicial to women, but they are also con-testable. Therefore, they argue, we need to rethink what it means to be "qualified."

A call for accountability in the standards that are set is entirely reasonable. However, those with competing views of what constitutes being (equally) qualified will have to justify their respective positions independently of whether a given conception yields the outcome they want to have produced. That is to say, the criteria for being qualified must be assessed on their own terms and not in terms of whether employing them leads to appointments of more women or more men. The question of who is qualified is distinct from the question how many people of each sex are qualified.

Even when the criteria of "being qualified" are assessed on their own terms (and not in terms of the gender outcome), there may be disagreement about what the appropriate criteria are.[3] There may also be disagreement about which impediments to equal pay are unfair. For example, it has been suggested that women, particularly those with children, want to have shorter commuting times to work than do men. This, it is said, limits the range of jobs available to women, which in turn "potentially leads to the crowding of women into those jobs available locally," which depresses women's wages.[4] Some argue that this is an unfair impediment to wage equality because women bear the bulk of child-rearing responsibilities and it is thus unfair to them if they are paid less because, as a result of their child rearing, they are constrained to take only jobs with a shorter commute. Others, however, argue that those willing to commute further will have a wider range of job options, including ones that pay more, and that it is not unfair if those willing to commute further are paid more.

Although there will be such disagreements, everybody would agree that any hidden barriers there might be to *fairness* should be removed. The disagreement is about *which* barriers are unfair – or, at least, sufficiently unfair that something should be done about them. Opponents of other forms of affirmative action are accordingly untroubled by equal opportunity affirmative action.[5]

All forms of affirmative action other than the equal opportunity form involve some kind of preference based on a person's sex. The preference in all (or almost all) actual cases is in favor of females. These forms of affirmative action are distinguished from one another on the basis of how much preference they accord women. Sometimes a person's sex is used as a tie-breaker between two candidates who are otherwise equally qualified. Sometimes a person's sex is accorded greater weight. And sometimes certain positions, or a proportion of positions, are set aside for women, as they are in (minimum) quotas. The more weight that is attached to a person's sex in admissions or hiring decisions, the more controversial the form of affirmative action. While all these forms of preference affirmative action apply most directly to the under-representation issue, they indirectly also affect the wage gap. This is because increasing the representation of women in certain positions would also reduce the wage gap.

Rectifying Injustice

There are two kinds of arguments that justify affirmative action policies on the grounds that they are necessary for rectifying injustice. One says that the injustices in need of rectifying are the product of past discrimination, while the other claims that the relevant injustices are the product of current, ongoing discrimination.

The past discrimination argument

Injustices should be rectified. The appropriate way to do this is to compensate those particular people who suffered the injustice (and to punish those who perpetrated it). An injustice done to a person is rectified by compensating that individual, rather than by compensating other individuals, even if those other individuals share some characteristic with the victim of injustice. This is true even if the shared characteristic was the basis for the discrimination against the individual who suffered the injustice. Herein lies the primary problem with affirmative action policies that appeal to the past discrimination argument and that grant preference to people on the basis of sex. They typically bestow benefits on some members of a group in response to past discrimination against other members of that group. That does not rectify injustice. Instead it recreates it.[6]

Those who think otherwise might do well to consider the application of the past discrimination argument to past instances of the second sexism. For example, given that males have borne the brunt of conscription in the past, should we rectify that injustice by conscripting only – or at least disproportionately many – women in those countries that retain conscription? Should those countries that do not currently conscript resolve to conscript only or disproportionately many women when conscription is next necessary? Some might answer these questions negatively because they think that this will compromise military effectiveness. I have responded to those arguments already (in Chapter 4), but the crucial issue here is that those people most likely to be impressed by the military effectiveness argument against conscripting only women are also those least likely to defend affirmative action policies at all. Those most likely to defend affirmative action for women are least likely to be impressed by the military effectiveness argument because they typically think that females could function as effectively or nearly as effectively as male soldiers. Those defending this view need to explain why past discrimination against women requires preferences for women today, whereas past discrimination against men does not require favoring men (by targeting more women than men for conscription). After all, women are even more under-represented in conscript forces than they are in those desirable positions for which defenders of sex-based affirmative action seek preferences for females.

It is true that defenders of affirmative action do not propose that women be forced into other positions. However, that is not a response to my thought experiment. Although men were not previously forced into those desirable positions to which defenders of affirmative action now want women to have preferred access, they *were* forced into the military. Thus the purported way to rectify the injustice resultant from that discrimination is to divert that burden to the opposite sex, which involves forcing women.

To clarify, I am not seriously recommending that women be conscripted *instead of* men or at greater rates than men. I raise the case to show how preposterous it is to think that one is rectifying an injustice caused by past discrimination against people of one sex by favoring a subsequent generation of people of the same sex. If conscription discriminated against men in 1916, we do not rectify that injustice by conscripting women instead of other men in 2016. The same is true in cases of discrimination against women. If women were excluded from professional positions in the past, we do not rectify that injustice by favoring other women today. Although women today share with the earlier victims of (anti-female) sexism the attribute of being female, we do not rectify the earlier injustice by favoring different individual women – women who were not the victims of the past sex discrimination. Put another way, injustices are rectified at the level of individuals rather than groups. Rectifying the injustices done to many members of a group has aggregative results for the group, but the rectification must be directed to those individuals who were the victims of injustice.

Of course, it is not always possible to rectify injustices. For example, most victims and perpetrators of past discrimination are now no longer alive and thus they cannot, respectively, be compensated or punished. However, when it is not possible to rectify injustice caused by past discrimination there is no point pretending that it can still be rectified.

Now it might be argued that past discrimination against members of a group can have lingering effects that impact on subsequent members of that group. In this way members of a group can be the victims of discrimination that took place much earlier, even before they were born. I do not think that preferential (as opposed to equal opportunity) affirmative action is an appropriate response even to these ongoing effects of past discrimination, but I shall not here say why this is the case. This is because defenders of sex-based affirmative action cannot appeal to the lingering effects of past discrimination in the way that defenders of race-based affirmative action can do so. This is because of the different kinds of discrimination to which women and blacks respectively were subjected. The kinds of discrimination against women in the past have not had the enduring effect on the opportunities of women today than much past discrimination against disadvantaged racial groups has had on most (but not all) current members of those groups. Many of those today who belong to racial groups that were discriminated against in the past continue to suffer severe ill-effects of that past discrimination. They often live deprived lives. The same is not true of females (from advantaged groups). The lingering *effects* of *past* discrimination are to be distinguished from lingering (present) discrimination. Until now I have been speaking about the former. I now turn to the latter.

The present discrimination argument

When the past discrimination argument fails, some defenders of affirmative action might wish to appeal to what I call the present discrimination argument. According to this argument, women are still being unfairly discriminated against, and an affirmative action policy that favors females is the way to rectify this. The evidence offered for the claim that women are still discriminated against is sometimes no more than the observation that they are under-represented in the sorts of positions mentioned earlier and that they earn less than men. Women, it is said, are about half of the adult population, and thus would, in the absence of discrimination, fill about half of these positions.

However, the inference from unequal outcomes to unfair discrimination is a problematic one. If the inference were a valid one then we could conclude that men are being unfairly discriminated against when they constitute more than half of those imprisoned or executed, or more than half of those who drop out of school or who die on the job. In these cases (almost) nobody leaps to the conclusion that males are unfairly discriminated against, even though males significantly exceed half of those whom these fates befall. While discrimination may account for some of the difference, as we saw in Chapter 4, much of the difference is attributable to other factors. Men commit more crimes, for example.

Similar caution is necessary when there are disproportionately few women in desirable positions or when women earn less than men. Discrimination against women is not the only explanation. Even to the extent that discrimination *is* the explanation, affirmative action may not be the way to rectify it. To show why this is so it will be helpful to distinguish four possible explanations for the fact that women have less than equal participation in various employment sectors and earn less:

(1)   discrimination in those specific sectors where women are under-represented;
(2)   discriminatory features of the wider society;
(3)   non-discriminatory sex differences;
(4)   some combination of the above.

Among the items to which the first explanation refers is implicit bias in hiring and promotion decisions. The claim here is that even those who are self-consciously committed to gender equality may have unconscious biases, which operate to the detriment of women. Females may be viewed, subconsciously, as less capable, and this leads to fewer of them being appointed. Another item to which the first explanation refers is the so-called "hostile environment." The idea here is that certain professional and other environments are hostile or at least unfriendly to women, thereby making those environments less attractive or unattractive to women. For example, they may have a very "masculine" ethos or require long or inflexible hours,[7] which do not fit well with the domestic duties that women disproportionately bear.

This last example connects the first explanation with the second. This is because, it is argued, the fact that women still bear the bulk of domestic duties is indicative of broader societal discrimination. This, however, is not the only way in which broader social discrimination is said to contribute to there being disproportionately few women in the sorts of positions under discussion. For example, it is often said that girls are raised to think that they are less suited to particular kinds of positions and thus they are less motivated to pursue them.

The third explanation claims that there are average differences between males and females that are not the product of discrimination and which do explain why males are found in disproportionately large numbers (and women in disproportionately small numbers) in some positions, and why men earn more on average. It is said, for example, that males, on average, are more assertive than women, that they respond more positively to competitive situations and display more dominance-seeking.[8] Men, it is said, are also inclined to take more risks, including professional risks,[9] and are less nurturing and empathic.[10]

These differences are said to explain why males are more likely to enter higher-paying professions and to advance up various hierarchies. Those who are more assertive, who thrive on competition and who seek status are more likely to seek (and win) political office, to rise up corporate and other ladders and to enter and succeed in fields that require drive. Risk-taking has a toll on those who lose, but it favors those who succeed. Insofar as these sex differences are the product of biology they do not constitute discrimination. They might be regarded as unfair in just the way that being born with or without some trait might be viewed as unfair – that is, losing out in the natural rather than the social lottery – but they cannot be regarded as unfair *discrimination*. Unfair discrimination may ensue, on some views, if due regard is not given for the unfairness of the natural lottery.

The fourth explanation of the under-representation of women in professions and positions of power, and derivatively their lower pay, is a combination of the previous three. It claims that sex differences play some part, but that discrimination does, too. This fourth explanation is the most plausible one. First, as I argued in Chapter 3, it is highly unlikely that human psychology is unaffected by human biology, and that *all* psychological traits, unlike physical traits, are equally distributed across both sexes. Those who think that psychological attributes are equally distributed need to explain why the over-representation of males in desirable positions is *fully* attributable to discrimination against females, but the over-representation of males in undesirable positions is not at all attributable to discrimination against males. Indeed, while this seems to be a position that some feminists do hold, they do not explain how it could be the case. They blame men for the fact that there are disproportionately few women in leadership positions, and they blame men for constituting the majority of those incarcerated. Men are at fault whether they are winning or losing.

Contrary to this view, (at least some) evolutionary psychologists claim that the greater successes and greater failures of men may well be related. Ambition, competitiveness, a desire for status and risk-taking can all contribute to a greater number of males at the extremes. Endorsement of this claim does not imply acceptance of the "costs-of-dominance" argument discussed in Chapter 5. Even if the greater successes and failures of males are related, it does not follow that the failures are the costs of dominance. This is because those who pay the costs are not those who are dominant, even if they happen to be members of the same sex.

The greater extremes characteristic of males might also be partially explained by the hypothesis that the distribution of *some* cognitive capacities, for example, is flatter among males than it is among females. That is to say, according to this hypothesis there are more males than females at the extremes of some cognitive capacities. Recollect, here, Helena Cronin's image, mentioned earlier, of there being, among males, both more "Nobels" and more "dumbbells."

These considerations suggest that the first and second explanations are probably not the sole explanations of the under-representation of women. It is not clear whether anybody holds the view that the third explanation fully accounts for the under-representation of women. Those who think that sex differences play a role do not typically think that biology explains the *full extent* of women's under-representation.[11] It is very likely, as I indicated in Chapter 3, that any biological differences between the sexes would be recognized and amplified by society. Thus social forces very probably play some role over and above any biological differences.

Among those who accept the fourth explanation, the disagreement is about how much of the difference is explained by biology and how much by social forces. The question of who is right is immensely difficult to determine with any precision. That, however, is partly why affirmative action is such a poor mechanism for dealing with whatever component is the product of discrimination. If the aim of affirmative action is to correct for discrimination and we do not know how much discrimination is taking place, we cannot tell how much of a corrective is required. Some feminists may suggest that we should nonetheless impose some counterbalance to whatever discrimination there is, even if we run the risk of overcompensating. However, there are a few problems with this suggestion.

Overcompensating would result in unfair discrimination in favor of some females and against some males. While not compensating at all would, given implicit bias against females, result in unfair discrimination in favor of some men and against some women, the difference is that affirmative action is an intentional policy favoring some over others. Faced with a choice, a policy of trying as hard as possible to avoid discrimination (even if one does so imperfectly) is arguably better than a policy of specifically trying to favor some people. The latter is more corrupting and more open to abuse. In other words, trying to give preference is more dangerous than trying not to give preference. The better one gets at not preferring, the closer one gets to fairness. By contrast, in the case of preferring, one gets closer to fairness to the extent that one is compensating for implicit bias, but then one gets further and further from fairness as one continues to give preference. Since one cannot accurately determine the extent of bias, the danger is that one will not know when one is becoming less and less fair.

Moreover, there is reason to think that the pressure in favor of preferential policies and practices will cause an excess of preference. As long as there are relatively few women in a given profession and the current concern for the position of women continues, there will be ongoing political incentives to attain a better balance of the sexes even if the residual difference is not a product of discrimination. Indeed that is exactly what those who accept the first and second explanations alone will be advocating. No affirmative action efforts will satisfy such people until any discrepancy is eliminated.[12]

Those who deny that affirmative action is the more dangerous option should consider whether they would recommend affirmative action to counter discrimination against men. Consider, for example, an affirmative action policy applicable to judges making custody decisions following divorce. Such a policy would be problematic because it would be inappropriate for judges consciously to favor fathers, even though we know that fathers are currently the victims of implicit bias in custody decisions. It is preferable for judges to work to overcome their biases rather than to replace them with new ones.

So far my focus has been on affirmative action as a corrective for direct, albeit unintentional and unconscious discrimination. Some people think that such discrimination explains both why women are under-represented in some employment sectors and why they are paid less. The evidence, however, does not support this (any more[13]). Consider the wage gap, for example. Once one controls for various crucial variables, one finds that the wage gap is negligible, if it exists at all.[14] The variables include how many hours people work (full-time work pays more than part-time work, and overtime is rewarded), how risky and unpleasant the work is and whether one is willing to commute longer distance to higher-paid positions.[15] Indeed, there is thus something misleading about reference to the pay gap. It is not that women are being paid less for doing the same jobs as men. They are doing different jobs.

Consider next the so-called glass ceiling. Several female clerks at one Fortune 500 company sued the company. They noted that the female proportion of staff promoted was less than the female proportion of the entry-level positions, and they alleged discrimination on these grounds. The company, mystified by the accusation, approached an independent consulting firm to conduct a study of its personnel practices. The study found that discrimination did not explain the imbalance.[16] For example, males had applied for promotion at a much greater rate than had females. Moreover, a higher proportion of women than men who applied were successful.[17] Roughly equal numbers of males and females were asked whether they were interested in promotion. However, a much larger proportion of the males who were asked responded affirmatively.[18] Men were also willing to give up more to obtain a promotion. For example, they were more willing to have a less than optimal shift assignment or to accept a transfer.[19]

There is also some evidence that gender imbalances among university academic staff are not attributable to discrimination. A study of Canadian universities showed that while women were under-represented, and especially at the higher levels, this was not a consequence of discrimination against females.[20] The study looked at the average age of people in each of the academic ranks and calculated when each cohort would have been appointed. This was then compared to the number of women earning PhDs immediately before that. It was found that "figures from the 1960s are consistent with there being a modest degree of discrimination against women during the hiring process at this time."[21] However, it was also found that "for all other ranks, the data are consistent with there being significant discrimination in favor of women and against men."[22] Indeed, "the discrepancy ... is much larger than the reverse discrepancy at the rank of full professor."[23]

There are also interesting differences between academic disciplines, with women even more under-represented in some disciplines. It is implausible to think that discrimination in university admissions explains why women are an especially small minority of engineering students, for example. Are we really to believe that while medical schools are now unbiased in their admissions, because women now constitute a majority of medical students, engineering schools are still pervaded by prejudice?[24] It is much more likely that females are choosing medicine over engineering. And if that is not the case, are we to conclude that medical schools are now biased against males, given that they now constitute fewer than half of all medical students in some countries?

Denying that these phenomena are explained primarily by proximate discrimination does not mean that discriminatory features of the wider society are not at play. Perhaps gender roles and other aspects of socialization make girls and boys more or less likely to enter specific professions, to be more or less inclined to seek promotion, to opt for part-time employment.

However, an affirmative action policy that grants preferential treatment to women is even harder to justify if one is attempting to correct for this upstream discrimination.

To see why this is so, consider the following. After divorce, fathers gain custody of children much less often than mothers and this is not simply because of implicit bias of judges. Men request custody less often. Perhaps it is even the case that fathers are less often the better custodial parent. Even if one thinks that biology is part of the explanation why males seek and are suited to custody less often, gender roles and other social factors also play a role. However, it does not follow that we should implement an affirmative action policy that aims to attain the levels of paternal custody that would have existed in the absence of those roles and factors. In deciding who gets custody, judges need to consider which parent or parents want custody and whether one parent is better suited to having custody. Custody decisions should not be made on the basis of what the paternal custody proportions would have been if fathers had been reared differently and thus made them want custody and be suited to it more often. Indeed, it seems repugnant consciously to aim at awarding custody to fathers more often even though one knew that fewer men wanted custody and that fewer would be the better custodial parent. This is true even if one knew that in the absence of socially reinforced gender roles men would have accounted for a greater proportion than they now do of parents wanting and worthy of custody.

It is similarly inappropriate to favor women in hiring or promotion merely because, in the absence of socially reinforced gender roles, more women would have chosen to become engineers or pilots, for example. In deciding who should gain custody, each parent's relative interest in and suitability to serve as the custodial parent is central. In deciding who should be appointed or hired, a person's capacity to do the job is central. That there are fewer female engineers and pilots from whom to choose does not mean that those hiring engineers and pilots should put any weight on a woman's sex in deciding whether to hire her. Doing so would put proportionately less weight on attributes that are relevant to how well she will do the job.

The same problem would arise for affirmative action policies that favor males in traditionally female professions. Imagine, for example, that a pool of applicants for a pre-primary school teacher position is 95% female. One can try to broaden the pool such that the proportion of males in the pool increases. However, if males are uninterested in applying, even if this is a product of socially contrived gender roles, then one might still have only 5% of the applicants being male. If one then favors those who constitute that 5% just because they are male, one will end up hiring some males who are weaker than the females one would otherwise have appointed. The more weight one attaches to being male, the relatively less other attributes will count. Thus, the stronger the form of affirmative action, the weaker, on average, will be those selected from the preferred sex. This is true if the favored sex is male, but it is equally true if the favored sex is female.

This is *not* to say that men cannot make good pre-primary school teachers (or that women cannot make good engineers or pilots). Instead it is to say that in hiring decisions, a person's sex is (generally) not relevant.[25] If it is made a consideration, then other considerations invariably count proportionately less and that would lead to the appointment of people who are less qualified for the position.

The underlying issue here is how we respond to the choices people do make, even if those choices would have been different if conditions had been different. Now, sometimes the conditions under which people choose are obviously such that their choices cannot be said to be free. If Dick Turpin offers you the choice of "your money or your life" and you choose to part with your money, your choice is not free. That, however, is not the kind of case about which we are speaking. Such cases are easy and we know what to do about such injustices – remove the threat.

We are speaking about more difficult cases – cases where one acts on the basis of preferences or attributes formed at least in part by social influences, but with which one identifies. The preferences are yours and you choose freely in accordance with them. If there are background injustices in the influences that lead to the formation of the preferences, then those injustices must be rectified upstream, where they occur. They cannot be rectified by overriding or ignoring people's choices or by favoring the very members of a group who were immune to the upstream influences.

Put another way, you should not be favored by how many other people of your sex have chosen as you did. Thus, if you are a woman who chose to become an engineer or a man who chose to become a pre-primary teacher, whether you get the job should not depend at all on the fact that your choice was relatively uncommon for somebody of your sex.[26] Similarly, if you are a man who chose to become an engineer or a woman who chose to become a pre-primary teacher, whether you get a particular job should not depend at all on the fact that most other people who made that choice are of the same sex.

Moreover, even if we thought it appropriate to correct for disadvantages caused by socially influenced preferences, it would be impossible to do so with any accuracy. So many of our preferences fall into this category and it is possible to know just how much better off each one of us would have been had our preferences been influenced in myriad alternative ways.

According to the view I have been presenting, the differing preferences of males and females, even if socially influenced, are not appropriate grounds for giving preference to either females or males. This does not mean, of course, that other things should not be done about background discrimination that affects the formation of preferences. We should take steps to avoid forcing girls and boys into gender roles. We should avoid characterizing certain jobs as either male or female. However, none of these sorts of intervention amount to giving preference to either sex. They are instances of equal opportunity affirmative action rather than preference affirmative action and are thus not problematic.

However, we should not assume that disproportionate representation of one or other sex in specific jobs or activities implies that societal discrimination is still at play. Natural differences might influence choices. Even when they do not, men and women might gravitate at different times and in different places at different rates into various positions and activities.

The present discrimination version of the rectification argument, like the past discrimination version, is much more problematic than its advocates realize. Taking note of the application of these arguments to the second sexism, as I have done, may highlight those difficulties that defenders of sex-based preference affirmative action might otherwise not see. Indeed, the implications of the second sexism for affirmative action might explain, at least in part, why some people are so reluctant to admit that there is a second sexism.

Lessons from "Summers School"

I argued above that discrimination does not fully account for the different participation rates by men and women in particular professions, jobs or activities. Feminists typically offer no complaint about that if the professions, jobs or activities are undesirable or unpleasant ones. However, the suggestion that discrimination does not fully account for women's under-representation in desirable positions is sometimes met with outrage.

Consider, for example, the case of Lawrence Summers. While president of Harvard University, Professor Summers was invited to speak in his capacity as an economist, rather than as university president, at a conference of the National Bureau of Economic Research.[27] The topic of the conference was diversifying the science and engineering workforce. He was asked to be provocative. Notwithstanding the uproar it caused, the speech itself was mild. Professor Summers noted that women are under-represented in "tenured positions in science and engineering at top universities and research institutions." He said that he wanted to "try to think about and offer some hypotheses as to why we observe what we observe" without passing judgment about this. He distinguished three hypotheses.

The first, what he called the "high-powered job hypothesis," was that "there are many professions and many activities, and the most prestigious activities in our society expect of people who are going to rise to leadership positions in their forties near total commitments to their work" and that "it is a fact of about our society that that is a level of commitment that a much higher fraction of married men have been historically prepared to make than of married women." He hastened to add that that was "not a judgment about how it should be" but rather just a description of the way things seem to be.

The second hypothesis is what he called the "different availability of aptitude at the high end." According to this hypothesis, regarding "many, many human attributes ... there is relatively clear evidence that whatever-difference in means ... there is a difference in the standard deviation, and variability of a male and a female population." He said that "physicists at a top twenty-five research university ... are people who are three and a half, [or] four standard deviations above the mean." Thus although there will be some very talented women at the high end, they would probably, according to this hypothesis, be outnumbered by men. In other words, the pool of high-end physicists, although not exclusively male, is disproportionately male.

The third hypothesis is the "socialization" hypothesis. As its name suggests, it attributes the gender imbalance under discussion to the different ways in which boys and girls are reared. Professor Summers indicated that while he thought that socialization may play some role, he provided reasons why not too much weight should be assigned to this hypothesis. His reluctant conclusion was that a combination of the first two hypotheses "probably explains a fair amount of this problem." He was clearly uncomfortable with even that mild and tentative conclusion, which he described as being, in his estimate, "the unfortunate truth," noting that he "would far prefer to believe something else." He also proposed a series of practical questions which he said were "ripe for research" – questions that would go some way to testing the hypotheses.

Professor Summers described his conclusions as his "best guesses," noting that they "may be all wrong" and that he will have served his purpose if he "provoked thought on this question and provoked the marshalling of evidence to contradict" what he had said.

It really is difficult to imagine a more tentative, reticent, even apologetic presentation of the *possibility* that discrimination may not be the major factor explaining the under-representation of women in certain areas. Yet it met with outrage and indignation. At least one professor at the talk walked out,[28] and that was only the beginning.

Almost immediately his remarks were misinterpreted, albeit subtly. The chair of Harvard's sociology department said that "the president of Harvard University didn't think that women scientists were as good as men."[29] That, however, was not what he said. He raised the *possibility* that there might be *fewer* women at the highest end of scientific ability. That is not the same as the claim that female scientists are not as good as male scientists. The *New York Times* itself attributed to Professor Summers the view that "innate sex differences might leave women *less capable* of succeeding at the most advanced mathematics,"[30] whereas it would have been more accurate to say that he thought that innate sex differences might result in there being *fewer* women capable of succeeding at the most advanced levels of subjects like mathematics.

The misinterpretation persisted even once the transcript of the remarks was released and people could read it for themselves. Several Harvard professors, it was reported, said "they felt he believed women were intellectually inferior to men."[31] Again, that is not what he said, nor is it an implication of what he said. The claim that there are more males at the highest levels of ability in areas like mathematics and engineering does not entail the claim that most women are intellectually inferior to men. There are disciplines other than engineering and mathematics, and even in those areas nothing he said implied that no women are capable of high-level intellectual activity. Professor Summers' remarks no more entail the conclusion that females are intellectually inferior than the claim that there are more males at the lowest levels of intellectual ability entails the claim that women are intellectually superior to men.

The outrage was not attributable only to misinterpretation. Even those who seem to have understood correctly what Professor Summers said were angry. Within a week Professor Summers, while not repudiating what he said, was apologizing that his words had "resulted in an unintended signal of discouragement to talented girls and women."[32] However, this did not appease his critics. He came under severe criticism at a meeting of the faculty of arts and sciences.[33] Harvard professors took a vote of no confidence, which passed by 218 to 185 votes.[34] Professor Summers resigned as President of Harvard early the following year.[35]

There are a number of lessons to be learned from this case. The first is a lesson about the extent to which the dogma that all sex differences are attributable to socialization has penetrated universities (and perhaps especially the social sciences). It is a dogma because alternative views are dismissed out of hand and reasonable proposals to test it are met with indignation rather than open-mindedness.

Second, we see just how intolerant some social constructionists are. The view Professor Summers was raising is one that enjoys support from a vast number of very respectable scholars. This is not a fringe, crackpot view, even if it is also not a unanimous one. To respond as vehemently as many of them did to the mention of it is alarming.

Third, it is also indicative of the insatiability of the affirmative action appetite, to which I referred earlier. Professor Summers' comments were not an attempt to justify failing to do anything about the relatively small proportion of women in some areas. Indeed Harvard had already taken measures to address this issue and continued to do so. The problem is that no matter how much is done, many defenders of affirmative action are not satisfied unless men and women are roughly equally represented – in desirable positions, that is. They treat the mere differential as evidence of discrimination, yet they make no such inference when the differential favors women. In the latter cases the very suggestion that men are the victims of discrimination is met with indignation, if not hostility.

Consequentialist Arguments

Consequentialist arguments for affirmative action, like all consequentialist arguments, are forward- rather than backward-looking. Affirmative action is justified, according to these arguments, by the good outcomes it is alleged to yield. Many, but not all, such arguments appeal to the value of diversity. They claim that the greater diversity produced by affirmative action is necessary to attain certain desirable goals. Thus affirmative action is a means to greater diversity, and diversity is said to be a means to one or more of a number of goods. I shall refer to arguments of this kind as *diversity arguments* and will focus on those that are most relevant to sex-based (rather than race-based) affirmative action.[36]

The viewpoint diversity argument

The first diversity argument suggests that gender diversity is valuable because it promotes a diversity of viewpoints. This in turn is important either for the pursuit of truth in those institutions such as universities, where the pursuit of truth is crucial, or for greater creativity or innovation in other institutions and in corporations. The pursuit of truth version draws on John Stuart Mill. In his famous defense of freedom of speech, he argued that those who suppress an opinion do so to their detriment. "If the opinion is right," he said, "they are deprived of the opportunity of exchanging error for truth: if wrong, they lose ... the clearer perception and livelier impression of truth, produced by its collision with error."[37] In other words, a diversity of views facilitates the pursuit of truth. One can see similarly how a mix of viewpoints could foster creativity and innovation in organizations where these goals are more central than the "pursuit of truth," narrowly conceived.

If the viewpoint-diversity argument is accepted, it would apply not only to women (and to disadvantaged racial groups) but also to political and religious views. Among academic staff of universities (and especially in certain disciplines), political conservatives and religious fundamentalists, for example, are under-represented[38] and thus should also be favored, according to the viewpoint-diversity argument. It would also apply to males in those professions where women predominate. Since advocates of affirmative action tend not to support preferences for such groups, it becomes questionable whether their advocacy of affirmative action really is based on this version of the diversity argument. However, they could (even if they will not) bite the bullet and extend the argument to religious and political views.

If the "pursuit of truth" argument is saved in this way, it remains questionable whether it does the kind of work that advocates of affirmative action think it does. For instance, diversity is not proportionality,[39] as many advocates of affirmative action mistakenly think. Thus insofar as women have different opinions from men, the viewpoint-diversity argument requires only that there be *some* women in each of the various sectors. It does not require that the number of women be proportionate to their share of the overall population. Since there are already a significant number of women in all or almost all those sectors where feminists suggest that sex-based affirmative action is required, affirmative action cannot be justified on this basis. The goal it justifies has already been met. This suggests that the "viewpoint-diversity" argument is not the real reason for their endorsement of affirmative action. Their choice, then, is either to accept the implications of the diversity argument or to abandon it.

The viewpoint-diversity argument assumes that sex-based affirmative action would foster a diversity of opinions. It is easy to understand, given the differing experiences of males and females, how having both sexes present might enhance a diversity of views in areas of inquiry such as psychology and sociology. It is much less clear, however, how having both men and women increases diversity of *opinion* in those areas, such as mathematics and physics, where the differing experience of each sex is unlikely to bear on the subject matter. Yet defenders of sex-based affirmative action want to see it employed across all disciplines and employment sectors (where women but not men are under-represented).

The role-model argument

A second diversity argument for affirmative action is that hiring (and promoting) women provides other women and girls with role models, which it is said are necessary to encourage other females to enter a given area of study and work.

It is hard to deny that a role model can be advantageous. The question is whether the role-model argument is strong enough to defend affirmative action. Put another way, the question is whether the benefit of role models is great enough to warrant a departure from a more sex-blind policy of equality of opportunity.

One common response to the "role-model" argument draws on the observation I made earlier that women are not disadvantaged in the ways in which, for example, blacks in America and South Africa are. Women (unless they are also members of such disadvantaged groups) have social and educational privilege. It is unclear that people of this sort really require role models to succeed. There have been other groups entering tertiary education and other sectors for the first time (at least for the first time in a new society if they are immigrants). Where such groups have not been deprived of decent education at the primary and secondary levels, they have succeeded and thrived at university and beyond without having role models. For example, the first generation of Jews to enter universities in the United States that often had quotas limiting their numbers succeeded without (many) role models among the professoriate.[40]

Unless they are also members of a particularly disadvantaged racial or ethnic group, women are no more disadvantaged, and often a lot less disadvantaged, than those ethnic groups who have successfully entered the realms of academia, the professions, business and industry. The "role-model" argument is thus considerably weaker in defending affirmative action for women than it is in defending affirmative action for blacks.[41]

Moreover, it is unclear that the role-model argument requires that the number of women in a given employment sector be proportional to their number in the population. Girls do not have to see that half of all engineers are female in order to have role models. It is sufficient that there be a few successful female engineers. Since there are already some such role models, it is hard to see how affirmative action could be justified on the basis of the role-model argument.

If the response is that, contrary to what I have just claimed, one *does* need at least many more women in those professions in which they are under-represented, then the argument would apply also to those professions and employment sectors in which males are under-represented. It would justify affirmative action for males in pre-primary education, in nursing and in secretarial services.

A common response to this suggestion is that there is a crucial difference between male under-representation in these areas and female under-representation in other areas.[42] The alleged difference is that whereas prevailing prejudices would have it that females are *incapable* of being mathematicians or scientists, males are not taught that they are incapable of becoming pre-primary teachers or nurses. Instead they are taught that such work is beneath them and is fit only for women.

This response is unconvincing. It was once thought that women were incapable of (or unsuited to) entering the professions, but it is extremely implausible to think that this is still the case in free societies. Indeed, female enrolment in medical schools, for example, now outstrips that of males in a number of countries. Perhaps it will be said that while females are no longer thought incapable of becoming doctors, they are still thought incapable of becoming engineers. Much more likely, however, is that those advancing the argument that women are perceived to be incapable are sticking to that hypothesis until females choose a given profession in numbers comparable to or exceeding those of males. To do this is to make the mistake of treating under-representation of women in a given profession as evidence of the prejudice. There are alternative possible explanations, including the view that women prefer some professions to others. There may well be complicated social reasons why women have those preferences, but that is different from claiming that women are perceived to be incapable. There do seem to be enough female engineers, for example, to refute the suggestion that women are perceived as incapable of entering that profession.

What of the suggestion that males are taught that those professions in which they enter in disproportionately small numbers are beneath them? If that is the message that is conveyed to boys and men, it unfairly disadvantages certain men. Some people might prefer to become a nurse than to become a doctor. Of those who would prefer to become a doctor, that option might not be open to all of them. Some might lack the academic qualifications necessary to gain admittance to medical school, or they might lack the resources to pay for the lengthy education required to become a doctor. For such people, becoming a nurse might well be a social advancement. Insofar as gender roles discourage males from entering such professions, they may well find themselves instead in those often dangerous jobs (such as mining, construction and logging) in which men have historically predominated. This may be to their disadvantage.

To clarify once again, I am not recommending that affirmative action policies be introduced for males in professions where they are under-represented. I am showing instead that those who do defend affirmative action for women on the basis of the role-model argument should be committed to affirmative action for males in certain contexts. Yet many (but not all) of them reject affirmative action for males. I think that they have good reasons for rejecting it, but these same reasons also apply to affirmative action for females.

The legitimate-sex-preference argument

According to this third argument, people sometimes have a legitimate preference that a person of a particular sex performs a specific job. Thus, if there are insufficient females in that line of work, females may be favored. For example, it might be argued that some women have a legitimate preference for a female gynecologist and thus if there is a dearth of female gynaecologists, gynecological training programs may favor female candidates in admission decisions. Similarly, gynecological practices with too few female practitioners may favor female candidates in their hiring decisions.

I shall not explain here why I think that a female's preference for a (heterosexual) female gynecologist is reasonable.[43] On the assumption that it is, a policy of favoring the appointment of female gynaecologists is not unreasonable. However, there are at least two things to note about the legitimate-sex-preference argument.

First, like the others, it also supports favoring males under certain circumstances. Some males may prefer (heterosexual) male nurses, for example. Second, the argument has limited application. It might apply to doctors, nurses, prison guards, those responsible for physical searches in security screening and so forth. Moreover, many of the jobs or professions in which women are most under-represented are also those to which the legitimate sex preference does not apply. For example, it cannot apply to the training or hiring of engineers, pilots or mathematicians. This is because a preference for an engineer, pilot or mathematician of a particular sex is not legitimate in the way that a same-sex preference in the other cases may be.

The ideal argument

Ronald Dworkin discerns two senses in which a society may be said to be "better off" as a result of affirmative action. The first is utilitarian. The three diversity arguments I have just considered are arguments that affirmative action makes society better off in this sense. The second sense in which a society may be said to be "better off" is in what Professor Dworkin calls the "ideal" sense. A society is better off in an ideal sense if it is "more just, or in some other way closer to an ideal society."[44]

The obvious question that arises, however, is whether affirmative action does indeed produce a society that is either more just or that comes closer to an ideal. Those who think it does argue that had there not been powerful gender roles then the gender profile of various professions would be very different. The assumption, then, is that if affirmative action is the most effective way of attaining the gender profile that would have existed in the absence of injustice, it is an effective way of making a society more just.

One problem for this view is that we do not know what gender profile would have existed in any given job in the absence of injustice. Even in the absence of unfair discrimination, we cannot expect that both sexes will be represented proportionately in all professions, trades and activities. Defenders of sex-based affirmative action may have difficulty seeing this and they may assume that unequal representation is always the consequence of discrimination. They should consider that other groups are often dispro-portionately prevalent without this being the consequence of discrimina-tion. For example, there was a disproportionately large number of Jews at the University of Vienna in the late nineteenth and early twentieth century, despite discrimination *against* them.[45] In early twentieth-century India, Parsees held a disproportionate number of university degrees, especially in sciences and engineering.[46] In the Catholic Church in the United States, disproportionately many priests and bishops were Irish and disproportionately few were Italian.[47] There was a disproportionately large number of female doctors in the Soviet Union.[48] More recently, Cambodian immigrants ran 80% of doughnut shops in California,[49] and a disproportionately large number of African-born residents of the United States, relative to any other immigrants or US citizens, hold doctoral degrees.[50] Most Canadian hockey players shoot left-handed, but south of the border, in the United States, the majority of hockey players shoot right-handed.[51]

If unequal distributions are possible in the absence of discrimination in the case of these ethnic and national groups, it could also be true of the sexes. We do not know how much of the differential proportion is attributable to discrimination. However, even if we did know, there is a problem with the assumption that approaching the gender profile that *would have* obtained in the absence of discrimination makes a society more just or closer to an ideal society. Even if the absence of *that* gender profile is the consequence of discrimination, it does not follow that the use of any means to attain that profile makes the society more just. Some ways of achieving that profile would simply plaster over unfairness and create a mere appearance of rectification. This would be the case if making the gender profiles correct required selecting women who would not have been selected in the absence of preference and failing to select men who would have been selected in the absence of preference for females – and vice versa. Affirmative action is a very poor mechanism for making a society more just, even if it happens to be good at making a society *appear* more just to those who confuse particular sex profiles with justice. Such people need to look beyond appearances to reality.

Conclusion

Except in its equal opportunity form, affirmative action involves a preference for people of one sex. Not only opponents but also many defenders of such affirmative action agree that there is a moral presumption against such preference in admissions, appointments and promotions decisions (except in the rare cases of legitimate sex preference to which I referred earlier). They are divided only on the question whether that presumption is defeated by other considerations in the case of affirmative action. That many defenders of affirmative action agree that there is a presumption against favoring people of one sex is borne out by the fact that they believe it should be implemented only as an interim measure until the problem it seeks to address is either fixed or sufficiently alleviated. I have argued that none of the arguments for preference affirmative action are successful. It follows that none of them can defeat a presumption against gender preference.

There may be some defenders of affirmative action who deny that there is even a presumption against the preference for women that is involved in most forms of affirmative action. Some defenders of affirmative action deny that it amounts to "reverse discrimination," "reverse sexism" or, to use my phrase, "second sexism." This, they say, is because unlike discrimination against women, which is predicated on views of women as inferior, affirmative action implies no contempt for males and is thus not presumptively wrong.

This argument is flawed even if we grant that affirmative action embodies no negative assumptions about males. Defenders of affirmative action would surely be opposed to disadvantaging women even if that discrimination did not emanate from beliefs in the inferiority of women. Although belief in the inferiority of those against whom one discriminates may well exacerbate sexism, the basic wrong of sexism lies in the discriminatory mistreatment.

It is because sex-based affirmative action is sexist discrimination that my rejection of it is continuous with my rejection of sexism and the second sexism. Men and women may have average differences but these do not justify discriminating in favor of or against individual members of either sex. For example, women are, on average, shorter and lighter than males. However, we may not, as a consequence, use a person's sex as a proxy for these attributes when appointing people to positions that require greater height and weight. Doing so would be unfair to those women who have the relevant attributes, and it would be counterproductive to hire those men who lack them and who are thus less able to perform the tasks.[52] But the same rationale extends to affirmative action. There may be fewer women in a given kind of job. It does not follow that we may use a female applicant's sex as a proxy for the attribute "victim of discrimination," and thus favor her via affirmative action.

While average differences between the sexes do not justify discriminatory treatment, they are nonetheless relevant, because they should lead us not to presume that males and females will be found in equal numbers in the ranks of every profession and among school dropouts, criminals and prison inmates, for example.

There are complicated reasons why members of each sex gravitate to particular jobs and certain sectors of society. Even when gender roles play a part in this, affirmative action is a problematic strategy. Appointments are not gifts for the benefit of those who receive them (even though those who are appointed often do benefit). We appoint people to do a job – indeed, the best possible job. For that we need to choose the best possible people for the particular job. Although we are less likely to appoint the best possible person if the candidate pool from which we are making the appointment is unduly limited, we do not compensate for that limitation by giving extra weight to the sex of those people within the pool. In other words, there is no problem, as I indicated earlier, with what I called equal opportunity affirmative action, which merely aims to remove impediments to equality of opportunity. Such affirmative action could indeed broaden the pool of applicants. However, once we have a pool of applicants, we do not increase the likelihood of appointing the best person by giving weight to the sex of some people, whether male or female. This is because giving weight to sex must mean giving relatively less weight to other, relevant attributes.

Defenders of sex-based preference affirmative action often assume that when women are under-represented in desirable positions, this is a product of discrimination. They make no such assumption when women are under-represented in undesirable positions. Moreover, while they propose preferential policies to address the under-representation of women in desirable positions, they usually make no such proposals to reduce the proportion of males in undesirable positions. These asymmetries are curious and suggest that many defenders of sex-based affirmative action are not as interested in equality as they are in advancing the position of women. Sometimes there is a happy coincidence of the two, but it is when they come apart that the guiding principle is exposed. In any event, while equal opportunity affirmative action can advance equality, those forms of affirmative action that give preference to some people on the basis of their sex fail to do so, even when there is real discrimination to be overcome.

Notes

1 Even if women do not experience the same degree of preference in all affirmative action policies, they do in some.
2 I have discussed race-based affirmative action in David Benatar, "Justice, diversity and racial preference: a critique of affirmative action," *South African Law Journal*, 125(2), 2008, pp. 274–306.
3 Although there may be some disagreement, there is also a limit to reasonable disagreement about what the criteria are.
4 Women and Work Commission, "Shaping a Fairer Future," London: UK Commission for Employment and Skills, 2006, p. 4.
5 Equal opportunity affirmative action would rule out favoring the children of alumni in admissions decisions. Curiously, some defenders of the controversial form of affirmative action – what I shall call preference affirmative action – like to note that children of alumni enjoy greater preference than beneficiaries of preference affirmative action. (See Deborah L. Rhode, *Speaking of Sex: The Denial of Gender Inequality*, Cambridge, MA: Harvard University Press, 1997, p. 166.) However, the practice of favoring the children of alumni is not an axiom justifying preference for other groups. Instead, it is a form of preference to be eliminated.
6 The same is true, *mutatis mutandis*, in many cases of race-based affirmative action.

7   Rarely is it noted that stereotypically masculine environments, as well as inflexible hours, may also be hostile to some (even if not as many) men.

8   Kingsley Browne, "Sex and temperament in modern society: a Darwinian view of the glass ceiling and the gender gap," *Arizona Law Review*, 37(4), Winter 1995, pp. 971–1106, at pp. 1017–1028.

9   Ibid., pp. 1028–1033.

10   Ibid., pp. 1033–1037.

11   Ibid., p. 984.

12   For more on the political power and insatiability of such people, see the next section, "Lessons from 'Summers School'."

13   At one time, the salaries for men and women performing the same job were explicitly different – women's lower than men's. This is no longer the case, at least in the developed world.

14   In the United Kingdom, single women "earn as much on average as single men" and "women in the middle age groups who remain single earn more than middle-aged single males." (J.R. Shackleton, *Should We Mind the Gap? Gender Pay Differentials and Public Policy*, London: Institute of Economic Affairs, 2008, pp. 29–30.)

15   Ibid., esp. pp. 45–66.

16   Carl Hoffmann and John Reed, "When is imbalance not discrimination?" in W.E. Block and M.A. Walker (eds), *Discrimination, Affirmative Action, and Equal Opportunity: An Economic and Social Perspective*, Vancouver: The Fraser Institute, 1982.

17   Ibid., p. 193.

18   Ibid.

19   Ibid., p. 198.

20   A.D. Irvine, "Jack and Jill and employment equity," *Dialogue*, 35(2), 1996, pp. 255–291.

21   Ibid., p. 259. The author says that during "the time that today's full professors were first being hired, the percentage of applicants who were women is estimated to have been 8.6%. At the same time, the percentage of job recipients who were women was only 7.6%."

22   Ibid., p. 260.

23   Ibid.

24   Steven Pinker makes the same point. See *The Blank Slate: The Modern Denial of Human Nature*, New York: Penguin Books, 2002, p. 355.

25   I say "generally" because there are exceptions. For a discussion of this see the section below on the "legitimate-sex-preference" argument.

26   The few possible exceptions to this are discussed in the discussion of the "legitimate-sex-preference" argument below.

27   Lawrence H. Summers, "Remarks at NBER conference on diversifying the science and engineering workforce," January 14, 2005. A transcript of the speech is available at http://www.president.harvard.edu/speeches/summers_2005/nber.php (accessed February 15, 2010).

28   Lisa Wogan, "Summersgate," *Ms*, Summer 2005, pp. 57–59, at p. 57.

29   Sam Dillon and Sara Rimer, "No Break in the Storm over Harvard President's Words," *New York Times*, January 19, 2005.

30 Ibid.; my emphasis.

31 Sara Rimer and Patrick D. Healy, "Furor Lingers as Harvard Chief Gives Details of Talk on Women," *New York Times*, February 18, 2005.

32 Lawrence H. Summers, "Letter from President Summers on women and science," January 19, 2005. Online at http://www.harvard.edu/president/speeches/summers_2005/womensci.php (accessed August 30, 2011).

33 Sara Rimer, "Professors at Harvard Confront Its President," *New York Times*, February 16, 2005.

34 Alan Finder, Patrick D. Healy and Kate Zernike, "President of Harvard Resigns, Ending Stormy 5-Year Tenure," *New York Times*, February 22, 2006. Professor Summers had had previous clashes with some members of the Harvard faculty and those earlier issues likely also factored into the no confidence vote. However, his remarks about women in science and engineering played a very significant part.

35 Ibid.

36 My discussion of the diversity arguments is drawn from my "Diversity limited," in Laurence M. Thomas (ed.), *Contemporary Debates in Social Philosophy*, Oxford: Wiley-Blackwell, 2008, pp. 212–225.

37 John Stuart Mill, *On Liberty*, in *On Liberty and Other Essays*, ed. J. Gray, Oxford: Oxford University Press, 1991, p. 21.

38 See, for example, Stanley Rothman, S. Robert Lichter and Neil Nevitte, "Politics and professional advancement among college faculty," *The Forum*, 3(1), 2005, online at http://www.bepress.com/forum/vol3/iss1/art2/; John F. Zipp and Rudy Fenwick, "Is the academy a liberal hegemony?" *Public Opinion Quarterly*, 70(3), Fall 2006, pp. 304–326.

39 David Wasserman, "Diversity and stereotyping," *Report from the Institute for Philosophy and Public Policy*, 17(1/2), Winter / Spring 1997, pp. 32–36, at p. 32.

40 Lewis S. Feuer, "The stages of the social history of Jewish professors in American Colleges and Universities," *American Jewish History*, 71(4), June 1982, p. 432. This author, citing earlier sources, says that "by the mid-[nineteen-]twenties there were still probably less than one hundred Jews among the college and university professors in the liberal arts and sciences faculties in the United States ... As late as April, 1930, the institution which had the largest Jewish student body in the world had not a single Jewish professor." That institution was the Washington Square College of New York University, where 93% of the students were Jews (p. 455).

41 The role-model argument for preferring "blacks" fails for more complex reasons.

42 See, for example, Kenneth Clatterbaugh, "Benatar's alleged second sexism," *Social Theory and Practice*, 29(2), April 2003, p. 218.

43 The argument is implicit in my discussion, in Chapter 4, of whether it is worse to be seen naked by (non-intimate) members of the opposite sex than by people of the same sex. In suggesting that it is reasonable for a woman to have a preference for a (heterosexual) female gynecologist, I am not suggesting that having no preference for the sex of one's gynecologist is unreasonable. That too might be reasonable.

44 Ronald Dworkin, *Taking Rights Seriously*, London: Duckworth, 1987, p. 232.

45   In 1910, for example, Jews constituted 8.6% of the Viennese population, but
     accounted for between 39.2% and 43.9% of academics at the University of
     Vienna. Jews were, however, more highly represented in some faculties than in
     others. In the faculty of medicine, for example, they accounted for between
     51.2% and 59.4% of academics. In the faculty of philosophy, they accounted
     for "only" 21.6% of academics. (Steven Beller, *Vienna and the Jews: 1867–1938*,
     Cambridge: Cambridge University Press, 1989, pp. 36, 44.) Advocates of the
     proportionality view would have to insist that Jews should have been
     proportionately represented in each of the relevant faculties.

46   According to the Indian Census of 1920/1921 and 1921/1922, the Parsees
     constituted only 0.03% of the Indian population, yet they held 6.8% of
     engineering degrees, 4.7% of degrees in medical fields and 1.7% of the degrees
     in science. (Robert E. Kennedy, Jr., "The Protestant ethic and the Parsis,"
     American Journal of Sociology, 68(1), July 1962, p. 19.)

47   Nathan Glazer and Daniel Patrick Moynihan, *Beyond the Melting Pot: The
     Negroes, Puerto Ricans, Jews, Italians, and Irish of New York City*, 2nd edn,
     Cambridge, MA: MIT Press, 1970, pp. 204–205.

48   In 1973, for example, 70% of all doctors were women. See Maria D. Piradova,
     "The role of women in the public health care system in the USSR," in *Proceedings
     of the International Conference on Women in Health*, Washington, DC:
     Department of Health, Education, and Welfare, 1975, p. 23.

49   Jonathan Kaufman, "How Cambodians Came to Control California
     Doughnuts," *Wall Street Journal*, February 22, 1995, p. A1. Would a more just
     California be one where immigrants from Korea or Mexico or Europe were
     more equitably represented among doughnut-shop owners? Although I fol-
     lowed this example to its source, I first learned of it in Thomas Sowell's
     Barbarians inside the Gates, Stanford: Hoover Institution Press, 1999, p. 168.

50   "African-born U.S. residents are the most highly educated group in American
     society," *Journal of Blacks in Higher Education*, 13, Autumn 1996, pp. 33–34;
     "African immigrants in the United States are the nation's most highly educated
     group," *Journal of Blacks in Higher Education*, 26, Winter 1999/2000, pp. 60–61.

51   Jeff Z. Klein, "It's Not Political, but More Canadians Are Lefties," *New York
     Times*, February 16, 2010.

52   Sometimes sexist discrimination excludes only one sex, while still imposing
     qualification requirements on members of the other sex. However, in some
     cases, those qualification requirements are set very low. Thus, in conscripting
     males, for example, the burden of proof is on males (of the targeted age) to
     show that they do not meet the minimum requirements rather than on the state
     to prove that they do meet them.

7

Conclusion

[My father] and my mother kept insisting that as the man of the family I was responsible for my sisters, even though my four siblings were my equals in every respect. They gave me the duty without the privilege; on the contrary, I felt that my sisters were shown far greater consideration and I neither accepted the burden of responsibility nor agreed with it in principle. I felt that my father often favored my sisters over me as an act of chivalry.

Edward Said, *Out of Place*, New York:
Alfred Knopf, 2000, p. 273.

I have argued that males are the victims of a second sexism – an unrecognized (or, at least, under-recognized) and neglected form of sexism. In this concluding chapter, I take up three resultant questions that arise in at least some people's minds. The first is whether feminism discriminates against men. My answer is that it need not, but it sometimes does. The second question concerns whether men or women are worse off. My answer is that women have been and continue to be more badly discriminated against than men in many places, but not in all places. The final question concerns what we should do about the second sexism. I suggest that we should take it seriously, and I provide some indication of what we might do to oppose it.

Does Feminism Discriminate against Men?

Sometimes the question whether males are the victims of unfair discrimination is confused with another question – whether feminism discriminates

The Second Sexism: Discrimination Against Men and Boys, First Edition. David Benatar.
© 2012 John Wiley & Sons, Inc. Published 2012 by John Wiley & Sons, Inc.

(unfairly) against men.[1] These are distinct questions. Many examples of the second sexism long predate the advent of feminism and thus feminism cannot be responsible for those. For those who recognize this, the question whether feminism discriminates unfairly against men is a question about whether feminism contributes something extra to the second sexism.

Part of the answer to this question depends on what kind of feminism one has in mind. In Chapter 1, I distinguished between egalitarian feminists and partisan feminists. The former seek equality of the sexes, whereas the latter seek the advancement of female interests (irrespective of whether that advances equality). Partisan feminism does entail some unfairness to men. Since its goal is the advancement of female interests irrespective of whether this promotes or compromises equality, it will sometimes advance the interests of women even when this is unfair to men. By contrast, there is nothing about egalitarian feminism that commits it to unfairness to men. Egalitarian feminism may sometimes require diminishing men's relative position but that is not unfair if the inequality it is correcting is the result of unfair discrimination. Egalitarian feminists would similarly be willing to diminish women's relative position when that is necessary to promote equality. (They would, for instance, remove a prohibition on conscripting women, at least where conscription of anybody is justified.[2])

However, although egalitarian feminism never aims at inequality, it might sometimes slip into it. For example, in attempting to correct an unfair male advantage, it may be too effective. Consider, for example, the case of child custody. As we saw earlier, children were once automatically awarded to the father in the event of divorce. That was certainly unfairly discriminatory against mothers and was in need of correction. Feminists rightly took up that matter. However, the problem has now been over-corrected. Although custody is not now *always* awarded to the mother, we saw that mothers are now much more likely to gain custody even when one controls for other variables. Thus child-custody decisions are now discriminatory against men.

Another such example is sexual harassment. Women previously had insufficient protection against unwanted sexual comments and advances from men. Feminism rightly sought a corrective to this. While the problem persists in some ways, it is also the case that in some quarters there is now a hypersensitivity about these matters. Men have become very vulnerable to accusations of sexual harassment. No matter how frivolous or unfounded such an accusation may be, a man can be seriously harmed by it. The challenge is to strike the right balance, but this is not easy. Victims of genuine sexual harassment need to be taken seriously and given protection. But victims of bogus sexual harassment charges also need protection from malicious, opportunistic and delusional accusers, even if there are not many of these.[3] It is also noteworthy that, for reasons explained earlier, women are not similarly vulnerable to sexual harassment accusations. Men who complain of sexual harassment, especially harassment by women, are unlikely to be taken as seriously and this will lead men to level such accusations less often.

Feminism has also been much more successful at breaking down the female gender role than the male gender role. Thus while many of the former advantages of being male have been lost, the disadvantages remain. The response to this is not to turn the clock back and regain the unfair advantages, but rather to finish the job by focusing more on unfair male disadvantages.

Some people deny that there has been greater success in breaking down the female than the male gender role. However, there is plenty of evidence that this is exactly what has happened. Consider, for example, the different attitudes towards "tomboys" (girls who have traditionally masculine dispositions) and "sissies" (boys with allegedly feminine characters). The former were for a very long time not as despised as the latter. Some have claimed that the term "tomboy" no longer makes any sense given how much girls' roles have expanded.[4] Whether or not that is true, it is certainly the case that many activities that used to be termed tomboyish – such as wearing pants or playing sport – no longer are. Boys playing with dolls are likely to be ridiculed in a way that girls playing with trucks are not. They are also likely to concern their parents in a way in which the girls with their trucks are not.

Another example of how the female gender role has been broken down more successfully comes from the extent to which women have entered historically male professions. The phenomenon of female doctors and lawyers is now unremarkable but male nurses and pre-primary school teachers are still much more of a rarity. One author has suggested that the restrictions of a gender role do not constitute oppression[5] unless the restrictions are imposed because of a perceived lack of abilities (which he thinks is not true in the case of restrictions on males).[6] He says that whereas young women are told they *cannot* be doctors, young men are being told that although they *could* be nurses it would be unworthy of them. But the evidence of men's and women's actual success in entering professions traditionally reserved for the opposite sex suggests that today in western societies, women *can* become doctors. Only the paranoid could think otherwise. Even if it is still true that men are not being told that they *cannot* become nurses, and even if they are not thereby being oppressed, it is still true that some individual men are *unfairly disadvantaged* (in ways that women are not) by societal pressures that militate against their becoming nurses.

Feminism has also produced a number of catch-22 situations for males. Consider what we might call the "chivalry bind." Feminists criticize the practice of men opening doors for women or letting women through the door first.[7] Even a man who, as a courtesy often allows others, male or female, through the door first, may be subjected to a rebuke when the person is a female feminist who takes offense.[8] Yet men are sometimes also rebuked for *not* letting women through the door first. This happens when the woman the man precedes is one who still expects the chivalrous gestures. When each kind of woman offers her rebuke, she does not think of the other kind of woman, and the bind in which these mixed messages leave men.

A further problem lies in certain excesses. Thus, it is not uncommon to hear the sort of insulting, demonizing or untrue comments about men that would cause outrage if said about women. While some of these comments are of minor significance, others feed and are fed by a culture of political correctness that protects female speech about men, but has a silencing effect in the reverse direction. Moreover, the comments are usually left unchallenged. As a result those making them are rarely given an opportunity to see just how inappropriate or unfounded they are. This is neither good for men nor fair to them. The following are but a few of the very many examples that could be cited.

In the question-and-answer session following a lecture by husband-and-wife team Nicholas Kristof and Sheryl Dunn-Wu,[9] one brash young woman prefaced her question by saying that "behind every enlightened, intelligent man is an even more enlightened, intelligent woman." Now, of course, it is no insult to be called an "enlightened, intelligent man," but it is a kind of backhand compliment when one's having these attributes is implicitly attributed to one's wife. Feminists would be outraged if the reverse were said or implied.

I can think of two responses that defenders of this sort of comment might offer. First, they might say that such comments really are very minor and inconsequential and not something men should complain about. I agree, of course, that they are minor matters, but then presumably the same attitude should be taken to similar comments about women. However, when the comments are about women they are typically met with indignation. Second, defenders of the comment might remark that men and women are differently situated. Women are the underdogs and thus jibes at them would be unfair in a way that jibes at males are not. But this response is also problematic. As I shall argue in the next section, it really is not clear that women are the underdogs in places like the United States, where this comment was made. And even if women are, it really is not the case that women like Sheryl Dunn-Wu are. I cannot imagine that women like her need that sort of affirmation or that men like Nicholas Kristof deserve the compliment in its backhanded form.

Some people will object that I have referred to only one stupid comment. However, that sort of comment is far from uncommon. Here is another:

> There is, then, an insult, whether intentional or not, in gallant behavior, and women, recognizing that they are at least equal if not superior in most respects to most men, can hardly be expected to respond with gratitude.[10]

Here we have a feminist who, while objecting to the insult *implicit* in a man's opening a door for a woman, *explicitly* insults men.

One regularly hears those sorts of jibes.[11] Since they are socially acceptable and opposing ones are not, they create a certain climate in which unreflective criticism of men is condoned. To be clear, I am not recommending limitations on freedom of speech. Instead I am making a comment on the ethics of speech – on how one uses one's legally protected freedoms. Nor do I think that *jocular* jibes routinely violate the ethics of speech. However, to the considerable extent that they are permissible, they are permissible whether the butt of the joke is the male or female. The unfairness to men is thus not that these jokes are made, but that if the joke goes in the opposite direction the response is indignation or outrage.

Nor is humor the only situation in which feminist concerns are used as a cudgel to beat the politically incorrect. We saw earlier what happened to the (now former) president of Harvard University, Lawrence Summers. Some feminists also berate those who use the male pronoun when referring to people of both or indeterminate sex, even though it is far from clear that morality dictates the use of the female pronoun or a disjunction of the male and female pronouns.[12] There have also been feminist campaigns to ensure that females are included among keynote speakers at conferences, even though there are dozens of feminist conferences at which there are no male keynote speakers.[13]

One comment heard not infrequently is that if men had wombs, abortion would be freely available. By that logic you would think that if men suffered more lung cancer than breast cancer, more money would be spent on research into the former rather than the latter. Yet men *do* suffer more lung cancer, but we find that research into breast cancer is better funded. Perhaps, then, men do not have as much power as they are purported to have, or they have the power but are not very good at utilizing it to their own advantage, or they quite knowingly exercise their power for the benefit of others. Whatever the reason, it is clear that men are not ensuring that public resources are devoted to alleviating their health problems rather than those of women. Moreover, it cannot be assumed that if men had wombs, abortion would be freely available.

Feminist excesses are also to be found in the rationalizations that are frequently employed. As we have seen repeatedly in earlier chapters, some feminists attempt to portray females as the victims of all unfair sex discrimination, even when they are not the victims. And when some feminists make a moral argument about what should be done, they curiously always reach the conclusion that it is the interests of females that ought to prevail. There is always some reason, as we have also seen, why the interests of females are of paramount importance.

Rationalizations are also employed to exculpate women.[14] For example, some feminists make much of how war is carried out by men, implying and sometimes even explicitly claiming that women are above this kind of behavior.[15] But there are obvious social and gender-role explanations that can account for why men become soldiers. Where women have had the opportunity to kill, torture and perpetrate other cruel acts, they have proved very capable of doing so.[16] There is disingenuousness in the arguments of those feminists who will discount the opportunity differentials between men and women for the violence of war, but who rush to explain the greater incidence of (non-sexual) child abuse by women as being a function of sexism. It is women, they correctly note, who have most contact with children and therefore have the greatest opportunity to abuse children. Moreover, we are told that female abusers of children "would probably not have become child abusers had the culture offered them viable alternatives to marriage and motherhood."[17] If this line of argument (contrary to my own view) is acceptable, why can a similar explanation for participation in war not be given for young men "whose culture does not offer them viable alternatives" to machismo and the military?

Some feminists not only excuse women's violence in the way that they refuse to excuse men's violence, they also resist the very changes which would make the violence of warfare a less male affair – namely parity in enlistment of the sexes. They oppose conscription of women.[18] Feminist defenders of women's absence from combat assume that women are different and unsuited to war. They maintain that so long as there is (or must be) war, it is men who must wage it. There are a number of problems with this view.

First, by seeking to preserve the status quo, they suppress the most effective test of whether men really are better suited to war. Notice how the real test of female competence to perform other tasks has been most unequivocally demonstrated by women's actually performing those tasks. Whereas when there were almost no female lawyers, people could have appealed to that fact to support claims of female unsuitability to the legal profession, that same line of argument is simply not available when there are vast numbers of successful female lawyers.

Second, those who argue that women are ill-suited to war assume that men (unlike women) want to participate in war. Alternatively, male preferences on this score are a matter of indifference to them. The overwhelming majority of men do not wish to be part of the military. Were it otherwise, conscription would never be necessary. Why should these men be forced into the military, while women are not? It simply will not do, as I explained before, to justify this by saying that men are naturally more aggressive than women and thus more suitable to military activity.

Perhaps the most serious cases of feminist excess are those in which scholars – many themselves feminists – have been threatened or harassed by highly partisan and intolerant feminists who have deemed their work threatening. The feminists offering these threats are a small minority, but they are nonetheless noteworthy for the harm they cause individuals. Two scholars among those who have come under threat are Suzanne Steinmetz and Murray Straus. Professors Steinmetz and Straus conducted studies that showed that males were the victims of intimate partner violence as often as were females. In no way did they deny the seriousness of domestic violence against female partners. Instead they showed only that there was a further neglected problem. This met with outrage in some quarters. Professor Steinmetz received phone calls threatening her children. When she spoke at an American Civil Liberties Union conference, threats were received that if she were allowed to speak, the place would be bombed. Murray Straus was heckled, booed, picketed and slandered in the most appalling and groundless ways.[19] Obviously the direct victims of this harassment are the particular targets, both male and female. In this regard, feminist excesses can be bad for both men and women. The broader way in which males specifically are disadvantaged is that the threatening and harassing behavior is aimed at silencing views that highlight male disadvantage.

I said earlier that the question whether feminism treats men unfairly is distinct from the question whether men are the victims of a second sexism. The questions intersect in the following way. Insofar as feminism does treat men unfairly, it contributes to the second sexism. This is *not* to say that feminism causes – is the sole or even the major cause – of the second sexism.[20] However, it is to say that those feminists who really are interested in equality of the sexes should oppose both the first and second sexism. The first step to opposing the second sexism is to acknowledge that it exists.

In noting that some feminists contribute to the second sexism I do not and need not deny that non-feminist males are often the perpetrators of what I take to be the second sexism.[21] Tom Digby is reluctant, given the context of the cultural ideals of manhood in which they operate, to *blame* males for what they do to other males.[22] However, he thinks that talk of a second sexism is inappropriate (partly) because the harm being inflicted on males is done by other *males*.[23] I cannot see how this makes a difference. We know that blacks can be agents of racism (against blacks), that Jews can succumb to prejudices about Jews and that women can be complicit in (anti-female) sexism.

As an example of the latter, consider female genital excision, which is almost always performed by women. Women are also amongst the most vigorous defenders of the practice. Nevertheless, feminists argue, entirely appropriately, that given how damaging the procedure is to the girls on whom it is performed, it cannot reasonably be claimed to serve the interests of women (except, perhaps, those few female performers of the ritual, as they may have a vested interest in it).[24] Why should similar reasoning not be applied to the conscription of only males, for example? While it has historically been mainly men who have sent other men to war, why should that undermine the claim that those males sent to war are the victims of sexism? Why are the female agents of genital excision serving the interests of men, while the male – and now also female – agents of government, the bureaucracy and the military who send men to war, are serving men's interests? And why may we not say that males can be perpetrators of the second sexism?

One answer may be that for members of a targeted group to be agents of racism or sexism, they must be serving the interests of some dominant group. But there are two problems with such an answer. First, as I shall argue in the next section, it is not clear that males are any longer the dominant sex in some societies. However, even where they are, I cannot see why that would preclude the possibility that males could be among those who perpetrate the second sexism. It is entirely possible, as I am suggesting is actually the case, for gender roles to be internalized by both men and women and for each group to perpetuate these to their own unfair advantage in some circumstances and unfair disadvantage in others. Moreover, the attributes that each sex looks for in a mate might reinforce those roles. Whether this is inevitable, as some evolutionary psychologists suggest, or whether it could be altered, it is certainly the case that "mate selection" is often (but not always) a two-way street. Women have played a role in "selecting in" certain (biological and cultural) male traits. If females valued different things in males, there would exist different kinds of males.

Are Men Worse off than Women?

Strangely, people are sometimes driven to vie for the status of being more or most victimized. Yet comparisons of suffering are often invidious. It is often notoriously difficult to compare different kinds of suffering. Is it worse to be raped or to be maimed? Is it worse to lose one's sight or to lose one's memory? Is it worse to lose a child or a spouse? And insofar as one can compare and weigh up different kinds of suffering, the exercise of doing so is prone to trivializing the suffering of those who have not suffered the most. This is unfortunate because a person's suffering can be considerable even if others suffer more. Matters become still more complicated when the suffering of groups is compared. This is because groups are made up of individuals. Even if we could work out which group, on the whole, suffers more, there is a temptation to infer that every member of that group suffers more than the contrast group. This is the fallacy of division.

This is not to say that comparisons of suffering are never useful. If, for example, some or other instance of suffering (but not both) is unavoidable, one might aim to avoid the greater suffering, all things being equal. Yet this is not usually the choice we face in comparing the first and second sexisms. It is possible to oppose both.

Why is it, then, that some people are so keen to know whether it is men or women who are worse off? The most charitable explanation, I think, has something to do both with issues about the definition of "sexism" that I raised in Chapter 1 and with various objections to the second sexism that I considered in Chapter 5.

For example, some people deny that males are the victims of sexism because they think that in order for unfair sex discrimination to be sexism it must be both systemic and to the advantage of those who hold power. The assumption is that it is still males who hold power and thus females who are worse off. On this conception of sexism, if neither males nor females are worse off in a given society then sexism no longer exists in that society, even if both sexes are wrongfully discriminated against in different ways but to an equal extent.[25] However, there is a still more troubling implication if it turns out that males are worse off than females in a given society. It then becomes the case that not only is there is a second sexism but there is no first sexism in that society.

Or consider the distraction argument. According to that argument we should not designate unfair discrimination against males as sexism because that will distract us from attending to the first sexism. This argument assumes, contrary to what I said before, that we cannot oppose both the first and second sexisms simultaneously or that opposition to one would diminish the effectiveness of our opposition to the other. However, there is also the further assumption that unfair discrimination against females is worse, because otherwise there would be no reason why we should prioritize efforts to oppose the first sexism rather than the second sexism.

The costs-of-dominance argument also assumes that women are worse off than men, in the sense that whatever disadvantages men have, they are at least dominant, according to this argument. If males were not dominant then the costs-of-dominance argument would obviously fail.

Given the role it plays in the above objections, there is some value in broaching the question whether it is males or females who are worse off. My answer to this question is that while in many or most places women are generally worse off than men, this is not true everywhere. Consider, first, those places were women are worse off. In some societies, as I noted in the introduction, girls are deprived of even basic education. Their brothers are prioritized for limited food and thus the girls often suffer greater malnutrition. They are married while still children, and run terrible risks during pregnancy and childbirth. It is possible, of course, that males can also be the victims of sexist discrimination in such societies, but that discrimination is often not as bad overall as that directed against females. There may be individual males who suffer more sexist discrimination than individual females even in such societies, and that discrimination should not be ignored. However, this would not undermine the claim that in general women are worse off than men in those places.

Consider next those societies in which the position of females has been substantially advanced. There is, of course, a continuum. It is not the case that women either suffer pervasive discrimination or suffer no discrimination at all. However, we might consider those countries in which the most progress has been made – generally the "western" liberal democracies – because if women are worse off there then they are probably worse off everywhere. And if they are not worse off in such societies then the excesses of those who claim they are will be demonstrated.

Feminists typically think that women remain substantially worse off than men even in those places where the position of women has most improved. Indeed, they go so far as to say that women remain *oppressed* in such societies. Marilyn Frye says that it "is a fundamental claim of feminism that women are oppressed."[26] Kenneth Clatterbaugh adds that Professor Frye "and other feminists argue that men are *not* oppressed."[27]

The claim that women remain oppressed in Norway, Sweden, the Netherlands, the United Kingdom and the United States, for example, sounds ludicrous. At least some feminists are aware that if we employ the traditional sense of "oppression," women in such countries may not plausibly be thought of as oppressed.[28] This is because talk of "oppression" conjures up images of tyrannical regimes. Accordingly, we are told that the meaning of "oppression" has "shifted."[29] It is worth considering this new meaning in order to determine whether, employing it, women are (and men are not) oppressed in the developed world.

Iris Marion Young provides a detailed account. She says that the new usage designates not only the tyrannical power of the traditional usage but also the disadvantage and injustice that people suffer "because of the everyday practices of well-intentioned liberal society."[30] It is, she says, "embedded in unquestioned norms, habits and symbols, in the assumptions underlying institutional rules and the collective consequences of following these rules."[31] Quoting Marilyn Frye, she says that "oppression" names "an enclosing structure of forces and barriers which tends to the immobilization and reduction of a group or category of people."[32] Professor Young identifies five faces of oppression, the presence of any one of which, she says, "is sufficient for calling a group oppressed."[33]

The first face is *exploitation*, a "steady process of transfer of the results of the labor of one social group to benefit of another."[34] The second is *marginalization*, which is what happens to "people the system of labor cannot or will not use."[35] The third is *powerlessness*. Those who are oppressed in this sense are "those over whom power is exercised without their exercising it."[36] They are those who "have little or no work autonomy, exercise little creativity or judgement in their work."[37] The powerless "lack the authority, status, and sense of self that professionals tend to have."[38] The fourth face of oppression is *cultural imperialism*, which "involves the universalization of a dominant group's experience and culture."[39] Under conditions of cultural imperialism, "the dominant meanings of a society render the particular perspective" of an oppressed "group invisible at the same time as they stereotype" the oppressed group.[40] The fifth and final face of oppression is *violence*. Members of groups oppressed in this sense "live with the knowledge that they must fear random unprovoked attacks on their person and property."[41] Professor Young says that what "makes violence a face of oppression is less the particular acts ... than the social context surrounding them, which makes them possible and even acceptable."[42]

Professor Young thinks that women are subject to four of the faces of oppression: exploitation, powerlessness, cultural imperialism and violence. She does not think that they are the victims of marginalization, which she describes as "perhaps the most dangerous form of oppression."[43] Is she correct that women are oppressed in the other ways (in the developed world)?

Consider exploitation first. Professor Young says that women's "oppression consists not merely in an inequality of status, power, and wealth resulting from men's excluding them from privileged activities."[44] In addition, she says, the "freedom, power, status, and self-realization of men is possible precisely because women work for them."[45] More specifically, she says that exploitation of women "has two aspects, transfer of the fruits of material labor to men and transfer of nurturing and sexual energies to men."[46]

There are a number of problems with saying, on these grounds, that women are exploited. First, it is not clear that men are still excluding women from privileged activities (in developed countries). It is true that disproportionately few women occupy the *most powerful* positions. For example, there are relatively (but not absolutely) few women in the highest positions in government, the professions, academia and industry. However, that is a distinct issue from whether women are being *excluded* from such positions. Just because women occupy disproportionately few such positions does not mean that they are being excluded from them. There is also a difference between "the most powerful positions" and "privileged activities," the latter being a larger category and the one to which Professor Young refers. Women are now found amply among the ranks of lawyers, doctors and accountants, for example. Determining *to what extent* women are participating in privileged activities depends in part on what activities are deemed privileged. Is teaching schoolchildren a privileged activity? I think it is: consider this profession relative to the many forms of hard, and often dangerous, manual labor typically performed by men. If I am correct that teaching schoolchildren is a privileged activity, then it will be even harder to say that women, who predominate in professions like this, are excluded from privileged activities. And if it is not deemed a privileged activity, how does one determine which activities are and which are not privileged? If the bar for what is considered a privileged activity is set very high then most *men* are also not engaged in privileged activities. Many men, after all, work in low-status jobs, many of which (unlike teaching, some would say) are also unfulfilling, not to mention dangerous. Some of them may also be more poorly paid than teaching.

A second problem with Professor Young's argument is that it is not clear that the "freedom, power, status, and self-realization of men is possible precisely because women work for them."[47] If this were true, then the freedom, power, status and self-realization that men are said to have would not be possible without women working for them. But there are men – and women – who enjoy freedom, power, status and self-realization without women working for them at home,[48] which suggests that the former are possible without the latter.

Third, it is not clear that there is a net transfer of fruits of material labor from women to men. It is true that women do more unpaid work within the home and family, but insofar as a man's income is conjugally pooled, there is also a transfer of the fruits of his labor to his wife or female partner.

To this Carole Pateman may respond that we should not "confuse particular examples of married couples with the *institution* of marriage."[49] While some couples may share the husband's income, the institution of marriage itself does not grant her equal access. But that objection also fails. First, if a large proportion of married couples in a given area or group operate in the way I have mentioned, then *de facto* there is not the unidirectional transfer to which Professor Young refers. Thus, in the absence of suitable empirical evidence, one cannot make the sweeping claim that there is a net transfer of the fruits of material labor from women to men. Second, how does one determine what the institution of marriage is like? One way is to examine the *de facto* institution. If we do this, then the first response suffices if the net transfers are not actually from women to men. The alternative is to examine the *de jure* institution.[50] It might then be suggested that because men retain the power to determine whether their incomes will be shared with their wives, the institution of marriage favors men.[51] One problem with this argument, however, is that it confuses the actual transfer of resources with the power to transfer them. If the claim is that women are exploited because there is a net transfer of resources from them to men, then the claim is refuted if, in fact, the net transfer is not in that direction. This is true even if men control the extent to which they transfer their resources to their wives. It may still be a good idea to equalize this power, but that is a distinct issue.

A fourth problem with Professor Young's argument is that even if we assume that there is a net transfer of nurturing and sexual energies from women to men, it will not follow that women are exploited. There seems to be something selective about focusing on those transfers that are towards men rather than in the reverse direction. What if we focused instead on the transfer of protective energies? Perhaps then the "exploitation" would be in the opposite direction. I use the scare quotes because it is really not clear that any of the transfers mentioned here amount to exploitation.

Next consider powerlessness. Is it really the case that women in developed countries constitute a group "over whom power is exercised without their exercising it"?[52] I do not think so. Women exercise power through their votes, their opinions and their professional roles, for example. Nor would it be fair to say that women, as a group, "have little or no work autonomy, exercise little creativity or judgement in their work." There certainly are many women of whom this true, but there are also very many men of whom this true. Perhaps it will be suggested that insofar it is true of men, this is not because they are men but rather because they are members of some other oppressed group. However, the very same thing may be said about those women who have little or no work autonomy and exercise little creativity or judgment in their work. Women who are not members of poorer classes and oppressed ethnic, racial or religious groups seem to enjoy levels of work autonomy and creativity that rival those of comparable men. Indeed there are very many women in the professions who have the authority, status and sense of self that Professor Young says the powerless lack.

Feminists in developed countries have made great strides in countering the cultural imperialism under which women previously suffered. They have exposed many of the hidden assumptions that disadvantage women. There may well be residues of this, but the extent of these is comparable to those suffered by males. For instance, Professor Young says that members of oppressed groups are "marked out by stereotypes" which "confine them to a nature which is often attached in some way to their bodies, and which thus cannot easily be denied. These stereotypes so permeate the society that they are not noticed as contestable."[53] Yet, as we have seen, there are many powerful stereotypes about males – such as their toughness – that mark them out for discrimination. Moreover, these stereotypes are less noticed than the contrasting ones about women now are in the developed world. It is thus false that white "males ... escape group marking."[54]

Consider, finally, the violent face of oppression. As we have seen, it is males rather than females who constitute the overwhelming majority of victims of violence. While females are more vulnerable than males to sexual violence, males are far more vulnerable to almost every other form of violence. It is true that in some situations it is males of a particular social class or ethnic, religious or racial group who are most vulnerable to violence. However, then the oppressions are intersecting. Their maleness is clearly playing a role – they are experiencing violence in part because they are males – as evidenced by the fact that females in the same social class or ethnic, religious or racial groups are not subjected to similar levels of violence.

The social context, as we have seen, makes violence against males much more acceptable and much more tolerated than violence against females.

Given the above, it is by no means obvious that women in developed countries are oppressed or, on the stated criteria of oppression, that men are not oppressed. I am not recommending that we do accept these criteria, but even if one does accept them, it does not follow that women are and men are not oppressed.

The claim that women are worse off than men is a more modest claim than the claim that they, but not men, are oppressed. It is accordingly harder to evaluate. Obviously the more equally discrimination against males and females is distributed, the more difficult it will be to determine who is worse off.

What evidence might be provided for the claim that women are worse off? One recent opinion article in the *Washington Post* offers the following evidence for the United States: "women are being shot dead in the streets," "more than 1000 women were killed by their partners in 2005," women continue to be the victims of sexual assault, women "hold 17 percent of the seats in Congress," while abortion is legal "more than 85% of counties in the United States have no provider," "women ... make about 76 cents to the man's dollar and make up the majority of Americans living in poverty" and that Hillary "Clinton and Sarah Palin were the targets of sexism during the 2008 campaign."[55]

This justification is typical of arguments for the claim that women do not yet enjoy equality, and indeed overlaps with the arguments that women remain oppressed. Yet the argument is highly selective, engages in what I have called inversion and makes mistaken inferences.

Women are indeed shot dead in the streets and are killed by their partners, but it is *males*, as we have seen, who constitute the overwhelming majority of victims of violence in the United States and elsewhere. If such violence is indicative of sex discrimination, then this speaks to discrimination against males rather than females.

Women do constitute the majority of victims of sexual assault. Although the margin by which they are the majority is, as we saw in Chapter 2, not as large as is generally thought, the net disadvantage is to females. But this must be balanced against the greater violence against males.

Women do constitute a minority of members of Congress. They also earn less than men. However, we saw that such differentials are not necessarily evidence of discrimination. And insofar as they are, the fact that women are the minority of those incarcerated and executed should similarly be seen as evidence of discrimination against males. These two kinds of discrimination would then need to be weighed against one another. Such comparisons, as I indicated above, are very difficult to make. Those who boldly assert that the net effect favors men and discriminates more against women are overly confident.

Abortion facilities are in short supply, but this too does not demonstrate a net disadvantage to being female. After all, males die younger and thus however healthcare resources are being distributed, males are faring worse.

While female candidates may well have experienced sexism in the 2008 campaign, it is quite common for males to experience sexism in American presidential campaigns. This often takes the form of questioning their military record. Former draft dodgers, for example, are frowned upon (even if they are eventually elected), but draft dodging is not a problem any female candidate faces. Of course, she might face sexist preconceptions about whether she could be a suitable Commander-in-Chief, but that is the very sort of question that is asked about male draft-dodging candidates.

It is very easy to point to ongoing discrimination against women. It obviously exists and it may even be systemic. But one cannot, in determining whether the sexes are equal, ignore all the discrimination against males, which may be as systemic. Because most people are not aware of the second sexism they could not make an informed judgment about which sex is the greater victim of discrimination. Even those who are sensitive to the phenomenon of the second sexism may be unaware of its full extent, given how little research has been undertaken on the subject.

It is true that women occupy fewer of the highest and most powerful positions, but this also does not show that women are in general worse off. To make the claim that women are worse off, one must compare all women with all men, rather than *only* the most successful women with the most successful men. Otherwise, one could as easily compare the least successful men with the least successful women and one would then find that men are worse off. This is because more boys drop out of school, fewer men earn degrees, more men die younger, more are incarcerated, and so forth. Indeed, insofar as one should give priority to improving the position of the worst off, attention would need to be focused primarily on males.

In defense of the claim that women are worse off than men it has been noted that "women bent on escape from the female sphere do not usually run into hordes of oppressed men swarming in the opposite direction, trying to change places with their wives and secretaries"[56] and that this is evidence for "where the real advantage lies."[57]

This is not a strong argument. The observation that men (generally[58]) do not want to change places with women should not be invested with too much significance. If people's satisfaction or dissatisfaction with their socially mandated roles were determinative (or even suggestive) of whether such roles were advantageous to their bearers, then a few conclusions which are unfortunate for feminists would follow.

First, many women forced into traditional female roles could not be viewed as being the victims of sexism, so long as those roles were internalized by those women and found by them to be satisfying. Just such an attitude characterized most women until the dawn of the women's movement, and it is an attitude that is still widespread among women in more traditional societies, if not with respect to every feature of their position then at least to many of its features.

Second, the women most dissatisfied with their condition are to be found in disproportionately large numbers amongst women who are subject to the least sexist discrimination and restrictions. For instance, female feminist professors in western societies are arguably among the most liberated women in the world – the women least restricted or disadvantaged by sexism. Yet they are also more concerned about the disadvantages they do face than are many less fortunate women.[59] If the level of one's satisfaction with one's role is what determines the severity of the discrimination to which one is subjected, then the sexism experienced by contemporary western feminists really is worse than that endured by those women in more traditional societies, past or present, who are satisfied with their position. Whether one takes that to be absurd will depend, at least in part, on what view one takes about such matters as adaptive preferences and false consciousness.

It would be unwise to attempt to settle these issues here. All I wish to observe is that if men's apparent contentment with their position is taken to be evidence that they are not the victims of discrimination, then from that follow some conclusions that should be unsettling to most feminists. If, by contrast, it is thought that somebody might be the victim of discrimination without realizing it, then the way is opened to recognizing that men may be worse off than women even if they do not realize it.

Thus it is far from clear that women today are worse off than men in those countries were feminism has had the greatest successes. It is thus disturbing not only how commonly it is claimed that women are worse off or even oppressed, but also how little public resistance there is to such comments.

To deny that women are clearly worse off than men is not to claim that it is men who are worse off. Perhaps men do fare less well and perhaps they do not. It really is very hard to say. What we can conclude, however, is that those arguments that rely on the claim that women are substantially worse off must fail in many places today. Those who think it is a precondition of sexism that one sex predominates over the other will find that at least some societies are already post-sexist. Because that will be, as it should be, an unpalatable conclusion, they would be advised to rethink their conception of sexism to eliminate that feature.

Taking the Second Sexism Seriously

The first step to taking the second sexism seriously is to acknowledge its very existence. If it is not acknowledged it cannot be confronted. This may seem like a small step. However, given how many people are in denial about the existence of the second sexism, it is a much bigger step than one would hope. Indeed, I have devoted this book to arguing that there is a second sexism.

The sort of recognition of the second sexism that is required to take it seriously is not the implicit or begrudging sort. For example, in response to the observation that almost everywhere it has been only men who have been conscripted and sent into combat, many feminists respond that they do not want *anybody*, male or female, forced into combat. Yet they will not explicitly acknowledge that males have been and continue to be unfairly discriminated against by being the only ones conscripted. Nor do they appear really interested in ending this form of discrimination.

I also do not wish to see anybody forced into combat, and I have noted that both conscription and war are justified much less often than they are practiced. Nevertheless to leave the matter there is to ignore two scenarios. The first, and more common, scenario is one in which conscription is unjustified but men (and only men) are being conscripted. If conscription cannot be ended in such cases, should women be exempt?[60] The second scenario, much less common, is when war and conscription are justified. Some people may want to deny either that war or that conscription is ever permissible.[61] I find such views implausible, but I shall not argue for that conclusion here. Instead, I shall focus on those who recognize that war and conscription are sometimes justified. There needs to be a clear recognition that males have unfairly borne the brunt of the combat burden in the past and that women should not be exempt when war and conscription next become morally justifiable.

It is also common for feminists to complain about harsh treatment to which women entering historically male professions are subjected, without acknowledging that males in these positions have been enduring that treatment, and worse, since time immemorial. For example, the harsh treatment of recruits elicited no criticism until the recruits were female, and then the harsh treatment of the female recruits was sometimes construed as the sole problem. The environment, we are told, is hostile to women, instead of recognizing that the environment is hostile to everybody.[62] The conditions for women are then sometimes alleviated, without any similar relief for males.[63]

A full recognition of the second sexism will also require much more research into discrimination against men. Given how little research there has been into the second sexism relative to the first sexism, we have every reason to think that the full extent of discrimination against males has not been revealed. If it has taken all the research it has to show the many facets of discrimination against women and girls, it surely will take as much to show the many ways in which men and boys suffer disadvantage.

The current paucity of such research both results from and further entrenches the neglect of the second sexism. That is to say, it is at least partly because such discrimination is not taken seriously that so little research time and money are devoted to it. But because it is not in vogue to examine such discrimination, much less is known about it, and this perpetuates the impression that is not worthy of detailed consideration. The lopsided information we have about sexism creates a climate in which the research bias is preserved and reinforced. This is dangerous. We have every reason to think that academic neglect of a problem is not an indication of its absence. For example, it was not long ago that sexual abuse of children was thought to be a rare phenomenon. That issue has since become a popular academic and social cause, with the result that we now know much more about it and it is now widely recognized to be more common than was previously thought. Thus one important way of responding to the second sexism is to enable more research, or at least not discourage it. The relevant research might be focused on the second sexism or it might examine questions of sexism more generally but without limiting the focus only to the first sexism.

Once the second sexism is explicitly recognized, the fitting response is to oppose it in the same way that we oppose those sexist attitudes and practices of which women are the primary victims.

This applies even in those societies were women are still worse off. One reason for this is that while it is sometimes permissible to prioritize the worst injustice for attention, we can often oppose both greater and lesser injustices simultaneously. When we can do so, there is no reason to ignore the lesser injustice merely because there is a still worse injustice.

The case for addressing multiple injustices simultaneously becomes strengthened when it is the case that they are intertwined and thus confronting one is best done also by confronting another. I noted in Chapter 5 that the first and second sexisms are intertwined – even if contingently rather than necessarily. That is to say, although it would be logically possible to eliminate all discrimination against women without eliminating any discrimination against men, it is actually the case that the two are connected (even if the connection is not linear). For example, the very same attitude that leads to women being excluded from combat also leads to their being exempted.

Moreover, confronting only the first sexism, while ignoring the second sexism arguably has the effect of unnecessarily alienating potential allies. Those concerned about the second sexism might be more supportive of efforts to counter the first sexism if they saw that opponents of the first second sexism applied their arguments consistently and were also opposed to the second sexism.

Many of the remedies for the second sexism are implicit in my explanations of the ways in which males are the victims of discrimination. However, these remedies can now be made explicit, at least in outline.

The most difficult part is changing attitudes. How does one get people to value male life as much as they value female life, to abhor violence against males as much as they do violence against females, to take as seriously the fact that men can be victims of sexual assault and to recognize that fathers can make good custodial parents in the event of a divorce? It is certainly not easy, but presumably one tries many of the techniques that have been used to change people's attitudes about females. For example, one rears new generations of children in relevant ways that differ from the past. One does not *force* males and females into particular gender roles. Thus, one would desist from telling boys that "big boys don't cry"[64] or to take adversity "like a man."[65] Nor are the needed changes only in how we speak to children. Thus the media and others should desist from the pervasive practice of singling out female casualties for special mention. Instead of referring to the number of dead and adding that they include a specified number of women, one might simply refer to the total number of dead. Even the practice of referring to the victims as "men, women and children" puts an undue emphasis on the sex of the adults, which is irrelevant. The children, after all, are referred to in a gender-neutral way, rather than as "boys and girls." Similarly, campaigns to "end violence against women and children" should be broadened to "end violence."[66] The endless repetition of untruths – for example, that girls and women are the main victims of violence – must end. They are uttered so often that people are genuinely surprised to hear that they are false. And truths that are often suppressed – such as the fact that men are often targeted for violence – should be brought to the fore.

Less difficult than changing attitudes, at least where there is a will to make changes, is the end to *de jure* wrongful discrimination. For example, there should be an end to male-only conscription and to male-only draft registration. Nor should women be exempted (or excluded) from combat. Suitable anesthesia should be used when circumcision is performed on infant boys. When corporal punishment is morally unacceptable, it should no longer be inflicted on males. Insofar as it is justified, it should not be restricted to males or inflicted more frequently or severely on them than on girls, controlling for the relevant wrongdoing. Laws governing corporal punishment should not discriminate between males and females. Similarly, equal regard should be given to male and female bodily privacy. Thus male prisoners should enjoy the greater bodily privacy currently enjoyed by female prisoners. (The alternative is that female prisoners should not enjoy the privileges they currently do, but the burden of proof lies with those who wish to make the lesser protection the norm for all.) Another legal change required to address the second sexism is to ensure that rape legislation and other sexual offenses legislation is gender-neutral. Males can be raped, and they can be raped by women. The law should recognize this and stipulate the same punishments as are inflicted on those males who rape girls and women.

Finally, there are practical interventions that although not as straightforward as the foregoing are also not as difficult as changing attitudes. For example, special attention should be given to those students who are most at risk of failure. Although such attention should be regardless of their sex, the actual rates of failure among boys and girls will mean that this will benefit boys more than girls. Shorter male life expectancy also merits special attention. This involves investigating its causes and undertaking public health and other interventions to address the problem. The question of judicial prejudice in child-custody and penal decisions should also be examined very carefully. There should also be more attention to rehabilitating prisoners. Feminists, in arguing for more women in senior corporate positions, often argue that this is not only good for women but also good for business,[67] and detailed recommendations are provided about how to achieve this.[68] Rehabilitating male prisoners would similarly be good not only for the men who are incarcerated but would also do immense good for society. Prisons, as they currently operate, are notoriously poor at rehabilitation. Indeed, they often reinforce criminality.

These are but a few examples of the many things that could and should be done. Given my arguments in Chapter 6, I have not recommended any remedies that involve preference affirmative action for males. That is to say, I do not propose that males be granted any kind of preference on the grounds of being male. However, this does mean that affirmative action policies and practices that give preference to females should also be terminated. None of this precludes what I called equal opportunity affirmative action – for men and women. This might include specific attempts to counter implicit bias. For example, Victor L. Streib has suggested that juries could be instructed that they must not consider the sex of the defendant or, put another way, that a jury "must not recommend a sentence of death unless it has concluded that it would recommend a sentence of death for the crime in question no matter what the … sex of the defendant … may be."[69] Such instructions, of course, are no guarantee of success, but they are one measure, among others, that might help.[70]

Some men favor the establishment of men's groups to focus on and find solutions to men's problems. I have the same view towards these as I do towards women's groups. Under certain limited conditions they might do some good. Focused advocacy groups, for example, can effectively promote the cause of their members. However, some men's groups, like some women's groups, also run certain risks. They can, for example, become fora for self-pity and for venting hyperbolic views that are not checked or moderated by alternative opinions.[71]

That people are prone to partiality in their thinking about such matters provides one reason why it is helpful, in thinking about remedies to sexism, to consider the first and second sexism together. Any biases in thinking about what constitutes unfair sex discrimination are more likely to be corrected if we are simultaneously thinking about comparable disadvantages of the other sex. Thus, I have suggested that thinking about male disadvantage can help block the common feminist inference from the existence of female disadvantage to the existence of anti-female discrimination. Similarly, any biases in thinking about how to correct sex discrimination are more likely to be exposed if we think about adopting the same correctives for the unfair discrimination against the other sex. I suggested, for example, that reflection on preference affirmative action for men might help some feminists to see why similar preference policies for females may be more problematic than they previously thought. These comparative perspectives are a helpful remedy for ideology and political correctness.

What would a society devoid of sexism (of both the first and the second kinds) look like? The short answer is that I do not know – and neither does anybody else, even if they think they do. This is partly because we do not know the precise extent to which disparities between the sexes are a consequence of sexism, and the precise extent to which they are a consequence of differences (in tendencies) between the sexes. It is also because we do not know exactly how we should respond to whatever differences there may be. For example, to what extent should we reduce those differences if we can do so, and to what extent should we compensate for them if we cannot or should not reduce them?

The inability to say precisely what a society would look like once it had shed the last vestiges of sexism is not such bad news. It need not stop us from acting to end very clear instances of sexism that now exist. Moreover, as we make progress, the bounds of the possible and the appropriate will become clearer. The extent to which the first sexism has been eroded in some contemporary societies would have been unimaginable to most people a century or two ago. It is thus possible that things unimaginable now might yet occur. While changes often occur slowly, they accumulate and can open new vistas. That said, it is extremely unlikely that a society devoid of all sexism will ever exist, for the simple reason that it is extremely unlikely that any utopian ideal will be attained. Rather than focusing on an unattainable utopia, we should direct our attention to the changes that clearly can and should be made.

Conclusion

What I have written cannot be the last word on this topic. There are thousands of articles and books about discrimination against women. Even if this book were a much longer one it could not be comprehensive. Each one of the forms of disadvantage could by itself be the subject of a separate volume, and there may very well be additional disadvantages I have not discussed. My goal has not been to be exhaustive, but rather to provide a relatively wide-ranging discussion of the issues in order to demonstrate that males are also the victims of wrongful sex discrimination and to show that this is overdue for further attention. Uncovering and discussing the full details of the second sexism will require the labors of many more people.

The same is true of responses to my inevitable critics. The claim that there is a second sexism should not be controversial, but it is. Criticism abounds. However, because there are all too few people responding to those criticisms, the criticisms are thought, by those who advance them, to be stronger than they really are. Until now, very few philosophers have raised their heads above the parapets to respond to the academy's orthodoxies on these questions. It would be good to see more of them speaking out.

I have demonstrated that males suffer considerable disadvantage and that much of this is a consequence of discrimination. It is extremely unlikely that all of this discrimination is fair but that no discrimination against females is fair. Yet this is just what some deniers of the second sexism would have us believe. We should be extremely skeptical of such an unlikely scenario. Others will concede that some discrimination against males is unfair, but deny that this is sufficient to constitute sexism. To merit the latter title, they say, the unfair or wrongful discrimination must be against a sex that is subordinated or oppressed. We have seen that there are serious flaws in that argument. Even if we concede that definition of sexism, wrongful discrimination against males should nonetheless be opposed precisely because it is wrong. But conceding to the definition precludes designating as sexism much of what we would ordinarily call sexism. If, as I have argued, women are no longer dominated or oppressed by men in some societies, then on the plausible assumption that women do not now dominate or oppress men, there is no such thing as sexism in such societies, which might be designated as post-sexist. Yet it seems highly implausible to think that sexism ceases to exist once one sex does not dominate or oppress another. This suggests, I have argued, that alternative definitions of sexism ought to be abandoned in favor of the one I proposed in the introduction. Once one does that, the last remaining obstacle to recognizing the second sexism is removed.

Notes

1   See, for example, Warren Farrell and James P. Sterba, *Does Feminism Discriminate against Men? A Debate*, New York: Oxford University Press, 2008.
2   The National Organization for Women (NOW) in the United States seems to have gone further than this in suggesting that even when conscription is *not* justified, women should not be exempt if men are being conscripted. In January 1980, NOW resolved as follows:

   Be it resolved, that NOW opposes the reinstatement of registration and draft for both men and women. NOW's primary focus on this issue is on opposition to registration and draft. However, if we cannot stop the return to registration and draft, we also cannot choose between sisters and brothers. We oppose any registration or draft that excludes women as an unconstitutional denial of rights to both young men and women. And we continue to oppose all sex discrimination by the volunteer armed services.

National Organization for Women, "Opposition to Draft and Registration." Online at http://www.now.org/issues/military/policies/draft2.html (accessed December 23, 2010).

It is unclear from this resolution whether NOW thinks that conscription could *ever* be justified. However it is clear that it was of the view that irrespective of whether conscription is justified it would be wrong to conscript only males.

The 1980 resolution was preceded by another, in 1971, in which the "sexist basis for compulsory military service" was condemned. Online at http://www.now.org/issues/military/policies/war.html (accessed December 23, 2010).

3   It is obviously difficult to know what proportion of sexual harassment accusations are false. Part of the difficulty is determining when an action is sexual harassment. There are broader and narrower definitions. It is even difficult to determine the extent of false rape accusations. One study, operating with an unambiguous definition of rape, tracked the proportion of false rape accusations in a small metropolitan community over a nine-year period. Accusations were deemed false when the accuser recanted. This study found that 41% of rape accusations were false. (See Eugene J. Kanin, "False rape allegations," *Archives of Sexual Behavior*, 23(1), 1994, pp. 81–92.) The author explicitly cautions against generalizing from this sample. He concludes that "false rape accusations are not uncommon" (p. 90). At the very least we can conclude that this possibility cannot be excluded.

4   Myra and David Sadker, *Failing at Fairness: How America's Schools Cheat Girls*, New York: Charles Scribner's Sons, 1994, p. 205. See pp. 205–209 of the Sadkers' book for further examples of how robust the male gender role still is.

5   I am not claiming that males are *oppressed* because they have not entered historically female professions in great numbers, but I do think that their failure to enter those professions indicates the greater resilience of the male gender role.

6   Kenneth Clatterbaugh, "Are men oppressed?" in Larry May, Robert Strikwerda and Patrick D. Hopkins (eds), *Rethinking Masculinity: Philosophical Explorations in the Light of Feminism*, Lanham, MD: Rowman & Littlefield, 1996, p. 299.

7   Linda A. Bell, "Gallantry: what it is and why it should not survive," *Southern Journal of Philosophy*, 22, 1984, pp. 165–173.

8   I do not claim that all feminists take offense or express it. Instead I refer to those– that subset of – feminists who do.

9   The lecture took place at the Woodrow Wilson School of Public and International Affairs at Princeton University on February 4, 2010.

10   Linda A. Bell, "Gallantry," p. 172.

11   For dozens more, see Paul Nathanson and Katherine K. Young, *Spreading Misandry*, Montreal and Kingston: McGill-Queen's University Press, 2001.

12 David Benatar, "Sexist language: alternatives to the alternatives," *Public Affairs Quarterly*, 19(1), January 2005, pp. 1–9. Curiously, departures from the zealous advocacy of gender-inclusive language are employed when this better serves the script of male perpetrators and female victims. See, for example, Sharon Lamb, "Note on terminology," in *The Trouble with Blame: Victims, Perpetrators, and Responsibility*, Cambridge, MA, Harvard University Press, 1996, p. viii; and an interview with Mark Hess, quoted by Philip W. Cook, *Abused Men: The Hidden Side of Domestic Violence*, 2nd edn, Westport, CT: Praeger, 2009, p. 143.

13 Here is one ironic example: A call for papers for a conference entitled "Under-represented Groups in Philosophy" (Cardiff University, November 26, 2010) makes reference to the strategy of "[a]lerting conference organisers as to the problems of homogenous speaker programs and encouraging them to consider speakers from a more diverse pool." The two advertised keynote speakers for this conference were both women. That is not gender diverse and thus it seems that the organizers of this conference did not heed their own advice.

14 For many examples, see Patricia Pearson, *When She Was Bad: Violent Women and the Myth of Innocence*, New York: Viking, 1997 (for example, pp. 52, 61).

15 Jean Bethke Elshtain (*Women and War*, Brighton: Harvester Press, 1987, p. 235) attributes this sort of view to Virginia Woolf (in her *Three Guineas*) and Jane Addams (in her *The Long Road to Woman's Memory*, *Peace and Bread in Time of War* and *Newer Ideals of Peace*).

16 See, for example, Jean Bethke Elshtain, *Women and War*, pp. 167–169,181, 196. See also, "Women as perpetrators," in Truth and Reconciliation Commission of South Africa, *Truth and Reconciliation Commission of South Africa Report*, Cape Town: Truth and Reconciliation Commission, 1998, vol. 4, pp. 313–314; and African Rights, *Rwanda: Not So Innocent – When Women Become Killers*, London: African Rights, 1995.

17 Wini Breines and Linda Gordon, "The new scholarship on family violence," *Signs: Journal of Women in Culture and Society*, 1983, 8(3), p. 495.

18 Many feminists ignore the question of drafting females. However, feminists were challenged to comment on the matter when the United States Supreme Court considered a sex-discrimination challenge to the males-only draft. The National Organization for Women expressed support for drafting females. Other feminist groups, however, opposed drafting females. (See Judith Wagner DeCew, "The combat exclusion and the role of women in the military," *Hypatia*, 10(1), Winter 1995, p. 72.)

19 Philip W. Cook, *Abused Men*, pp. 114–117.

20 Although I have stated this explicitly before, it has not stopped some critics from attributing to me the claim that feminism is responsible for the second sexism. See Carol Quinn and Rosemarie Tong, "The consequences of taking the second sexism seriously," *Social Theory and Practice*, 29(2), April 2003, p. 245; and Kenneth Clatterbaugh, "Benatar's alleged second sexism," *Social Theory and Practice*, 29(2), April 2003, p. 213.

21 Some have suggested that I am denying this. See, for example, Tom Digby, "Male trouble: are men victims of sexism?" *Social Theory and Practice*, 29(2), April 2003, pp. 252–253; and Carol Quinn and Rosemarie Tong, "The consequences of taking the second sexism seriously," p. 244.

22 Tom Digby, "Male trouble," p. 253.

23 Ibid., p. 252.

24 Some may seek to claim that girls are benefited by the procedure because without it they would be ostracized. It is true that in societies in which the practice is widespread, individuals who are not cut may be ostracized. It is a further question whether the benefit of not being ostracized outweighs the harm of being cut. However, whatever the answer to this, the feminist critique is most plausibly understood as a critique of the general practice rather than of individual instances of it in the context of a general practice.

25 As I said in the Introduction, even if this does not count as sexism, it would still be wrong.

26 Marilyn Frye, *The Politics of Reality: Essays in Feminist Theory*, Freedom, CA: The Crossing Press, 1983, p. 1. Others use slightly different language. Allison Jaggar says that feminism is "dedicated to ending the *subordination of women*" (my emphasis). (Alison Jaggar (ed.), *Living with Contradictions: Controversies in Feminist Social Ethics*, Boulder, CO: Westview Press, 1994, p. 2.)

27 Kenneth Clatterbaugh, "Are men oppressed?" p. 289.

28 Iris Marion Young, *Justice and the Politics of Difference*, Princeton: Princeton University Press, 1990, pp. 40–41.

29 Ibid., p. 41.

30 Ibid.

31 Ibid.

32 Marilyn Frye, *The Politics of Reality*, pp. 10–11, cited by Iris Marion Young, *Justice and the Politics of Difference*, p. 41.

33 Iris Marion Young, *Justice and the Politics of Difference*, p. 64.

34 Ibid., p. 49.

35 Ibid., p. 53.

36 Ibid., p. 56.

37 Ibid.

38 Ibid., p. 57.

39 Ibid., p. 59.

40 Ibid., pp. 58–59.

41 Ibid., p. 61.

42 Ibid.

43 Ibid., p. 53.

44 Ibid., p. 50.

45 Ibid.

46 Ibid.

47 Ibid.

48 How many such men and women there are depends on what one means by "women working for them at home." If one means women with whom they are partnered or married, then the number is much larger than if one includes hired (usually female) domestic labor. But the problem with interpreting the phrase in the broader way to include hired labor is that those "who enjoy freedom, power, status and self-realization" are reliant not only on (paid) domestic labor but also on much other paid labor – the labor of those who grow their food, remove their refuse and fix their cars, for example. Since much of this work is done by

men, those "who enjoy freedom, power, status and self-realization" could not enjoy those things without the work of both men and women.

49   Carole Pateman, *The Sexual Contract*, Cambridge: Polity Press, 1988, p. 158.

50   It should go without saying that in determining the current *de jure* situation, it will not suffice to cite historical evidence. Professor Pateman's focus in *The Sexual Contract* is almost exclusively historical. She writes at great length about the relationship of men and women, husbands and wives, in the past. When she refers to the present, it is almost always an unsubstantiated sweeping statement. For example, she says that in "modern civil society all men are deemed good enough to be women's masters" (p. 219). She refers, in a few sentences, to contemporary female disadvantage in the developed world (on p. 228, for example), but the examples are selective and even some of those (for example, the claim that "women's economic circumstances still place them at a disadvantage in the termination of the marriage contract") are contested. (See the section on "Custody" in Chapter 5, above.)

51   To rectify this, Susan Moller Okin has suggested that both partners to a marriage should have "*equal legal entitlement* to all earnings coming into the household" (*Justice, Gender, and the Family*, New York: Basic Books, 1989, pp. 181–183).

52   Iris Marion Young, *Justice and the Politics of Difference*, p. 56.

53   Ibid., p. 59.

54   Ibid.

55   Jessica Valenti, "For Women in America, Equality Is Still an Illusion," *Washington Post*, February 21, 2010, p. B02.

56   Janet Radcliffe Richards, "Separate spheres," in Peter Singer (ed.), *Applied Ethics*, Oxford: Oxford University Press, 1986, p. 198.

57   Ibid.

58   I say "generally," because there are some men who have wanted to change places with women, and not because of a so-called "gender-identity disorder." Men's dressing in women's clothing in order to secure places on lifeboats is one example.

59   This is not to say that these female feminist philosophers think that they are worse off than women in more traditional societies. They do not think this. However, it is the case that they are more dissatisfied with their own situation than *some* of the more restricted women in more traditional societies are dissatisfied with theirs.

60   Feminists need to take a stand – as the National Organization for Women did (see note 2 above) – on whether women should be exempt under such conditions.

61   Pacifists think this, and some feminists are pacifists. It is presumably an implication of at least some forms of pacifism that a woman may not use (deadly) violence to defend herself against a man attempting to rape her, even if that is the only way she can prevent the assault.

62   In his letter to the *New York Times* about the mistreatment of female recruits at the Citadel in South Carolina, USA, Dan Patterson writes "It is indeed a sad state of affairs when it takes the abuse of female cadets to make the Citadel's 'deviant conduct' newsworthy. Where was this indignation during the scores of years that male cadets suffered abuse?" "Citadel's Culture Abused Men before

Women," *New York Times*, January 17, 1997. I do not deny that a lone female recruit may be singled out for a special kind of harsh treatment, but this has also been true of male recruits who have been different in some way.

63   For some examples see Kingsley Browne, *Co-Ed Combat: The New Evidence That Women Shouldn't Fight the Nation's Wars*, New York: Sentinel, 2007, pp. 208–229.

64   Some might suggest an alternative strategy – that continuing to tell boys this would be acceptable if one also told girls that "big girls don't cry." The problem with this strategy is that the effect of the admonition to girls is unlikely, at least for now, to have the same effect on girls that the comparable admonition would on boys and thus the same treatment would have a disparate impact.

65   If the phrase "taking it like a woman" ever came to mean the same as "taking it like a man," then the meaning of both phrases will have changed.

66   Or, more accurately, to end violence against those, including men, who do not deserve it.

67   Federal Glass Ceiling Commission, *Good for Business: Making Full Use of the Nation's Human Capital*, Washington, DC: Federal Glass Ceiling Commission, 1995.

68   Women and Work Commission, "Shaping a Fairer Future," London: UK Commission for Employment and Skills, 2006, p. xii.

69   Victor L. Streib, "Gendering the death penalty: countering sex bias in a masculine sanctuary," *Ohio State Law Journal*, 63, pp. 464–465, quoting 18 U.S.C §3593(f) 1997.

70   For evidence that these sorts of ethical reminders can impact on behavior, see Dan Ariely, *Predictably Irrational: The Hidden Forces That Shape Our Decisions*, rev. and expanded edn, New York: Harper, 2009, pp. 207–214.

71   Deborah Rhode objects that the "American public gets endless accounts of what is wrong with the women's movement" but "rarely do we hear about what is wrong with the men's movement" (*Speaking of Sex: The Denial of Gender Inequality*, Cambridge, MA: Harvard University Press, 1997, p. 217). One good reason for the asymmetrical attention, however, is that the men's movement is much smaller and less influential than the women's movement. Many people do not take it seriously, but they have a much more difficult time dismissing the women's movement. The focus on (some parts of) the women's movement is thus understandable, even if many of the same flaws characterize (some parts of) the men's movement.

Bibliography

African Rights (1995) *Rwanda: Death, Despair and Defiance*, rev. edn. London: African Rights.

African Rights (1995) *Rwanda: Not So Innocent – When Women Become Killers*. London: African Rights.

Albert, D.J., Walsh, M.L. and Jonik, R.H. (1993) "Aggression in humans: what is its biological foundation?" *Neuroscience and Behavioral Review*, 17: 405–425.

Allen, A. (1993) "Women's health," *New England Journal of Medicine*, 329(24): 1816–1817.

Allen, C.M. (1990) "Women as perpetrators of child sexual abuse: recognition barriers," in A.L. Horton, B.L. Johnson, L.M. Roundy and D. Williams (eds), *The Incest Perpetrator: A Family Member No One Wants to Treat*. Newbury Park, CA: Sage Publications, pp. 108–125.

Aloisi, A.M., and Bonifazi, M. (2006) "Sex hormones, central nervous system and pain," *Hormones and Behavior*, 50: 1–7.

Altermatt, E.R., Jovanovic, J. and Perry, M. (1998) "Bias or responsivity? Sex and achievement-level effects on teachers' classroom questioning practices," *Journal of Educational Psychology*, 90(3): 516–527.

Alvarez, L. (2009) "G.I. Jane Breaks the Combat Barrier as War Evolves," *New York Times*, August 16, http://www.nytimes.com/2009/08/16/us/16women.html (accessed August 16, 2009).

Amato, P.R., and Keith, B. (1991) "Parental divorce and adult well-being: a meta-analysis," *Journal of Marriage and the Family*, 53: 43–58.

American Academy of Pediatrics, Committee on Bioethics (2010) "Policy Statement – Ritual Genital Cutting of Female Minors," *Pediatrics*, published online April 26, 2010. DOI: 10.1542/peds.2010-0187.

American Academy of Pediatrics (2010) "American Academy of Pediatrics Withdraws Policy Statement on Female Genital Cutting," May 27, www.aap.org/advocacy/releases/fgc-may27-2010.htm (accessed July 4, 2010).

The Second Sexism: Discrimination Against Men and Boys, First Edition. David Benatar.
© 2012 John Wiley & Sons, Inc. Published 2012 by John Wiley & Sons, Inc.

American Association of University Women (1991) *Shortchanging Girls, Shortchanging America*. Washington, DC: American Association of University Women.

American Association of University Women (1992) *The AAUW Report: How Schools Shortchange Girls*. Washington, DC: American Association of University Women.

American Association of University Women (2001) *Beyond the "Gender Wars": A Conversation about Girls, Boys and Education*. Washington, DC: American Association of University Women.

Anderson, K.G. (2006) "How well does paternity confidence match actual paternity?" *Current Anthropology*, 47(3): 513–520.

Anderson & Travis, PC (2004) Statement: "Army drops all legal action against SSG Georg-Andreas Pogany," July 16.

Angell, M. (1993) "Caring for women's health: what is the problem?" *New England Journal of Medicine*, 329(4): 271–272.

Anonymous (1996) "African-born U.S. residents are the most highly educated group in American society," *Journal of Blacks in Higher Education*, 13 (Autumn): 33–34.

Anonymous (1999/2000) "African immigrants in the United States are the nation's most highly educated group," *Journal of Blacks in Higher Education*, 26 (Winter): 60–61.

Anonymous (2006) "Circumcisions have claimed 102 lives since 1996," *Cape Times*, October 5, p. 6.

Anonymous (2010) "Not Anyone's Daughter," *New York Times*, June 30, http://nytimes.com/2010/07/01/opinion/01thu4.html?scp=1&sq=not%20anyone's%20daughter&st=cse (accessed July 1, 2010).

Anonymous (n.d.) "Berit Mila Program of Reform Judaism: Ceremonies for Girls," http://beritmila.org/Ceremonies%20for%20girls.html (accessed August 10, 2005).

Anonymous (n.d.) "Caning in Singapore," *Wikipedia*, http://en.wikipedia.org/wiki/Caning_in_Singapore#Military_Caning (accessed October 12, 2009).

Anonymous (n.d.) "Conscription," *Wikipedia*, http://en.wikipedia.org/wiki/Conscription (accessed March 21, 2010).

Anonymous (n.d.) "Eton College," *Wikipedia*, http://en.wikipedia.org/wiki/Eton_College#Corporal_punishment (accessed December 24, 2010).

Anonymous (n.d.) "Judicial corporal punishment," *Wikipedia*, http://en.wikipedia.org/wiki/Judicial_corporal_punishment (accessed October 12, 2009).

Anonymous (n.d) "Parental leave," *Wikipedia*, http://en.wikipedia.org/wiki/Parental_leave (accessed January 3, 2011).

Arias, I., and Johnson, P. (1989) "Evaluations of physical aggression among intimate dyads," *Journal of Interpersonal Violence*, 4(3): 298–307.

Ariely, D. (2009) *Predictably Irrational: The Hidden Forces That Shape Our Decisions*, rev. and expanded edn, New York: Harper.

Associated Press (2009) "Pregnant G.I.s Could Be Punished," *New York Times*, December 20, http://www.nytimes.com/2009/12/20/us/20general.html?pagewanted=print (accessed December 20, 2009).

Associated Press (2009) "U.S. General Backs Off Pregnancy Policy," *New York Times*, December 23, http://www.nytimes.com/2009/12/23/us/23baghdad.html?fta=y&pagewanted=print (accessed December 23, 2009).

Associated Press (2009) "Commander to Rescind a Provision on Pregnancy," *New York Times*, December 26, http://www.nytimes.com/2009/12/26/us/26military.html?th=&emc=th&pagewanted=print (accessed December 26, 2009).

Auvert, B., Taljaard, D., Lagarde, E. *et al.* (2005) "Randomized, controlled intervention trial of male circumcision for reduction of HIV infection risk: the ANRS 1265 trial," *PLoS Medicine*, 2(11): 1112–1122.

Bailey, R.C., Moses, S., Parker, C.B. *et al.* (2007) "Male circumcision for HIV prevention in young men in Kisumu, Kenya: a randomised controlled trial," *The Lancet*, 369: 643–656.

Baldus, C., Woodworth, G. and Pulaski, Jr., C.A. (1990) *Equal Justice and the Death Penalty: A Legal and Empirical Analysis*. Boston: Northeastern University Press.

Barker, R. (2006) "Questions for Written Answer," New Zealand Parliament, July 27, http://www.parliament.nz/enNZ/PB/Business/QWA/0/f/d/QWA_09643_2006-9643-2006-Judy-Turner-to-the-Minister-for-Courts.htm (accessed April 5, 2011).

Bateman, C. (2005) "Blood service adjusts after 'racist' claims," *South African Medical Journal*, 95: 728–730.

Bax, E.B. (1908) "The Legal Subjection of Men," http://en.wikisource.org/wiki/The_Legal_Subjection_of_Men (accessed July 1, 2010).

Bell, L.A. (1984) "Gallantry: what it is and why it should not survive," *Southern Journal of Philosophy*, 22: 165–173.

Beller, S. (1989) *Vienna and the Jews: 1867–1938*. Cambridge: Cambridge University Press.

Benatar, D. (1996) "The child, the rod and the law," *Acta Juridica*: 197–214.

Benatar, D. (1997) "Same-sex marriage and sex discrimination," *American Philosophical Association Newsletter on Philosophy and Law*, 97(1): 71–74.

Benatar, D. (1998) "Corporal punishment," *Social Theory and Practice*, 24(2): 237–260.

Benatar, D. (2003) "The second sexism," *Social Theory and Practice*, 29(2): 177–210.

Benatar, D. (2003) "The second sexism, a second time," *Social Theory and Practice*, 29(2): 275–296.

Benatar, D. (2005) "Sexist language: alternatives to the alternatives," *Public Affairs Quarterly*, 19(1): 1–9.

Benatar, D. (2006) *Better Never to Have Been*. Oxford: Oxford University Press.

Benatar, D. (2008) "Diversity limited," in L.M. Thomas (ed.), *Contemporary Debates in Social Philosophy*. Oxford: Wiley-Blackwell, pp. 212–225.

Benatar, D. (2008) "Justice, diversity and racial preference: a critique of affirmative action," *South African Law Journal*, 125(2): 274–306.

Benatar, D. (2008) "Why do Jewish egalitarians not circumcise their daughters?" *Jewish Affairs*, 63(3): 21–23.

Benatar, D., and Benatar, M. (2001) "A pain in the fetus: toward ending confusion about fetal pain," *Bioethics*, 15(1): 57–76.

Benatar, D., and Benatar, M. (2003) "How not to argue about circumcision," *American Journal of Bioethics*, 3(2): W1–W9, http://www.bioethics.net/journal/pdf/3_2_LT_w01_Benatar.pdf (accessed August 29, 2011).

Benatar, M., and Benatar, D. (2003) "Between prophylaxis and child abuse: the ethics of neonatal circumcision," *American Journal of Bioethics*, 3(2): 35–48.

Benokraitis, N.V. (1997) *Subtle Sexism: Current Practices and Prospects for Change.* Thousand Oaks, CA: Sage Publications.

Benokraitis, N.V., and Feagin, J.R. (1995) *Modern Sexism: Blatant, Subtle, and Covert Discrimination*, 2nd edn. Englewood Cliffs, NJ: Prentice-Hall.

Berenbaum, S.A., and Resnick, S.M. (1997) "Early androgen effects on aggression in children and adults with congenital adrenal hyperplasia," *Psychoneuroendochrinology*, 22(7): 505–515.

Bevacqua, M. (2000) *Rape on the Public Agenda: Feminism and the Politics of Sexual Assault.* Boston: Northeastern University Press.

Bevan, D. (1972) *Drums of the Birkenhead.* Cape Town: Purnell & Sons.

Bickle, G.S., and Peterson, R.D. (1991) "The Impact of Gender-Based Family Roles on Criminal Sentencing," *Social Problems*, 38(3): 372–394.

Bleier, R. (1984) *Science and Gender: A Critique of Biology and Its Theories on Women.* New York: Pergamon Press.

Bloom, B.L., Asher, S.J. and White, S.W. (1978) "Marital disruption as a stressor: a review and analysis," *Psychological Bulletin*, 85(4): 867–894.

Bourke, J. (1996) *Dismembering the Male: Men's Bodies, Britain and the Great War.* Chicago: University of Chicago Press.

Bourke, J. (1999) *An Intimate History of Killing: Face-to-Face Killing in Twentieth-Century Warfare.* New York: Basic Books.

Bourke, J. (2007) *Rape: A History from 1860 to the Present Day.* London: Virago.

Bowlby, G. (2008) "Provincial drop-out rates: trends and consequences," http://www.statcan.gc.ca/pub/81-004-x/2005004/8984-eng.htm (accessed December 2, 2009).

Brake, E. (2005) "Fatherhood and child support: do men have a right to choose?" *Journal of Applied Philosophy*, 22(1): 55–73.

Braver, S.L. (1998) *Divorced Dads: Shattering the Myths.* New York: Jeremy P. Tarcher/Putman.

Breines, W., and Gordon, L. (1983) "The new scholarship on family violence," *Signs: Journal of Women in Culture and Society*, 8(3): 490–531.

Brinkeroff, M.B., and Lupri, E. (1988) "Interspousal Violence," *Canadian Journal of Sociology*, 13(4): 407–430.

Brody, L. (1999) *Gender, Emotion and the Family.* Cambridge, MA: Harvard University Press.

Browne, K. (1995) "Sex and temperament in modern society: a Darwinian view of the glass ceiling and the gender gap," *Arizona Law Review*, 37(4): 1017–1028.

Browne, K. (2007) *Co-Ed Combat: The New Evidence That Women Shouldn't Fight the Nation's Wars.* New York: Sentinel.

Browning, C. (1992) *Ordinary Men: Reserve Police Battalion 101 and the Final Solution in Poland.* New York: HarperCollins.

Browning, C. (2000) *Nazi Policy, Jewish Workers, German Killers.* New York: Cambridge University Press.

Brozan, N. (1998) "Religious Circumcision in a Changing World," *New York Times*, October 19, http://www.nytimes.com/1998/10/19/us/religious-circumcision-in-a-changing-world.html (accessed June 18, 2011).

Carlson, E.S. (2006) "The hidden prevalence of male sexual assault during war," *British Journal of Criminology*, 46(1): 16–25.

Carpenter, C. (2005) "'Women, children and other vulnerable groups': gender, strategic frames and the protection of civilians as a transnational issue," *International Studies Quarterly*, 49(2): 295–334.

Cascardi, M., Langhinrischen, J. and Vivian, D. (1992) "Marital aggression: impact, injury, and health correlates for husbands and wives," *Archives of Internal Medicine*, 152: 1178–1184.

Centers for Disease Control and Prevention. (1995) *Monthly Vital Statistics Report*, 43(9), Supplement, pp. 24–25.

Chivers, M., and Bailey, J.M. (2005) "A sex difference in features that elicit genital response," *Biological Psychology*, 70(2): 115–120.

Clark, R. (n.d.) "Female executions 2000 to date," http://www.capitalpunishmentuk. org/women.html (accessed February 24, 2010).

Clarke-Steward, K.A., and Hayward, C. (1996) "Advantages of father custody and contact for the psychological well-being of school-age children," *Journal of Applied Developmental Psychology*, 17(2): 239–270.

Clatterbaugh, K. (1996) "Are men oppressed?" in L. May, R. Strikwerda and P.D. Hopkins (eds), *Rethinking Masculinity: Philosophical Explorations in the Light of Feminism*, 2nd edn. Lanham, MD: Rowman & Littlefield, pp. 289–305.

Clatterbaugh, K. (2003) "Benatar's alleged second sexism," *Social Theory and Practice*, 29(2): 211–218.

Claver, S. (1954) *Under the Lash: A History of Corporal Punishment in the British Armed Forces*. London: Torchstream Books.

Coleman, D.L. (1998) "The Seattle compromise: multicultural sensitivity and Americanization," *Duke Law Journal*, 47: 717–783.

Conquest, R. (1968) *The Great Terror: Stalin's Purge of the Thirties*. Toronto: Macmillan.

Cook, P.W. (2009) *Abused Men: The Hidden Side of Domestic Violence*, 2nd edn. Westport, CT: Praeger.

Coughlin, A.M. (1994) "Excusing women," *California Law Review*, 82(1): 1–93.

Craft, R.M., Mogil, J.S. and Aloisi, A.M. (2004) "Sex differences in pain and analgesia: the role of gonadal hormones," *European Journal of Pain*, 8(5): 397–411.

Craven, D. (1997) "Sex Differences in Violent Victimization, 1994," Bureau of Justice Statistics Special Report. Washington, DC: US Department of Justice.

Cronin, H. (2008), "Mind the (Gender) Gap: It's More Than Cultural," *Cape Times*, 29 August, p. 11.

Cronin, H. (2008) "More dumbbells but more Nobels: why men are at the top," http://edge.org/q2008/q08_10.html (accessed January 11, 2010).

Curan, D.A. (1983) "Judicial discretion and defendant's sex," *Criminology*, 21(1): 41–58.

Dahl, R. (1984) *Boy: Tales of Childhood*. London: Puffin Books.

Daly, K. (1987) "Discrimination in criminal courts: family, gender, and the problem of equal treatment," *Social Forces*, 66(1): 152–175.

Daly, K., and Tonry, M. (1997) "Gender, race and sentencing," *Crime and Justice*, 22: 201–252.

DeCew, J.W. (1995) "Women, equality, and the military," in D.E. Bushnell (ed.), *Nagging Questions: Feminist Ethics in Everyday Life*. Lanham, MD: Rowman & Littlefield.

DeCew, J.W. (1995) "The combat exclusion and the role of women in the military," *Hypatia*, 10(1): 56–73.

Dempsey, J. (2007) "East German Shoot-to-Kill Order Is Found," *New York Times*, August 13, http://www.nytimes.com/2007/08/13/world/europe/13germany.html (accessed August 13, 2007).

Demuth, S., and Steffensmeier, D. (2004) "The impact of gender and race-ethnicity in the pretrial release process," *Social Problems*, 51(2): 222–242.

Department of Justice (1990) *Evaluation of the Divorce Act. Phase II: Monitoring and Evaluation*. Ottawa: Department of Justice Canada, Bureau of Review.

Digby, T. (1998) "Do feminists hate men? Feminism, antifeminism and gender oppositionality," *Journal of Social Philosophy*, 29(2): 15–31.

Digby, T. (2003) "Male trouble: are men victims of sexism?" *Social Theory and Practice*, 29(2): 247–273.

Dillon, S., and Rimer, S. (2005) "No Break in the Storm over Harvard President's Words," *New York Times*, January 19, http://www.nytimes.com/2005/01/19/education/19harvard.html (accessed January 19, 2005).

Drèze, J., and Sen, A. (1989) *Hunger and Public Action*. Oxford: Clarendon Press.

Dutton, D., and Nicholls, T. (2005) "The gender paradigm in domestic violence research and theory. Part 1: the conflict of theory and data," *Aggression and Violent Behavior*, 10(6): 680–714.

Dworkin, R. (1981) "What is equality? Part 2: equality of resources," *Philosophy and Public Affairs*, 10(4): 283–345.

Dworkin, R. (1987) *Taking Rights Seriously*. London: Duckworth.

Eagly, A.H., and Steffen, V.J. (1986) "Gender and aggressive behavior: a meta-analytic review of social psychological literature," *Psychological Bulletin*, 100(3): 309–330.

The Economist. (2006) *Pocket World in Figures*, 2007 edn. London: Profile Books.

Ehrhardt, A.A., and Baker, S.W. (1978) "Fetal androgens, human central nervous system differentiation, and behavior sex differences," in R.C Friedman, R.M. Richart and R.L. Vande Wiele (eds), *Sex Differences in Behavior*. Huntington, NY: Robert E. Krieger Publishing Co., pp. 33–51.

Ellis, L., Herschberger, S., Field, E. *et al.* (2008) *Sex Differences: Summarizing More Than a Century of Scientific Research*. New York: Psychology Press.

Ellsworth-Jones, W. (2008) *We Will Not Fight: The Untold Story of the First World War's Conscientious Objectors*. London: Aurum.

Elshtain, J.B. (1987) *Women and War*. Brighton: Harvester Press.

Estrich, S. (1987) *Real Rape*. Cambridge: Harvard University Press.

Enloe, C. (1994) "Some of the best soldiers wear lipstick," in A.M. Jaggar (ed.), *Living with Contradictions*, pp. 599–608.

Farrell, C. (n.d.) "Singapore: school CP," http://www.corpun.com/rules2.htm#singsch (accessed October 13, 2009).

Farrell, W., and Sterba, J.P. (2008) *Does Feminism Discriminate against Men? A Debate*. New York: Oxford University Press.

Fausto-Sterling, A. (1985) *Myths of Gender: Biological Theories about Men and Women*, rev. edn. New York: Basic Books.

Federal Bureau of Investigation (2008) "Hate Crime Statistics," http://www.fbi.gov/ucr/hc2008/documents/incidentsandoffenses.pdf (accessed December 21, 2009).

Federal Glass Ceiling Commission (1995) *Good for Business: Making Full Use of the Nation's Human Capital*. Washington, DC: US Department of Labor.

Feinberg, J. (1985) *Offense to Others*. New York: Oxford University Press.

Felson, R.B. (2000) "The normative protection of women from violence," *Sociological Forum*, 15(1): 91–116.

Fergusson, D.M., Horwood, L.J. and Ridder, E.M. (2005) "Partner violence and mental health outcomes in a New Zealand birth cohort," *Journal of Marriage and the Family*, 67(5): 1103–1119.

Feuer, L.S. (1982) "The stages of the social history of Jewish professors in American colleges and universities," *American Jewish History*, 71(4): 432–465.

Fiebert, M.S. (n.d.) "References examining assaults by women on their spouses or male partners: an annotated bibliography," http://www.csulb.edu/~mfiebert/assault.htm (accessed March 5, 2010).

Fillingim, R. (2003) "Sex-related influences on pain: a review of mechanisms and clinical implications," *Rehabilitation Psychology*, 48(3): 165–174.

Finder, A., Healy, P.D. and Zernike, K. (2006) "President of Harvard Resigns, Ending Stormy 5-Year Tenure," *New York Times*, February 22, http://www.nytimes.com/2006/02/22/education/22harvard.html (accessed February 22, 2006).

Fischer, H. (2009) "United States Military Casualty Statistics: Operation Iraqi Freedom and Operation Enduring Freedom." Washington, DC: Congressional Research Service, March 25.

Friedan, B. (1974) *The Feminine Mystique*. New York: Dell.

Fritz, G.S., Stoll, K. and Wagner, N.N. (1981) "A comparison of males and females who were sexually molested as children," *Journal of Sex and Marital Therapy*, 7(1): 54–59.

Frodi, A., Macaulay, J. and Thome, P.R. (1977) "Are women always less aggressive than men? A review of the experimental literature," *Psychological Bulletin*, 84(4): 634–660.

Frye, M. (1983) *The Politics of Reality: Essays in Feminist Theory*. Freedom, CA: The Crossing Press.

Gettleman, J. (2003) "Soldier Accused as Coward Says He Is Guilty Only of Panic Attack," *New York Times*, November 6, http://www.nytimes.com/2003/11/06/national/06SOLD.html (accessed November 6, 2003).

Giroud, M. (1981) *The Return to Camelot: Chivalry and the English Gentleman*. London: Yale University Press.

Glanz, J. (2009) "Historians Reassess Battle of Agincourt," *New York Times*, October 25, http://www.nytimes.com/2009/10/25/world/europe/25agincourt.html?pagewanted=all (accessed October 25, 2009).

Glazer, N., and Moynihan, D.P. (1970) *Beyond the Melting Pot: The Negroes, Puerto Ricans, Jews, Italians, and Irish of New York City*, 2nd edn. Cambridge, MA: MIT Press.

Goldberg, S. (1993) *Why Men Rule: A Theory of Male Dominance*. Chicago: Open Court.

Goldhagen, D.J. (1997) *Hitler's Willing Executioners: Ordinary Germans and the Holocaust*. New York: Vintage Books.

Goldstein, J. (2001) *War and Gender*. Cambridge: Cambridge University Press.

Grall, T.S. (2009) "Custodial Mothers and Fathers and Their Child Support: 2007." Washington, DC: US Census Bureau.

Gray, R.H., Kigozi, G., Serwadda, D. *et al.* (2007) "Male circumcision for HIV prevention in men in Rakai, Uganda: a randomised trial," *The Lancet*, 369: 657–666.

Greenblat, C.S. (1983) "A hit is a hit is a hit ... or is it? Approval and tolerance of the use of physical force by spouses," in D. Finkelhor, R.J. Gelles, G.T. Hotaling and M.A. Straus (eds), *The Dark Side of Families: Current Family Violence Research*. Beverly Hills: Sage Publications, pp. 235–260.

Grossman, D. (1995) *On Killing: The Psychological Cost of Learning to Kill in War and Society*. Boston: Back Bay Books.

Groth, N., and Burgess, W. (1980) "Male rape: offenders and victims," *American Journal of Psychiatry*, 137(7): 806–810.

Gupta, S.C. (1986) *Capital Punishment in India*. New Dehli: Deep & Deep Publications.

Haas, J. (1998) "The cost of being a woman," *New England Journal of Medicine*, 338(23): 1694–1695.

Hales, S.D. (1996) "Abortion and fathers' rights," in J.M. Humber and R.F. Almeder (eds), *Reproduction, Technology, and Rights*. Totowa, NJ: Humana Press, pp. 5–26.

Hales, S.D. (1996) "More on fathers' rights," in J.M. Humber and R.F. Almeder (eds), *Reproduction, Technology, and Rights*. Totowa, NJ: Humana Press, pp. 43–49.

Hedderman, C., and Hough, M. (1994) "Does the Criminal Justice System Treat Men and Women Differently?" Research Findings 10. Croydon: Home Office Research and Statistics Department.

Hines, D.A., Brown, J. and Dunning, E. (2007) "Characteristics of callers to the domestic abuse helpline for men," *Journal of Family Violence*, 22(2): 63–72.

Hines, M., and Kaufman, F.R. (1994) "Androgen and the development of human sex-typical behavior: rough-and-tumble play and sex of preferred playmates in children with congenital adrenal hyperplasia (CAH)," *Child Development*, 65(4): 1042–1053.

Hochschild, A. (1999) *King Leopold's Ghost*. Boston: Mariner Books.

Hoffmann, C., and Reed, J. (1982) "When is imbalance not discrimination?" in W.E. Block and M.A. Walker (eds), *Discrimination, Affirmative Action, and Equal Opportunity: An Economic and Social Perspective*. Vancouver: The Fraser Institute, pp. 187–216.

Holden, C. (1987) "Why do women live longer than men?" *Science*, 238, October 9, pp. 158–160.

Holdstock, T.L. (1990) "Violence in schools: discipline," in B. McKendrick and W. Hoffmann (eds), *People and Violence in South Africa*. Cape Town: Oxford University Press, pp. 341–372.

Holmes, G., and Offen, L. (1996) "Clinicians' hypothesis regarding clients' problems: are they less likely to hypothesize sexual abuse in male compared to female clients?" *Child Abuse & Neglect*, 20(6): 493–501.

Holmes, W.C., and Slap, G.B. (1998) "Sexual abuse of boys: definition, prevalence, correlates, sequelae, and management," *Journal of the American Medical Association*, 280(21): 1855–1862.

Home Office (2009) *Crime in England and Wales 2008/9: A Summary of the Main Findings*. London: HMSO.

Hood, R., and Hoyle, C. (2008) *The Death Penalty: A Worldwide Perspective*, 4th edn. Oxford: Oxford University Press.

Howard League Working Party. (1985) *Unlawful Sex*. London: Waterlow Publishers.

Hubin, D.C. (1999) "Parental rights and due process," *Journal of Law and Family Studies*, 1(2): 123–150.

Hubin, D.C. (2003) "Daddy dilemmas: untangling the puzzles of paternity," *Cornell Journal of Law and Public Policy*, 13(1): 29–80.

Hyman, I.A. (1990) *Reading, Writing, and the Hickory Stick*. Lexington, MA: Lexington Books.

"Investigator" and Farrell, C. (2008) "Judicial caning in Singapore, Malaysia and Brunei," http://www.corpun.com/singfeat.htm (accessed October 12, 2009).

Irvine, A.D. (1996) "Jack and Jill and employment equity," *Dialogue*, 35(2): 255–291.

Izraeli, D.N. (1997) "Gendering military service in the Israel Defense Force," *Israel Social Science Research*, 12(1): 129–166.

Jack, I. (1999) "Leonardo's grave," *Granta*, 67: 7–37.

Jagger, A.M., ed. (1994) *Living with Contradictions: Controversies in Feminist Social Ethics*. Boulder, CO: Westview Press.

Johnson, K., Asher, J., Rosborough, S. *et al.* (2008) "Association of combatant status and sexual violence with health and mental health outcomes in postconflict Liberia," *Journal of the American Medical Association*, 300(6): 676–690.

Jones, A. (2000) "Gendercide and genocide," *Journal of Genocide Research*, 2(2), pp. 185–211.

Jones, A., ed. (2004) *Gendercide and Genocide*. Nashville: Vanderbilt University Press.

Jones, A. (2009) *Gender Inclusive: Essays on Violence, Men, and Feminist International Relations*. New York: Routledge.

Jurado, R. (1998/1999) "The essence of her womanhood: defining the privacy rights of women prisoners and the employment rights of women guards," *Journal of Gender, Social Policy and the Law*, 7(1): 1–53.

Kanin, E.J. (1994) "False rape allegations," *Archives of Sexual Behavior*, 23(1): 81–92.

Kaufman, A., Divasto, P., Jackson, R. *et al.* (1980) "Male rape victims: noninstitutionalized assault," *American Journal of Psychiatry*, 137(2): 221–223.

Kaufman, J. (1995) "How Cambodians Came to Control California Doughnuts," *Wall Street Journal*, February 22, p. A1.

Keegan, J. (1978) *The Face of Battle*. New York: Penguin Books.

Keegan, J., and Holmes, R. (1985) *Soldiers: A History of Men in Battle*. London: Hamish Hamilton.

Kennedy, R.E., Jr. (1962) "The Protestant ethic and the Parsis," *American Journal of Sociology*, 68(1): 11–20.

Kirby, R. (2000/2001) "Spoil the Rod, Spare the Child," *Mail & Guardian* (Johannesburg), December 22–January 4, p. 41.

Klein, J.Z. (2010) "It's Not Political, But More Canadians are Lefties," *New York Times*, February 16, http://www.nytimes.com/2010/02/16/sports/olympics/16lefty.html (accessed February 2, 2010).

Kposowa, A.J. (2000) "Marital status and suicide in the national longitudinal mortality study," *Journal of Epidemiological Community Health*, 54(4): 254–261.

Kropotkin, Prince Peter Alekseevich (1898) "Discipline in the Russian Army," *New York Times*, 16 October, http://query.nytimes.com/gst/abstract.html?res=F50F1FFA3 F5C11738DDDAF0994D8415B8885F0D3 (accessed October 7, 2009).

Kuper, L. (1981) *Genocide: Its Political Use in the Twentieth Century*. New Haven: Yale University Press.

Lamb, S. (1996) *The Trouble with Blame: Victims, Perpetrators, and Responsibility*. Cambridge, MA: Harvard University Press.

Leach, F., and Humphreys, S. (2007) "Gender violence in schools: taking the 'girls-as-victims' discourse forward," in G. Terry with J. Hoare (eds), *Gender-Based Violence*. Oxford: Oxfam.

Lentin, R., ed. (1997) *Gender and Catastrophe*. London: Zed Books.

Levin, M. (1987) *Feminism and Freedom*. New Brunswick, NJ: Transaction Books.

Liederman, J., Kantrowitz, L. and Flannery, K. (2005) "Male vulnerability to reading disability is not likely to be a myth: a call for new data," *Journal of Learning Disabilities*, 38(2): 109–129.

Lin, Y., Chen, C. and Luo, J. (2008) "Gender and age distribution of occupational fatalities in Taiwan," *Accident Analysis and Prevention*, 40(4): 1604–1610.

Lyman, R. (2006) "In Many Public Schools, the Paddle Is No Relic," *New York Times*, September 30, http://nytimes.com/2006/09/30/education/30punish.html (accessed October 3, 2006).

Maccoby, E.E., and Mnookin, R.H. (1992) *Dividing the Child: Social and Legal Dilemmas of Custody*. Cambridge, MA: Harvard University Press.

McGinn, C. (2003) *The Making of a Philosopher*. New York: Perennial.

McKendrick, B., and Hoffman, W., eds (1990) *People and Violence in South Africa*. Cape Town: Oxford University Press.

MacKinnon, C.A. (1987) *Feminism Unmodified*. Cambridge, MA: Harvard University Press.

McLeod, M. (1984) "Women against men: an examination of domestic violence based on an analysis of official data and national victimization data," *Justice Quarterly*, 1(2): 171–193.

Maimonides, M., trans. M. Friedländer (1956) *The Guide for the Perplexed*, 2nd edn. New York: Dover Publications.

Malone, J., Tyree, A. and O'Leary, K.D. (1989) "Generalization and containment: different effects of past aggression for wives and husbands," *Journal of Marriage and the Family*, 51: 687–697.

Matthews, J. (1992) "A system rated NC-17," *Newsday* (Long Island, NY), November 22, p. 5.

Meier, M.H., Slutske, W.S., Heath, A.C. and Martin, N.G. (2009) "The role of harsh discipline in explaining sex differences in conduct disorder: a study of opposite-sex twin pairs," *Journal of Abnormal Psychology*, 37(5): 653–664.

Meinert, C.L., Gilpin, A.K., Unalp, A. and Dawson, C. (2000) "Gender representation in trials," *Controlled Clinical Trials*, 21(5): 462–475.

Mendel, M.P. (1995) *The Male Survivor: The Impact of Sexual Abuse*. Thousand Oaks, CA: Sage Publications.

Mercurio, J. (1972) *Caning: Educational Rite and Tradition*. Syracuse, NY: Syracuse University Division of Special Education and Rehabilitation and the Center on Human Policy.

Merkatz, R.B., Temple, R., Sobel, S. *et al.* (1993) "Women in clinical trials of new drugs: a change in Food and Drug Administration policy," *New England Journal of Medicine*, 329(4): 292–296.

Mezey, G.C., and King, M.B., eds (2000) *Male Victims of Sexual Assault*, 2nd edn. Oxford: Oxford University Press.

Middleton, J. (2008) "The experience of corporal punishment in schools, 1890–1940," *History of Education*, 37(2): 253–275.

Mill, J.S. (1991) "The subjection of women," in *On Liberty and Other Essays*, ed. J. Gray. Oxford: Oxford University Press, pp. 469–582.

Millar, P. (2009) *The Best Interests of Children: An Evidence-Based Approach.* Toronto: University of Toronto Press.

Millar, P., and Goldenberg, S. (1998) "Explaining child custody determinations in Canada," *Canadian Journal of Law and Society*, 13(1): 209–225.

Money, J., and Ehrhardt A.A. (1972) *Man and Woman, Boy and Girl.* Baltimore: Johns Hopkins University Press.

Money, J., and Schwartz, M. (1976) "Fetal androgens in early treated adrenogenital syndrome of 46XX hermaphroditism: influence on assertive and aggressive types of behavior," *Aggressive Behavior*, 2: 19–30.

Moreau, S. (2010) "What is discrimination?" *Philosophy and Public Affairs*, 38(2): 143–179.

Morgan, R., ed. (1970) *Sisterhood Is Powerful: An Anthology of Writings from the Women's Liberation Movement.* New York: Vintage Books.

Moyer, I.L. (1981) "Demeanor, Sex, and Race in Police Processing," *Journal of Criminal Justice*, 9(3): 235–246.

Mnookin, R.H., and Kornhauser, L. (1979) "Bargaining in the shadow of the law: the case of divorce," *Yale Law Journal*, 88(5): 950–997.

Mustard, C.A., Kaufert, P., Kozyrskyj, A. and Mayer, T. (1998) "Sex differences in the use of health care services," *New England Journal of Medicine*, 338(23): 1678–1683.

Myers, S.L. (2006) "Hazing Trial Bares Dark Side of Russia's Military," *New York Times*, August 13, http://www.nytimes.com/2006/08/13/world/europe/13hazing.html (accessed October 7, 2009).

Myers, S.L. (2009) "Living and Fighting alongside Men, and Fitting In," *New York Times*, August 16, http://www.nytimes.com/2009/08/17/us/17women.html?scp=1&sq=living+and+fighting+alongside+men+and+fitting+in&st=nyt (accessed August 16, 2009).

Nathanson, P., and Young, K.K. (2001) *Spreading Misandry*. Montreal and Kingston: McGill-Queen's University Press.

National Cancer Institute (2011) "Male Breast Cancer Treatment: Incidence and Mortality," www.cancer.gov/cancerinfo/pdq/treatment/malebreast/patient (accessed June 15, 2011).

National Organization for Women (1971) "Women and War," http://www.now.org/issues/military/policies/war.html (accessed December 23, 2010).

National Organization for Women (1980) "Opposition to Draft and Registration," http://www.now.org/issues/military/policies/draft2.html (accessed December 23, 2010).

Nationmaster (n.d.) "Military statistics: conscription (most recent) by country," http://www.nationmaster.com/graph/mil_con-military-conscription (accessed March 21, 2010).

Nessen, S.C., Lounsbury, D.E. and Hetz, S.P., eds (2008) *War Surgery in Afghanistan and Iraq*. Falls Church, VA: Office of the Surgeon General, United States Army; and Washington, DC: Walter Reed Army Medical Center, Borden Institute.

Nichols, P., and Chen, T. (1981) *Minimal Brain Dysfunction: A Prospective Study*. Hillsdale, NJ: Lawrence Erlbaum Associates.

Nussbaum, M. (1999) *Sex and Social Justice*. New York: Oxford University Press.

Nussbaum, M., and Glover, J., eds (1995) *Women, Culture, and Development*. Oxford: Clarendon Press.

O'Donnell, K. (1999) "Lesbian and gay families," in G. Jagger and C. Wright (eds), *Changing Family Values*. London: Routledge, pp. 77–97.

Okin, S.M. (1989) *Justice, Gender, and the Family*. New York: Basic Books.

O'Leary, K.D., Barling, J., Arias, I. *et al.* (1989) "Prevalence and stability of physical aggression between spouses: a longitudinal analysis," *Journal of Consulting and Clinical Psychology*, 57(2): 263–268.

O'Leary, K.D., Smith Slep, A.M., Avery-Leaf, S. and Cascardi, M. (2008) "Gender differences in dating aggression among multiethnic high school students," *Journal of Adolescent Health*, 42(5): 473–479.

Oosterhoff, P., Zwanikken, P. and Ketting, E. (2004) "Sexual torture of men in Croatia and other conflict situations: an open secret," *Reproductive Health Matters*, 12(23): 68–77.

Oppel, R.A., and Nordland, R. (2010) "U.S. Is Reining In Special Forces in Afghanistan," *New York Times*, March 15, http://www.nytimes.com/2010/03/16/world/asia/16afghan.html (accessed March 16, 2010).

Organisation for Economic Co-operation and Development (2008) *Education at a Glance 2008 (OECD Indicators)*, http://www.oecd.org/document/9/0,3343,en_2649_39263238_41266761_1_1_1_1,00.html (accessed June 16, 2011).

Organisation for Economic Co-operation and Development (2009) *Education at a Glance 2009 (OECD Indicators)*, http://www.oecd.org/document/24/0,3746,en_2649_39263238_43586328_1_1_1_1,00.html (accessed December 2, 2009).

Organization for Security and Co-operation in Europe (1999) *Kosovo: As Seen, As Told: An analysis of the human rights findings of the OSCE Kosovo Verification Missions, October 1998 to June 1999*. Warsaw: OSCE, Office for Democratic Institutions and Human Rights.

Parke, R.D. (1981) *Fathers*. Cambridge, MA: Harvard University Press.

Pasterski, V., Hindmarch, P., Geffner, M. *et al.* (2007) "Increased aggression and activity level in 3- to 11-year-old girls with congenital adrenal hyperplasia (CAH)," *Hormones and Behavior*, 52(3): 368–374.

Pateman, C. (1988) *The Sexual Contract*. Cambridge: Polity Press.

Patterson, D. (1997) "Citadel's Culture Abused Men before Women," *New York Times*, January, 17.

Pearson, P. (1997) *When She Was Bad: Violent Women and the Myth of Innocence*. New York: Viking.

Peel, M., Mahtani, A., Hinshelwood, G. and Forrest, D. (2000) "The sexual abuse of men in detention in Sri Lanka," *The Lancet*, 355: 2069–2070.

Perel, S. (1997) *Europa Europa*. New York: John Wiley & Sons, Inc.

Pinker, S. (2002) *The Blank Slate: The Modern Denial of Human Nature*. New York: Penguin Books.

Pino, N.W., and Meier, R.F. (1999) "Gender differences in rape reporting," *Sex Roles*, 40(11/12): 979–990.

Piradova, M.D. (1975) "The role of women in the public health care system in the USSR," in *Proceedings of the International Conference on Women in Health*. Washington, DC: Department of Health, Education, and Welfare.

Presidential Commission on the Assignment of Women in the Armed Forces (1992) *Women in Combat: Report to the President*. McLean, VA: Brassey's (US).

Pritchard, C. (1995) *Suicide – The Ultimate Rejection? A Psycho-Social Study*. Buckingham: Open University Press.

Quinn, C., and Tong, R. (2003) "The consequences of taking the second sexism seriously," *Social Theory and Practice*, 29(2): 233–245.

Radcliffe Richards, J. (1986) "Separate spheres," in P. Singer (ed.), *Applied Ethics*. Oxford: Oxford University Press, pp. 185–214.

Radcliffe Richards, J. (1994) *The Sceptical Feminist*. London: Penguin Books.

Ramsey, G.V. (1943) "The sexual development of boys," *American Journal of Psychology*, 56(2): 217–233.

Rawls, J. (1973) *A Theory of Justice*. Oxford: Oxford University Press.

Reuters (2010) "Khmer Rouge Prison Chief Sentenced," *Cape Times*, July 27, p. 2.

Reynolds, M. (2000) "War Has No Rules for Russian Forces Fighting in Chechnya," *Los Angeles Times*, September 17.

Rhode, D.L. (1997) *Speaking of Sex: The Denial of Gender Inequality*. Cambridge, MA: Harvard University Press.

Rimer, S. (2005) "Professors at Harvard Confront Its President," *New York Times*, February 16, http://www.nytimes.com/2005/02/16/education/16harvard.html (accessed February 16, 2005).

Rimer, S., and Healy, P.D. (2005) "Furor Lingers as Harvard Chief Gives Details of Talk on Women," *New York Times*, February 18, http://www.nytimes.com/2005/02/18/education/18harvard.html (accessed February 18, 2005).

Rohde, D. (1997) *Endgame: The Betrayal and Fall of Srebrenica, Europe's Worst Massacre Since World War II*. Boulder, CO: Westview Press.

Rosen, M., ed. (1995) *The Penguin Book of Childhood*. London: Penguin.

Rothman, S., Lichter, S.R. and Nevitte, N. (2005) "Politics and professional advancement among college faculty," *The Forum*, 3(1), http://www.bepress.com/forum/vol3/iss1/art2/.

Rubin, R.T. (1987) "The neuroendocrinology and neurochemistry of antisocial behavior," in S.A. Mednick, T.A. Moffit and S.A. Stack (eds), *The Causes of Crime: New Biological Approaches*. Cambridge: Cambridge University Press.

Rummel, R.J. (1994) *Death by Government*. New Brunswick, NJ: Transaction Books.

Sadker, M., and Sadker, D. (1994) *Failing at Fairness: How America's Schools Cheat Girls*. New York: Charles Scribner's Sons.

Said, E. (2000) *Out of Place*. New York: Alfred A. Knopf.

Sang-Hun, C. (2007) "Spirits Sag in South Korea at Death of Hostage," *New York Times*, July 27, http://query.nytimes.com/gst/fullpage.html?res=9802E3D8143E F934A15754C0A9619C8B63 (accessed July 27, 2007).

Sapa-AFP (2011) "Mass Grave Contains 800 Saddam Victims," *Cape Times*, April 15, p. 2.

Sapa-AP (1986) "Two Women among the Victims," *Cape Times*, January 23, p. 1.

Sarrel, P.M., and Masters, W.H. (1982) "Sexual molestation of men by women," *Archives of Sexual Behavior*, 11(2): 117–131.

"Scalpel" (pseudonym) (1851) "The Female Medical Pupil," *Daily Evening Transcript* (Boston), January 3, p. 2.

Scott, G. (1950) *The History of Capital Punishment*. London: Torchstream Books.

Segal, M.W. (1982) "The arguments for female combatants," in N.L. Goldman (ed.), *Female Soldiers: Combatants or Noncombatants? Historical and Contemporary Perspectives*. Westport: Greenwood Press, pp. 267–290.

Sen, A. (1990) "More Than 100 Million Women Are Missing," *New York Review of Books*, December 20, pp. 61–66.

Shackleton, J.R. (2008) *Should We Mind the Gap? Gender Pay Differentials and Public Policy*, London: Institute of Economic Affairs.

Sharp, D. (2006) "Shocked, shot, and pardoned," *The Lancet*, 368: 975–976.

Sharpe, A., and Hardt, J. (2006) "Five Deaths a Day: Workplace Fatalities in Canada, 1993–2005." Ottawa: Centre for the Study of Living Standards.

Shaw, S.R., and Braden, J.P. (1990) "Race and gender bias in the administration of corporal punishment," *School Psychology Review*, 19(3): 378–383.

Singer, P. (1990) *Animal Liberation*, 2nd edn. New York: New York Review of Books.

Singer, P. (1999) *A Darwinian Left: Politics, Evolution and Cooperation*. New Haven: Yale University Press.

Slackman, M. (2009) "Reformer in Iran Publishes Account of a Prison Rape," *New York Times*, August 24, http://www.nytimes.com/2009/08/25/world/ middleeast/25iran.html (accessed October 18, 2009).

Slate, J.R., Perez, E., Waldrop, P.B. and Justen, J.E., III (1991) "Corporal punishment: used in discriminatory manner?" *Clearing House*, 64: 362–364.

Sloth-Nielsen, J. (1990) "Legal violence: corporal and capital punishment," in B. McKendrick and W. Hoffmann (eds), *People and Violence in South Africa*. Cape Town: Oxford University Press, pp. 73–95.

Smith, B.V. (2003) "Watching you, watching me," *Yale Journal of Law and Feminism*, 15: 225–288.

Smith, D. (2003) *The State of the World Atlas*. Brighton: Earthscan.

Smith, H.D., Fromouth, M.E. and Morris, C.C. (1997) "Effects of gender on perceptions of child sexual abuse," *Journal of Child Sexual Abuse*, 6(4): 51–62.

Smith, R.E., Pine, C.J. and Hawley, M.E. (1988) "Social cognitions about adult male victims of female sexual assault," *Journal of Sex Research*, 24: 101–112.

Sommers, C.H. (1994) *Who Stole Feminism?* New York: Simon & Schuster.

Sommers, C.H. (2000) "The War against Boys," *Atlantic Monthly*, May: 59–74.

Sommers, C.H. (2000) *The War against Boys: How Misguided Feminism Is Harming Our Young Men*. New York: Simon & Schuster.

Sowell, T. (1999) *Barbarians inside the Gates*. Stanford: Hoover Institution Press.

Spencer, M., and Dunklee, P. (1986) "Sexual abuse of boys," *Pediatrics*, 78(1): 133–137.

Spiegel, P.B., and Salama, P. (2000) "War and mortality in Kosovo, 1988–9: an epidemiological testimony," *The Lancet*, 355: 2205–2206.

Spohn, C., and Beichner, D. (2000) "Is preferential treatment of female offenders a thing of the past? A multisite study of gender, race, and imprisonment," *Criminal Justice Policy Review*, 11(2): 149–184.

Stattin, H., Janson, H., Klackenberg-Larsson, I. and Magnusson, D. (1995) "Corporal punishment in everyday life: an intergenerational perspective," in J. McCord (ed.), *Coercion and Punishment in Long-Term Perspectives*. Cambridge: Cambridge University Press, pp. 315–347.

Steffensmeier, D., Kramer, J. and Streifel, C. (1993) "Gender and imprisonment decisions," *Criminology*, 31(3): 411–446.

Steffensmeier, D., Ulmer, J. and Kramer, J. (1998) "The interaction of race, gender and age in criminal sentencing: the punishment cost of being young, black and male," *Criminology*, 36(4): 763–798.

Stiehm, Judith Hicks (1994) "The protected, the protector, the defender," in A.M. Jaggar (ed.), *Living with Contradictions: Controversies in Feminist Social Ethics*, Boulder, CO: Westview Press, pp. 582–592.

Sterba, J. (2003) "The wolf again in sheep's clothing," *Social Theory and Practice*, 29(2): 219–232.

Stets, J.E., and Straus, M.A. (1989) "The marriage license as a hitting license: a comparison of assaults in dating, cohabiting, and married couples," *Journal of Family Violence*, 4(2): 161–180.

Stets, J.E., and Straus, M.A. (1990) "Gender differences in reporting marital violence and its medical and psychological consequences," in M.A. Straus and R.J. Gelles (eds), *Physical Violence in American Families*. New Brunswick, NJ: Transaction Publishers, pp. 151–165.

Stolnitz, G. (1955) "A century of international mortality trends: I," *Population Studies*, 9(1): 24–55.

Stolnitz, G. (1956) "A century of international mortality trends: II," *Population Studies*, 10(1): 17–42.

Stolzenberg, L., and D'Alessio, S.J. (2004) "Sex differences in the likelihood of arrest," *Journal of Criminal Justice*, 32(5): 443–454.

Straus, M.A. (1990) "Victims and aggressors in marital violence," *American Behavioral Scientist*, 23(5): 681–704.

Straus, M.A. (1994) *Beating the Devil Out of Them: Corporal Punishment in American Families*. New York: Lexington Books.

Straus, M.A., and Gelles, R.J. (1986) "Societal change and change in family violence from 1975 to 1985 as revealed by two national surveys," *Journal of Marriage and the Family*, 48: 465–479.

Streib, V.L. (1990) "Death penalty for female offenders," *University of Cincinnati Law Review*, 58: 845–880.

Streib, V.L. (2002) "Gendering the death penalty: countering sex bias in a masculine sanctuary," *Ohio State Law Journal*, 63(1): 433–474.

Streib, V.L. (2006) "Rare and inconsistent: the death penalty for women," *Fordham Urban Law Journal*, 33(2): 609–636.

Struckman-Johnson, C., and Struckman-Johnson, D. (1992) "Acceptance of male rape myths among college men and women," *Sex Roles*, 27(3/4): 85–100.

Struckman-Johnson, C., and Struckman-Johnson, D. (1994) "Men pressured and forced into sexual experience," *Archives of Sexual Behavior*, 23(1): 93–114.

Struckman-Johnson, C., and Struckman-Johnson, D. (2000) "Sexual coercion rates in seven prison facilities for men," *Prison Journal*, 80(4): 379–389.

Struckman-Johnson, C., Struckman-Johnson, D., Rucker, L., Bumby, K. *et al.* (1996) "Sexual coercion reported by men and women in prison," *Journal of Sex Research*, 33(1): 67–76.

Sugarman, D.B., and Hotaling, G.T. (1991) "Dating violence: a review of contextual and risk factors," in B. Levy (ed.), *Dating Violence: Young Women in Danger*. Seattle: Seal Press, pp. 100–118.

Summers, L.H. (2005) "Remarks at NBER conference on diversifying the science and engineering workforce," January 14, http://www.president.harvard.edu/speeches/summers_2005/nber.php (accessed February 15, 2010).

Summers, L.H. (2005) "Letter from President Summers on women and science," Cambridge, MA: Harvard University, 19 January, http://www.harvard.edu/president/speeches/summers_2005/womensci.php (accessed August 30, 2011).

Tanay, E. (2004) *Passport to Life*. Ann Arbor, MI: Forensic Press.

Taylor, S.P., and Epstein, S. (1967) "Aggression as a function of the interaction of the sex of the aggressor and the sex of the victim," *Journal of Personality*, 35: 474–486.

Tjaden, P.G., and Tjaden, C.D. (1981) "Differential treatment of the female felon: myth or reality?" in M.Q. Warren (ed.), *Comparing Female and Male Offenders*. London: Sage Publications, pp. 73–88.

Truth and Reconciliation Commission of South Africa (1998) "Children and Youth" and "Women," in *Truth and Reconciliation Commission of South Africa Report*. Cape Town: Truth and Reconciliation Commission, vol. 4, pp. 250–283 and 284–318.

Truth and Reconciliation Commission of South Africa (1998) "Methodology and Process," in *Truth and Reconciliation Commission of South Africa Report*. Cape Town: Truth and Reconciliation Commission, vol. 1, pp. 135–173.

UK Office of National Statistics (2005) "Prison population, 2003," March 22, http://www.statistics.gov.uk/cci/nugget.asp?id=1101 (accessed February 3, 2010).

University of California, Berkeley (USA) and Max Planck Institute for Demographic Research (Germany) (n.d.) The Human Mortality Database, www.mortality.org/ (accessed January 28, 2010).

US Bureau of the Census (1949) *Historical Statistics of the United States, 1789–1945*. Washington, DC: US Department of Commerce.

US Bureau of Justice Statistics (2008) "Prison Inmates at Midyear 2007." Washington, DC: US Department of Justice.

US Bureau of Labor Statistics (2009) "Current Population Survey and Census of Fatal Occupational Injuries." Washington, DC: U.S. Department of Labor, www.bls.gov/iif/oshwc/cfoi/cfch0007.pdf (accessed January 17, 2010)

US Department of Commerce (2010) US Census Bureau News, "Women's History Month, 2010." Washington, DC: US Department of Commerce, http://www.census.gov/Press-Release/www/releases/pdf/cb10ff-03_womenshistory.pdf (accessed March 21, 2010).

US Department of Labor (2008) "Fatal Occupational Injuries, Total Hours, and Rates of Fatal Occupational Injuries by Selected Worker Characteristics, Occupations, and Industries, Civilian Workers." Washington, DC: US Department of Labor, http://www.bls.gov/iif/oshwc/cfoi/cfoi_rates_2008hb.pdf (accessed January 17, 2010).

US Digest of Educational Statistics (2007) "Table 191: College enrolment and enrolment rates of recent high school completers, by sex: 1950 through 2006," http://nces.ed.gov/programms/digest/d07/tables/dt07_191.asp (accessed October 25, 2009).

US Digest of Educational Statistics (2008) "Table 403: Average mathematics literacy, reading literacy, and science literacy scores of 15-year-olds, by sex and country: 2006," http://nces.ed.gov/programms/digest/d08/tables/dt08_403.asp. (accessed October 25, 2009).

US Digest of Educational Statistics (2008) "Table 109: Percentage of high school dropouts among persons 16 through 24 years old (status dropout rate), by sex and race/ethnicity: selected years, 1960 through 2007," http://nces.ed.gov/programms/digest/d08/tables/dt08_109.asp (accessed October 25, 2009).

US Institute of Education Sciences, National Center for Education Statistics (2010) "Fast facts: what is the percentage of degrees conferred by sex and race?" http://nces.ed.gov/fastfacts/display.asp?id=72 (accessed October 25, 2009).

Valenti, J. (2010) "For Women in America, Equality Is Still an Illusion," *Washington Post*, February 21, p. B02.

Valle, J.E. (1980) *Rocks and Shoals: Order and Discipline in the Old Navy, 1800–1861*. Annapolis: Naval Institute Press.

van Creveld, M. (2001) *Men, Women and War*. London: Cassell & Co.

van Emden, R. (2005) *Boy Soldiers of the Great War*. London: Headline.

Vasquez, D., and Falcone, R.E. (1997) "Cross-gender violence," *Annals of Emergency Medicine*, 29(3): 427–428.

Visher, C.A. (1983) "Gender, police arrest decisions, and notions of chivalry," *Criminology*, 21(1): 5–28.

Walmsley, R. (2003) "World Prison Population List," 4th edn. London: Home Office.

Walmsley, R. (2006) "World Female Imprisonment List." London: International Centre for Prison Studies.

Warren, M.A. (1985) *Gendercide*. Totowa, NJ: Rowman & Allanheld.

War Resisters' International. (1998) "World Survey of Conscription and Conscientious Objection to Military Service," http://www.wri-irg.org/programmes/world_survey (accessed March 21, 2010).

Wasserman, D. (1997) "Diversity and stereotyping," *Report from the Institute for Philosophy and Public Policy*, 17(1/2): 32–36.

Wasserstrom, R. (1997) "On racism and sexism," in C. Gould (ed.), *Gender*. Atlantic Highlands, NJ: Humanities Press, pp. 337–358.

Watkins, Bill and Bentovim, Arnon (2000) "Male children and adolescents as victims: a review of current knowledge," in G.C. Mezey and M.B. King (eds), *Male Victims of Sexual Assault*, pp. 35–78.

Weiss, M. (2001) "A Woman's Touch: Lillian Schapiro Is Charting New Territory as an Atlanta Mohelet," *Atlanta Jewish Times*, June 8, http://atlanta.jewish.com/archives/2001/060801cs.htm (accessed August 15, 2005).

Weitzman, L. (1985) *The Divorce Revolution: The Unexpected Social and Economic Consequences for Women and Children in America*. New York: The Free Press.

Wenger, N.K., Speroff, L. and Packard, B. (1993) "Cardiovascular health and disease in women," *New England Journal of Medicine*, 329(4): 247–256.

Werner, E.E., and Smith, R.S. (1982) *Vulnerable but Invincible: A Longitudinal Study of Resilient Children and Youth*. New York: Adams Bannister Cox.

Whitaker, D.J., Halleyesus, T., Swahn, M. and Saltzman, L.S. (2007) "Differences in frequency of violence and reported injury between relationships with reciprocal and nonreciprocal intimate partner violence," *American Journal of Public Health*, 97(5): 941–947.

Wogan, L. (2005) "Summersgate," *Ms*, Summer, pp. 57–59.

Women and Work Commission (2006) "Shaping a Fairer Future." London: UK Commission for Employment and Skills.

Wright, A.E. (1913) *The Unexpurgated Case against Woman Suffrage*. New York: Paul Hoeber.

Young, I.M. (1990) *Justice and the Politics of Difference*. Princeton: Princeton University Press.

Yuval-Davis, N. (1985) "Front and rear: the sexual division of labor in the Israeli Army," *Feminist Studies*, 11(3): 649–675.

Zipp, J.F., and Fenwick, R. (2006) "Is the academy a liberal hegemony?" *Public Opinion Quarterly*, 70(3): 304–326.

List of Cases

Bagley v. Watson, 579 F. Supp. 1099 (D.C.Or., 1983).

Bradwell v. The State (Illinois) 83 U.S. 16 Wall.

Carlin v. Manu, 72 F.Supp.2d 1177 (D.Or., 1999).

County of San Luis Obispo v. Nathaniel J., 50 Cal.App.4th 842, 57 Cal.Rptr.2d 843.

Forts v. Ward, 621 F.2d 1210 (2nd Cir. 1980).

Frontiero v. Richardson, 411 US 677 (1973).

Griffin v. Michigan Dept. of Corrections, 654 F.Supp. 690 (E.D.Mich.1982).

Grummett v. Rushen, 779 F.2d 491 (9th Cir. 1985).

Jevning v. Cichos, 499 N.W.2d 515.

Johnson v. Phelan, 69 F.3d 144 (7th Cir. 1995).

Jordan v. Gardner, 986 F.2d 1521 (9th Cir. 1993).

Louisiana and Rojas v. Frisard, 694 So.2d 1032, 96-368 (La.App. 5 Cir. 4/29/97).

Mercer County Dept. of Social Services on Behalf of Imogene T. v. Alf M., 155 Misc.2d 703, 589 N.Y.S.2d 288.

Michenfelder v. Sumner, 860 F.2d 328 (9th Cir. 1988).

Nguyen v. I.N.S, 121 S.Ct 2053 (2001).

Oliver v. Scott, 276 F.3d 736 (5th Cir. 2002).

President of the Republic of South Africa v. Hugo, 1997 (4) SA 1 (CC).

Robino v. Iranon, 145 F.3d 1109 (9th Cir. 1998).

S.F. v. State ex rel. *T.M.*, 695 So.2d 1186.

Smith v. Fairman, 678 F.2d 52 (7th Cir. 1982).

Somers v. Thurman, 109 F.3d 614 (9th Cir. 1997).

State of Kansas ex rel. *Hermesmann v. Seyer*, 252 Kan. 646, 847 P.2d 1273.

Timm v. Gunter, 917 F.2d 1093 (8th Cir. 1990).

Torres v. Wisconsin Department of Health & Social Services, 838 F. 2d 944 (7th Cir. 1988).

Tyrer v. United Kingdom (1978) 2 E.H.R.R 1.

Weatherall v. Canada (Attorney General), [1993] 2 S.C.R. 872.

List of Legislation and Other Legal Instruments

Michigan Penal Code Act 328 of 1931, Section 750.520, 1974 Amendment, http://www.legislature.mi.gov/(S(24i0ub45icnmus55zkfdd32r))/documents/mcl/pdf/mcl-750-520a.pdf (accessed December 2, 2009).

National People's Congress (July 1, 1979) as amended. "Criminal Law of the People's Republic of China," http://www.cecc.gov/pages/newLaws/criminalLawENG.php (accessed December 1, 2009).

Penal Code of Japan, Act No. 45 of 1907, as amended, http://www.cas.go.jp/jp/seisaku/hourei/data/PC_2.pdf (accessed December 1, 2009).

Sexual Offences Act 2003 (UK), http://www.opsi.gov.uk/Acts/acts2003/ukpga_20030042_en_2#pt1-pb1-l1g1 (accessed 19 October, 2009).

Sexual Offences Act 2009 (Scotland) (asp 9), http://www.opsi.gov.uk/legislation/scotland/acts2009/pdf/asp_20090009_en.pdf (accessed December 1, 2009).

Singapore Criminal Procedure Code, Chapter 25, 231(a).

Singapore Criminal Procedure Code 2010, Part XVI, Division 2, 325(1)(a).

Singapore Ministry of Education (1957) "Schools Regulation Act," Regulation No. 88, http://www.corpun.com/sgscr1.htm (accessed February 18, 2002).

South African Criminal Law (Sexual Offences and Related Matters) Amendment Act 32 of 2007, http://www.justice.gov.za/legislation/acts/2007-032.pdf (accessed December 1 2009).

"Standard Minimum Rules for the Treatment of Prisoners," adopted by the First United Nations Congress on the Prevention of Crime and the Treatment of Offenders, held in Geneva in 1955, and approved by the Economic and Social Council by its resolutions 663 C (XXIV) of 31 July, 1957 and 2076 (LXII) of 13 May, 1977, http://www2.ohchr.org/english/law/pdf/treatmentprisoners.pdf (accessed January 6, 2010).

Index

The Second Sexism: Discrimination Against Men and Boys, First Edition. David Benatar.
© 2012 John Wiley & Sons, Inc. Published 2012 by John Wiley & Sons, Inc.

CPSIA information can be obtained
at www.ICGtesting.com
Printed in the USA
BVOW10s0157060917
494063BV00006B/119/P